50 FABULOUS GAY-FRIENDLY PLACES TO LIVE

By

GREGORY A. KOMPES

CAREER
PRESS

Franklin Lakes, NJ

50 FABULOUS GAY-FRIENDLY PLACES TO LIVE
EDITED BY JODI BRANDON
TYPESET BY EILEEN DOW MUNSON
Cover design by Johnson Design
Printed in the U.S.A. by Book-mart Press

To order this title, please call toll-free 1-800-CAREER-1 (NJ and Canada: 201-848-0310) to order using VISA or MasterCard, or for further information on books from Career Press.

The Career Press, Inc., 3 Tice Road, PO Box 687,
Franklin Lakes, NJ 07417
www.careerpress.com
www.newpagebooks.com

Library of Congress Cataloging-in-Publication Data

Kompes, Gregory A.
　50 fabulous gay-friendly places to live / Gregory A. Kompes
　　　p.cm.
　ISBN 1-56414-827-0 (paper)
　　　1. Gay communities—United States—Directories. I. Title: Fifty fabulous gay-friendly places to live. II. Title.

HQ76.3.U5K66 2005
306.76'6'0973080511—dc22

2005050173

► **Dedication**

This book is dedicated to

all the fabulous past and future Family,

Gay Activists and Urban Pioneers

who have boldly emerged to make our world

more gay friendly.

► **Acknowledgments**

A work of this size and depth wouldn't be possible without generous help and support. Thanks to my literary agent, Margot Mailey-Hutchinson, and everyone at Waterside Productions, Inc., for assisting me in being in the right place at the right time; Kirsten Dalley, Michael Pye, Linda Rienecker, Jodi Brandon and everyone at Career Press; my friend and mentor Eva Shaw for her nudging support; Mary Ann Cooper, Matt Kompes, Joan Heppert, Don Rhynard, Kathleen Shaputus, and Charles Goetz for their constant support. I extend my grateful thanks to the hundreds who helped with research, including the fabulous 50 city mayors and their staffs, members of convention, visitor, and tourism bureaus, area chambers of commerce, and everyone who took the time to tell me about their cities. And, finally, thanks to the love of my life, my partner, Todd Isbell. You make all things possible.

CONTENTS

Most city guides reduce gay-friendly places to lists: lists of bars, lists of dance clubs, and lists of hotels. *50 Fabulous Gay-Friendly Places to Live* has a different goal: to present gay-friendly cities and towns from a local point-of-view. There's no point in telling someone considering relocating about the best gay dance clubs and bars because these are often out of favor before a city guide goes to press. Instead, this book will offer city dwellers, visitors, and potential relocating residents a sense of an area's local gay communities, neighborhoods, and resources.

The 50 Fabulous Gay-Friendly Cities

The task of choosing the 50 cities for this book was a challenge. The good news is there are many more than 50 fabulous gay-friendly American cities. The original list included more than 400 cities. These were collected with the help of several books, personal exploration, Websites, and articles. It turns out that members of the gay-lesbian-bisexual-transgender (GLBT) community call just about every city and town in America home and a majority of those same people say their hometown is gay-friendly.

In his book, *The Rise of the Creative Class* (Basic Books, 2002), Richard Florida creates a ranking system called the Creative Index. Cities that rank highest on this index are diverse. This is a new city model: No longer are the best businesses attracting workers; instead, workers are attracting the businesses. The highest-ranking Creative Index cities attract creative, successful people who demand active, cultural, diverse cities to live in. In turn, these cities attract businesses that require creative workers for success.

Gary Gates and Jason Ost, in their book, *The Gay & Lesbian Atlas* (Urban Institute Press, 2004), analyzed the 2000 census data and compiled a collection of maps and lists of the cities most populated by same-sex couples. Although the census data is not absolutely reliable, in that the United States census contains no direct questions related to a person's sexual orientation, the analysis of current data provides a view of a widespread gay community.

Interestingly, the creative cities in Mr. Florida's work and the high gay population cities from the demographic work of Mr. Gates and Mr. Ost are frequently the same cities.

But, there's more to finding a gay-friendly place to live than moving to cities with large gay populations. There's a need for a high quality of life that includes economic, cultural, recreational, and GLBT community opportunities.

The field of cities narrowed after hundreds of interviews were conducted with gay business owners, gay and lesbian center board members, city mayors, city council members, convention and tourism staffs, chamber of commerce members, real estate agents, and individuals living in cities they consider gay-friendly. Fortunately, there were still too many possible cities. To further narrow the field, a criteria list was created based on what people said were the most important aspects of a gay-friendly place to live.

The Criteria

1. **An active gay community.** Whether the gay community is large or small, it's important that it's a vibrant, active community. Having people, groups, government, and businesses that support the community is essential to feeling that important sense of inclusion. Historic events and people help connect a community.

2. **Positive gay health programs.** Staying healthy is a key to happiness. Having health programs that support the needs of the GLBT community is important.

3. **Youth outreach.** One of the hardest issues facing GLBT community members can be feeling alone. Gay teen suicide is a large, yet avoidable problem when programs and services are provided for a community's younger members.

4. **Gay-friendly politics.** Having groups, organizations, and elected officials fighting for GLBT community, city, state, and federal issues of equality help create gay-friendly environments from both the grassroots and the larger environmental levels.

5. **Gay-owned and gay-friendly businesses.** People live where they work. A strong foundation of gay-owned business not only enhances gay-friendly places, but the GLBT community as well. And, having employers who provide domestic partner benefits enhances the GLBT community and retains creative, well-educated employees.

6. **Employment opportunities.** Creative and diverse job opportunities and a strong economic outlook are essential for the future of a gay-friendly place.

7. **Fun nightlife.** Gay-friendly communities often connect at local bars, restaurants, and community centers. Historically, The Stonewall Inn in Greenwich Village, New York, set the stage for the gay political movement of the past 40 years. Of course, hanging out at the clubs and bars, with your own community, can be fun, too.

8. **Cultural opportunities.** There's more to finding fun in a community than the nightlife. Museums, symphonies, ballets, theaters, and galleries are just a few of the essentials creative communities search out for entertainment, personal growth, and employment.

9. **Recreational opportunities.** A well-balanced life includes active opportunities and sports, clubs, and natural area attractions offer a part of that balance.

10. **Housing options.** Everyone needs somewhere to call home. A diverse community has diverse housing needs.

Estimating Gay Populations

Estimating a city's GLBT population is virtually impossible. Although the 2000 U.S. census data provides estimates on same-sex couples, there is no reliable census or survey of America's total gay population. Many still cling to the Kinsey 10% as a way of estimating the gay population. Gary Gates and some gay marketing firms put a more realistic estimate at 3 to 5 percent of the American population. Yet even the revised percentages become skewed. Many of the cities profiled have gay populations that are noticeably higher than either of these estimates. Because there is no reliable source of gay-population estimates, these numbers have been left out of the city profiles, but all of the cities included have large, active GLBT communities.

Size Matters

After combining the interviews and criteria, one conclusion surfaced: Size matters. Some people want the electricity and opportunities provided by a big city, others want that Mayberry feel, and most folks want a gay-friendly place somewhere in between. The major goal then was to compile a collection of cities from each category to help those in search of a gay-friendly place to call home find a place of their size. The collection of places included fall into four different sizes: big (million+), medium (100–900K), small (25–100K) and tiny (25K or less). There's a city for everyone's taste, dreams, and desires in these city profiles.

The Result

The result is a collection of 50 cities that vary in size. They all are home to unique and creative gay-friendly communities. You'll find many of the expected big cities such as New York, Los Angeles, Chicago, Dallas, and Boston. But, you'll also discover some small gems such as Bellaire, Guerneville, Lakewood, and Wilton Manors.

If your gay-friendly hometown is missing it's not because it isn't one of America's gay-friendly places to live. Instead, it's simply a matter of the limits of choosing only 50 cities. Thankfully, there are more than 50 gay-friendly places to live in America with more entering the fold every day.

Creating a Gay-Friendly Life

It's important to develop a personal philosophy that supports and encourages your gay-friendly life. For some that means being out and political activists; others might choose to keep their personal lives to themselves. The majority of our GLBT community falls somewhere in between. Whether we choose to live in a gay-friendly place or turn our current hometown into a gay-friendly place, it's important to know that we're not alone. The GLBT community spans our nation and the world and has for a very long time.

History tells us that world leaders, artists, business moguls, sports figures, and countless uncounted citizens of the world are members of our GLBT community. A few clicks at the GLBTQ (*www.glbtq.com*), an online encyclopedia of gay, lesbian, bisexual, transgender, queer culture, leads to a discovery of thousands of GLBT community members who have had an impact on the last three centuries of Western culture, science, and society. Though some community members have visible impact on the world, others, including unnamed local activists, politicians, and community members living and enjoying their gay-friendly lives, have a more subtle influence on their local GLBT communities.

America continues to evolve into a more gay-friendly place. More employers offer domestic partner benefits. More elected officials are gay and gay-friendly. There are more publications, groups, and events for the gay communities around the country. Cities and towns, big and small are not only gay-friendly places, but encouraging and catering to their creative and diverse populations.

With these shifting and encouraging attitudes, it's easier to live your life as an out gay person in America and the world. And, as more people continue to come out of the closet, more attitudes will shift. It's much harder to promote hate when you know someone who is gay.

It's been a right of passage for young members of the GLBT community to leave their hometown for a larger city to come out. Big cities, such as Los Angeles, New York City, and Chicago, make the transition out of the closet easier. These cities provide large gay communities and general environments where a person can literally get lost in the crowds. This helps make some parts of the self-discovery process easier. If no one knows you, you don't have to worry so much about what they think.

Because of their large gay communities, big cities create a sense of safety in numbers. These cities offer support groups in many forms. Just seeing lots of different people happy and comfortable with their own sexuality provides a sense of safety. Large communities also offer more formal support systems through gay and lesbian community centers, organized sports, and recreational groups and social clubs. The big gay ghetto or gay Mecca provides dwellers and visitors a safety net as they explore and grow through self-discovery.

The country's economy is shifting to high-tech, personal services, and entrepreneurial start-ups. It's becoming understood that creating and supporting a gay-friendly, diverse community supports this economic growth. Smaller cities and towns have begun to actively court the GLBT community. They don't want to loose their creative, diverse workforce to the big cities, but instead hope to draw creative companies to their cities.

As Richard Florida discusses in his book, *The Rise of the Creative Class* (Basic Books, 2002), companies seeking creative, diverse work forces are now moving their operations to cities with large creative-class populations. These companies are coming to better understand and support the needs of their work forces by creating supportive environments for the GLBT community.

Businesses recognize the benefits of employing a diverse and create staff. A growing number of companies are now gay-friendly. They offer domestic partner benefits, "sensitivity training" for all employees, and support groups, both social and emotional, for their gay employees. By taking advantage of all the benefits these companies offer, you not only improve the quality of your own life, but prove to your company that offering such programs is a positive thing. Such encouragement leads to more companies offering similar benefits. It's important to participate. And, if your company doesn't offer these benefits, approach your boss, human resources contact, or even the owner and ask for the benefits you deserve.

The Human Rights Campaign (HRC) puts out the *Corporate Index Report(CEI)* (*www.hrc.com*). The *CEI* is a business survey that collects data on companies' gay-friendly policies. The result is a list of the most gay-friendly employers in America. HRC also tracks domestic partner benefits and policies.

There are thousands of gay-owned businesses in the country. Maybe you own or work for one of them. While it's impossible to actually estimate the number of GLBT community dollars spent, it is estimated that the community spends approximately $48 billion annually on travel alone. Considering this figure, there are many billions more spent on day-to-day living. In our commercial-based democracy, money talks.

It's important to spend your dollars within the GLBT community whenever possible. Purchasing goods and services from within the community supports, enhances and increases visibility for the community. GLBT community centers, chambers of commerce, and gay publications frequently compile a "Gay-Yellow Pages" or "Pink Pages" publication listing area businesses that are gay-owned or gay-supportive.

If you're interested in exploring and acting on your own entrepreneurial spirit there are many organizations to help. The National Gay & Lesbian Chamber of Commerce (NGLCC) (*www.nglcc.org*) is the only national not-for-profit advocacy organization specifically dedicated to expanding the economic opportunities and advancements of the LGBT business community. NGLCC offers a wide array of services and advice for helping you start, expand, or support gay-owned businesses. NGLCC also maintains a current list of GLBT chambers around the country.

Financially supporting the GLBT community is one form of activism. Political activism is another important aspect of support. There are GLBT groups that go to extremes such as Act/Up (*www.actupny.org*). In the spirit of the Stonewall drag queens, radical groups are important groundbreakers for our community. Someone going to an extreme first helps define the middle ground. But, creating a definition is useless if no one steps into that open space. It's important that those middles are filled by supportive community members living average, everyday lives. Being someone who fills in that middle ground and lives a normal, gay-friendly, day-to-day life is the position most of us take. After all, the vast majority of us are simply normal in our own extraordinary ways.

Part of that everyday life includes supporting political candidates from the local to the national level who believe in the ideals of equality and inclusion. Voting for such candidates is an excellent way to support the GLBT community. Making financial contributions or volunteering for those same candidates or other organizations that support gay-friendly policies is another. And, running for office as such a candidate is another great option.

Positive political change that supports the GLBT communities refines the equality levels enjoyed by individuals and families within our communities. Families come in all shapes and sizes. Many of us have a personal goal of belonging to a group that loves and supports us just the way we are. We all have the families we are born into and those we create. In the best of worlds, these two types mix and blend to form a safe, loving environment where you can grow into the person you're meant to be. Your family can be whatever you want it to be and filled with whomever you choose.

The current debate about legalizing same-sex marriage is the latest request by our GLBT community to achieve equality. It's the latest sign that our community and its members are actually just the same as everyone else. This position may be the most threatening to conservative society. That realization that we are the same as the majority—that we love and need support just as everyone else does—is the greatest realization our community can share with society and the world at large.

Along with this realization comes the need for support. If you're spiritually inclined you have many gay-friendly options. The first is to travel your own path of spiritual self-discovery by reading any of the thousands of texts on the subject. Another choice is to join a group that promotes and supports your spiritual being without judgment. There are groups such as Dignity (*www.dignityusa.org*) and the Metropolitan Community Church (*www.mccchurch.org*) that provide spiritual direction for the GLBT community. The Unitarian Universalists (*www.uua.org*) are another. There are also gay Jewish and Muslim congregations, Pagan groups, and gay atheists, too.

This desire to find and feel support, whether spiritual, emotional, or social, is possibly the most important factor determining whether GLBT community members choose to stay or leave their hometowns.

Relocation is a big step. It's important to understand why you're moving, what you're looking for, and to do your homework when choosing your new hometown.

1. **Do your homework.** What needs, dreams, and desires do you have for your new hometown? Every place is different, with varying services, opportunities, attitudes, and styles. Decide what factors are important to you: community, economy, climate, location. Make a list and use it to narrow the field of possible locations. If you don't find the perfect city among the 50 presented here take your list and the criteria used in these city profiles and use them to search for other cities.

2. **Decide why you're moving.** If your goal is to find a gay-friendly place to live, the 50 city profiles in this book are a fabulous place to start. The descriptions, details, and resources provided in each profile provide an overview of what each city has to offer. If retirement is your plan, your additional needs or requirements will be met by *50 Fabulous Places to Retire in America* (Career Press, 2005). Likewise, if your goal is to find a family-friendly place, check out *50 Fabulous Places to Raise Your Family in America* (Career Press, 2005).

3. **Do more research.** When you've decided on a few potential cities contact their convention and visitor's bureau, chamber of commerce, and city hall. It's their job to sell their cities, and they'll be happy to provide detailed information and guides. Local realtors can also provide a wealth of information and contacts. Head to the Internet. The 50 city profiles each contain dozens of Web addresses to start your search. You'll find huge amounts of information online for just about any town or city. Just remember that the reliability of information you find on unofficial Websites might be questionable.

4. **Get a feel for daily life.** Subscribe to your potential hometown's Sunday newspaper for a few weeks. The newspaper will provide current information about jobs, housing, community priorities, shopping, local arts, and recreation. Many cities and states have glossy magazines that promote them. Check to see if your local library already has a subscription to these publications or if there's an online version available for free.

5. **Visit.** Plan to visit your new hometown. From your research you might have some potential neighborhoods. Seeing how your future neighbors live might help narrow your search. A local realtor will be willing to give you a tour of these neighborhoods, too. Visit the areas of town you might work or spend your recreational time. Stop into a few grocery stores and the nearby restaurants and businesses to discover your comfort level. Remember: No city or town is perfect. Every place has its drawbacks, but what's a negative to someone else might be your most desired attribute.

Arizona	1. Phoenix
	2. Tucson
California	3. Guerneville
	4. Laguna Beach
	5. Los Angeles
	6. Palm Springs
	7. Sacramento
	8. San Francisco
	9. West Hollywood
Colorado	10. Boulder
	11. Denver
District of	12. Washington
Columbia	
Florida	13. Key West
	14. Miami Shores
	15. St. Petersburg
	16. West Palm Beach
	17. Wilton Manors
Georgia	18. DeKalb County
Hawaii	19. Kihei
Illinois	20. Chicago
Louisiana	21. New Orleans
Maine	22. Portland
Maryland	23. Takoma Park
Massachusetts	24. Boston
	25. Provincetown
Michigan	26. Ferndale
Minnesota	27. Minneapolis
MIssouri	28. St. Louis
Nevada	29. Las Vegas
New Jersey	30. Collingswood
New Mexico	31. Santa Fe
New York	32. Ithaca
	33. Manhattan
North Carolina	34. Asheville
	35. Durham
Ohio	36. Columbus
	37. Lakewood
Oregon	38. Portland
Pennsylvania	39. Harrisburg
	40. Philadelphia
Rhode Island	41. Providence
Tennessee	42. Nashville
Texas	43. Austin
	44. Bellaire
	45. Dallas
Vermont	46. Burlington
Virginia	47. Alexandria
Washington	48. Olympia
	49. Seattle
Wisconson	50. Madison
Utah	51. Salt Lake City

50 Fabulous Gay

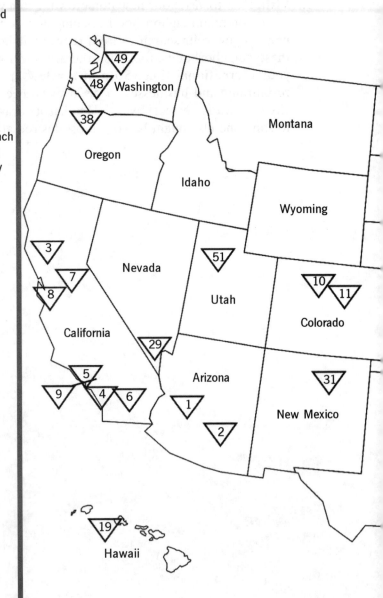

Friendly Places to Live

How to Use the Area Profiles

Throughout the profiles you'll see the letters "GLBT." This is a common gay-friendly acronym for gay, lesbian, bisexual, and transgender. The GLBT community profiles and organizations listed are often just a place's tip of the iceberg. Community centers, local GLBT publications, and GLBT chambers of commerce are excellent organizations for further research, and these are all included in the city profiles. Keep in mind that many local GLBT organizations are all-volunteer-staffed and under-funded. These organizations can move, disband, or change contact phone numbers and Website addresses without warning.

Frequently, you'll find a Website address for groups, organizations, and businesses listed in the city profiles. In our electronic world it's much easier to find information online, and having a reliable starting Website will help you further research the cities, organizations, and companies listed.

Local connections: The listed local providers for gas, electric, phone and cable services companies are often only suggestions. With deregulation and mergers, companies change or extend services to new areas.

Tax rate information: Tax rates change based on current economic factors. For the most up to-to-date tax information, contact city and state tax authorities. The Federal Tax Administrators (*www.taxadmin.org*) and BankRate.com (*www.bankrate.com*) provide online state-by-state tax comparisons. Both of these sites were helpful in finding local and state tax information for the city profiles.

Income figures: The per capita and median household income figures provided for each city profile are based on recent U.S. census data (2000). For comparison, average per capita income is $22,711 and average median household income is $47,493.

1 ▶ Phoenix, Arizona

A Look at Phoenix

Phoenix rests next to the Salt River between two mountain ranges and boasts more than 325 sun-filled days a year. This fabulous weather and location in the Sonoran Desert make for exceptional recreation opportunities including golfing at one of more than 200 courses, hiking, biking, hot-air ballooning, and horseback riding in glorious desert mountains and plains. Plus, there are swimming, sailing, and water skiing opportunities in the region's 75 lakes and rivers. Arizona is home to 21 different Native American tribes on 23 reservations. This rich Native American culture is represented within a collection of museums that serve as display cases for Western, Native American, Spanish, and other cultural heritages. These regional influences, mixed with the area's other international influx, create a wide variety of cuisine options often presented in unique atmospheres that include views of majestic mountains, serene desert, and amazing sunsets, making hunger an exciting opportunity. This array of environment, recreation, and cultural opportunities is further enhanced by a city *Governing* magazine selected the "Best Managed" city in 2000. Excellent management and services have created an environment rich with job and business opportunities in high-tech manufacturing, tourism, and construction.

Possible drawbacks: It's the desert and therefore hot in the summer. Though it's a dry heat (and yes, that does make a difference), it's still hot, with average July and August temperatures topping one hundred degrees.

Arizona

• *Flagstaff*

Phoenix
▼

Tucson •

▶ Nickname:
Sun Valley

▶ County:
Maricopa

▶ Area codes:
480; 602; 623

▶ Time zone:
Mountain (no DST)

▶ Population: 1,421,298

▶ County population:
3,072,149

▶ Region:
Southwest Arizona

▶ Average home price:
$210,000

▶ Fabulous reasons to live here:
Affordable housing, growing GLBT community, nightlife, culture, recreation, outstanding medical care, solid economy

Climate

Elevation 1117'	Avg. high/low (F°)	Avg. inches rain	Avg. inches snow	Avg. # days precip.	Avg. % humidity
Jan.	66/41	0.9	–	4	48%
April	84/54	0.3	–	2	29%
July	104/78	0.9	–	4	31%
Oct.	87/59	0.8	–	3	35%
YEAR	72.6	7.66	–	37	36%
# days 32° or below: 4			# days 90° or warmer: 169		

Local Connections

Gas company: Southwest Gas Corp. (602–395–4703; *www.swgas.com*)

Electric companies: Arizona Public Service (602–371–7171/800–253–9405; *www.aps.com*); Salt River Project (602–236–8888; *www.srpnet.com*)

Phone companies: Sprint (888–723–8010; *www.sprintpcs.com*); AT&T (800–222–0300; *www.att.com*); Verizon (800–483–4000; *www.verizon.com*); Qwest (800–491–0118; *www.qwest.com*)

Water and sewer: Phoenix Water and Sewer (602–262–6251; *phoenix.gov/WATER*)

Cable company: Cox (623–594–1000; *www.cox.com*)

Car registration/License: Arizona Department of Motor Vehicles (602–255–0072; *www.dot.state.az.us*)

New residents must obtain an Arizona driver's license and registration upon establishing residency (out-of-state college students exempt). Registration and title fees are $12. The driver's license is a one-time purchase with fees based on age: 16–39, $25; 40–44, $20; 45–49, $15; 50 and older, $10. An annual vehicle license tax (VLT) is charged based on the annual assessed car value. For example, the VLT on a new $25,000 vehicle would be $420.00 in the first year and $363.06 in the second year. License plates stay with the owner, not the vehicle.

The Tax Ax

Sales tax: 8.1 percent; prescription drugs exempt

State income tax: 2.87–5.04 percent graduated, depending on income

Property tax: Assessor's Office (602–506–3406); Arizona Department of Revenue (800–843–7196; *www.revenue.state.az.us*)

Tax rates vary considerably from area to area. The current average levy is $1.82 per $100 of assessed valuation.

Local Real Estate

Overview: Current growth in Phoenix is explosive, along with appreciation rates in most areas; many homeowners that would be sellers simply aren't because they are nearing the point of not being able to buy a replacement home. The number of buyers exceeds the number of sellers, further adding to the escalating prices. Ranch and traditional styles are common in the older areas; custom homes on hillsides include everything from hacienda and territorial to very industrial. Frank Lloyd Wright made his winter home here, so his style can be seen through the valley. (His winter home, Taliesin West, is a local and national tourist attraction.)

Median price for a single-family home: $190,000

Average price for a single-family home: $210,000

Average price for a 2BR condo: $195,000

Rental housing market: Rental vacancies are a bit high currently, so there are some good deals if you are looking to. Average two-bedrooms are renting for about $850.

Gay-friendly neighborhoods: The GLBT community makes its home throughout the valley. There's no gay center in Phoenix. Central Phoenix (also called Central Corridor and North Central Phoenix), with its historic neighborhoods, and Northern are popular.

Nearby areas to consider: As the Phoenix area's population continues to escalate, many GLBT community members are heading to the suburbs of Tempe, Chandler, Glendale, Fountain Hills, and Apache Junction. The GLBT community calls all of these cities home, and a growing number of community businesses, bars, and restaurants are popping up to accommodate the growing community. You'll also get a little more bang for your housing buck in most of these cities.

Earning a Living

Per capita income: $19,833

Median household income: $41,207

Business climate: Phoenix has a diversified economic base and an annual growth rate of about 4 percent, making it one of the top growing cities in the nation. The greater Phoenix area is a $50 billion marketplace driven by technology. Intel, Avnet, Motorola, AlliedSignal, Honeywell, and Boeing Company have their corporate and regional headquarters in Phoenix.

Help in starting a business: The Greater Phoenix Chamber of Commerce is a portal for the Employment Channel and hosts a series of Small Business Programs. The Greater Phoenix Gay & Lesbian Chamber of Commerce provides opportunities for its members to promote, network, and socialize.

Job market: Services, trade, government, manufacturing, finance, insurance, and real estate account for the biggest area industry sectors. The top five employers are American Express, America West Holdings, Arizona State University, Banc One Corp., and Banner Health System.

The Community

Overview: "You're Welcome Here Anytime." That's the community's motto for this large, active gay population. The community is well integrated into the city, making it possible to live downtown or in a nearby suburb and fit into the live-and-let-live attitude of the city. The Greater Phoenix Gay & Lesbian Chamber of Commerce (*www.gpglcc.org*) sponsors several major community events throughout the year, maintains a directory of gay-owned and gay-friendly businesses, and hosts two comprehensive Websites with up-to-date listings: Visit Gay Arizona (*www.visitgayarizona.com*) and Visit Lesbian Arizona (*www.visitlesbianarizona.com*).

Community organizations: Although the GLBT community lacks the central focus of a formal community center, there is a large collection of organized groups providing support and social opportunities for the Phoenix GLBT community. Whether bowling, choral singing, political action, human rights, biking, or rock climbing, there's a group or organization you'll fit right into. In addition, Phoenix is home to one of America's few GLBT retirement communities, The Calamus Communities (401 W. Clarendon; 602–870–7679; *www.calamuscommunities.com*), which also has a hotel on site.

Medical care: There are 42 hospitals with more than 8,100 beds in Greater Phoenix. Among the many fabulous health programs in Phoenix is the Southern Arizona AIDS Foundation (SAAF) (520–628–7223; *www.saaf.org*) with a mission of creating and sustaining a healthier community through a compassionate, comprehensive response to HIV/AIDS. SAAF provides direct services and programs in safe, supportive environments that enhance the quality of life for those living with and affected by HIV/AIDS; assisting people in avoiding HIV infection; and empowering people to lead healthy, productive lives. Another compassionate program is the Lesbian Cancer Project (602–263–5622; *www.lcparizona.org*), which provides support, education, direct services, and advocacy for lesbians and their families of choice who have been touched by cancer.

Nuptials: The state of Arizona has a law similar to DOMA defining marriage as between a man and a woman. The state doesn't acknowledge same-sex marriges from other jurisdictions. Many area employers extend benefits to domestic partners.

Getting Around Town

Public transportation: Valley Metro (602–253–5000; *www.valleymetro.org*) provides regional bus service (standard fare $1.25; all-day pass $3.60; express $1.75) and is constructing a light-rail to better connect the greater Phoenix area.

Roads: US60; US79; US85; I-17; I-40

Airport: Phoenix Sky Harbor International Airport (airport code: PHX) (602–273–3300; *www.phoenix-phx.com*) is one of the nation's busiest, served by more than 20 airlines. J.D. Power & Associates ranks it as one of the nation's top two airports for customer service. Ground transportation costs are about $10 to downtown.

It's a Gay Life

Annual events: There are plenty of annual events, festivals, and fairs to keep everyone busy in Phoenix throughout the year and the GLBT community adds many of its own. Arizona Central Pride (*www.azpride.org*) hosts the annual pride weekend in April. Other events include the AGRA Road Runner Regional Rodeo (*www.agra-phx.com*) and the all-women's professional rodeo event Sierra Stampede (*www.sierrastampede.com*) in January, February's Outfar Gay and Lesbian Film Festival (*www.outfar.org*), *Echo Magazine*'s Gays and Friends Day at the Renaissance Festival (*www.echomag.com*), where knights joust in March, the September Sedona Jazz on the Rocks Jazz Festival (*www.sedonajazz.com*), and the Rainbows Festival (*www.rainbowsfestival.com*) in October.

Nightlife: There are breweries, comedy clubs, dance bars, sports bars, and lounges throughout the city as well as more than 35 GLBT bars sprinkled across Phoenix. Cactus Mountain offers casino action. Although there's no central gay zone within the city, the downtown shopping district, which includes 5th Avenue, Old Town, Main Street, and Marshall Way, is active between Camelback Road and Indian School Road, and 7th Street North is home to a half dozen GLBT bars. Visit The Bookstore (4230 N. 7th Avenue; 602–279–3910) to pick up a copy of *Echo Magazine* (*www.echomag.com*) with current listings, events, and community news.

Culture: Museums, galleries, symphonies, theaters, and arenas create a well-balanced cultural scene in Phoenix. A variety of museums offer indigenous history, national history, and contemporary art. Of exceptional interest are the Heard Museum (2301 N. Central Avenue; 602–252–8848; *www.heard.org*), well known for its Native American art exhibits; the Phoenix Art Museum (1625 N. Central Avenue; 602–257–1222; *www.phxart.org*), host of the Cowboy Artists Show and home to a permanent collection of nearly 16,000 pieces ranging the past six centuries; the Arizona Science Center (600 E. Washington Street; 602–716–2000; *www.azscience.org*), with 350 hands-on exhibits; and the Hall of Flame Museum of Firefighting (6101 E. Van Buren Street; 602–275–3473; *www.hallofflame.org*), with its display of three centuries of firefighting equipment. More than two dozen theater groups offer everything from Broadway plays to lyric opera. The Phoenix Symphony Orchestra (602–495–1999; *www.phoenixsymphony.org*) performs at Symphony Hall fall through spring. The Herberger Theater Center (222 E. Monroe; 602–254–7399; *www.herbergertheater.org*) hosts Ballet Arizona (602–381–1096; *www.balletaz.org*), the Arizona Opera Company (602–266–7464; *www.azopera.com*), and the Arizona Theatre Company (602–256–6995; *www.aztheatreco.org*). Also of importance is the longest continuously running community theater in the nation, the Phoenix Theatre (100 E. McDowell; 602–254–2151; *www.phxtheatre.org*). Touring shows and performers appear at America

West Arena (201 E. Jefferson Street; 602–379–2000; *www.americawestarena.com*), Bank One Ballpark (4300 N. Miller Road; 480–994–0471; *www.bankoneballpark.com*), Dodge Theatre (400 W. Washington Street; 602–379–2888; *www.dodgetheatre.com*), the outdoor Cricket Pavilion (2121 N. 83rd Avenue; 602–254–7200; *www.cricket-pavilion.com*), ASU's Gammage Auditorium (1200 S. Forest Avenue; 480–965–3434; *www.asugammage.com*), Red River Music Hall (*www.redrivermusichall.com*), and the Sundome (19403 R. H. Johnson Boulevard; 623–975–1900; *www.asusundome.com*), as well as area nightclubs.

Recreation: With more than 1,700 acres of traditional park land, the world's largest municipal park (South Mountain Park), and excellent year-round weather Phoenix boasts more than 200 golf courses, countless tennis courts, hundreds of miles of trails for hiking, biking, and horseback riding, and six lakes within 75 minutes to provide a lifetime of recreational opportunities. The nearby mountains are perfect for skiing and sledding during the winter months. For spectators, there are regular tournament stops for the PGA FBR Open (602–870–4431; *www.phoenixopen.com*), the LPGA Safeway International (602–495–GOLF; *www.safewaygolf.com*), and the PGA Gila River Classic (*www.pgatour.com*) in Phoenix. The city is home to the Tostitos Fiesta Bowl (480–350–0900; *www.tostitosfiestabowl.com*), the NFL's Arizona Cardinals (623–266–5000; *www.azcardinals.com*), MLB's Arizona Diamondbacks (602–514–8400; *www.azdiamondbacks.com*), the NBA's Phoenix Suns (602–379–SUNS; *www.nba.com/suns/*), the NHL's Phoenix Coyotes (623–463–8800; *www.phoenixcoyotes.com*), arena football's Arizona Rattlers (602–514–8300; *www.azrattlers.com*), and the WNBA's Phoenix Mercury (602–514–8333; *www.wbna.com.mercury*). Each spring, Phoenix hosts the Cactus League (*www.cactus-league.com*), consisting of nine major league baseball teams. To round things out, Phoenix International Raceway (125 S. Avondale Boulevard, Avondale; 602–252–2227; *www.phoenixintlraceway.com*) hosts Indy Car and NASCAR events, and there's drag racing at Manzanita Speedway (3417 W. Broadway Road; 602–276–7575; *www.manzanitaspeedway.us*) and boat racing at Firebird International Raceway (20000 W. Maricopa Road; 602–268–0200; *www.firebirdraceway.com*).

For the Visitor

Accommodations: With more than 55,000 hotel rooms and numerous four- and five-diamond resorts (AAA rating), finding a place to stay during your visit shouldn't be a problem. There are plenty of gay-friendly accommodations, too. Arizona Biltmore Resort and Spa (2400 East Missouri; 866–950–1039; *www.arizonabiltmore.com*) is the "Jewel of the Desert"; Downtown's historic Hotel San Carlos (202 N. Central Avenue; 866–253–4121; *www.hotelsancarlos.com*) is a luxury boutique hotel within walking distance to attractions and the convention center; Maricopa Manor Bed & Breakfast (15 W. Pasadena Avenue; 800–292–6403; *www.maricopamanor.com*) is an in-city B&B with fireplaces and jet tubs; Yum Yum Tree Guest House (90 W. Virginia; 602–265–2590; *www.yytguesthouse.com*) has five unique guest suites located in a historic neighborhood; and Arizona Royal Villa Resort (1110 E. Turney Avenue; 888–266–6884; *www.royalvilla.com*) is a men's-only, clothing-optional resort.

For More Information

Publications

Echo Magazine
P.O. Box 16630
Phoenix, AZ 85011-6630
602–266–0550
www.echomag.com

The Arizona Republic
200 E. Van Buren Street
Phoenix, AZ 85004
602–444–8000
www.arizonarepublic.com

East Valley Tribune
120 W. First Avenue
Mesa, AZ 85210
480–898–6500
www.eastvalleytribune.com

Convention and Visitors Bureau

Greater Phoenix Convention and
Visitors Bureau
400 E. Van Buren Street, Suite 600
Phoenix, AZ 85004
602–254–6500
www.phoenixcvb.com

Chambers of Commerce

Greater Phoenix Chamber of
Commerce
Bank One Center
201 North Central Avenue,
27th Floor
Phoenix, AZ 85073
602–254–5521
www.phoenixchamber.com

Greater Phoenix Gay and Lesbian
Chamber of Commerce
P.O. Box 2097
Phoenix, AZ 85001-2097
888–429–2948
www.gpglcc.org

Realtor

Ron Houston
Realtor
Coldwell Banker Success Realty
6330 N. 7th Avenue
Phoenix, AZ 85013
602–402–2459
www.RonHoustonHomes.com

Tucson, Arizona

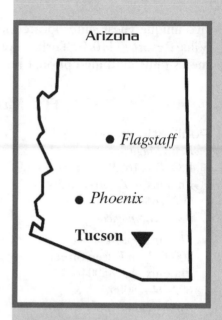

A Look at Tucson

Having been continuously settled for more than 12,000 years, Tucson is one of the oldest towns in the United States. It celebrates a diversity of cultures, architecture, and peoples. Tucsonans enjoy a low-key lifestyle. The pace is naturally relaxed, the weather mild, dress casual, the cost of living low, and the natural and cultural attractions plentiful. Tucson's rich cultural heritage is centered around a unique blend of Native American, Spanish, Mexican, and Anglo-American influences. Blessed with the natural beauty of the Sonoran Desert and an unsurpassed climate of 360 sunny days a year, Tucsonans embrace a rare lifestyle and are committed to preserving that quality of life. The City's dry desert air and winter sunshine make it a popular health and winter resort. Tucson is set to become one of the "Mega-Trend" cities of the 21st century with the Optics Valley, premier health services center for the Southwest, the astronomy center of the world, a tourism destination, and home to a premier research institution, the University of Arizona. Tucson boasts the best of both worlds: the progress and innovation of a metropolitan community and the friendly, caring atmosphere of a small town.

Possible drawbacks: Urban sprawl is the name of the game. The city of Tucson is spread over 156 square miles of desert that gets extremely hot in the summer months. You'll need a car with excellent air conditioning if you make Tucson your home.

▸ Nickname:
Old Pueblo

▸ County:
Pima

▸ Area code:
520

▸ Time zone:
Mountain (no DST)

▸ Population:
486,699

▸ County population:
843,746

▸ Region:
Southeast Arizona

▸ Average home price:
$150,000

▸ Fabulous reasons to live here:
Arts, culture, history, scenic environment, relaxed pace, affordable housing, new-knowledge-based economy

Climate

Elevation 2483'	Avg. high/low(F°)	Avg. inches rain	Avg. inches snow	Avg. # days precip.	Avg. % humidity
Jan.	66/40	1.0	0.3	4	47%
April	83/52	0.3	0.1	2	29%
July	101/75	1.9	–	10	42%
Oct.	86/58	1.2	–	3	38%
YEAR	84/56	12	0.9	52	38%
# days 32° or below: 11			# days 90° or warmer: 144		

Local Connections

Gas company: Southwest Gas Corporation (520–889–1888; *www.swgas.com*)

Electric company: Tucson Electric Power Company (520–623–7711; *www.tucsonelectric.com*)

Phone companies: Qwest (800–491–0118; *www.qwest.com*); AT&T (520–615–4400; *www.att.com*); Sprint (520–888–1930; *www.sprint.com*); MCI (520–918–8000; *www.mci.com*)

Water and sewer: Tucson Water Department (520–791–3242; *www.ci.tucson.az.us/water*)

Cable companies: Comcast (800–COMCAST; *www.comcast.com*); Cox Communications (520–884–0133; *www.cox.com*)

Car registration/License: Arizona Department of Motor Vehicles (602–255–0072; *www.dot.state.az.us*)

New residents must obtain an Arizona driver's license and registration upon establishing residency (out-of-state college students exempt). Registration and title fees are $12. The driver's license is a one-time purchase with fees based on age: 16–39, $25; 40–44, $20; 45–49, $15; 50 and older, $10. An annual vehicle license tax (VLT) is charged based on the annual assessed car value. For example, the VLT on a new $25,000 vehicle would be $420.00 in the first year and $363.06 in the second year. License plates stay with the owner, not the vehicle.

The Tax Ax

Sales tax: 5.6 percent; prescription drugs exempt

State income tax: 2.87–5.04 percent graduated, depending on income

Property tax: Arizona Department of Revenue (800–843–7196; *www.revenue.state.az.us*)

Residential real estate is assessed at 10 percent of fair market value. The average tax rate is $16 per $100 of assessed value or roughly 1.1 percent of the sales price.

Local Real Estate

Overview: The Tucson housing market is consistent, although at times experiences periods of low inventory in terms of resale, but, being a military and college town, there is always movement. It is estimated that 420 people visit Tucson on a daily basis, with some 4,000 moving here a month. New home construction is at an all-time high. The Tucson real estate market does not experience the peaks and valleys of larger towns when it comes to market pricing. There's a small but steady increase in housing prices dictated primarily by the area of town.

Median price for a single-family home: $185,000

Average price for a single-family home: $150,000

Average price for a 2BR condo: $125,000

Rental housing market: 49 percent of Tucson residents are renting college students, military personnel, and temporary Raytheon position workers. Rents fluctuate with demand (that is, cheaper in spring and summer, higher in fall and winter).

Gay-friendly neighborhoods: Tucson as a whole is gay-friendly. GLBT members live all over the city and are quite happy with their neighborhoods. The 4th Street area near campus is popular because of its "Old Tucson" charm with bungalows and Victorians scattered about.

Nearby areas to consider: An hour southeast of Tucson is the small, ex-mining town of Bisbee. Popular with artists, this small community has many boutiques, art galleries, and bed and breakfasts. Oro Valley, about 15 miles to the north of Tucson, is a smaller community with fabulous parks. Catalina, about 45 minutes to the north of Tucson, is a small, rural town run by a volunteer village council and popular with the retirement community.

Earning a Living

Per capita income: $16,322

Median household income: $30,981

Business climate: Tucson has become a leader in the new knowledge-based economy. The City of Tucson, Pima County, the State of Arizona, and the private sector have all made commitments to create a growing, healthy economy with high-tech industries as its foundation. Tucson is seeing growth with new business including a new research center co-developed with the nation's pharmaceutical companies.

Help in starting a business: Recognizing the importance of linking regional economic expansion with the needs of the community, the Office of Economic Development (520–791–5093; *www.ci.tucson.az.us/oed*) strives to promote neighborhood commercial revitalization and the economic well-being of Tucson's neighborhoods with a primary focus on growth, retention, and expansion of local businesses through facilitation, communication, and advocacy. Both the Tucson

Metropolitan Chamber of Commerce and the Tucson Hispanic Chamber of Commerce offer networking, advertising, and small business advice. The Community Business Association (*www.tucsonglbtchamber.org*) provides a forum for Tucson's GLBT business community for the purpose of networking to create increased visibility and strengthen business relationships.

Job market: Tucson is home to the University of Arizona and Davis-Monthan Air Force Base. Advanced technology companies such as Raytheon Missile Systems, Texas Instruments, IBM, and America Online call Tucson home. Other industries include electronics and missile production, education, and professional services.

The Community

Overview: The GLBT community of Tucson is active and organized, both politically and socially. The city of Tucson has a GLBT Commission (*www.tucsonglbtcommission.org*) to foster conditions that promote the welfare of GLBT people of metropolitan Tucson through education, advocacy, and collaborative and advisory relationships with government, community organizations, businesses, and individuals.

Community organizations: There are scores of groups and organizations that offer services and social activities throughout the city. Wingspan (*www.wingspan.org*) operates the Southern Arizona GLBT Community Center, providing services and resources and organizing activities and events for the GLBT community. Wingspan maintains the most comprehensive list of contact information for the varied health, service, and social GLBT groups in Tucson.

Medical care: Before state-of-the-art medical facilities existed, the dry desert air in Arizona was recommended by doctors across the country for patients with respiratory problems. Tucson now boasts some of the most sophisticated healthcare available anywhere; healthcare statewide is a multi-billion dollar industry and one of the largest sectors of its economy. The University of Arizona Health Sciences Center (520–621–2211; *www.ahsc.arizona.edu*), Tucson Medical Center (502–327–5461; *www.tmcaz.com*), and University Medical Center (520–694–0111; *www.azumc.com*) are among the leaders in area full-service providers. Tucsonans also have access to alternative medical treatments in the form of acupuncture and oriental medicine, hypnotherapy, massage therapy, biofeedback, bioenergetics manipulation, homeopathy, and chiropractic care. A number of local doctors are familiar with the benefits of alternative therapies and are trained to provide such services or can refer patients to an alternative practitioner.

Nuptials: The city of Tucson sponsors a domestic partner registry through its GLBT Commission (*www.tucsonglbtcommission.org*). The ordinance lists just two rights or benefits for registered partners in the City of Tucson: (1) a right to visitation of one's partner in a health care facility, as long as the patient consents, and (2) extending use of and access to city facilities to a registered domestic partner as if the domestic partner were a spouse. Registration fee: $50.

Getting Around Town

Public transportation: Sun Tran (520–792–9222; *www.suntran.com*) provides city bus service. Fare: $1 (all-day pass $2). In the downtown area, catch a free ride on the Tucson Inner City Express Transit (TICET) (520–791–5071).

Roads: I-10, I-19, US79, US86

Airport: Tucson International Airport (airport code: TUS) (520–573–8000; *www.tucsonairport.com*) is located approximately 10 miles from the center of town and services 11 airlines.

It's a Gay Life

Annual events: Tucson Pride (*www.tucsonpride.com*) produces three events each year: Pride Week in June, Gay West in May, and OUToberFEST in October. The Screening Room, Tucson's premiere venue for independent film, hosts the annual Arizona International Film Festival (*www.azfilmfest.com*). Other city events of note are the Tucson Gem & Mineral Show (*www.tucsonshowguide.com*), the Pima County Fair (*www.swfair.com*), the Fourth Avenue Street Fair (*www.fourthavenue.org*), and community events such as La Fiesta de los Vaqueros (*www.tucsonrodeo.com*), Cinco de Mayo, and the Fiesta de los Chiles (*www.tucsonbotanical.org*). Contact the Metropolitan Tucson Convention and Visitors Bureau for times and dates.

Nightlife: There are more than 3,000 eateries in Tucson. More than 150 serve authentic Mexican cuisine, from Sonoran to Mexico City style and local hybrids in between. Tucson's restaurants feature some local landmarks, such as the oldest continuously family-owned restaurant in the country; others, such as the Wild West Steakhouse that prohibits neckties, inject fun and entertainment into the dining experience. Several bars serve the GLBT community, including the Venture-N (1239 N. 6th Avenue; 520–882–8224), a leather/Levi bar; the dance bar IBT's (516 N. 4th Avenue; 520–882–3053; *www.ibts.net*); the Biz (2900 E. Broadway; 520–318–4838), popular with women during the week/mixed crowd on the weekends; Yard Dog (2449 N. Stone; 520–624–3858) with a patio; Woody's (3710 N. Oracle Road; 520–292–5702) with weekly events and activities; and Novembers Bar & Grill (4001 N. Romero Road; 520–407–9622) with pool, food, a dance floor, and drag shows. Visit Antigone Books (411 N. 4th Avenue; 520–792–3715; *www.antigonebooks.com*) and pick up *The Weekly Observer* (520–622–7176; *www.tucsonobserver.com*) for current listings and events.

Culture: Downtown is the historic and cultural heart of Tucson, and Congress Street is the center of the action. The Tucson Convention Center (260 S. Church Avenue; 520–791–4101; *www.tucsonaz.gov/tcc*) and the Temple of Music and Art (330 S. Scott Avenue) host performances by the Tucson Symphony (520–822–8585; *www.tucsonsymphony.org*), the Arizona Opera (520–293–4336; *www.azopera.com*), the Arizona Friends of Chamber Music (520–577–3769; *www.arizonachambermusic.org*), the Arizona Ballet (602–381–1096; *www.balletaz.org*), the Theater League, and Arizona Theatre Company (520–622–2823; *www.aztheatreco.org*). Old Town

Artisan galleries are located in a 150-year-old adobe that was built on the foundation of the original walled Presidio of Tucson. The Tucson Museum of Art (140 N. Main Avenue; 520–624–2333; *www.tucsonarts.com*) is renowned for its pre-Columbian artifacts and Western art collection, and the Historic Block features five of Tucson's oldest homes, art galleries, museum shop, school, library, and Cafe a la C'Art. The University of Arizona (*www.arizona.edu*) is home to The Arizona State Museum (1013 E. University Boulevard; 520–621–6302; *www.statemuseum.arizona.edu*), the Southwest's oldest and largest anthropology museum, with one of the nation's most significant cultural resources, the largest and most comprehensive collection of whole-vessel Southwest Indian ceramics, and The Center for Creative Photography (1030 N. Olive Road; 520–621–7968; *www.creativephotography.org*), founded by Ansel Adams and home to his prints. Other museums of note are the Pima Air and Space Museum (6000 E. Valencia Road; 520–574–0462; *www.pimaair.org*), the world-famous Arizona-Sonora Desert Museum (2021 N. Kinney Road; 520–883–2702; *www.desertmuseum.org*), Tucson Botanical Gardens (2150 N. Alvernon Way; 520–326–9686; *www.tucsonbotanical.org*), Reid Park Zoo (1030 S. Randolph Way; 520–881–4753; *www.tucsonzoo.org*), and Old Tucson Studios (201 S. Kinney Road; 520–883–0100; *www.oldtucsonstudios.com*). Mission San Xavier del Bac (1950 W. San Zavier Road; 520–294–2624; *www.sanxaviermission.org*), known as the "White Dove of the Desert," provides a peaceful respite.

Recreation: Tucson's climate varies from the 2,400-foot desert basin to the 9,100-foot forests of the Santa Catalina mountains. It's surrounded by five mountain ranges with hundreds of trails creating a year round "hiker's heaven." Mount Lemmon ski resort (*www.mt-lemmon.com*) is a favorite among skiers. Tucson is home to one of the United States' newest national parks: Saguaro National Park (*www.saguaro.national-park.com*), with the world's largest concentration of saguaro cactus. Colossal Cave (*www.colossalcave.com*) is one of the largest dry caverns in the world where explorers will enjoy a constant 70 degrees. The mild climate and outstanding courses also make Tucson a favorite golf destination and home to the PGA Tour's Chrysler Classic of Tucson (520–571–0400; *www.Tucson.pgatour.com*). Take your best shot on a challenging desert golf course or enjoy a more traditional links-style layout, playing the same courses the PGA pros do. For spectator sport enthusiasts, Tucson is the Spring Training venue for three major league baseball teams: the Arizona Diamondbacks (602–514–8400; *www.azdiamondbacks.com*), the Chicago White Sox (312–674–1000; *Chicago.whitesox.mlb.com*), and the Colorado Rockies (303–ROCKIES; *www.coloradorockies.com*).

For the Visitor

Accommodations: The Royal Elizabeth Bed & Breakfast Inn (204 S. Scott Avenue; 877–670–9022; *www.royalelizabeth.com*) is a beautiful 1878 Victorian adobe mansion in Historic Downtown Tucson. The Casa de San Pedro Bed & Breakfast Inn (8933 South Yell Lane, Hereford; 888–257–2050; *www.bedandbirds.com*) is located on 10 acres adjacent to the San Pedro River and Riparian National Conservation Area and perfect for bird watching, outdoor adventures, or a romantic getaway in the high desert. Tucson also has 10 major destination resorts: Canyon Ranch (8600 E. Rockliff Road; 800–742–9000; *www.canyonranch.com*), Dove Mountain (13900 N. Dove Mountain Boulevard; 888–603–7600; *www.dovemountain.com*), La Tierra Linda (7501 N. Wade Road; 888–872–6241; *www.bkmcreativeservices.com/latierralinda.com*), Loews Ventana Canyon (7000 N. Resort Drive; 800–234–5117; *www.loewshotels.com*), Miraval (5000 E. Via Estancia Mirval; 800–232–3969; *www.miravalresort.com*), Hilton Tucson El Conquistador Golf & Tennis Resort (10000 N. Oracle Road; 800–445–8667; *www.hiltonconquistador.com*), Tanque Verde Guest Ranch (14301 E. Speedway; 520–296–6275; *www.tanqueverderanch.com*), Omin Tucson National Golf Resort (2727 W. Club Drive; 520–297–2271; *www.tucsonnational.com*), Westin La Paloma (3800 E. Sunrise Drive; 800–937–8461; *www.westinlapalomaresort.com*), and Westward Look Resort (245 E. Ina Road; 800–722–2500; *www.westwardlook.com*).

For More Information

Gay & Lesbian Center
Wingspan
300 E. Sixth Street
Tucson, AZ 85705
520–624–1779
www.wingspan.org

Publications
Arizona Star
4850 S. Park Avenue
Tucson, AZ 85714
520–573–4511
www.azstarnet.com

Tucson Citizen
P.O. Box 26767
Tucson, AZ 85726-6767
520–573–4561
www.tucsoncitizen.com

Convention and Visitors Bureau
Metropolitan Tucson Convention
and Visitors Bureau
100 S. Church Avenue
Tucson, AZ 85701
520–624–1817/800–638–8350
www.visittucson.org

Chambers of Commerce
The Community Business
Association
P.O. Box 14312
Tucson, AZ 85732
520–615–6436
www.tucsonglbtchamber.org

Tucson Metropolitan Chamber of
Commerce
P.O. Box 991
465 W. St. Mary's Road
Tucson, AZ 85701
520–792–1212
www.tucsonchamber.org

Realtor
Steven McGarrigle
Realtor, ABR, Notary
Coldwell Banker Success Southwest
8872 E. Tanque Verde Road
Tucson, AZ 85749
520–247–6355
www.imasoldman.com

3 ▶ Guerneville, California

A Look at Guerneville

What began as loggers' cabins and vacation homes 140 years ago gradually turned into small communities of foresters, farmers, and merchants. Among these hamlets, Guerneville, once the hub of the redwood timber mills, offers great opportunities in a town known for its social and cultural diversity. A gay-friendly, year-round haven just 75 miles north of San Francisco, Guerneville combines the finest wine with dining, a flourishing arts community, interesting history, and the bounty of northern California's great outdoors in one location. Though still a favorite getaway for retreats and vacations, many of the attractive and unique 1920s cabins and historic cottages have become year-round homes. The beauty of the area has attracted artists and craftsman colonies, rejuvenating spas, and some of the finest dining experiences in the United States. Hills covered in cows and woolly sheep, orchards, and gardens where the freshest, often organic, produce is grown for your dinner table and farms of every variety are all to be discovered in this wondrous country. Life here can be relaxing and rejuvenating or fast-paced and exciting, depending on your tastes and desires. The Russian River area inspires a diverse lifestyle where one can savor the delights of country living near larger city commerce.

Possible drawbacks: The Russian River is a weekend getaway spot for northern California, especially San Francisco. This could be the best of both worlds, unless you're looking to totally escape the big city.

▶ Nickname:
Russian River
▶ County:
Sonoma
▶ Area code:
707
▶ Time zone:
Pacific
▶ Population:
2,441
▶ County population:
458,614
▶ Region:
Northern California
▶ Closest metro area:
Santa Rosa–Petaluma
▶ Average home price:
$443,000
▶ Fabulous reasons to live here:
Beautiful scenery, laid-back pace, excellent recreation, integrated GLBT community

Climate

Elevation 56'	Avg. high/low (F°)	Avg. inches		Avg. # days precip.	Avg. % humidity
		rain	snow		
Jan.	57/38	11.6	0.1	10	80%
April	69/43	3.2	–	5	63%
July	83/51	0.1	–	0	53%
Oct.	75/46	3.0	–	3	58%
YEAR	78/45	56.0	0.4	57	64%
# days 32° or below: 0			# days 90° or warmer: 0		

Local Connections

Gas and electric company: Pacific Gas and Electric Company (800–743–5000; *www.pge.com*)

Phone company: AT&T (800–924–9224; *www.att.com*)

Water and sewer: Sweetwater Springs Water District (707–869–4000; *www.sweetwatersprings.com*)

Cable company: Comcast Communications (707–584–4434; *www.comcast.com*)

Car registration/License: California Department of Motor Vehicles (800–777–0133; *www.dmv.ca.gov*)

You must get a California driver license within 10 days of establishing residency. License application fee: $25. If you have a valid license from another state, the driving test can be waived. Car registration and registration renewals are $31. The Vehicle License Fee (VLF) replaces property tax on vehicles. The formula for VLF assessment is based upon the purchase price or value of the vehicle and decreases with each renewal for the first 11 years. The VLF on a $25K vehicle for the first two years would be $163 and $147, respectively. The VLF is prorated for partial year registrations.

The Tax Ax

Sales tax: 7.5 percent

State income tax: 1.0–9.3 percent graduated, depending on income

Property tax: Assessor (707–565–1888; *www.sonoma-county.org/Assessor*)

The general tax levy is determined in accordance with State law and is limited to $1 per $100 of assessed value of your property. The Homeowner Exemption allows a homeowner to exempt up to $7,000 of property value from taxation each year if you owned and occupied your property on January 1. Once granted, the exemption remains in effect every year until it is terminated.

Local Real Estate

Overview: Guerneville and the Russian River area are a mix of historic, rustic cabins, river view homes of new construction, log homes, and large estate-style properties with many private acres.

Median price for a single-family home: $220,100

Average price for a single-family home: $443,000

Average price for a 2BR condo: $295,000

Rental housing market: The median rent in the Guerneville area is $651, with a two-bedroom rental at approximately $800.

Gay-friendly neighborhoods: All of Guerneville and the surrounding Russian River area are gay-friendly.

Nearby areas to consider: Sebastopol, Forestville, and Occidental are all small, gay-friendly cities in the Russian River area each with its own charms. Sebastopol is one of the area's cultural centers, with theater and the arts a city priority. The historic town of Occidental, nestled among the hills and redwoods, is renowned for its collection of unique shops and boutiques. Forestville is something of a resort area with wineries, first-class hotels, and a low-key, family atmosphere.

Earning a Living

Per capita income: $22,793

Median household income: $37,266

Business climate: Local businesses in Guerneville are small and tourist- or service-related. Agriculture and services are the main business focus in the Russian River area. These are supply-and-demand sectors reliant on the national economy as a whole. The advantage of Guerneville is its location. Within a 30-minute commute you have almost all of Sonoma County available to you and, with San Francisco about an hour away, you open up incredible markets and possibilities.

Help in starting a business: The Russian River Chamber of Commerce and Visitors Center (707–869–9000/877–644–9001; *www. russianriver.com*) offers job and business assistance, as well as networking and advertising opportunities. Redwood Empire Small Business Development Center (707–524–1770/888–346–7232; *www.santarosa.edu/sbdc*) in Santa Rosa provides help and information for small businesses. The Sonoma County Public Library system (Guerneville branch: 707–869–9004; *www.sonoma.lib.ca.us*) also offers a wide variety of information for small businesses.

Job market: Education, health, and social services; arts, entertainment, recreation, accommodation, and food services; and manufacturing make up the job markets. The county's top employers are Agilent Technologies, Inc., St. Joseph Health System, Sonoma State University, Kaiser Permanente, and Optical Coating Laboratory. Sonoma County Job Link (707–565–5550; *www.socojoblink.org*)

offers resources for both the employer and the job-seeker in Sonoma County with links to California and national employment resources, including jobs for youths.

The Community

Overview: Pick up your Russian River Gay Guide at the Russian River Visitor's center or at your lodge's concierge office. Sonoma County Gay and Lesbian Info Referral Line: 707–526–0442

Community organizations: The Russian River area and Sonoma County have dozens of well-organized community, political, social, health, and religious community organizations. Check out GaySonoma.com (*gaysonoma.com*) for the area's most comprehensive list of organizations as well as area classifieds, personals, a gay-friendly business directory, and a calendar of area events. The Russian River Sisters of Perpetual Indulgence (707–490–5995; *www.rrsisters.org*) lead the way in charitable fundraising and fabulous fun. The Metropolitan Community Church meets at Guerneville's Odd Fellows Hall (16219 First Street; 707–869–0552) at 10 a.m. on Sundays.

Medical care: Palm Drive Hospital (707–823–8511; *www.palmdrivehospital.com*) in Sebastopol provides a 24-hour emergency room, an intensive-care unit, outpatient surgery, laboratory services, radiology services, a women's imaging center, and pain management and rehabilitation services. Kaiser Permanente Santa Rosa Medical Center (707–571–5000; *www.kaiserpermanente.org*) provides a full range of medical care. Healdsburg District Hospital (707–431–6500; *www.h-g-h.org*) is a district hospital whose mission is to meet the healthcare needs of the population with a constant striving for the highest quality care and service, innovative and responsible use of resources, and compassion for its customers.

Nuptials: California offers a domestic partnership registration (*www.ss.ca.gov/dpregistry*). Registration isn't the same as marriage, but it does secure many important rights and responsibilities. Under current law, registration can protect your rights in times of family crisis, protect your children, and give you access to family benefits at work.

Getting Around Town

Public transportation: Sonoma County Transit (707–576–7433/800–345–7433; *www.sctransit.com*) provides bus service to the entire county. Local Route 28 (Monday–Friday only) connects Guerneville to the county. Fares are zone-based ($1.10–2.90). Bill's Taxi Service (707–869–2177) is available 24 hours.

Roads: SR116 (SR1, SR12, and US101 nearby)

Airport: San Francisco International (airport code: SFO) (650–821–8211; *www.flysfo.com*), 75 miles away, is the closest full-service airport. The Sonoma County Airport Express offers bus service between the Sonoma County Airport and San Francisco International for $26 one-way.

It's a Gay Life

Annual events: Women's Weekends (*www.russianriverwomensweekend.com*) are held in May and September. June events include Stumptown Daze, Mr. Russian River Resort Leather (*www.russianriverresort.com*), Sonoma County Pride (*www.SonomaPride.com*), and the Russian River Blues Festival (*www.russianriverbluesfest.com*). Along with fireworks, July offers the Lazy Bear Weekend and Rainbow Classic Softball (*www.rainbowclassic.com*). September is graced with the Russian River Jazz Festival (*www.russianrivereagle.com*). The Russian River Leather Weekend is in November, and you won't want to miss the Parade of Lights (707–869–9000) in early December. Gay Russian River (*www.gayrussianriver.com*) is the best online source for all the events and businesses serving the Russian River area.

Nightlife: Guerneville's plaza, shops, restaurants, cafes, pubs, clubs, and lodgings in its busy downtown draw people from all walks of life. Intimate evenings in front of the fire should be on your list. The Russian River Resort (Triple "R") (16390 4th Street; 707–869–0691/800–417–3767; *www.russianriverresort.com*) is the beautiful home of fabulous events including weekly comedy nights and special guest comedians, karaoke, psychic nights, drag shows, and community fundraisers. On Fridays and Saturdays check out Club Fab (16135 Main Street; 707–869–5708; *www.clubfab.com*). Housed in a converted 1930s movie theater in downtown Guerneville, it's the biggest dance club north of the Golden Gate. Fife's Resort and Bunkhouse (16467 River Road; 707–869–0656/800–734–3371) is a medium-sized club-house/disco. Even when the Bunkhouse is closed, Fife's bar by the swimming pool and restaurant are usually open. Other highlights include the Rainbow Cattle Company (16220 Main Street; 707–869–3400) and the Russian River Eagle (16225 Main Street; 707–869–3400). Mc T's Bullpen (16246 1st Street; 707–869–3377) is a sports bar located right downtown and is the perfect place for enjoying a regional beer and watching a game. The Stumptown Brewery (15045 River Road; 707–869–0705; *www.stumptown.com/brews*) is the place for ribs and local brewed beer.

Culture: The Russian River area of Sonoma County is home to hundreds of artists representing all the mediums. Each small hamlet has its own collection of galleries of the local artists' works. The local playhouses Pegasus Theater (20347 Highway 116, Monte Rio; 707–522–9043; *www.pegasustheater.com*) in Monte Rio, the Main Street Theater (104 N. Main Street, Sebastopol; 707–823–0177) in nearby Sebastopol, Sebastopol Center for the Arts (6780 Depot Street; 707–829–4797; *www.sebarts.org*), and Sonoma County Repertory Theatre – Sebastopol (104 N. Main Street, Sebastopol; 707–823–0177; *www.the-rep.com*) stage works throughout the season. The Luther Burbank Center for the Arts (500 Mark W. Springs Road, Santa Rosa; 707–546–3600; *www.lbc.net*) is about 20 miles away in Santa Rosa. The LBC is home to the Ruth Finley Person Theater, Carston Cabaret, and the Wells Fargo Stage where touring productions, headliners, and concerts are performed. The Museum of Contemporary Art exhibits provocative and significant contemporary work by local, regional, national, and international artists.

Recreation: Nestled among the Sequoia Redwoods, the rambling Russian River, Sonoma wine county, and Pacific coastal beaches, activities abound: hiking, bicycling, kayaking, horseback riding, hot air balloons, whale and seal watching, walking along miles of beaches, wine tasting and tours, and lying in the sun on the ocean or river beaches. The Russian River Valley is also home to several amazing spas and resorts so massages, enzyme baths, and other rejuvenating treatments are only moments away. Two miles north of town, Armstrong Redwood State Reserve (17020 Armstrong Woods Road; 707–869–2015) covers 700 acres of awe-inspiring trees, many of which are old-growth. Also nearby are Austin Creek State Recreation Area (17020 Armstrong Woods Road; 707–869–2015) and Fort Ross State Park and Salt Point State Park (19005 Coast Highway 1, Jenner; 707–847–4777). The world famous Korbel Champagne Cellars (13250 River Road; 707–824–7000; *www.korbel.com*) are only three minutes away, and within another 20 minutes you can reach another 50 wineries.

For the Visitor

Accommodations: Just about all accommodations in the Russian River Valley are gay-friendly. Russian River Resort (Triple "R") (16390 4th Street; 707–869–0691/800–417–3767; *www.russianriverresort.com*) has 24 motel rooms plus a bar, restaurant, piano bar, and live entertainment. Fifes Guest Ranch (16467 River Road; 707–869–9500/800–734–3371; *www. fifes.com*) has 50 rustic-style cabins, 75 campsites, a bar, restaurant, dance bar, pool, and more; the Woods Resort (707–869–0600/877–887–9218; *www.rrwoods.com*) offers 19 units and suites and has a clothing-optional pool; River Village Resort & Spa (14880 River Road; 707–869–8139/800–529–3376; *www.rivervillageresort.com*) has 19 intimate cottages and a full-service spa set amidst lush gardens, as well as a large outdoor Jacuzzi and pool. Huckleberry Springs Country Inn & Spa (8105 Old Beedle, Monte Rio; 707–865–2683/800–822–2683; *www.huckleberrysprings.com*) has four cabins on 56 acres in a secluded location 5 miles outside Guerneville.

For More Information

Publications

Petaluma Argus-Courier
P.O. Box 1091
Petaluma, CA 94953
707–762–4541
www.arguscourier.com

Santa Rosa Press Democrat
427 Mendocino Avenue
Santa Rosa, CA 95401
707–575–7500/800–696–5056
www1.pressdemocrat.com

Sonoma Index-Tribune
P.O. Box C
Sonoma, CA 95476
707–938–2111
www.sonomanews.com

Chamber of Commerce and Visitors Center

Russian River Chamber of Commerce Visitor Center
16209 First Street
P.O. Box 331
Guerneville, CA 95446
707–869–9000/877–644–9001
www.russianriver.com

Realtor

Russian River Realty
16190 Main Street
Guerneville, CA 95446
707–869–0608
www.rusrivrealty.com

4 ▶ Laguna Beach, California

A Look at Laguna Beach

The city of Laguna Beach is a unique beach community and artist's colony blessed with a landscape defined by 7 miles of platinum sand public beaches, swaying palms, gentle surf, canyons, and coastal hills. Sometimes called SoHo-by-the-Sea, it's located about halfway between Los Angeles and San Diego. The essence of Laguna Beach has altered little since the arrival of the plein-air artists more than a century ago. The town and its residents have eschewed the notion of over-development and blatant commercialism, staying true to their roots as an artist and eco-friendly community. In a time when communities are flooded with big-box retailers and chain restaurants, Laguna Beach prides itself on its collection of independently owned stores, restaurants, and galleries. During the summer, several million visitors are drawn to the resort environment for its picturesque beaches, art festivals, and the Pageant of the Masters. Laguna Beach's bluff top walkways and tram system create a pedestrian environment unique in Southern California. From its incorporation as a city in 1927, preservation and forward planning played a role in maintaining a character attractive to residents, visitors, and Hollywood film producers. This Laguna Beach Greenbelt Plan is designed to preserve the city's surrounding natural environment from further development. Consequently, the city and private citizens have purchased as much open space as possible. These principles help maintain the community's village character for both residents and visitors in spite of growth and commercialism. Bette

▶ Nickname:
A Resort for all Seasons

▶ County: Orange

▶ Area code:
949

▶ Time zone:
Pacific

▶ Population:
23,727

▶ County population:
2,846,289

▶ Region:
Southern California

▶ Closest metro area:
Los Angeles

▶ Average home price:
$3,250,000

▶ Fabulous reasons to live here:
Beautiful, sun-drenched beach setting; large arts community and arts festivals; recreation; progressive GLBT community

Climate

Elevation 70'	Avg. high/low(F°)	Avg. inches		Avg. # days precip.	Avg. % humidity
		rain	snow		
Jan.	67/44	2.7	–	6	53%
April	71/49	0.8	–	3	51%
July	77/60	–	–	0	54%
Oct.	76/55	0.5	–	2	54%
YEAR	72/47	13.3	–	31	54%
# days 32° or below: 0			# days 90° or warmer: 0		

Davis, Charlie Chaplin, Mary Pickford, Judy Garland, and Douglas Fairbanks are just of few of the city's historic residents who have fancied the serenity of Laguna Beach. Today's celebrities are no different. Heather Locklear, Richie Sambora, and Bette Midler are just a few of the stars calling Laguna Beach home today. Others among the rich and famous can be spotted at the Surf & Sand Hotel, Zinc Café, and the Sawdust Festival.

Possible drawbacks: Laguna Beach has been prone to natural disasters (earthquakes, mountain flooding, and landslides) for the past decade. The city is also a tourist haven, with more than 3 million annual visitors.

Local Connections

Gas company: Sempra Energy (800–411–7343; *www.sdge.com*)

Electric companies: Southern California Edison (800–655–4555; *www.sce.com*); Sempra Energy (800–411–7343; *www.sdge.com*)

Phone company: Verizon (800–483–4000; *www.verizon.com*)

Water and sewer: Laguna Beach County Water District (949–497–1041); South Coast Water District (949–499–4256; *www.scwd.org*)

Cable company: Cox Communications (949–720–2020; *www.cox.com*)

Car registration/License: California Department of Motor Vehicles (800–777–0133; *www.dmv.ca.gov*)

You must get a California driver license within 10 days of establishing residency. License application fee: $25. If you have a valid license from another state, the driving test can be waived. Car registration and registration renewals are $31. The Vehicle License Fee (VLF) replaces property tax on vehicles. The formula for VLF assessment is based upon the purchase price or value of the vehicle and decreases with each renewal for the first 11 years. The VLF on a $25K vehicle for the first two years would be $163 and $147, respectively. The VLF is prorated for partial year registrations.

The Tax Ax

Sales tax: 7.75 percent; many food products exempt

State income tax: 1.0–9.3 percent graduated, based on income

Property tax: Orange County Assessor (714–834–2727; *www.oc.ca.gov/assessor*)

Property is assessed at fair market value for tax purposes. The current rate in Laguna Beach combines city, school, and district rates with a total levy of $1.04834 per $1,000.

Local Real Estate

Overview: The housing market in Laguna Beach varies from the original cottage homes built in the 1950s to brand-new construction and remodels of present day. Any given street in Laguna Beach has both types of housing with neighbors having a two-bedroom cottage on one side of a property and a multi-million dollar mansion on the other.

Median price for a single-family home: $3,250,000

Average price for a single-family home: $3,250,000

Average price for a 2BR condo: $2,100,000

Rental housing market: The rental market in Laguna Beach is seasonal with rents for a two-bedroom home from $1,600 to $18,000, with an average of $3,942

Gay-friendly neighborhoods: The whole of Laguna Beach is gay-friendly.

Nearby areas to consider: The GLBT community calls all of Orange County home. Newport Beach, Corona Del Mar, Irvine, Dana Point, Garden Grove, and Newport Coast all combine the fabulous panorama of ocean or mountain views with fun nightlife, arts, and recreation opportunities. This collection of cities provides varied home styles, costs, and amenities. The Center Orange County (*www.thecenteroc.org*) offers residents a wide variety of support and services and acts as a GLBT community advocate on the local political scene.

Earning a Living

Per capita income: $58,732

Median household income: $75,808

Business climate: Tourism, the arts, and resident-serving businesses comprise the main components of the Laguna Beach economy. Laguna Beach attracts visitors from around the world to its beaches, art festivals, galleries, museum, restaurants, and unique shopping. The City also provides stores and services for its resident population. Subdivision ordinances promote development in the pristine hillsides and canyons; Lagunans developed the first access standards in 1964 in an effort to control and slow development.

Help in starting a business: The Laguna Beach Chamber of Commerce is the local political, networking, and PR advocate for businesses in the city. The

Orange County Business Council (949–476–2242; *www.ocbc.org*) provides information and advice on doing business in the county.

Job market: Laguna Beach's top employer is South Coast Medical Center. The city is home to many artists and a center for tourism. In addition, Orange County has one of the most diverse high-tech economies in the nation, with telecommunications and computer software identified as the fastest-growing sectors of Orange County's high-tech industry. Laguna Beach is home to an increasing number of high-tech businesses in the software, sales, and technical service categories.

The Community

Overview: It's estimated that 30 percent of the Laguna Beach population is gay. Priding itself on its progressive, slow-growth politics, in 1983 Laguna Beach was the first city in the nation to elect an openly gay mayor (Robert Gentry). It was also the first city in Orange County, and one of the first in the state, to adopt ordinances making it illegal to discriminate against gays or people with HIV/AIDS.

Community organizations: Laguna Outreach (949–497–4237; *www.lagunaoutreach.org*) is the area's nonprofit, all-volunteer social and educational group serving the gay and lesbian community in southern California's Orange County area. It provides social alternatives to the bars and clubs, including regular monthly activities and special events throughout the year. PFLAG Orange County (*www.ocpflag.com*) is available for support, and Gay Laguna Beach (*www.gaylagunabeach.org*) has listings of current events and gay-friendly clubs and businesses.

Medical care: South Coast Medical Center (949–499–1311; *www.southcoastmedcenter.com*) is 208-bed, community, not-for-profit general acute care hospital, providing a wide range of patient care services. It also has free physician referral services and a health resource center.

Nuptials: California offers a domestic partnership registration (*www.ss.ca.gov/dpregistry*). Registration isn't the same as marriage, but it does secure many important rights and responsibilities. Under current law, registration can protect your rights in times of family crisis, protect your children, and give you access to family benefits at work. Couples in Laguna Beach can exchange vows in a number of romantic locations, including the beach, public parks, waterfront resorts, avant-garde event venues, and gardens.

Getting Around Town

Public transportation: Laguna Beach Transit (949–497–0746; *www.lagunabeachcity.net*) provides intra-community transportation services. LBT has free Ride to Work passes and free ride passes for seniors. June through August the Summer Shuttle Service is a free four-line service for the Pageant of the Masters, local art festivals, and other day-tripping activities during the summer.

Roads: Pacific Coast Highway (US1); nearby SR133 and I-5

Airport: The area is primarily served by John Wayne/Orange County Airport (airport code: SNA) (949–252–5200; *www.ocair.com*), located 20 minutes away. In addition to shuttles and taxi service, Orange County Transportation Authority (714–636–7433; *www.octa.net*) provides public services to get you from the airport to Laguna Beach.

It's a Gay Life

Annual events: Laguna Beach is home to several summer art festivals, including the renowned Festival of Arts and Pageant of the Masters (*www.foapom.com*) presented in July and August. The Festival is a juried exhibit of fine, strictly original works by more than 140 gifted artists, and the Pageant presents a mesmerizing stage production of living art recreations. The Sawdust Art Festival (*www.sawdustartfestival.org*) is an outdoor event with nearly 200 local artists displaying their works in a village of booths connected by paths of sawdust; it runs from July through September. The Sawdust Festival also presents a series of winter weekend arts events. The Art-A-Fair Festival (*www.art-a-fair.com*) is a summer gathering showcasing several artists from around the world.

Nightlife: With the constant flood of tourists and exceptional weather, Laguna Beach is the perfect place to spend your evening sipping cocktails at an outdoor café and watching the world pass by. If you're interested in a more active evening, The Boom Boom Room (1401 South Coast Highway; 949–494–7588/800–653–2697; *www.boomboomroom.com*) is the must visit, classic of Laguna Beach. Club Main Street (1460 South Coast Highway; 949–494–0056) and Woody's at the Beach (1305 South Coast Highway; 949–376–8809; *www.woodysatthebeach.com*) are pleasant local spots to spend your evening. The combination dance and sushi bar, Club M (680 S. Pacific Coast Highway; 949–497–5646), is gay-friendly. Also of interest in nearby Long Beach are Falcon (1435 East Broadway; 562–432–4146; *www.thefalcon.us*), Fire Island (3325 Anaheim Street; 562–659–3057; *www.clubfireisland.com*), and Silverfox (411 Redondo Avenue; 562–439–6343; *www.silverfoxlongbeach.com*). Pick up a free copy of *The Orange County & Long Beach Blade* for current listings and events.

Culture: There are more than 80 galleries and 400 registered artists, with an additional 400 artists either living, working, or exhibiting in Laguna Beach. In addition to the three major art festivals there's also the Laguna Beach Film Festival, sponsored by the Laguna Beach Film Society, part of the Laguna Beach Art Museum (307 Cliff Drive; 949–494–8971; *www.lagunaartmuseum.org*), and the California Choreographer's Dance Festival (*www.cadancefest.com*). First Thursdays Art Walk (949–683–6871; *www.firstthursdaysartwalk.com*) is a festive cultural evening hosted the first Thursday of each month from 6 to 9 p.m., with free shuttle service to more than 40 galleries. Performing arts come alive at the award-winning Laguna Playhouse (Moulton Theatre, 606 Laguna Canyon Road; 949–497–ARTS; *www.lagunaplayhouse.com*), the West Coast's oldest, continuously operating professional theater company, and Laguna Beach Live (606 Laguna Canyon Road; *www.lagunabeachlive.org*), designed to nurture young talents, has concerts throughout the year and an annual Chamber Music Festival (949–553–2422; *www.philharmonicsociety.org*) in May. The Laguna Beach Community Concert Band (949–497–0986; *www.lagunacommunityconcertband.org*) presents frequent concerts.

Recreation: With its temperate climate, Laguna Beach is a prime destination for year-round outdoor fun. Water activities and sports run the gamut from guided kayak tours and seasonal whale-watching excursions, to surfing, boogie boarding, and diving. Marine reserves and wilderness parks add another element to an already picture-perfect afternoon. West Street Beach, about 4 miles from downtown, is the city's popular gay-friendly beach. Other activities of interest include tennis, golf, hiking, biking, and frolicking in the surf. Aside from a plethora of water sports you can also enjoy seaside picnics, lawn bowling, shuffleboard, hiking, cycling, tennis, golf, and botanical garden tours arranged through the Department of Parks (949–497–3311; *www.lagunabeachcity.net*).

For the Visitor

Accommodations: Laguna Beach boasts more than 30 inns, bed and breakfast hideaways, cozy cottages, beach-style bungalows, and full-service resorts. Visitors will find that no matter what their budget, there is a place that will accommodate their needs. From family-style retreats, complete with kitchens and kid-friendly services, to plush romantic resorts where couples can enjoy side-by-side massages, visitors can select from a myriad of settings: oceanfront, historic, contemporary, vintage, or intimate. The Coast Inn (1401 South Coast Highway; 949–494–7588) is a particular gay-friendly favorite.

For More Information

Gay & Lesbian Center

Laguna Outreach
P.O. Box 1701
Laguna Beach, CA 92652
949–497–4237
www.lagunaoutreach.org

Publications

Orange County & Long Beach Blade Magazine
P.O. Box 1538
Laguna Beach, CA 92651
949–376–9880
www.eyespyla.com

Orange County Register
625 N. Grand Avenue at the Santa Ana (5) Freeway
Santa Ana, CA 92701
877–469–7344
www.ocregister.com

Convention and Visitors Bureau

Laguna Beach Visitor and Conference Bureau
P.O. Box 221
Laguna Beach, CA 92651
949–497–9229/800–877–1115
www.lagunabeachinfo.org

Chamber of Commerce

Laguna Beach Chamber of Commerce
357 Glenneyre
Laguna Beach, CA 92651
949–494–1018, ext. 1
www.lagunabeachchamber.org

Realtor

Ariel Feir, Real Estate Consultant
First Team Real Estate
4040 Barranca Parkway, Suite 100
Irvine, CA 92604-4772
949–244–7700
www.feir.com

Los Angeles, California

5

A Look at Los Angeles

In a day, a weekend, or a week you can meander from world-famous attractions to a wealth of museums and galleries, from hip hop to pop to high culture, or view what's in vogue in the performing arts in an array of cinemas, clubs, and theaters. Whether it is the sunny skies you seek or the starry nights, the hot shopping or museum hopping, or just sinking your feet into the cool sand on a warm beach, this singular, serendipitous city has it all. LA's greatest asset has always been the rush of newcomers eager to start a new life and reinvent themselves. That means Easterners and Midwesterners and immigrants from every continent all come together here to create a powerful dynamic, encouraging creativity at its highest level and producing the richest possible cultural life for Angelenos and visitors alike. LA has more artists than any place ever in the history of the world, from world-renowned painters to Disney imagineers to those who spend their days designing cars of the future. LA is also home to more artists-in-residence than anywhere else. Fourteen local universities offer advanced degrees in the arts, driving the enormous imagination product and creating the next generation of cars, clothes, movies, and furnishings.

Possible drawbacks: Los Angeles is one of the most expensive cities in the nation. It's also an extensive urban sprawl creating a tangle of traffic congested roads and highways. You'll be spending a lot of time in your car if you have a daily work commute.

California

▶ Nickname:
City of Angels

▶ County:
Los Angeles

▶ Area code:
213

▶ Time zone: Pacific

▶ Population:
3,694,820

▶ County population:
9,519,338

▶ Region:
Southern California

▶ Average home price:
$1,200,000

▶ Fabulous reasons to live here:
Entertainment, nightlife, arts, culture, recreation, strong economy, diverse and large GLBT community, outstanding healthcare, progressive politics

Climate

Elevation 330'	Avg. high/low(F°)	Avg. inches		Avg. # days precip.	Avg. % humidity
		rain	snow		
Jan.	67/47	3.8	–	6	53%
April	71/52	0.8	–	3	51%
July	80/62	0.0	–	0	54%
Oct.	77/58	0.5	–	2	54%
YEAR	73/55	17.1	–	31	54%
# days 32° or below: 0			# days 90° or warmer: 26		

Local Connections

Gas company: Southern California Gas Company (800–427–2200; *www.socalgas.com*)

Electric company: Los Angeles Department of Water and Power (800–342–5397; *www.ladwp.com*)

Phone companies: SBC (800–310–2355; *www.sbc.com*); AT&T (800–222–0300; *www.att.com*); among others

Water and sewer: Los Angeles Department of Water and Power (800–342–5397; *www.ladwp.com*)

Cable companies: Time Warner Cable (818–700–6500; *www.timewarner.com*); Adelphia (888–683–1000; *www.adelphia.com*); Comcast (800–COMCAST; *www.comcast.com*)

Car registration/License: California Department of Motor Vehicles (800–777–0133; *www.dmv.ca.gov*)

You must get a California driver's license within 10 days of establishing residency. License application fee: $25. If you have a valid license from another state, the driving test can be waived. Car registration and registration renewals are $31. The Vehicle License Fee (VLF) replaces property tax on vehicles. The formula for VLF assessment is based upon the purchase price or value of the vehicle and decreases with each renewal for the first 11 years. The VLF on a $25K vehicle for the first two years would be $163 and $147, respectively. The VLF is prorated for partial year registrations.

The Tax Ax

Sales tax: 8.25 percent

State income tax: 1.0–9.3 percent graduated, depending on income

Property tax: LA County Tax Assessor (213–974–3211)

1 percent of assessed value plus bonded indebtedness. Current average is 1.25 percent. (Due to Prop 13, property taxes cannot rise by more than 2 percent per year unless the property is reassessed because of being sold or expanded.)

Local Real Estate

Overview: Los Angeles property styles include 1920s bungalows, 1940s traditional and ranch houses, high-rises, state-of-the-art condos, and multi-million-dollar estates. Currently there are many new loft-style condos being built. The market has been tight recently, which continues to drive prices up.

Median price for a single-family home: $900,000

Average price for a single-family home: $1,200,000

Average price for a 2BR condo: $642,000

Rental housing market: The rental market is very strong because people can't afford to buy properties. Prices continue to rise steadily. Expect to pay $1,700–2,500 for a two-bedroom apartment.

Gay-friendly neighborhoods: Most of Los Angeles and the surrounding suburbs are gay-friendly. Price and amenities are the biggest factors in choosing a neighborhood to call home.

Nearby areas to consider: There's no shortage of gay-friendly places near LA. Beyond housing costs, the biggest attractions of one area over another are employment and recreation. The entertainment industry draws large numbers of GLBT community members to Studio City, North Hollywood, Hollywood, and West Hollywood. Silverlake, with the Elysian Park, Silver Lake, Mt. Washington, Dodger Stadium, and a nice collection of GLBT bars, restaurants, and businesses, is another nearby winner. Van Nuys, Newport Beach, Riverside, Sherman Oaks, and Resida are only a few of the other LA suburbs that the gay community calls home in Los Angeles County.

Earning a Living

Per capita income: $20,671

Median household income: $36,687

Business climate: The five-county area that includes Los Angeles is ranked No. 10, with an economy larger than that of Mexico. And California has the fifth-largest economy in the world, surpassing most countries. Currently, LA is the leading supplier of entertainment to the world and the largest import/export port in the United States. There are more than 4,500 technology firms in Los Angeles County. With a diverse economy that includes business and professional services, media, technology, health sciences, and tourism, Los Angeles will continue to grow economically and be a world economic leader.

Help in starting a business: The Los Angeles Area Chamber of Commerce serves the needs of the Los Angeles business community through its public policy and advocacy initiatives and its business development programs and services. The Chamber's wide range of programs and services will help you attract new customers, expand your business base, reduce your costs of doing business, and assist with connections that will further your business goals.

Job market: Major market sectors providing employment include arts, entertainment, educational, health, and social services; manufacturing, professional, scientific, management, and administrative services; retail trade; and tourism.

The Community

Overview: The Los Angeles area is widespread and home to a diverse GLBT community. LA was one of the first cities in the country to adopt a law prohibiting discrimination on the basis of sexual orientation and an early leader in providing domestic partner benefits to city employees. Numerous openly gay and lesbian people serve at the highest levels and at all levels of city government.

Community organizations: The L.A. Gay & Lesbian Center (323–993–7400) stands as a model for centers around the country. The center provides a broad array of services for the lesbian, gay, bisexual, and transgender community, welcoming nearly a quarter-million client visits from ethnically diverse youth and adults each year. The Center offers health, legal, social, cultural, and educational services, with unique programs for seniors, families, and youth, including a 24-bed transitional living program for homeless youth. Los Angeles is an extremely gay-friendly city and is home to numerous organizations serving the gay and lesbian community, including numerous gay- and lesbian-friendly religious institutions with large and vibrant congregations.

Medical care: Los Angeles is home to many of the world's medical specialists practicing at technically advanced hospitals including Cedars-Sinai Medical Center and the UCLA and USC hospitals. The City of Los Angeles provides leadership and funding on AIDS and HIV issues through the Office of the AIDS Coordinator. In addition, through its Jeffrey Goodman Special Care Clinic (323–993–7500; *www.laglc.org*) and on-site pharmacy, the L.A. Gay & Lesbian Center offers free and low-cost health, mental health, HIV/AIDS medical care, and HIV/STD testing and prevention.

Nuptials: California offers a domestic partnership registration (*www.ss.ca.gov/dpregistry*). Registration isn't the same as marriage, but it does secure many important rights and responsibilities. Under current law, registration can protect your rights in times of family crisis, protect your children, and give you access to family benefits at work.

Getting Around Town

Public transportation: Los Angeles County Metropolitan Transportation Authority (Metro) (800–266–6883; *www.metro.net*) provides subway, light-rail, and bus service; Southern California Regional Rail Authority (Metrolink) (800–371–5465; *www.metrolinktrains.com*) offers commuter train service; Los Angeles Department of Transportation (213–808–2273; *www.ladottransit.com*) provides DASH, Commuter Express, City Ride shuttles and buses, City Hall Shuttle, Metrolink Shuttle downtown, San Pedro Electric Trolley, and the Los Angeles Charter Bus Program.

Roads: I-5, I-405, I-10, I-110; US101; State Highway 1 (Pacific Coast Highway)

Airports: Los Angeles International Airport (airport code: LAX) (310–646–5252; *www.lawa.org/lax*) provides free ground transportation to the City Bus Center and the Metro Rail Green Line. Bob Hope Airport (airport code: BUR) (818–840–8840; *www.bobhopeairport.com*), formerly Burbank Glendale Pasadena Airport, is the closest airport to downtown LA, Hollywood, and popular attractions.

It's a Gay Life

Annual events: There are more than 40 major annual city events and hundreds more in the varied communities of Los Angeles. Christopher Street West hosts the Gay Pride Celebration (*www.lapride.org*), culminating with a parade in June. There are more than 2,000 festivals, street fairs, parades, and other special events held each year in LA. The core of LA's festival life is the kaleidoscopic celebrations hosted by LA's richly diverse ethnic groups—Angelenos from 140 countries eager to share their food, music, dance, and crafts. These festivals—year-round in LA's mild weather—showcase the traditions of Mexico, China, Japan, Greece, Cuba, Thailand, Africa, Samoa, and many more places. All 300-plus possibilities are listed in the Festival Guide put out by LA's Cultural Affairs Department (213–473–7700; *www.culturela.org*).

Nightlife: Whether sitting down for a dinning extravaganza, standing up and snacking at a multi-ethnic festival, or touring eye-catching spaces and places to experience design and architecture, old and gracious or new and arresting, LA is a diverse delight. The beauty of a metropolis is having options. Lipstick chic, leather and Levi, classic disco, pounding house, or cool jazz, you'll find it in multiples. LA bars and clubs are clustered downtown with the baths, but they're also scattered through the vast mileage of LA. The free rags and magazines, available at all the bars, are the best way to keep up with the city scene. Pick up Frontier Magazine (323–848–2222; *www.frontiersnewsmagazine.com*), In Los Angeles (323–848–2200; *www.inmagla.com*), Odyssey (415–621–6514; *www.odysseymagazine.net*), or FAB! (323–655–5716; *www.gayfab.com*), LA's only gay and lesbian bi-weekly newspaper, for all the nightlife details.

Culture: Los Angeles County is home to more than 250 live performance theaters, more than 250 galleries, and more than 300 museums, plus a few zoos and nature preserves. Downtown is home to the city's latest attraction, the internationally acclaimed Walt Disney Concert Hall (151 S. Grand Avenue; 323–850–2000; *wdcg.laphil.com*): a glimmering, billowing stainless-steel structure designed by LA's renowned architect Frank Gehry and home to the equally praised Los Angeles Philharmonic Orchestra (323–850–2000; *www.laphil.org*). The city's burgeoning visual arts scene can also be experienced at the Museum of Contemporary Art (MOCA) (213–626–6222; *www.moca.org*) in its main galleries (250 S. Grand Avenue) and its addition in Little Tokyo (152 N. Central Avenue). Then there are also the scattered artworks that enliven the plazas, parks, and walkways of the area. The area of Little Tokyo east of Downtown offers the Japanese American National Museum (369 E. First Street; 213–625–0414; *www.janm.org*), appropriately housed in a converted Buddhist Temple and a brand new facility. The Asian influence in LA also can be experienced across from Union Station at the recently opened Chinese American Museum (425 N. Los Angeles Street; 213–626–5240; *www.camla.org*) and the nearby shops and restaurants. Just south of Downtown, Exposition Park (888–LA–PARKS; *www.laparks.org*) is home to the LA Memorial Coliseum—of 1932 and 1984 Olympic fame (3911 S. Figueroa Street; 213–747–7111; *www.lacoliseum.com*), the Sports Arena, and a cluster of museums focusing on science, aerospace, and natural history, with world-class collections and ever diverting exhibits. Across the street is the 150-acre campus of the University of Southern California (213–740–2311; *www.usc.edu*).

Recreation: Edged to the west by the Pacific and surrounded by mountains large and small, Los Angeles has much to offer. Lesser known than its famous beaches, Los Angeles butts up against a series of snow-capped mountains. From Snow Summit to Snow Valley to Mountain High to Big Bear, there are many local skiing and snowboarding peaks averaging around only a two-hour drive from downtown LA (*www.skisocal.org*). Endless beaches are one of LA's calling cards, and you can surf dozens of miles of waves, from Malibu's Surfrider to San Pedro. Life in the City of Angels is just one continuous game. Thanks to a never-ending parade of sporting events, spectators have something to cheer about with baseball, basketball, arena football, soccer, horse racing, tennis, and polo taking place on almost any given Sunday, as well as just about any other day of the week. There are more than 200 sports venues, including the Staples Center (1111 S. Figueroa Street; 213–742–7340; *www.staplescenter.com*), home to the L.A. Lakers (310–426–6031; *www.lakers.com*) and the Los Angeles Clippers (888–895–8662; *www.clippers.com*); the Home Depot Center (18400 Avalon Boulevard, Carson; 310–630–2000; *www.homedepotcenter.com*) is home to Los Angeles Galaxy (310–630–2200; *www.lagalaxy.com*) soccer; and Dodger Stadium (1000 Elysian Park Avenue; 866–363–4377; *www.dodgers.com*), home to the Los Angeles Dodgers (866–DODGERS; *www.dodgers.com*).

For the Visitor

Accommodations: Los Angeles boasts more than 93,000 hotel rooms, ranging from hostels to luxurious five-star resorts, with a diverse selection of amenities to meet individual needs and budgets. There are more than 8,500 hotel rooms in approximately 40 hotels in downtown Los Angeles alone. Among LA's many gay-friendly options is The Georgian Hotel (1415 Ocean Avenue; 310–395–9945/800–538–8147; *www.georgianhotel.com*). The hotel is rich in history, dating back to the late 1920s, and features spectacular ocean sunsets and panoramic Santa Monica Bay views.

For More Information

Gay & Lesbian Center

L.A. Gay and Lesbian Center
1625 N. Schrader Boulevard
Los Angeles, CA 90028
323–993–7400
www.laglc.org

Publications

Los Angeles Times
202 W. 1st Street
Los Angeles, CA 90012
213–237–5000
www.latimes.com

Daily News
P.O. Box 4200
Woodland Hills, CA 91365
818–713–3000
www.dailynews.com

Convention and Visitors Bureau

LA INC.
The Convention and Visitors Bureau
685 Figueroa Street
Los Angeles CA 90071
213–624–7300
www.VisitLAnow.com

Chamber of Commerce

Los Angeles Area Chamber of Commerce
350 S. Bixel Street
Los Angeles, CA 90017
213–580–7500
www.lachamber.org

Realtor

Prudential California Realty, John Aaroe
Division
227 N. Larchmont Boulevard
Los Angeles, CA 90004
323–769–3349
www.prudentialcal.com

6 ▶ Palm Springs, California

California

Sacramento
San Francisco
Los Angeles
Palm Springs

A Look at Palm Springs

Palm Springs, rich in history and glorious weather (with 354 days of sunshine), is the jewel among desert cities. Geography gives Palm Springs its famed warm, dry climate because it's sheltered by the Little San Bernardino Mountains to the north, the Santa Rosa Mountains on the south, and the San Jacinto Mountains to the west, with the towering 10,831-foot Mt. San Jacinto, site of the Palm Springs Aerial Tramway. From a simple hike to picnicking by a peaceful stream, to adventurous jeep excursions and horseback riding deep into the canyon, the Indian Canyons are not to be missed. The world-famous Tahquitz Canyon is open for guided tours. The village atmosphere, preserved and embellished over the years, presents a downtown area with quaint lampposts, benches, and Mexican-tile-paved enclaves inviting strollers to linger among the shops, galleries, eateries, and coffeehouses. The mission-style architecture throughout the village is a big part of the charisma one feels in Palm Springs. A stroll on Palm Canyon Drive with its Walk of Stars, honoring pioneers and entertainment celebrities, offers shops, galleries, and coffeehouses and, when you turn the corner, there's Lucille Ball holding court on her bronze bench.

Possible drawbacks: The dry desert heat of summer pushes daytime temperatures into the 100s, and during the winter the city population doubles as snow birds take advantage of the temperate climate.

▶ Nickname:
Golf Capital of the World

▶ County: Riverside

▶ Area code: 760

▶ Time zone: Pacific

▶ Population: 44,260

▶ County population:
1,545,387

▶ Region:
Southwest California

▶ Closest metro area:
San Diego

▶ Average home price:
$382,000

▶ Fabulous reasons to live here:
Nightlife, arts, recreation, dry desert climate, beautiful setting, strong economy, historically accepted and integrated GLBT community

Climate

Elevation 487'	Avg. high/low(F°)	Avg. inches		Avg. # days precip.	Avg. % humidity
		rain	snow		
Jan.	70/44	1.4	–	6	65%
April	87/55	0.1	–	4	66%
July	108/75	0.2	–	0	69%
Oct.	90/61	0.1	–	2	68%
YEAR	89/56	5.2	–	33	67%
# days 32° or below: 0			# days 90° or warmer: 122		

Local Connections

Gas company: Southern California Gas Company (800–427–2200; *www.socalgas.com*)

Electric company: Southern California Edison Company (800–655–4555; *www.sce.com*)

Phone company: Verizon (800–483–4000; *verizon.com*)

Water and sewer: Water: Desert Water Agency (760–323–4971; *www.dwa.org*); Sewer: operated by USFilter for the City of Palm Springs (760–323–8226; *www.ci.palm-springs.ca.us*)

Cable company: Time Warner Cable (760–340–2225; *www.timewarnercable.com*)

Car registration/License: California Department of Motor Vehicles (800–777–0133; *www.dmv.ca.gov*)

You must get a California driver's license within 10 days of establishing residency. License application fee: $25. If you have a valid license from another state, the driving test can be waived. Car registration and registration renewals are $31. The Vehicle License Fee (VLF) replaces property tax on vehicles. The formula for VLF assessment is based upon the purchase price or value of the vehicle and decreases with each renewal for the first 11 years. The VLF on a $25K vehicle for the first two years would be $163 and $147, respectively. The VLF is prorated for partial year registrations.

The Tax Ax

Sales tax: 7.75 percent; some food products exempt

State income tax: 1.0–9.3 percent graduated, depending on income

Property tax: Office of the Treasurer—Tax Collector (951–955–3900)

Property taxes are 1 percent of the sales price and remain the same until the property re-sells. Some areas have small additional assessments, bringing the average annual tax to about 1.1 percent of the sales price.

Local Real Estate

Overview: Palm Springs has an eclectic, adventurous architectural style, which is drawing significant attention worldwide. Residential Palm Springs consists of single-family homes, condominiums, villas, and townhouses. The Palm Springs resurgence is in full swing and expected to continue in the decades ahead. Palm Springs has many mid-century architecture homes and, though the supply of available housing has increased slightly, prices remain strong. Many Baby Boomers are planning for retirement by purchasing now in Palm Springs.

Median price for a single-family home: $345,000

Average price for a single-family home: $382,000

Average price for a 2BR condo: $290,000

Rental housing market: The rental market is strongest November through May. During this season the rent for two-bedroom condos runs $1,200 to $1,800 per month and houses rent from $2,500 per month. An annual lease for a three-bedroom home in South Palm Springs has a range of $1,800 to $5,000 a month. Rental prices are expected to increase, as home prices continue to rise.

Gay-friendly neighborhoods: All of Palm Springs is gay-friendly, as are most of the other nearby desert cites. The most concentrated areas for gay families are Central and South Palm Springs.

Nearby areas to consider: As you move away from Palm Springs, housing prices begin to drop and lot sizes increase. The natural beauty of the area, combined with the vast array of recreation and amenity options, draw the GLBT community to Rancho Mirage, Desert Hot Springs, Thousand Palms, and Palm Desert. Cathedral City Cove has one of the nation's largest per capita GLBT communities. All of these places are popular and areas that the GLBT community calls home. Each has its own attractions, yet is close enough to Palm Springs to take advantage of the city nightlife and cultural offerings.

Earning a Living

Per capita income: $25,957

Median household income: $35,973

Business climate: High-tech manufacturing, exporting, and service businesses; the motion picture industry; and being a renowned desert city resort create a strong economy. This strength is expected to continue because of new residential and retail developments and the ongoing expansion of the area's tourism industries.

Help in starting a business: The Palms Springs Chamber of Commerce is an advocate for local business. It also provides contacts, assistance, advertising, and networking opportunities for area businesses. The Desert Business Association is the Coachella Valley's "Gay Chamber of Commerce," a network of gay, lesbian, and gay-friendly businesses that promote and support each other and also educate the community about the many products and services available through the GLBT-friendly stores, hotels, restaurants, and other businesses.

Job market: The Palm Springs education system is one of the best in the nation and a major area employer. Construction, arts, services, and high-tech manufacturing jobs will continue to drive the Palm Springs market.

The Community

Overview: Palm Springs is a well-organized gay enclave. The GLBT community is well integrated into the area and a driving factor politically and economically.

Community organizations: The Desert Pride Center (*www.desertpridecenter.org*) is a community hub, providing classes, workshops, and meeting space for many of the community's organizations and sponsoring social events throughout the year. Palm Springs has dozens of organizations, including social groups and social and recreational organizations. The Desert Pride Center maintains a current list of groups and events.

Medical care: Desert Regional Medical Center (760–323–6511; *www.desertmedctr.com*) is a 394-bed, acute-care regional medical center and home to the Coachella Valley's only designated trauma center. The AIDS Assistance Program (760–325–8481; *www.aidsassistance.org*) is a volunteer organization sponsoring programs supporting low-income men, women, and children living with HIV/AIDS. Desert AIDS Project (760–323–2118; *www.desertaidsproject.org*) meets the evolving medical and social service needs of people living with HIV/AIDS by providing direct services and advocacy while working to prevent new infections through education and outreach.

Nuptials: California offers a domestic partnership registration (*www.ss.ca.gov/dpregistry*). Registration isn't the same as marriage, but it does secure many important rights and responsibilities. Under current law, registration can protect your rights in times of family crisis, protect your children, and give you access to family benefits at work.

Getting Around Town

Public transportation: The Amtrak Palm Springs platform (800–872–7245) is located at N. Indian Canyon Drive just south of I-10; SunLine Transit Agency (760–343–3451; *www.sunline.org*) provides local bus service for the city. Regular fare: $1; transfer 25 cents; unlimited-ride day pass $3.

Roads: US111, I-10

Airport: Palm Springs International Airport (airport code: PSP) (760–318–3800; *www.palmspringsairport.com*) is served by 12 airlines, providing up to 60 daily departures to 1.3 million passengers a year.

It's a Gay Life

Annual events: Greater Palm Springs Pride (*www.pspride.org*) and Leather Pride (*www.pslod.com*) are both held in November. In January, the Nortel Palm Springs International Film Festival (*www.psfilmfest.org*) attracts the filmmakers of the world who show their wares and pay tribute to the legends of the silver screen. In July, the Palm Springs International Short Film Festival (*www.psfilmfest.org*) showcases the industry's talented filmmakers and animators. The Bob Hope Chrysler Classic (*www.bhcc.com*) and the Nabisco Dinah Shore Classic (*www.kncgolf.com*) are popular annual golfing events. The Dinah Shore Weekend (*www.dinahshoreweekend.com*) is a March women's event that draws thousands.

Nightlife: Downtown Palm Springs is a happening place. A stroll on Palm Canyon Drive, with its Walk of Stars honoring pioneers and entertainment celebrities, offers shops, galleries, restaurants, and coffeehouses. There are plenty of gay hot spots, including Badlands (200 S. Indian Canyon Drive; 760–778–4326), Dates Bar (67–670 Carey Road; 760–328–7211), HeadHunters (611 S. Palm Canyon Drive; 760–416–0950), Hunter's Video Bar (302 E. Arenas Road; 760–323–0700; *www.huntersnightclubs.com*), Rainbow Cactus Cafe (212 South Indian Avenue; 760–325–3868), and the Levi and leather bar Sidewinders (67–555 E. Palm Canyon Drive; 760–328–9919; *www.sidewindersbar.com*).

Culture: The Palm Springs Desert Museum (101 Museum Drive; 760–325–0189; *www.psmuseum.org*) is the cultural centerpiece of the community, with renowned traveling exhibitions and an extensive permanent collection. The Village Green Heritage Center (221–223 S. Palm Canyon Drive; 760–323–8297) houses the McCallum Adobe and the Cornelia White House with memorabilia of local pioneers; the charming Ruddy's 1930s General Store Museum; and the Agua Caliente Cultural Museum (760–323–0151). The many programs and flight demonstrations at the Palm Springs Air Museum (745 N. Gene Autry Trail; 760–778–6262; *www.air-museum.org*) bring the World War II era to life. The historic Plaza Theatre, the scene of many Jack Benny radio broadcasts in the 1940s as well as a Hollywood premiere or two, is the home of The Fabulous Palm Springs Follies (128 S. Palm Canyon Drive; 760–864–6514; *www.psfollies.com*), with top guest stars, hilarious variety acts, and a company of long-legged lovelies, all over 55! First Friday is held monthly on the first Friday each month, with stores in the Uptown Heritage District remaining open until 9:00 p.m.

Recreation: Excellent weather beckons the outdoors enthusiast. Primary Palm Springs pastimes include golf (at more than 100 courses in the Coachella Valley) and tennis courts citywide. Bike trails, such as Heritage Trail, are well marked throughout Palm Springs and the surrounding estate neighborhoods. Off-road biking is also available. Hiking trails abound in nearby wilderness areas, California state parks, and Joshua Tree National Park (*www.joshua.tree.national-park.com*) just to the east. Horseback riding and eco-jeep trips offer seated exploration. Spectator sports such as polo, the Tennis Masters Series Pacific Open at Indian Wells Tennis Garden(78–200 Miles Avenue, Indian Wells; 760–200–8000; *www.iwtg.atponline.net*), and golf tournaments such as the Bob Hope Classic (39000 Bob Hope Drive, Rancho Mirage; 760–346–8184; *www.bhcc.com*) and Nabisco Championship (34–600 Mission Hills Drive, Rancho Mirage; 760–324–4546; *www.kncgolf.com*) are enjoyed seasonally. At the edge of Palm Springs sits the

Knotts' Oasis Water Park (Gene Autry Trail and Mesquite Avenue; 714–220–5200; *www.knots.com*) with a beach with private cabanas, a wave pool for body surfing, thrilling water slides, and a wonderfully relaxing Whitewater River inner tube ride. The Palm Springs Aerial Tramway (One Tramway Road; 760–325–1391; *www.pstramway.com*) has been delighting visitors for 30 years with a short trip from the desert floor to an alpine forest at 8,516 feet. The tramway gives spectacular views of the mountains and valley below.

For the Visitor

Accommodations: With 130 hotels and 6,500 rooms in Palm Springs, there is something for every taste and price range. The desert landscape has been dotted with so many new gay and lesbian resorts that it has helped propel Palm Springs in gaining the image of being the most popular vacation destination in America. Feeling stressed out? Start your day with a visit to one of the famous spas. On the site of the original Agua Caliente mineral springs is the Spa Hotel & Casino (100 N. Indian Canyon; 888–9991–995; *www.sparesortcasino.com*), where you can luxuriate in a full-service spa, mineral baths, and the peaceful sounds of Native American music. There is also the elegant Givenchy Spa at Merv Griffin's Resort Hotel (4200 E. Palm Canyon Drive; 760–770–5000; *www.desertresorts.com/givenchy*), offering a complete European spa experience. Most accommodations are gay-friendly and many gay owned. Just a few to help you start planning are Viola's Resort (1200 S. Palm Canyon Drive; 760–318–8400; *www.violasresort.com*), a private resort for gays and lesbians, their families, and their friends; Alpine Gardens Hotel (1586 E. Palm Canyon Drive; 888–299–7455; *www.alpinegardens.com*); Casitas Laquitas (450 E. Palm Canyon Drive; 760–416–9999), a lesbian-friendly private retreat with a unique, fun, and comfortable environment where you can be yourself; and Caliente Tropics (411 E. Palm Canyon Drive; 866–HOT–9595; *www.calientetropics.com*), where you can sun bathe by a dramatic 65' pool.

For More Information

Gay & Lesbian Center
The Desert Pride Center
The Sun Center
611 South Palm Canyon, Suite 201
Palm Springs, CA 92264
760–327–2313
www.desertpridecenter.org

Publications
The Bottom Line Magazine
312 N. Palm Canyon Drive
Palm Springs, CA 92262
760–323–0552
www.psbottomline.com

The Desert Sun
P.O. Box 2734
Palm Springs, CA 92263
760–322–8889
www.thedesertsun.com

Convention and Visitors Bureau
Palm Springs Convention and
Visitor's Bureau
70–100 Highway 111
Rancho Mirage, CA 92270
760–770–9000
www.palmspringsusa.com

Chambers of Commerce

The Desert Business Association
777 East Tahquitz Canyon Way, Suite 200
Palm Springs, CA 92264
760–416–5183
wwww.dbaps.org

Palms Springs Chamber of Commerce
190 W. Amado Road
Palm Springs, CA 92262
760–325–1577
www.pschamber.org

Realtor

Harry Sterling
Realtor
Coldwell Banker Residential Brokerage
1555 S. Palm Canyon Drive, Suite C
Palm Springs, CA 92264
760–409–7977
www.harrysterling.com

7 ▶ Sacramento, California

A Look at Sacramento

Peacefully located in a leafy valley of scenic rivers and canopies of trees, Sacramento is a cosmopolitan convergence of tall, gleaming buildings, hearty Victorians, splendid restaurants and shops, a vibrant arts scene, and a virtual cornucopia of state-of-the-art meeting facilities. Sacramento is the capital of California, seat of the state government, and home to California State University Sacramento. Sacramento has been called a snapshot of Wild West history in a modern, world-class city. Its amenities combine with the rich history of California's Wild West. That history comes to life through interactive experiences on steam engine train rides, tours of the State Capitol Building, and historic museum tours. Sacramento's central location and low cost of living make this a fabulous city. It's in the middle of everything, just 90 miles from San Francisco and Lake Tahoe and only 50 miles from the Napa Valley. Sacramento is both the state capital and seat of Sacramento County. Located on the Sacramento River at its confluence with the American River, this city has a deepwater port via a 43-mile channel to Suisun Bay, making shipping a major job and income source. The city is known for its camellias; a camellia festival is held annually along with the California State Fair and Exposition.

Possible drawbacks: Sacramento is an old city, poorly designed for modern travel, and traffic congestion plagues the city. Unsuccessful and expensive attempts have been made to ease the problem through a light-rail system.

▶ Nickname:
Silicon Valley East

▶ County:
Sacramento

▶ Area code: 916

▶ Time zone:
Pacific

▶ Population:
407,018

▶ County population:
1,223,499

▶ Region:
Northern California

▶ Average home price:
$280,000

▶ Fabulous reasons to live here:
High-tech economy; excellent healthcare; large, organized GLBT community; museums; recreation

Climate

Elevation 17'	Avg. high/low(F°)	Avg. inches		Avg. # days precip.	Avg. % humidity
		rain	snow		
Jan.	55/40	4.0	–	10	80%
April	73/48	1.1	–	5	63%
July	93/60	0.0	–	0	53%
Oct.	79/52	0.9	–	3	58%
YEAR	75/50	19	–	57	64%
# days 32° or below: 8			# days 90° or warmer: 74		

Local Connections

Gas company: Pacific Gas & Electric (800–743–5000; *www.pge.com*)

Electric company: Sacramento Municipal Utilities District (888–742–7682; *www.smud.org*)

Phone company: SBC (800–310–2355; *www.sbc.com*)

Water and sewer: City of Sacramento Department of Utilities (916–264–5371; *www.cityofsacramento.org/utilities*)

Cable company: Comcast (800–722–3409; *www.comcast.com*)

Car registration/License: California Department of Motor Vehicles (800–777–0133; *www.dmv.ca.gov*)

You must get a California driver's license within 10 days of establishing residency. License application fee: $25. If you have a valid license from another state, the driving test can be waived. Car registration and registration renewals are $31. The Vehicle License Fee (VLF) replaces property tax on vehicles. The formula for VLF assessment is based upon the purchase price or value of the vehicle and decreases with each renewal for the first 11 years. The VLF on a $25K vehicle for the first two years would be $163 and $147, respectively. The VLF is prorated for partial year registrations.

The Tax Ax

Sales tax: 7.75 percent

State income tax: 1.0–9.3 percent graduated, depending on income

Property tax: Sacramento County Assessor (916–875–0700; *www.assessor.saccounty.net*)

Property is assessed at fair market value. Under Proposition 13, the property tax rate is fixed at 1 percent of assessed value plus any assessment bonds or fees approved by popular vote. As a result of various assessment bonds in addition to the 1 percent rate, property tax rates in Sacramento County average roughly 1.1 percent countywide.

Local Real Estate

Overview: Sacramento's housing styles range from Victorian to modern; there aren't too many brick homes. Most desirable are the Craftsman, Spanish, and Tudor homes from the early 1900s to 1940. These are typically two-bedroom and command premium prices per square foot. Although Sacramento has some modern mid-century homes built by Eichler and Streng, they don't command much of a premium. Some of these are located in very high-end areas, where they're often a great value compared to the neighbors. There's also a new loft market beginning to emerge in Sacramento.

Median price for a single-family home: $372,000

Average price for a single-family home: $403,000

Average price for a 2BR condo: $210,000

Rental housing market: Right now, there's lots to choose from, especially newer units. The rent on units that are 20 years or older is $800–1,000; recent construction rents for $1,000–1,200.

Gay-friendly neighborhoods: The older areas of town, such as downtown, Midtown, East Sacramento, Curtis Park, and Land Park, are very gay-friendly. These were all developed prior to the 1940s and have tree-shaded streets and unique homes.

Nearby areas to consider: To the south, Land Park Hills has quality ranch-style homes on large lots. There are quite a few mid-century modern homes there, too. Sierra Oaks, to the east, offers larger estate-style living on more acreage. This area contains the highest priced housing near downtown. There's a good school district in this area, so it's attractive to families. There are also some areas near Sacramento that can have great homes but neighborhoods that still contain some "rough spots." Tahoe Park, Oak Park, Colonial Park, and Fruitridge all have vintage homes for reasonable prices. These neighborhoods are seeing lots of activity from people priced out of other areas and willing to do a little "urban pioneering."

Earning a Living

Per capita income: $18,721

Median household income: $37,049

Business climate: Aerospace and computer and electronics industries contribute greatly to the city's economy. Sacramento is the shipping, rail, processing, and marketing center for the fertile Sacramento valley, where fruit, vegetables, grains, sugar beets, and dairy goods are produced. Cattle and poultry are raised, and food processing is a major industry.

Help in starting a business: There are several chambers of commerce in Sacramento. The Rainbow Chamber of Commerce promotes networking within the gay and lesbian business community and its supporters to enhance the awareness of political and social issues and to encourage involvement in charitable causes. The Sacramento Metro Chamber of Commerce is a champion for business and is committed to helping shape the region by creating networking, advertising, and educational opportunities for their members.

Job market: As the state capital, government is a major employer. In addition to shipping, agriculture, and the growing high-tech fields, other manufacturing includes printing and publishing, glass, wood products, and building materials.

The Community

Overview: Sacramento has a well-organized and well-supported GLBT community. At the center is the Lambda Community Center (*www.lambdasac.org*), a multi-purpose human service agency. Programs of the Lambda Community Fund serve to assist the GLBT community in leading self-sufficient, healthy, well-adjusted lives and to provide advocacy for issues of importance or special interest. The area's politics are progressive as well, without gay politicians helping to shape the city's future. Additionally, being only about an hour from San Francisco is drawing a GLBT commuter crowd.

Community organizations: This is a city of organizations. You'll discover sports, politics, social, spiritual, and youth outreach groups throughout the city. In addition to the online resources provided by Lambda Community Center, Out Sacramento (*www.outsacramento.com*) is an excellent place for information on the many groups in the city. The Valley Rainbow Pages (*www.vrp.info*) is available both online and around town and contains area news, information, classifieds, and more. Visit the community book store Open Book Ltd. (910 21st Street; 916–498–1004) for all the local rags.

Medical care: There are more than 38 hospitals, surgical centers, and clinics serving the greater Sacramento area. The City of Sacramento (916–808–5704; *www.thecityofsacramento.com/hospital*) provides contact information for all area hospitals. Sacramento Health Care Decisions (916–851–2828; *www.sachealthdecisions.org*) is a nonprofit, nonpartisan organization that gives the public a voice in improving healthcare policy and practice through inquiry, education, and collaboration.

Nuptials: California offers a domestic partnership registration (*www.ss.ca.gov/dpregistry*). Registration isn't the same as marriage, but it does secure many important rights and responsibilities. Under current law, registration can protect your rights in times of family crisis, protect your children, and give you access to family benefits at work.

Getting Around Town

Public transportation: Sacramento Regional Transit (916–321–2800; *www.sacrt.com*) provides bus and light-rail services. Fares: single trip $1.50; one-day pass $3.50; transfers are free and good for 90 minutes. Senior discounts begin at age 62.

Roads: I-5, I-80, US50, US99

Airport: Sacramento International Airport (airport code: SMF) (916–929–5411; *www.sacairports.org*) is served by all major airlines.

It's a Gay Life

Annual events: The Rainbow Festival (*www.rainbowfestival.com*) is Sacramento's three-day pride event in September, and the Sacramento International Gay & Lesbian Film Festival (*www.siglff.org*) is a five-day event in October. Other area annual events of note include the Sacramento Jazz Jubilee (*www.sacjazz.com*), California State Fair (*www.bigfun.org*), Gold Rush Days (*www.oldsacramento.com*), Juneteenth (*www.juneteenth.com*), Festival de la Familia (*www.strauspromotions.com*), Pacific Rim Street Festival (*www.oldsacramento.com*), and New Year's Eve Sky Concert (*www.cityofsacramento.org*).

Nightlife: If you think Sacramento is a sleepy little cow town, then you're simply not paying attention. The revitalization of downtown Sacramento has generated a surge of nightclubs, comedy clubs, live music venues, and much more throughout the region. Night clubs range from quiet piano bars to folk, pop, hip-hop, and country western to rock and roll. The Sacramento gay clubs include Club Bojangles inside Club 21 (1119 21st Street; 916–443–1537; *www.clubbojangles.com*), the Bolt (2560 Boxwood; 916–649–8420), a Levi and leather club; Mercantile Saloon (1928 L Street; 916–447–0792); the dance nightclub Faces - Sacramento (2000 K Street; 916–448–7798; *www.facesnightclub.com*); and the Depot (2001 K Street; 916–441–6823; *www.thedepot.com*), with more than 30 video screens and a spacious outdoor patio. Looking for an alternative to the nightclubs and bars? Sacramento offers other fabulous options, from a comedy show at Laughs Unlimited (1207 Front Street; 916–446–8128; *www.laughsunlimited.com*) or Punch Line Comedy Club (2100 Arden Way; 916–925–5500; *www.punchlinecomedyclub.com*) to a thrilling "who-done-it?" at Garbeau's Dinner Theatre (12401 Folsom Boulevard, Rancho Cordova; 916–985–6361; *216.92.56.121*) or Suspects Murder Mystery Dinner on the Delta King Riverboat (1000 Front Street; 800–825–5464; *www.deltaking.com*). The Esquire IMAX Theatre (1211 K Street; 916–443–4629; *www.imax.com/sacramento*) boasts a six-stories-tall screen with a state-of-the-art sound system. Even the film reels for these amazing movies are an impressive 5 feet tall! Catch an art, independent, or foreign film at the historic Tower and Crest Theatres (1013 K Street; 916–44–CREST; *www.thecrest.com*) or the newest box office hit at one of the many Cineplexes throughout Sacramento. For 24 hours of fun, Country Club Lanes (2600 Watt Avenue; 916–483–5105) has billiards and bowling. Finally, if you're feeling lucky, Thunder Valley (1200 Athens Avenue, Lincoln; 916–408–7777; *www.thundervalleyresort.com*) and several Indian Casinos are less than an hour's drive away.

Culture: Sacramento is home to performing arts, professional ballet, opera, and more than 32 theaters, galleries, and museums. Of community note are The Lambda Players (2427 17th Street; 916–484–4742; *www.lambdaplayers.com*), the area's GLBT theater company. The Sacramento Area Performing Arts (*www.lightsup.com*)

maintains a Website of current performances. As the state's capital, Sacramento is rich in California history, including the California State History Museum (1020 O Street; 916–653–7524; *www.californiamuseum.org*), the California State Railroad Museum (111 I Street; 916–445–96645; *www.csrmf.org*), the California State Indian Museum (2618 K Street; 916–324–0971; *www.csrmf.org*), the California Military Museum (1119 Second Street; 916–442–2883; *www.militarymuseum.org*), and the California State Capitol Museum (10th and L streets; 916–324–0333; *www.capitolmuseum.ca.gov*). If you really want to visit the past, step back in time to the California Gold Rush era in Old Sacramento, a 28-acre town of historic buildings, museums, and monuments. With strong preservation efforts, the wooden sidewalks, horse-drawn carriages, Pony Express monuments and Mississippi-style riverboats reflect the nostalgic appeal of early American history. Also of interest are the Crocker Art Museum (216 O Street; 916–264–5423; *www.crockerartmuseum.org*), Discovery Museum History Center (101 I Street; 916–264–7057; *www.thediscovery.org*), Towe Auto Museum (2200 Front Street; 916–442–6802), Wells Fargo History Museum (Wells Fargo Center, 400 Capitol Mall; 916–440–4161; *www.wellsfargo.com*), and the B.F. Hastings Building (1000 2nd Street; 916–440–4263). The Sacramento Association of Museums (*www.sacmuseums.org*) is the best source for information on the area's many museums. The Sleep Train Amphitheater (2677 Forty Mile Road, Marysville; 916–649–8497; *www.sacvalleyamp.com*) is an open-air venue hosting concerts that span the musical spectrum. Other attractions include the Old Sacramento Historic Area (916–558–3912; *www.oldsacramento.com*), Sutter's Fort (27th and L streets; 916–445–4422; *www.parks.ca.gov*), the Sacramento Zoo (3930 West Land Park Drive; 916–264–5885; *www.saczoo.com*), Eagle Theatre (925 Front Street; 916–323–6343), Governor's Mansion State Historic Park (16th and H streets; 916–323–3047; *www.parks.ca.gov*), Pony Express Monument (2nd and J streets), Delta King Hotel (1000 Front Street; 916–444–5464), and Leland Stanford Mansion (8th and N streets; 916–324–0575; *www.stanfordmansion.org*).

Recreation: In a city bound by two rivers, the American and the Sacramento, water recreation tops the list for outdoor activities: salmon and steelhead fishing, river rafting, boating. All can be done on the 1,000 miles of waterways around Sacramento and the Delta. Nearby Folsom Lake and Lake Natoma offer sailing and windsurfing. Sacramento municipal golf courses provide the surrounding community with 540 acres of quality fairways and greens. The selection is impressive, from Ancil Hoffman Park (6700 Tarshes Drive, Carmichael; 916–482–1206; *www.effieyeaw.org*)—listed as one of *Golf Digest*'s 75 Top Public Courses—to The Ridge (2020 Golf Course Road, Auburn; 530–888–PUTT; *www.ridgegc.com*), designed by legendary Robert Trent Jones II. Whether you favor links-style courses with gently rolling, driver-friendly fairways or challenging obstacle such as lakes and oak trees, you'll find the perfect course. More than 120 city parks encompassing 2,000-plus acres provide outstanding natural and developed parklands. For high-speed excitement, don't miss the annual Bridge-to-Bridge Waterfront Festival and Boat Race event (916–808–777; *www.discovergold.org*).

High-powered boat races thrill crowds at this two-day event as they speed down the Old Sacramento Waterfront between the Tower Bridge and the I Street Bridge. The timed cigarette-style boat races are accented with live entertainment and food vendors. Speed is of the essence again at the California International Marathon (916–983–4622; *www.runcim.org*) held each December. Watch some of the best runners in the world conquer this very fast course from the foothills to the State Capitol (10th and L streets; 916–324–0333; *www.assembly.ca.gov*). If you're interested in spectator sports Sacramento is represented by the NBA's Sacramento Kings (916–928–0000; *www.kings.com*), the WNBA's Sacramento Monarchs (916–928–0000; *www.sacramentomonarchs.com*), World Indoor Soccer League's Knights (916–912–6771; *www.sactoknights.com*), and the Sacramento River Cats (400 Ballpark Drive; 916–376–4700; *www.rivercats.com*), a AAA baseball team.

For the Visitor

Accommodations: There are approximately 10,000 hotel rooms in the Sacramento region. Full-service hotels, affordable inns, and historic bed and breakfasts create an extensive list of accommodations from which to choose. The historic Inn at Parkside (2116 6th Street; 800–995–7275; *www.innatparkside.com*), a grand mansion, built in 1936 as the official U.S. residence for the North American Ambassador from Nationalist China with views of the state capital, provides seven well-appointed guest suites, delicious three-course breakfasts, and an elegant setting for weddings or commitment ceremonies.

For More Information

Gay & Lesbian Center
Lambda Community Center
1927 L Street
Sacramento, CA 95814
916–442–0185
www.lambdasac.org

Publications
The Sacramento Bee
2100 Q Street
Sacramento, CA 95816
916–321–1000
www.sacbee.com

Mom Guess What Newspaper
1103 T Street
Sacramento, CA 95814
916–441–6397
www.mgwnews.com

Convention and Visitors Bureau
Sacramento Convention and Visitors Bureau
1608 I Street
Sacramento, CA 95814
916–808–7777
www.sacramentocvb.org

Chambers of Commerce
Rainbow Chamber of Commerce
1330 21st Street, Suite 201
Sacramento, CA 95814
916–817–2400
www.rainbowchamber.com

Sacramento Metro Chamber of Commerce
917 Seventh Street
Sacramento, CA 95814
916–552–6800
www.metrochamber.org

Realtor
David Rickert
Coldwell Banker Residential Brokerage
440 Drake Circle
Sacramento, CA 95864
916–717–2188
www.RickertProperties.com

## 8

San Francisco, California

A Look at San Francisco

San Francisco combines sheer physical beauty, cultural diversity, and leisure and recreational offerings with an ideal climate. In an age of freeways and urban sprawl, San Francisco remains a compact city with a thriving downtown business and retail center and attractive, friendly neighborhoods. Globally recognized as a gem, San Francisco boasts many famous landmarks: the Golden Gate Bridge, Fisherman's Wharf, Ghirardelli Square, Chinatown, the clanging cable cars pulling up the crests of Nob and Russian hills, and the angular construction of the pyramid-shaped Transamerica Building, the center of San Francisco's Financial District. Natural beauty notwithstanding, attitude more than latitude has made San Francisco the "world's gay and lesbian capital." The headquarters for a vast vacationland, the metropolis known variously as the Paris of the West, Baghdad-by-the-Bay, the Gateway to the Orient, and to locals, simply The City, San Francisco is the original "gay-friendly city," welcoming diversity since the days of the Gold Rush. One of the most culturally rich cities in the world, San Francisco values diversity, tolerance, individuality, and compassion.

Possible drawbacks: San Francisco remains one of the most expensive cities in the world. Homes with a view are offered at extreme premiums. The once-cheap, bohemian neighborhoods are now trendy and expensive.

▶ Nickname:
Gay Capital of the World

▶ County:
San Francisco

▶ Area code: 415

▶ Time zone: Pacific

▶ Population:
789,600

▶ County population:
789,600

▶ Region:
Northwest California

▶ Average home price:
$896,000

▶ Fabulous reasons to live here:
Beautiful and historic city; progressive politics; temperate climate; arts; culture; recreation; high-tech economy; large, organized GLBT community

Climate

Elevation 63'	Avg. high/low(F°)	Avg. inches rain	Avg. inches snow	Avg. # days precip.	Avg. % humidity
Jan.	58/46	4.7	0.1	10	80%
April	64/50	1.2	–	5	63%
July	68/54	–	–	0	52%
Oct.	70/55	1.2	–	3	58%
YEAR	65/51	22.1	0.4	57	63%
# days 32° or below: 1			# days 90° or warmer: 3		

Local Connections

Gas company: Pacific Gas and Electric (800–743–5000; *www.pge.com*)

Electric companies: Green Mountain Energy Resource (415–439–5310; *www.greenmountain.com*); Pacific Gas & Electric Co. (800–743–5000; *www.pge.com*); San Francisco Thermal (415–777–3415; *www.nrgenerg.com*); Sempra Energy Solutions (925–460–9830; *www.sempra.com*)

Phone companies: AT&T (800–222–0300; *www.att.com*); MCI Telecommunications (888–MCI–LOCAL; *www.mci.com*); Pacific Bell (800–310–2365; *www.pacbell.com*); Sprint (800–538–0943; *www.sprintps.com*)

Water and sewer: The San Francisco Public Utilities Commission (415–551–3000; *www.sfwater.org*); San Francisco Water Department (415–550–4911; *www.puc.sf.ca.us*)

Cable company: AT&T Cable Services (800–436–1999; *www.cable.att.com*)

Car registration/License: California Department of Motor Vehicles (800–777–0133; *www.dmv.ca.gov*)

You must get a California driver's license within 10 days of establishing residency. License application fee: $25. If you have a valid license from another state, the driving test can be waived. Car registration and registration renewals are $31. The Vehicle License Fee (VLF) replaces property tax on vehicles. The formula for VLF assessment is based upon the purchase price or value of the vehicle and decreases with each renewal for the first 11 years. The VLF on a $25K vehicle for the first two years would be $163 and $147, respectively. The VLF is prorated for partial year registrations.

The Tax Ax

Sales tax:　　　8.5 percent

State income tax: 1.0–9.3 percent graduated, depending on income

Property tax:　　Property taxes are currently 1.114 percent of the assessed value, which is based on the purchase price. Thanks to Proposition 13, there are no periodic re-assessments of property values, just increases limited to 2 percent annually.

Local Real Estate

Overview: The San Francisco real estate market is dynamic, consistent, and competitive. Housing stock includes everything from pre-earthquake (we're talking 1906 here) Victorians to sleek and modern condos to "live-work" lofts to a uniquely San Francisco hybrid called a "TIC" (tenancy in common) where two or more partners buy a multi-unit building using one mortgage. Inventory is generally good but most properties sell in less than 30 days and usually for more than the asking price.

Median price for a single-family home: $794,000

Average price for a single-family home: $896,000

Average price for a 2BR condo: $834,000

Rental housing market: The most popular rental is a one-bedroom plus formal dining room. A two-bedroom rental is likely to be priced in the range of $1,750–2,450 depending on condition, location, and whether it includes parking. The market is not moving dramatically at the moment. Rents dropped significantly after the dotcom bubble burst but have been increasing since then.

Gay-friendly neighborhoods: This is San Francisco, so pretty much every neighborhood qualifies as ethnically mixed, liberal, and gay-friendly, which allows you to choose where you want to live based on whatever criteria are important to you. There are some neighborhoods that stand out: the Castro/Eureka Valley (often considered the gay ghetto), Bernal Heights, and Noe Valley.

Nearby areas to consider: The high prices and competitiveness of the San Francisco real estate market often leads prospective home owners to look at East Bay areas including Berkeley, Emeryville, and parts of Oakland; Marin County (north of the Golden Gate Bridge), including Sausalito and Mill Valley, is also popular with the GLBT community. With such large numbers of the area population seeking residences in more affordable, outlying areas, daily commute times are beginning to increase and should be a factor when determining your potential new community.

Earning a Living

Per capita income: $34,556

Median household income: $55,221

Business climate: The San Francisco Bay Area is the hub of a nine-county complex and the financial and insurance capital of the West. Additionally, the arts are the fourth-largest growth industry in San Francisco, and one in 11 jobs are related to the arts through employment in such sectors as graphic design, advertising, architecture, publishing, broadcast, and film.

Help in starting a business: The Golden Gate Business Association was the first GLBT chamber of commerce in the nation and provides members with networking and mentoring opportunities, informal business advice, business leads, and referrals. The organization provides a sense of community for members facing the task of doing business in today's rapidly changing and challenging marketplace. In addition, The San Francisco Chamber of Commerce is recognized as the preeminent business organization for advocacy, networking, and economic growth in the city. It also runs The San Francisco Center for Economic Development and its many programs for businesses large and small.

Job market: The largest area employers are The City and County of San Francisco. The area is home to dozens of national headquarters and a few of the top employers include Bechtel Group Inc., Levi Strauss & Co., New United Motor, DHL Airways Inc., Lucasfilm Ltd., Chevron Corp., BankAmerica Corp., and AirTouch. Banking, finance, import/export, services, retail, and the arts are all prominent market sectors.

The Community

Overview: It's estimated one third of all voting adults in San Francisco are gay, and this is reflected in the openly gay elected officials, the so-called "lavender" ticket, and the pro-gay politics and policies of the city. The city prides itself on its respect for the diversity of its citizens and its overriding motto seems to be "live and let live."

Community organizations: San Francisco is rich with organizations and agencies serving the needs of the GLBT community. There are hundreds of groups and organizations in San Francisco providing social and recreation opportunities, as well as support. The Center (*www.sfgaycenter.org*) is the hub that links individuals and programs to each other and to the community. Rather than duplicating existing services, The Center works to foster connections among service providers, ensuring that people can find the services they need. The Center has a distinct role to strengthen both individuals and institutions in San Francisco's GLBT community. It develops programs that encourage peer leadership and focuses on empowering individuals to be active participants in building a shared community.

Medical care: The dozens of hospitals and clinics in San Francisco offer some of the nation's finest health treatment. Downtown San Francisco Health Online (415–956–3226; *www.downtownsfhealth.org*), a free health and news e-magazine, serves residents of San Francisco by providing health information to assist with making important everyday healthcare decisions. Its services include listings, newsletters, and information on the various health care options in the city.

Nuptials: California offers a domestic partnership registration (*www.ss.ca.gov/ dpregistry*). Registration isn't the same as marriage, but it does secure many important rights and responsibilities. Under current law, registration can protect your rights in times of family crisis, protect your children, and give you access to family benefits at work.

Getting Around Town

Public transportation: The San Francisco transit system includes 9,860 miles of transit routes. There are about two dozen transit providers in and around the city. A few include San Francisco Municipal Railway, operating buses, cable cars, and streetcars; Bay Area Rapid Transit, offering light-rail; and Golden Gate Bridge, Highway & Transportation District, providing buses and ferry service between San Francisco and Marin County. 511 Transit is a free phone (511) and Web (*www.511.org*) service that consolidates Bay Area transportation information, making it easy to find routes, carriers, schedules, and fares.

Roads: I-80, US1, US101

Airport: San Francisco International Airport (airport code: SFO) (650–877–0118 *www.flysfo.com*) is about 11 miles from downtown; Oakland International Airport (airport code: OAK) (510–563–3300; *www.flyoakland.com*) is about 16 miles from downtown. Both offer quick and easy ground transportation options to get you to the city.

It's a Gay Life

Annual events: San Francisco Pride (*www.sfpride.org*) sponsors pride events the entire month of June, culminating with the world's largest GLBT pride parade and rally. Also of note are the International Gay & Lesbian Film Festival (*www.frameline.org*), the Queer Arts Festival (*www.queerculturalcenter.org*), Bay to Breakers fundraising marathon (*www.baytobreakers.com*), the San Francisco Waterfront Festival (*www.pier39.com*), several jazz and blues festivals, the San Francisco Shakespeare Festival (*www.sfshakes.org*), the San Francisco Fringe Festival (*www.sffringe.org*), the Folsom Street Fair (*www.folsomstreetfair.com*), and the Castro Street Fair (*www.castrostreetfair.org*).

Nightlife: A metropolis in every sense of the word, San Francisco is renowned for the quality of its more than 3,300 restaurants. The City has more restaurants per capita than any other in the United States. With 30 GLBT bars and clubs and dozens of restaurants throughout the city that cater to the GLBT community, it's no wonder entire books have been written about San Francisco's gay nightlife. Without question, the epicenter of gay life is Castro Street. San Francisco Gate (*www.sfgate.com*) provides news and listings of bars and events around the city.

Culture: San Francisco supports an opera with a glittering tradition, a world-class symphony orchestra, a ballet that has won international acclaim, an annual International Film Festival, four public art museums, dozens of galleries, legitimate theaters presenting top offerings from New York and London and the local production circuit, and a resident repertory company of exceptional caliber, the American Conservatory Theater (30 Grant Avenue; 415–834–3200; *www.act-sfbay.org*). The City's principal attractions are the century-old cable cars, America's only mobile National Historic Landmark; Fisherman's Wharf (Pier 39 and the Embarcadero; 415–391–2000; *www.fishermanswharf.org*), with its bay-view restaurants and resident sea lions; Alcatraz (Pier 41, Fisherman's Wharf; 415–705–5555; *www.blueandgoldfleet.com*), once the site of the United States' toughest maximum security prison and now a National Park; Chinatown (*www.sanfranciscochinatown.com*), the largest Asian enclave outside of Asia; Golden Gate Park (*www.parks.sfgov.org*), with its Japanese Tea Garden (415–752–1171), Steinhart Aquarium and Morrison Planetarium (875 Howard Street; 415–321–8000; *www.calacademy.org*), outstanding museums, and 1,000 wooded acres; Mission Dolores (3321 16th Street; 415–621–8203; *www.californiamissions.com*), founded by the Spanish padres in 1776; the pagoda-crowned Japan Center (2211 Bush Street, the Fillmore District); the Victorian shopping sector known as Cow Hollow on outer Union Street, Ocean Beach and Seal Rocks; Union Square (Powell and Post streets), home of major-league shopping; and North Beach, the Little Italy of the West.

Recreation: Created in 1972, The Golden Gate National Recreation Area (*www.nps.gov/goga*) is the largest urban park in the world and the most popular in the national system. Bird watchers, beachcombers, hikers, cyclists, surfers, surf fishers, picnickers, and nature lovers flock to both sides of the Golden Gate and the coastal range to the city's south. The Steinhart Aquarium (875 Howard Street; 415–321–8000; *www.calacademy.com*) features a roundabout tank that is 180-feet in diameter. Sharks, seals, dolphins, penguins, and alligators are among the popular residents of the aquarium. For spectators, the 42,000-seat SBC Park (24 Willie Mays Plaza; 415–972–1800; *www.sbcpark.com*) is home to National League's San Francisco Giants (415–972–2000; *www.sfgiants.com*); Across the bay, the American League's Oakland Athletics (7000 Coliseum Way, Oakland; 510–638–4900; *oakland.athletics.mlb.com*) have been Oakland's home team for 29 seasons. The National Football League's San Francisco 49ers (Monster Park; 415–656–4900; *www.sf49ers.com*) was the first professional sports franchise on the West Coast. The National Football League's Oakland Raiders (7000 Coliseum Way; 510–569–2121; *www.raiders.com*) play in the McAfee Coliseum (7000 Coliseum Way; 510–569–2121; *www.coliseum.com*), just next door to the NBA's Golden State Warriors (1011 Broadway; 510–986–2200; *www.nba.com/warriors*). Rounding out the field are the NHL's San Jose Sharks (525 West Santa Clara; 408–287–7070; *www.sj-sharks.com*) and soccer's San Jose Earthquakes (100 North Almaden Avenue, San Jose; 408–985–GOAL; *www.sjearthquakes.com*). For racing fans there's the Bay Meadows Race Course (2600 S. Delaware Street, San Mateo; 650–574–RACE; *www.baymeadows.com*) and the Golden Gate Fields Race Track (1100 Eastshore Highway, Berkeley; 510–559–7300; *www.ggfields.com*).

For the Visitor

Accommodations: Most of San Francisco's hoteliers would be surprised if two men traveling together asked for separate rooms. Among the many gay-friendly favorites are Hotel Triton (342 Grant Avenue; 415–394–0500/800–828–6544; *www.hoteltriton.com*), a hip, eco-sensitive boutique hotel at Union Square. The Clift (495 Geary Street; 415–775–4700/800–606–6090; *www.clifthotel.com*), described as a masterpiece of urban chic, is steps from Union Square and the Theatre District. Joie de Vivre Hospitality (800–738–7477; *www.jdvhospitality.com*) provides travelers on a budget with two excellent choices: The Maxwell Hotel (386 Geary Street; 415–986–2000/800–828–6544), a stylish restored masterpiece with a Deco flair located in the heart of Union Square, and the Phoenix Hotel (601 Eddy Street; 415–776–1380/800–828–6544; *www.jdvhospitality.com*), once a popular 1950s celebrity hangout, at the edge of the gritty Tenderloin neighborhood and popular with musicians and artists.

For More Information

Gay & Lesbian Center

The Center
1800 Market Street
San Francisco, CA 94102
415–865–5555
www.sfcenter.org

Publications

San Francisco Chronicle
901 Mission Street
San Francisco, CA 94103
415–777–1111
www.sfgate.com/chronicle

San Francisco Examiner
450 Mission Street
San Francisco, CA 94105
866–733–7323
www.examiner.com

Bay Area Reporter (LGBT)
395 Ninth Street
San Francisco, CA 94103
415–861–5019
www.ebar.com

Convention and Visitors Bureau

San Francisco Convention and Visitors Bureau
201 Third Street, Suite 900
San Francisco, CA 94103
415–391–2000
www.sfvisitor.org

Chambers of Commerce

The Golden Gate Business Association
1800 Market Street, Suite Q32
San Francisco, CA 94102
415–865–5545
www.ggba.com

The San Francisco Chamber of Commerce
235 Montgomery Street, 12th Floor
San Francisco, CA 94104
415–392–4520
www.sfchamber.com

Realtor

Jim Hedges, Manager
Prudential California Realty
2241 Market Street
San Francisco, CA 94114
415–575–5599
www.prurealty.com/sfmarket

West Hollywood, California

9

California

Sacramento

San Francisco

Los Angeles

West Hollywood

A Look at West Hollywood

From award show parties, celebrity appearances and exclusive promotions to events highlighting this city's diversity and love for living, West Hollywood is the destination for those seeking the finest and most exciting diversions in life. Its 19th-century roots as Rancho La Brea sprouted Moses Sherman's Los Angeles Pacific Railway terminal (the original Red Line) and the un-incorporated township of Sherman. By the early '20s, it was far too hot a spot to be "Sherman." The little rebel cast aside its given name and began to call itself "West Hollywood." By the time of its incorporation (1984), it had become the entertainment, music, film, art, design, and cuisine capital of the new West. West Hollywood is beautiful. You look to the north and see the gorgeous Hollywood Hills, where it appears that one house is built right on top of another. Driving down Sunset Boulevard or Melrose Avenue in the winter months you see snow-capped mountains. With the nightlife, restaurants, art, fashion, and gay and lesbian diversions, there's never a dull moment in the 1.9-square-mile "Creative City."

Possible drawbacks: West Hollywood is a small and desirable location that keeps the housing market tight and expensive. The city is home to many attractive, young men; this is a plus or minus, depending on how hard you're willing to work out.

▶ Nickname:
The Creative City

▶ County: Los Angeles

▶ Area codes: 323; 310

▶ Time zone: Pacific

▶ Population: 35,716

▶ County population:
9,519,338

▶ Region:
Southern California

▶ Closest metro area:
Los Angeles

▶ Average home price:
$1,200,000

▶ Fabulous reasons to live here:
Progressive politics, large GLBT community, arts, entertainment, nightlife, historic setting, great weather

Climate

Elevation 287'	Avg. high/low(F°)	Avg. inches rain	snow	Avg. # days precip.	Avg. % humidity
Jan.	67/47	3.7	–	6	64%
April	71/52	0.8	–	3	65%
July	80/62	–	–	0	68%
Oct.	77/87	0.5	–	2	67%
YEAR	67/54	17	–	31	67%
# days 32° or below: 0			# days 90° or warmer: 26		

Local Connections

Gas company: The Southern California Gas Company (800–427–2200; *www.socalgas.com*)

Electric company: Southern California Edison (800–684–8123; *www.sce.com*)

Phone company: SBC Communications (800–310–2355; *www.sbc.com*)

Water and sewer: Los Angeles Department of Water & Power (323–481–5800; *www.ladwp.com*)

Cable company: Adelphia Cable (323–654–5600; *www.adelphia.net*)

Car registration/License: California Department of Motor Vehicles (800–777–0133; *www.dmv.ca.gov*)

You must get a California driver's license within 10 days of establishing residency. License application fee: $25. If you have a valid license from another state, the driving test can be waived. Car registration and registration renewals are $31. The Vehicle License Fee (VLF) replaces property tax on vehicles. The formula for VLF assessment is based upon the purchase price or value of the vehicle and decreases with each renewal for the first 11 years. The VLF on a $25K vehicle for the first two years would be $163 and $147, respectively. The VLF is prorated for partial year registrations.

The Tax Ax

Sales tax: 8.25 percent; some food exempt

State income tax: 1.0–9.3 percent graduated, depending on income

Property tax: L.A. County Tax Assessor (213–974–3211)

Property is assessed and taxed at fair market value. The current levy is 1.25 percent of the new sales price.

Local Real Estate

Overview: West Hollywood consists of many bungalows from the 1920s and traditionals from the '40s. There are several high-end, full-service, high-rise buildings built in the 1960s. In the '70s, with great city and ocean views, many of these have been converted to condominiums. Currently there are many new mid-century and loft-style condos being built.

Median price for a single-family home: $850,000

Average price for a single-family home: $1,200,000

Average price for a 2BR condo: $550,000

Rental housing market: The rental market is very strong because people can't afford to buy properties. Prices continue to rise steadily.

Gay-friendly neighborhoods: All of West Hollywood is gay-friendly.

Nearby areas to consider: Unfortunately all of the surrounding areas are not that much less expensive. The areas immediately south and east of West Hollywood are not as gay-friendly and not as beautiful. The entertainment industry draws large numbers of GLBT community members to Studio City, North Hollywood, Hollywood, and West Hollywood. Silverlake, with the Elysian Park, Silver Lake, Mt. Washington, Dodger Stadium, and a nice collection of GLBT bars, restaurants, and businesses, is another nearby winner. Van Nuys, Newport Beach, Riverside, Sherman Oaks, and Resida are only a few of the other LA suburbs that the gay community calls home in Los Angeles County.

Earning a Living

Per capita income: $38,302

Median household income: $38,914

Business climate: The entertainment industry is vital to the economy of West Hollywood. As early as the 1950s, the design and decorating industry found a home in West Hollywood; the 750,000-square-foot Pacific Design Center anchors the burgeoning Avenues of Art & Design. In the last decade, the City has undertaken projects to strengthen its economy, including revitalization of the city's East Side and approval of the Sunset Specific Plan to guide and promote quality development along historic Sunset Boulevard.

Help in starting a business: The West Hollywood Chamber of Commerce provides resources on how to start a new business, how to jump-start an existing business, and how to get involved in the community. Additionally, the chamber offers networking, referral, and exposure opportunities for West Hollywood businesses.

Job market: Market sectors providing most of the area employment are information and technology; professional, scientific, management, administrative, and waste management services; arts, entertainment, recreation, accommodation, and food services; and education, health, and social services.

The Community

Overview: The City of West Hollywood was founded as a gay enclave city. The GLBT community is a third of West Hollywood's population. It's an organized, out, and vocal community with strong ties and support from local government. It's common for a majority of the city council members to be out GLBT community members.

Community organizations: The L.A. Gay & Lesbian Center (323–993–7400) stands as a model for centers around the country. The center provides a broad array of services for the lesbian, gay, bisexual, and transgender community, welcoming nearly a quarter-million client visits from ethnically diverse youth and adults each year. The Center offers health, legal, social, cultural, and educational services, with unique programs for seniors, families, and youth, including a 24-bed transitional living program for homeless youth.

Medical care: Cedars-Sinai Medical Center (310–423–3277; *www.cedars-sinai.edu*) has more than 1,800 physicians in virtually all medical specialties. Cedars-Sinai physicians are leaders in basic and clinical research, bringing advancements in medicine directly from the laboratory to the bedside. In addition, more than 245 residents and fellows in nearly 60 graduate medical education programs are taught at Cedars-Sinai. UCLA Medical Center (310–206–3410; *healthcare.ucla.edu*), with more than 600 beds, offers patients of all ages comprehensive care, from routine to highly specialized medical and surgical treatment with specialized intensive care units, state-of-the-art inpatient and outpatient operating suites, a Level-1 trauma center, the latest diagnostic technology, and a high level of commitment from our dedicated and experienced staff of more than 1,000 physicians and 3,500 nurses, therapists, technologists, and support personnel. The Spot (745 N. San Vicente Boulevard; 323–993–7440; *www.laglc.org*) is a weekday clinic run by the L.A. Gay & Lesbian Center offering Free Rapid HIV Testing and STD screening.

Nuptials: California offers a domestic partnership registration (*www.ss.ca.gov/ dpregistry*). Registration isn't the same as marriage, but it does secure many important rights and responsibilities. Under current law, registration can protect your rights in times of family crisis, protect your children, and give you access to family benefits at work. In addition, the City of West Hollywood provides its own domestic partnership registration, enabling any two individuals, regardless of sexual orientation, to have their relationship officially recognized by the City of West Hollywood. The couple need not reside in West Hollywood in order to register, nor does the length of their relationship have to be of any particular duration in order to qualify.

Getting Around Town

Public transportation: Metropolitan Transit Authority (MTA) (800–COM-MUTE; *www.mta.net*): Metro Red line (800–266–6883; *www.mta.net*) base fare $1.25; all-day pass $3. The nearest metro station is located at Western and Wilshire. The Fairfax Dash (323–808–2273; *www.mta.net*) provides access to the Fairfax District, Melrose Avenue, Park La Brea, Cedars-Sinai, and the Beverly/La Cienega areas, Farmer's Market, La Brea Avenue, and the Miracle Mile.

Roads: Historic Route 66 (nearby I-10, I-5, I-405, US101)

Airports: Los Angeles International Airport (airport code: LAX) (310–646–5252; *www.lawa.org/lax*) provides free ground transportation to both the City Bus Center and the Metro Rail Green Line. Bob Hope Airport (airport code: BUR) (818–840–8840; *www.bobhopeairport.com*), formerly Burbank Glendale Pasadena Airport, is the closest airport to downtown LA, Hollywood, and popular attractions.

It's a Gay Life

Annual events: Christopher Street West (*www.lapride.org*) hosts the Gay, Lesbian and Transgender Pride Parade and Festival in June. The two-day festival, the second largest on the West Coast, celebrates diversity and culture with booths, food, exhibits, and performances. Other annual events include the Rose Bowl Parade on January 1st (*www.tournamentofroses.com*) and Outfest (*www.outfest.org*) in July, the largest film festival in Southern California and the region's largest gay and lesbian arts event. The West Hollywood Halloween Costume Carnival on October 31st (*www.weho.org*) draws more than 400,000 participants to "The Boulevard" for food, merriment, and costume contests.

Nightlife: West Hollywood has no shortage of gay establishments, and the nightlife is exciting. Among the dozens of area hotspots, O-Bar (8279 Santa Monica Boulevard; 323–822–3300), Here Lounge (696 N. Robertson Boulevard; 310–360–8455; *www.herelounge.com*), and the Abbey (692 N. Robertson Boulevard; 310–855–9977; *www.abbeyfoodandbar.com*) are the perennial favorites; the Gold Coast (8228 Santa Monica Boulevard; 323–656–4879) is one of the city's oldest neighborhood gay bars; the Revolver (8851 Santa Monica Boulevard; 310–659–8851) runs the gamut with nightly events ranging from drag to karaoke; Micky's (8857 Santa Monica Boulevard; 310–657–1176; *www.mickys.com*) is the trendy gay video and dance bar; Rage is a fun disco; the Palms (8572 Santa Monica Boulevard; 310–652–6188) is a lesbian bar with nightly specials; and anything goes at gender-bending Club 7969 (7969 Santa Monica Boulevard; 323–654–0280; *www.club7969.com*). Also of interest for music fans are the House of Blues (8430 Sunset Boulevard; 323–848–5100; *www.hob.com*) and the famous-club Whiskey-a-Go-Go (8901 Sunset Boulevard; 310–652–4202; *www.whiskyagogo.com*), a fabulous venue to see rock 'n' roll's top names. Pick up the gay and lesbian biweekly newspaper *FAB!* (*www.gayfab.com*) and *Frontiers Magazine* (*www.frontiersmagazine.com*) for all the current bar listings and events; both are available at Book Soup (8818 Sunset Boulevard; 310–659–3110) or A Different Light (8853 Santa Monica Boulevard; 310–854–6601).

Culture: West Hollywood is one of the nation's centers for art and design. The Pacific Design Center (87 Melrose Avenue; 610–657–0800; *www.pacificdesigncenter.com*) has 1.2 million square feet of showrooms and unusual exhibits and is home to the Museum of Contemporary Art (MOCA) West (250 S. Grand Avenue; 213–626–6222; *www.moca-la.org*). West Hollywood's design district, concentrated on Melrose, Beverly, and Robertson, also boasts more than 30 art galleries catering to an international clientele with a passion for original art and sculpture. West Hollywood Arts and Cultural Affairs Commission (213–485–2433; *www.weho.org*) has created a fabulous public art program: Art on the Outside, bringing art out from the museums and galleries and into public spaces; many of these public art spaces are along Santa Monica Boulevard. The architectural landmark Schindler House (835 N. Kings Road; 323–651–1510; *www.makcenter.org*), a model of Modernist design, is home to the MAK Center, where exhibitions of art and architecture are displayed. Music lovers will love every note of West Hollywood Orchestra's (866–WHO–CALL; *www.whorchestra.org*) exciting and enlightening performances. Each season, renowned WHO artistic director and conductor Nan Washburn leads West Hollywood musicians in concerts of contemporary music and best-loved classics. Summer Sounds Series are outdoor musical concerts held on Sundays in June, July, and August in West Hollywood parks (*www.weho.org*). These performances represent different cultures and sounds of the community—from Broadway show tunes to Eastern European Klezmer—and are a perfect excuse to have a picnic with the family while listening to great music. Times and dates vary. The Celebration Theatre (7051 Santa Monica Boulevard; 323–957–1884; *www.celebrationtheatre.com*) is the area's LGBT theater.

Recreation: The City of West Hollywood has four parks, one softball field (West Hollywood Park), a swimming pool, and tennis and paddle courts. West Hollywood Park (647 N. San Vicente Boulevard; 323–848–6534; *www.weho.org*) and Plummer Park (7377 Santa Monica Boulevard; 323–845–0174; *www.weho.org*) facilities are available for recreational events, community meetings, and sports activities. Plummer Park is also home to the award-winning Helen Albert Certified Farmers' Market (1200 N. Vista Street at Fountain Avenue), featuring organic and farm fresh fruits and vegetables, baked goods, fresh fish, flowers, and even crepes. It runs every Monday from 9:00 a.m. until 2:00 p.m. (including most holidays); William S. Hart Park (8341 De Longpre Avenue; 323–848–6308; *www.weho.org*) is available for outdoor weddings and memorials only. For spectators, Los Angeles County is home to more than 200 sports venues, including the Staples Center (1111 S. Figueroa Street; 213–742–7340; *www.staplescenter.com*), home to the L.A. Lakers (310–426–6031; *www.lakers.com*) and the Los Angeles Clippers (888–895–8662; *www.clippers.com*); the Home Depot Center (18400 Avalon Boulevard, Carson; 310–630–2000; *www.homedepotcenter.com*), home to soccer's Los Angeles Galaxy (310–630–2200; *www.lagalaxy.com*); and Dodger Stadium (1000 Elysian Park Avenue; 866–363–4377; *www.dodgers.com*), home to the Los Angeles Dodgers (866–DODGERS; *www.dodgers.com*).

For the Visitor

Accommodations: West Hollywood's 14 hotels run the gamut from the landmark art deco Argyle to the intimate and secluded Sunset Marquis Hotel & Villas (1200 Alta Loma Road; 310–657–1333; *www.sunsetmarquishotel.com*). In addition to being where those in the know lay their heads, WeHo hotels are the perfect spot for enjoying sweeping sunset vistas, admiring often-imitated architecture, and sampling exotic cuisine. San Vicente Inn/Resort (845 N. San Vicente Boulevard; 310–854–6915; *www.gayresort.com*), West Hollywood's only gay guesthouse, is a relaxing, intimate retreat close to Santa Monica Boulevard. Comfortable cottages and rooms overlook the tropical gardens surrounding the heated pool and clothing-optional sundecks. The Argyle Hotel (8358 Sunset Boulevard; 323–654–7100/800–225–2637; *www.argylehotel.com*) is the ultimate art deco experience, offering 15 stories of elegance in the heart of the Sunset Strip.

For More Information

Gay & Lesbian Center

L.A. Gay and Lesbian Center
1625 N. Schrader Boulevard
Los Angeles, CA 90028
323–993–7400
www.laglc.org

Publications

Los Angeles Times
202 W. 1st Street
Los Angeles, CA 90012
213–237–5000
www.latimes.com

The Los Angeles Independent
4201 Wilshire Boulevard,
Suite 600
Los Angeles, CA 90010
323–556–5720
www.laindependent.com

Convention and Visitors Bureau

West Hollywood Convention and
Visitors Bureau
8687 Melrose Avenue, Suite M-38
West Hollywood, CA 90069
310–289–2525/800–368–6020
www.visitwesthollywood.com

Chamber of Commerce

West Hollywood Chamber of Commerce
8278 1/2 Santa Monica Boulevard
West Hollywood, CA 90046
323–650–2688
www.wehochamber.com

Realtor

Ron Thomas, Realtor/Designer
Sotheby's Int'l.
9200 Sunset Boulevard, Suite 200
West Hollywood, CA 90069
310–650–7115

## 10

Boulder, Colorado

Colorado

Boulder ▼ *Denver* •

Colorado Springs •

A Look at Boulder

Nestled against the Flatiron Mountains 35 miles west of Denver, Boulder's picturesque setting alone distinguishes it from other urban communities in the Rocky Mountain States. Yet beyond the breathtaking scenery lies a town filled with culture, history, and unique qualities that give Boulder its personality and make it one of Colorado's most desired places to live. It's no wonder that *Men's Journal* ranked Boulder number one in its 50 Best Places to Live, calling it "the healthiest, sexiest, most fun, and most affordable towns in the land" (March 2005). The look of the city won't change anytime soon. Several city programs, such as the Boulder Open Space Program and Boulder's Growth Management System, have set building limits, building height limits, and population growth limits and secured almost 60,000 acres of land to prevent development. The outdoor, active lifestyle is a big part of this city in the hills, as apparent from another city highlight: the 6-mile greenway running through the middle of the community perfect for recreation and biking and walking to work. Sound planning and management combine with world-class shopping, recreation, fine dining, culture, and arts in this tucked-away city that has it all.

Possible drawbacks: Building limits and the growing popularity of Boulder are pushing housing costs higher on an annual basis. Although walking and biking are encouraged, the city remains without a solid, public transportation program.

▶ County:
Boulder

▶ Area code:
303

▶ Time zone:
Mountain

▶ Population:
93,051

▶ County population:
291,288

▶ Region:
North Central Colorado

▶ Closest metro area:
Denver

▶ Average home price:
$624,277

▶ Fabulous reasons to live here:
Scenic beauty, eco-environment, active outdoor community, recreation, arts, culture

Climate

Elevation 5344'	Avg. high/low(F°)	Avg. inches		Avg. # days precip.	Avg. % humidity
		rain	snow		
Jan.	45/19	0.7	5.9	5	54%
April	62/33	2.9	7.8	9	53%
July	87/55	1.9	–	12	55%
Oct.	66/37	1.3	3.4	5	55%
YEAR	65/36	20.1	83.3	93	53%
# days 32° or below: 101			# days 90° or warmer: 34		

Local Connections

Gas and electric company: Xcel Energy (303–623–1234/800–895–4999; *www.xcelenergy.com*)

Phone company: Qwest Communications at (800–244–1111; *www.qwest.com*)

Water and sewer: City of Boulder Department of Public Works (303–441–3260; *www.ci.boulder.co.us*)

Cable company: AT&T Broadband (303–930–2001; *www.att.com*)

Car registration/License: Denver Department of Revenue (303–376–2200 *www.revenue.state.co.us*)

New residents have 30 days to obtain a Colorado driver's license, but titles and registration must be changed immediately. Surrender a valid driver's license from another state to avoid the written test. Driver's license fees: $15.60, adults ages 21 to 60, valid for 10 years; $8.10, adults ages 61 and older, valid for five years. Registration fees are based upon the year, weight, taxable value, and date of purchase of the vehicle. For most passenger vehicles: $20–30 per year. Annual property taxes are assessed on personal vehicles based on county. In Boulder, fees are based on a rate of 85 percent of the MSRP times a diminishing tax based on car age. The tax for a new $25K car would be $446 in year one and $319 in year two. For cars 10 years and older the tax is a flat fee of $3.

The Tax Ax

Sales tax: 8.16 percent

State income tax: 4.63 percent (flat rate)

Property tax: Assessed property valuation is 29 percent of the market value for non-residential properties and 9.74 percent of the market value for residential properties. The mill levy rate is 10.502.

Local Real Estate

Overview: Boulder has an evolved style of housing, from Victorian to contemporary, both remodeled and new. It is not uncommon to find very different styles adjacent to each other, as many older bungalows continue to be upgraded and expanded as homeowners remodel to meet their needs. Housing offerings in the city include everything from condos, town homes, and patio homes on small clustered lots to larger residences on small lots bordering open space to mini estates on substantial acreage located in the non-incorporated county bordering the city.

Median price for a single-family home: $535,000

Average price for a single-family home: $624,277

Average price for a 2BR condo: $276,569

Rental housing market: Being a college town, home to the University of Colorado Boulder, there's a large rental market catering to the student population. Average rent per bedroom is approximately $450–550. A two-bedroom unit therefore would rent for approximately $1,000–1,200/month.

Gay-friendly neighborhoods: Boulder has nondiscrimination city ordinances for both housing and employment, and the GLBT population calls all of Boulder home.

Nearby areas to consider: Surrounding Boulder to the east, north, and south, at a distance of about 8 to 15 miles (10–15 minutes commute from Boulder), are the towns of Longmont, Superior, Erie, Lyons, Lafayette, and Louisville. Louisville has one of the largest per-capita populations of lesbian couples in the United States. All offer housing at approximately 15 percent less cost for equal housing compared to Boulder. At one time they were considered bedroom communities to Boulder, but now they enjoy their own vibrant shopping, entertainment, and community amenities.

Earning a Living

Per capita income: $27,262

Median household income: $44,748

Business climate: The city of Boulder established its Economic Vitality Program (*www.ci.boulder.co.us*) in 2003 to promote a healthy economy, which is a part of the outstanding quality of life enjoyed by its residents. Boulder is following a sustainable path to economic development, adopting strategies to improve the business climate for both retail and primary businesses, while enhancing community character and preserving environmental quality. Economic Vitality responsibilities include general business development (retention, expansion, and attraction) along with redevelopment and efforts focused on the downtown and University Hill commercial areas.

Help in starting a business: In addition to the Economic Vitality Program, the Boulder Chamber of Commerce provides many programs and services for area businesses including the Small Business Development Center (SBDC) and the Boulder Economic Council. The SBDC provides business people with access to a wide array of resources to help them start, grow, and thrive.

Job market: Boulder, the eighth-largest city in the state, has a dynamic economy supported by computer, aerospace, scientific, and research firms. *Forbes Magazine* recently named Boulder one of its Best Places for Business and Careers (March 2005).

The Community

Overview: The Boulder GLBT community is organized, active, political, and fun. The area's many groups and organizations span the gamut of ages and life experiences. The remarkable foundation of this community is the open connections people make both to one another and to the community as a whole, and newcomers are welcomed. Openly gay and lesbian individuals have served as elected officials of Boulder and neighboring cities from city council to school boards.

Community organizations: In addition to its many planned social events, Boulder Pride provides services to the GLBT community including health, youth outreach, and support groups through their location downtown called Pride House. The GLBT Resource Center at the University of Colorado at Boulder (303–492–1377) provides resources and support for both the campus and Boulder's GLBT community at large. The Open Door Fund (*www.opendoorfund.org*) raises money and distributes grants for programs that enhance the lives of the city's gay, lesbian, bisexual, and transgender people.

Medical care: Boulder Community Hospital (303–440–2273; *www.bch.org*) has approximately 200 beds and is known for its outstanding cardiology and advanced neurology services. It has a 26-bed emergency department, a 22-bed intensive-care unit, and offers complete laboratory and imaging services, including CT, MRI, and PET scanners. Maternity and pediatric services are offered at the Foothills Hospital campus. More than 600 physicians in 48 medical specialties have privileges at BCH. Many of their registered nurses and technologists have earned national certification in their specialties.

Nuptials: The State of Colorado currently has a law similar to DOMA that defines marriage as between a man and a woman and doesn't recognize same-sex marriages from other jurisdictions.

Getting Around Town

Public transportation: Regional Transportation District (RTD) (303–299–6000; *www.rtd-denver.com*) offers 175 fixed routes to almost 80 million riders a year including both light-rail and bus service. The RTD's focus is primarily the Denver area, though several RTD bus lines serve Boulder, including the Skyride line from the airport to downtown Boulder. Fares: one-way $1.25; express $2.75; regional $3.75.

Roads: US36, SR7, SR119, SR157

Airport: Denver International Airport (airport code: DEN) (303–342–2000; *www.flydenver.com*), about 40 miles south, has the largest public art program in

American history, with a $7.5 million budget for local and national artists to create works specifically for this unique setting. The art focuses on several themes including western life, travel, light, and space.

It's a Gay Life

Annual events: Boulder Pride (*www.boulderpride.org*) presents community events throughout the year including the Dancing Diva's Summer Dance in June, Boulder Gay & Lesbian Film Festival in September, summer softball tournaments, pool parties, and a PrideFest Blockparty in September. From food and wine festivals to cooking demonstrations and farmer's markets, diners are only limited by time and imagination. The Colorado Music Festival (*www.coloradomusicfest.org*) runs for two weeks beginning in late June.

Nightlife: As an environmentally conscientious town, it's only appropriate that Boulder's hub of shopping and dining, Pearl Street, is a four-block, pedestrian-only mall. The lively atmosphere of a variety of outdoor cafes, restaurants, coffee houses, and street performers gives Pearl Street its "personality" and creates a unique opportunity to experience the local culture that makes Boulder such a special place to visit and live. Boulder's progressive lifestyle includes an affinity for a variety of ethnic foods, brought to this mountain community from natives of Nepal, Japan, Thailand, Vietnam, Greece, and Italy, to name a few. Coupled with many award-winning chefs who specialize in regional cooking, Boulder's dining experience is unparalleled in its offerings for a city of its size. The Foundry (1109 Walnut; 303–447–1803) is Boulder's GLBT bar. Denver, less than a half-hour away, has dozens of GLBT nightlife options. For all the latest news, events, and listings, pick up a copy of *Out Front in Colorado*, the statewide GLBT publication, at Left Hand Books (1200 Pearl Street; 303–443–8252) or Word is Out (1731 15th Street; 303–449–1415)

Culture: Boulder is home to more than 30 art galleries, four local museums, 32 movie and stage theaters, and many annual festivals. Unique performance venues, such as the historic Boulder Theater (2032 14th Street; 303–786–7030; *www.bouldertheater.com*), the Fox Theatre (1135 13th Street; 303–447–0095; *www.foxtheatre.com*), Chautauqua Music Hall (900 Baseline Road; 303–440–7666; *www.chautauqua.com*), Mary Rippon Outdoor Theater (University of Colorado–Boulder Campus; University Avenue at 17th Street; *www.colorado.edu*), and Macky Auditorium (University of Colorado–Boulder Campus; University Avenue at 17th Street; 303–492–6309; *www.colorado.edu*), provide intimate settings for Boulder's annual Shakespeare (University of Colorado–Boulder Campus; University Avenue at 17th Street; 303–492–0554; *www.colorado.edu*), Bach (303–652–9101; *www.boulderbachfest.org*), Dance (719–389–6098; *www.coloradocollege.edu*), and Music (303–449–1397; *www.coloradomusicfest.org*) Festivals, as well as live concerts by well-known performers. Visiting and aspiring musicians consider Boulder home due to the personalized experiences these concert halls offer both performers and visitors. The Boulder Museum of Contemporary Art (1750 13th Street; 303–443–2122; *www.bmoca.org*) is free on Saturdays and Wednesdays during the Farmer's Market. The Museum is dedicated to bringing our time's important works of art and performance to Boulder. The free Leanin' Tree Museum of Western Art (6055 Longbow Drive; 303–530–1442; *www.leanintreemuseum.com*) exhibits the private art collection of Ed Trumble, which includes American Western contemporary (1950–present) paintings and sculpture. On Saturdays from May through October, the Boulder Outdoor Market (Boulder High School; 14th and Arapahoe; 720–272–7467; *www.bouldermarket.com*) offers up the works of local artists, great food, live entertainment, and a blend of antiques, jewelry, furniture, and services. Also of interest is the Columbia Cemetery (between 9th and Columbia) where Tom Horn and a collection of notorious Old West figures are laid to rest.

Recreation: Boulder is home to many world-class athletes and runners as well as residents who choose to live here due to the community's variety of sports and recreational opportunities. From kayaking and tubing in the Boulder Creek to cycling, roller blading, jogging, and walking along the Boulder Bike Path, leisure sports enthusiasts have a number of options to choose from within Boulder's city limits. Close by, there are four golf courses and three city-owned and -operated state-of-the-art recreation centers, including more than 40 tennis courts. For more serious adventurers, there's rappelling and rock climbing in the neighboring mountains and state parks. Moreover, strong local support to protect and retain open space provides an additional hundreds of miles of hiking and mountain biking trails within Boulder County for every ability level. Within easy driving distance from Boulder, world renowned ski resorts, national parks, and attractions abound. Thirty miles northwest are Rocky Mountain National Park and Eldora Mountain Ski Area and Nordic Center. Within 60 miles are a variety of dude and guest ranches, historic gambling towns, such as Black Hawk and Central City, and Winter Park Ski Resort. Ninety miles away are the ski resort communities of Summit County and Vail.

For the Visitor

Accommodations: Boulder's unique and varied lodging options provide guests with glimpses of the city's rich history and heritage, with many bed and breakfasts, inns, and hotels residing in preserved and historic landmarks for a total of more than 2,000 guest rooms in the city. Two gay-friendly options include The Briar Rose Bed & Breakfast (2151 Arapahoe Avenue; 303–442–3007; *www.briarrosebb.com*), offering a private retreat provided by the gardens and meditation room and daily full organic breakfasts, and the Historic Earl House Inn (2429 Broadway Street; 303–938–1400), a nationally acclaimed, 1882 grand stone Victorian mansion with antique-filled spacious guest rooms.

For More Information

Gay & Lesbian Center

Boulder Pride
2132 14th Street
Boulder, CO 80302
303–499–5777
www.boulderpride.org

Publications

Boulder Daily Camera
1048 Pearl Street
Boulder, CO 80302
303–442–1202
www.bouldernews.com

Longmount Daily Times-Call
350 Terry Street
Longmont, CO 80501
303–776–2244
www.longmontfyi.com

Convention and Visitors Bureau

Boulder Convention & Visitors Bureau
2440 Pearl Street
Boulder, CO 80302
303–442–2911/800–444–0447
www.bouldercoloradousa.com

Chamber of Commerce

Boulder Chamber of Commerce
2440 Pearl Street
Boulder, CO 80302
303–442–1044
www.boulderchamber.com

Realtor

Dan Kuchars
Realtor/Associate Broker
Coldwell Banker Residential Brokerage
2700 Canyon Boulevard, #200
Boulder, CO 80302
303–441–2436
www.ColoradoHomes.com/DanKuchars

Denver, Colorado

A Look at Denver

Denver is a clean, young, and green city with more than 200 parks and dozens of tree-lined boulevards. Contrary to popular belief, Denver is not *in* the mountains; it is *near* them. Denver itself is located on high, rolling plains and its architecture reflects the city's three boom periods: Victorian, when silver was discovered in Leadville; turn of the century, when gold was discovered in Cripple Creek; and contemporary, when the energy boom added 16 skyscrapers to the downtown skyline in a three-year period (1980–1983). Unlike some Western cities, Denver has a central downtown area. Here, within easy walking distance, are 5,200 hotel rooms, the city's convention complex, a performing arts complex, and a wide variety of shops, department stores, restaurants, and nightspots. Lower Downtown (called "LoDo" by locals) is on the northern edge of downtown Denver and offers one of the nation's greatest concentrations of Victorian buildings and warehouses, many of which have been refurbished to house restaurants, art galleries, offices, and shops. This is the center of the city's brewpubs, with six large brewpubs and microbreweries, each brewing six to eight exclusive beers, all within easy walking distance of each other. Downtown is also the home of Auraria Campus, where three colleges have more than 30,000 students.

Possible drawbacks: Although the sun shines about 300 days a year, the city temperatures drop below freezing nearly a third of the year. The boom cycles create economic swings that have an adverse effect on the city's economy.

Colorado

Boulder

Denver

Colorado Springs

- Nickname:
  Mile High City
- County:
  Denver
- Area codes:
  303; 720
- Time zone:
  Mountain
- Population:
  554,636
- County population:
  554,636
- Region:
  Central Colorado
- Average home price:
  $186,374
- Fabulous reasons to live here:
  Beautiful setting, affordable housing, recreation, culture, entertainment, nightlife, large GLBT community, high-tech economy

Climate

Elevation 5260'	Avg. high/low(F°)	Avg. inches		Avg. # days precip.	Avg. % humidity
		rain	snow		
Jan.	45/15	–	5.5	5	53%
April	61/33	–	6.7	8	50%
July	88/56	2.0	–	12	54%
Oct.	66/34	–	3.2	5	49%
YEAR	65/34	17	42.2	88	52%
# days 32° or below: 101			# days 90° or warmer: 34		

Local Connections

Gas and electric company: Xcel Energy (303–623–1234/800–895–4999; *www.xcelenergy.com*)

Phone company: Qwest Communications (800–244–1111; *www.qwest.com*)

Water and sewer: Denver Water Department (303–628–6000; *www.water.denver.co.gov*)

Cable company: AT&T Broadband (303–930–2001; *www.att.com*)

Car registration/License: Denver Department of Revenue (303–376–2200 *www.revenue.state.co.us*)

New residents have 30 days to obtain a Colorado driver's license, but titles and registration must be changed immediately. Surrender a valid driver's license from another state to avoid the written test. Driver's license fees: $15.60, adults ages 21 to 60, valid for 10 years; $8.10, adults ages 61 and older, valid for five years. Registration fees are based upon the year, weight, taxable value, and date of purchase of the vehicle. For most passenger vehicles: $20–30 per year. Annual property taxes are assessed on personal vehicles based on county. In Denver, fees are based on a rate of 85 percent of the MSRP times a diminishing tax based on car age. The tax for a new $25K car would be $446 in year one and $319 in year two. For cars 10 years and older the tax is a flat fee of $3.

The Tax Ax

Sales tax: 7.2 percent; most services exempt

City tax: Denver income tax withholding if gross annual wages are greater than $6,000 is $2.66 biweekly

State income tax: 4.63 percent (flat rate)

Property tax: Assessor's Office (720–913–4067)

The current mill levy in Denver is 64.402. For residential properties, the actual value is multiplied by the residential assessment rate in order to arrive at the assessed value (the residential assessment rate is set by the state, and the current rate is 7.96 percent). The assessed value is then multiplied by the mill levy to arrive at the property tax bill.

Local Real Estate

Overview: In the 1990s, the real estate market in Denver increased significantly with the median house price increasing more than 100 percent. The entire Denver economy, however, slowed down in the new millennium, and though the economic slowdown has stopped, Denver has not yet seen signs of recovery. Denver is in a "buyer's market" with the supply of properties currently greater than the demand. This gives buyers a great selection of properties to choose from and more negotiating power.

Median price for a single-family home: $210,000

Average price for a single-family home: $186,374 in Denver Southwest; $387,094 in Denver Southeast

Average price for a 2BR condo: $169,803 in Denver Southwest; $216,793 in Denver Northwest

Rental housing market: Rents vary by location as well as condition and amenities. The rent for a place with two bedrooms can range from $650 for a garden-level condominium to $950 for a house.

Gay-friendly neighborhoods: Denver has an ordinance banning discrimination based on sexual orientation in housing, employment, education, public accommodations, health and welfare services, and so on. In the mid-1970s, Capital Hill began emerging as Denver's gay neighborhood, and Cheesman Park became a gathering and socializing area for the gay community. Denver as a whole is a gay-friendly place and is filled with gay-friendly neighborhoods.

Nearby areas to consider: To the north of Denver, the cities of Wheat Ridge, Golden, Edgewater, Commerce City, and Arvada are popular areas for the GLBT community. Though each is its own city, all are considered part of the North Metro Denver region. These small towns provide a more rural setting and a great sense of belonging to a community. The lower real estate prices allow for larger home lots, and a good highway system makes for an easy commute from these bedroom suburbs.

Earning a Living

Per capita income: $24,101

Median household income: $39,500

Business climate: The Milken Institute predicts that Colorado will be a national leader in science and technology expansion, and the Beacon Hill Institute at Suffolk University in Boston ranked Metro Denver as the fourth-most-competitive out of the 50 largest metropolitan areas in the nation. These and other studies predict that Denver is positioned for a period of long-term, sustainable growth.

Help in starting a business: Housed within the Denver Metro Chamber of Commerce building is the Denver Small Business Development Center (SBDC), which helps nurture small business entrepreneurs by providing counseling, training, financial assistance, procurement, resource opportunities, and programs such as NxLeveL.

Job market: Colorado has the highest concentration of high-tech workers in the country and is viewed as a prime location for continued high-tech job growth. The major job sectors consist of professional and business services, educational and health services, information, and the leisure and hospitality industries.

The Community

Overview: The gay-friendly city of Denver is home to a large GLBT community. Capital Hill is Denver's gay neighborhood, and Cheesman Park, the starting point for the Pridefest Parade, is a popular meeting place for socializing and recreation. Local politics are supportive of the GLBT community.

Community organizations: The Gay Lesbian Bisexual Transgender Community Center of Colorado is a focal point and catalyst for community organizing, support services, social activities, and cultural events for Denver's GLBT community. The Center's Youth Services are provided through Rainbow Alley, Denver's only drop-in center for gay, lesbian, bisexual, transgender, queer, and questioning young people, aged 21 years and younger. Auraria Campus's Gay, Lesbian, Bisexual, and Trans Student Services (*www.glbtss.org*) is a tri-institutional office offering many services for students, faculty, and staff of Metropolitan State College of Denver, University of Colorado at Denver, and Community College of Denver.

Medical care: There are 13 hospitals in the Denver regional area providing state-of-the-art medical care to the community. The GLBT Center (1050 Broadway; *www.coloradoglbt.org*) offers a variety of community health services, including low-cost hepatitis vaccinations, anonymous HIV testing, free mammograms for uninsured women, a healthcare provider referral database, and resource referrals for individuals seeking emergency assistance. The Center also sponsors and co-sponsors numerous health- and wellness-related events.

Nuptials: The State of Colorado currently has a law similar to DOMA that defines marriage as between a man and a woman and doesn't recognize same-sex marriages from other jurisdictions.

Getting Around Town

Public transportation: Regional Transportation District (RTD) (303–299–6000; *www.rtd-denver.com*) offers 175 fixed routes to almost 80 million riders a year that include both light-rail and bus service to get you around Denver. Fares: one-way $1.25; express $2.75; regional $3.75.

Roads: I-25, I-70, I-76, I-225, US85, US285, SR51, SR28, SR470

Airport: Denver International Airport (airport code: DEN) (303–342–2000; *www.flydenver.com*) has the largest public art program in American history, with a $7.5 million budget for local and national artists to create works specifically for this unique setting. The art focuses on several themes, including Western life, travel, light, and space.

It's a Gay Life

Annual events: PrideFest (*www.pridefestdenver.org*) is hosted by The Center in June with a parade, festival, rally, and an afternoon of live entertainment. In addition, The Center also hosts a Gay and Lesbian Film Festival and "Jokers, Jewels & Justice" fundraiser. Other annual events of note in Denver are Buskerfest (*www.buskerfest.com*) in June, Cherry Creek Arts Festival (*www.cherryarts.org*) and LoDo Music Festival (*www.lodomusicfestival.com*) in July, and Oktoberfest (*www.oktoberfestdenver.com*) in September.

Nightlife: Downtown Denver is fabulous for a bar crawl, and microbrews are popular at most drinking holes around the city. Two things stand out about the Denver bar scene: Many of the bars also serve food, and, setting Denver apart from most cities, there are lots of lesbian establishments. Denver is home to more than 20 bars and a dozen restaurants and cafes catering to the GLBT community. Just a few of the favorites are JR's (1669 Clarkson Street; 303–813–1159; *www.jrsdenver.com*), a two-floor club with drag shows and go-go boys; the Wave (2101 Champa Street; 303–299–9283; *www.thewavenightclub.com*), where multiple dance floors come alive after midnight with pounding music and flare bartenders; Charlie's (900 E. Colfax Avenue; 303–839–8890; *www.charliesonline.com*), a gay country western bar that hosts lots of events; the Denver Detour (551 E. Colfax Avenue; 303–861–1497; *www.denverdetour.com*), a women's bar serving food; and the Brig (117 Broadway; 303–777–9378), a dive bar that's great for a lonely last call. *H Ink, Out in Colorado*, and *Pride Magazine* are the publications to keep you in the know. All are available at the bookstore Relatively Wilde (42 South Broadway; 303–777–0766; *www.relativelywilde.com*).

Culture: Denver has always had a long love affair with the arts. When Denver was a wild gold rush town in the 1870s, it boasted a theater with sold-out performances of *MacBeth,* long before it had either a school or a hospital. A mile-long pedestrian mall cuts through the heart of downtown and is surrounded by a series of parks and plazas that soften the towering skyscrapers and provide viewpoints from which to see and appreciate the modern architecture. The Mile High Trail is a series of six walking tours throughout the downtown area. Other attractions of note include the Denver Museum of Nature and Science (2001 Colorado Boulevard; 303–322–7009; *www.dmns.org*), Museo de las Américas (861 Santa Fe Drive; 303–571–4401; *www.museo.org*), Denver Mint (West Colfax at Cherokee Street; 303–405–4761; *www.usmint.treas.gov*), Molly Brown House Museum (1340 Pennsylvania Street; 303–832–4092; *www.mollybrown.org*), Denver Firefighters Museum (1326 Tremont Place; 303–892–1436; *www.denverfirefightersmuseum.org*), Byers-Evans House Museum (1310 Bannock Street; 303–620–4933; *www.coloradohistory.org*), Children's Museum of Denver (2121 Children's Museum

Drive; 303–433–7444; *www.mychildsmuseum.org*), and Denver Botanic Gardens (909 York Street; 720–865–3500; *www.botanicgardens.org*). The city is home to 30 live theaters and more than 100 cinemas. The Denver Performing Arts Complex (1245 Champa Street; 303–893–4100; *www.denvercenter.org*) is the second-largest performing arts center in the nation, after Lincoln Center in New York. Located downtown, the four-square-block center features Boettcher Concert Hall, the nation's first symphony hall in-the-round, the Denver Center Theater Company, and the Temple Buell Theater, which also boasts the world's first voice research laboratory. Downtown, within easy walking distance, are some of the city's top attractions, including the Denver Pavilions (500 16th Street; 303–260–6000; *denverpavilions.com*), Denver Art Museum (100 W. 14th Avenue Parkway; 720–865–5000; *www.denverartmuseum.org*), and Colorado History Museum (1300 Broadway; 303–866–3670; *www.coloradohistory.org*).

Recreation: With 300 days of sunshine a year, Denver is a sports capital. The city offers more than 450 miles of paved, designated bike paths, including two beautiful stretches through downtown along Cherry Creek and along the South Platte River. There are 70-plus golf courses in the area and more than 143 free tennis courts. Half of Colorado is public land open to all forms of recreation with two national parks, six national monuments, 11 national forests, three national recreation areas, and 30 state parks. Six Flags Elitch Gardens (2000 Elitch Circle; 303–595–4386; *www.sixflags.com*), in downtown Denver, is a year-round amusement park offering 48 thrill rides, formal gardens, restaurants, and shops. Denver has a full complement of professional sports teams including the NFL's Denver Broncos (303–649–9000; *www.denverbroncos.com*), the NBA's Denver Nuggets (303–405–1100; *www.nba.com/nuggets*), MLB's Colorado Rockies (303–292–0200; *www.coloradorockies.com*), and the NHL's Colorado Avalanche (303–575–1904; *www.coloradoavalanche.com*). Denver also has a professional lacrosse team, Colorado Mammoth (303–405–1100; *www.coloradomammoth.com*), and an arena sports team, the Colorado Crush (303–405–1100; *www.coloradocrush.com*). Other spectator sports include the world's largest rodeo, held each year at the National Western Stock Show (4655 Humboldt Street; 303–297–1166; *www.nationalwestern.com*) in January and pari-mutuel dog and horse racing.

For the Visitor

Accommodations: Denver has 5,200 hotel rooms that range from B&B accommodations to all the major chains. A few gay-friendly properties include: The Victoria Oaks Inn (1575 Race Street; 303–355–1818; *www.victoriaoaks.com*), within walking distance to nightlife, and Sheraton Denver West (360 Union Boulevard; 303–987–2000; *www.sheraton.com/denverwest.com*), offering city view rooms and all the amenities expected of a big chain hotel.

For More Information

Gay & Lesbian Center

The Gay Lesbian Bisexual
Transgender Community Center
of Colorado
P.O. Box 9798
Denver, CO 80209-0798
303–733–7743
www.coloradoglbt.org

Publications

H Ink Magazine
Quest Publications
P.O. Box 18325
Denver, CO 80218
303–752–4300
www.denvergay.com

Out Front Colorado
723 Sherman Street
Denver, CO 80203
303–778–7900
www.outfrontcolorado.com

Denver Post
1560 Broadway
Denver, CO 80202
303–832–3232
www.denverpost.com

Rocky Mountain News
100 Gene Amole Way
Denver, CO 80204
303–892–5000
www.denver.rockymountainnews.com

Convention and Visitors Bureau

Denver Metro Convention and Visitor's
Bureau
1555 California Street, Suite 300
Denver, CO 80202
303–892–1505/800–233–6837
www.denver.org

Chamber of Commerce

Denver Chamber of Commerce
1445 Market Street
Denver, CO 80202
303–534–8500
www.denverchamber.org

Realtor

Vicki Porter, Broker/Owner
Porter House Realty Company
3773 Cherry Creek North Drive, Suite 575
Denver, CO 80209
303–296–3666
www.PorterHouseRealty.com

## 12

Washington, District of Columbia

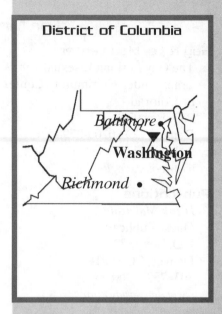

District of Columbia

A Look at Washington

Washington, DC is a town of much renown: It is a government town, a company town, a scandalous town, and the political capital of the world. The District of Columbia is filled with vibrant neighborhoods that are as diverse as its residents. Living in this world-class city has several advantages from the excitement of watching professional sports to having a picnic lunch in one of the city's beautifully manicured parks. Washington, DC's unforgettable skyline is dominated by some of the world's most celebrated monuments. The fantastic structures and statues that grace the green expanses of the National Mall tell fascinating stories through their history and design. The city is internationally known for the vast collection of art housed in its celebrated museums and galleries. Washington, DC, boasts some of the finest museums in the world, and many of the city's fabulous dining establishments have received national recognition. Washington, DC, offers the perfect atmosphere for open space, living, working, and playing. From intimate parks to the many unique neighborhoods, Washington, DC, has something for everyone.

Possible drawbacks: Because of the government's "don't ask/don't tell" mentality, some groups within the GLBT community are more out than others. Also, the long-lasting summer humidity can drain the life out of you.

▶ Nickname:
Hollywood on the Potomac

▶ County:
District of Columbia

▶ Area code: 202

▶ Time zone: Eastern

▶ Population:
572,059

▶ County population:
572,059

▶ Region:
Central East Coast

▶ Average home price:
$588,256

▶ Fabulous reasons to live here:
The nation's capital; museums; recreation; entertainment; nightlife; large, organized GLBT community; stable economy

Climate

Elevation 420'	Avg. high/low(F°)	Avg. inches		Avg. # days precip.	Avg. % humidity
		rain	snow		
Jan.	43/25	3.5	5.5	10	63%
April	67/43	3.2	–	10	59%
July	89/68	4.1	–	10	64%
Oct.	69/46	3.4	–	7	67%
YEAR	67/46	42.9	16.6	112	64%
# days 32° or below: 75			# days 90° or warmer: 36		

Local Connections

Gas company: Washington Gas (703–750–1000; *www.eservice.washgas.com*)

Electric company: PEPCO (202–833–7500; *www.pepco.com*)

Phone companies: AT&T (800–222–0300; *www.att.com*); Sprint (*www.sprint.com*); SBC (800–310–2355; *www.sbc.com*); Verizon (202–392–9900; *www.verizon.com*); among others

Water and sewer: DC Water and Sewer Authority (202–354–3600; *www.dcwasa.com*)

Cable companies: Comcast Cable Television (202–635–5100; *www.comcast.com*); Starpower Communications (888–782–7313; *www.starpower.net*)

Car registration/License: DC Department of Motor Vehicles (202–727–1000 *www.dmv.washingtondc.gov*)

A licensed driver who moves to the District from another jurisdiction is required to convert a valid out-of-state driver's license to a DC driver's license if remaining in DC for more than 30 days. A DC driver's license is valid for up to five years for U.S. citizens and may vary for non–U.S. citizens depending on visa classification. The written test is not required if your prior license is valid or has not been expired for more than 90 days. The road test is not required if your prior license is valid or has not been expired for more than 180 days. Fee: $39. If your vehicle has tags from another jurisdiction, you may go directly to the inspection station. Once your vehicle has passed inspection, you may apply for registration at a DMV. Fee is based on vehicle weight: less than 3,500 pounds $72/year; more than 3,500 pounds $115/year. Title Fee: $26.

The Tax Ax

Sales tax: 5.75 percent; total hotel tax including sales tax 14.5 percent; food and beverage tax 10 percent

City tax: Office of the Chief Financial Officer (202–727–2476; *www.cfo.dc.gov*) Approximately 12 percent; varies by income

Property tax: Assessment Division, Real Property Tax Administration, Office of Tax and Revenue (202–727–4TAX; *cfo.dc.gov*)

Property taxes are based on type and class. Residential property is taxed at $0.96 per $100 of the assessed value.

Local Real Estate

Overview: The housing stock in Washington, DC, varies significantly between neighborhoods. The city has a great mix of homes, ranging from large brownstones, Victorians, and stately Colonials to small row houses, cottages, and Beaux Arts–style apartment buildings. DC is booming with new construction that has added a number of contemporary buildings across the city.

Median price for a single-family home: $367,500

Average price for a single-family home: $588,256

Average price for a 2BR condo: $550,000

Rental housing market: The average two-bedroom rental in the city runs about $1,850. Apartments closer to the Metrorail start at $2,000.

Gay-friendly neighborhoods: Logan, DuPont Circle, Capitol Hill, Cleveland Park

Nearby areas to consider: With their easy commutes to DC, Silver Spring, MD, and Arlington, VA, provide fabulous alternatives. Silver Spring's downtown, a major shopping district in the 1950s and 1960s, is experiencing a renaissance, and there are plenty of opportunities for entrepreneurs. The city also offers older housing styles as well as modern construction, plus a bit of open countryside. Located across the Potomac River from DC, Arlington has a large, organized GLBT community. The Arlington Gay & Lesbian Alliance (*www.agla.org*) sponsors community and social events and provides support services to the community. (Also see the profiles for Alexandria, VA, and Takoma Park, MD, for other fabulous DC alternatives.)

Earning a Living

Per capita income: $28,659

Median household income: $40,127

Business climate: Washington, DC, is a world-class city that offers unparalleled opportunities to organizations and businesses, large and small. The nation's capital boasts a multifaceted economy tied to national and international markets and a well-educated and highly skilled workforce. World headquarters include USAirways, Marriott, AMTRAK, AOL, Gannett News, Mobil Oil, MCI Telecommunications, and International Monetary Fund.

Help in starting a business: The DC Chamber of Commerce works as an advocate for all DC businesses. The Washington DC Marketing Center (202–661–8670; *www.dcmarketingcenter.com*) provides both new and established DC businesses with resources, education, and assistance.

Job market: Washington, DC's primary industry after the federal government is tourism. Other important industries include trade associations, as Washington, DC is home to more associations than any other U.S. city; law; higher education; medicine and medical research; government-related research; publishing; and international finance.

The Community

Overview: Each neighborhood in Washington, DC, has a unique identity, expressed through architecture, business, and residents. The DuPont Circle neighborhood is a center for gay activity. Culture and entertainment collide at the many cafes and bars in the area, where patrons discuss the latest happenings in politics and art alike.

Community organizations: The Washington Center for Gay, Lesbian, Bisexual and Transgender People, known as The Center, has a mission of celebrating, strengthening, and supporting the GLBT residents and organizations of metropolitan Washington, DC. Additionally, there are hundreds of GLBT community groups in the metro DC and surrounding areas of Maryland and Virginia including health, support, social, and recreational organizations. Gay Washington (*www.gaywdc.com*) is a one-stop online resource for all the community organizations and businesses in the DC metro area. Also, check out DC Registry (*www.dcregistry.com*) for listings of dozens of clubs and organizations.

Medical care: Washington, DC, has 13 hospitals and almost 5,000 hospital beds. The 345-bed Howard University Hospital (202–865–6100; *www.huhosp.org*) offers a full range of outpatient services and the Division of Infectious Diseases provides comprehensive care to patients infected with HIV and conditions associated with AIDS using an approach to care that emphasizes self-care management using a chronic-care model.

Nuptials: The District of Columbia has no specific laws relating to same-sex marriages. Many large employers in DC offer domestic partner benefits.

Getting Around Town

Public transportation: Washington Metropolitan Area Transit Authority (202–637–7000; *www.wmata.com*) operates buses and subway lines throughout the city. Metrobus fare: $1.25; unlimited day pass $3. Metrorail one-way fare: $1.35–3.90.

Roads: I-66, I-95, I-370, US1, US5, US50, US301

Airports: Three major airports serve the Washington, DC, area: Ronald Reagan Washington National Airport (airport code: DCA) (703–417–8000 *www.mwaa.com*); Dulles International Airport (airport code: IAD) (703–572–2700; *www.mwaa.com*); and Baltimore-Washington International Airport (airport code: BWI) (410–859–7992; *www.bwiairport.com*).

It's a Gay Life

Annual events: Capital Pride (*www.capitalpride.org*) hosts 10 days of pride events and celebrations in June, including a film festival, awards ceremonies, parade, and rally. In April and May, the Washington, DC, International Film Festival (*www.filmfestdc.org*) features more than 100 features, documentaries, short films, and special programs. Thousands flock to Washington to see the elegant cherry trees that adorn the tidal basin with their spring blossoms. Also in June, the Barbecue Battle (*www.barbecuebattle.com*) features serious competition between top BBQ competitors. Fourth of July fireworks light up the National Mall (*www.nps.gov/nama*). The Smithsonian Folklife Festival (*www.folklife.si.edu*) in June, Kennedy Center Prelude Festival (*www.kennedy-center.com*) in September, National Christmas Tree Lighting (*www.whitehouse.gov*) in December, and Pageant of Peace (*www.pageantofpeace.com*), which runs throughout December, are just a few of the other DC annual events.

Nightlife: Washington, DC provides three dozen bars and clubs catering to the GLBT community. A few of the popular options in the DuPont Circle area are 1409 Playbill Café (1409 14th Street NW; 202–265–3055), a bar and restaurant; DC Eagle (639 New York Avenue NW; 202–347–6025; *www.dceagle.com*), which caters to leather fans; Green Lantern (1335 Green Court NW; 202–347–4533; *www.greenlanterndc.com*); Remington's (639 Pennsylvania Avenue SE; 202–543–3113; *www.remingtonswdc.com*), a popular destination for line dancers; Club Chaos (1603 17th Street NW; 202–232–4141; *www.chaosdc.com*), with a great dance floor; Hamburger Mary's, also home to the Titan Bar (1337 14th Street NW; 202–232–7009; *www.hamburgermarysdc.com*); and Phase One (525 8th Street SE; 202–544–6831), the oldest continually operating lesbian bar in DC (locally known as the Phase). Pick up copies of *Metro Arts & Entertainment Weekly* (*www.metroweekly.com*) and the *Washington Blade* (*www.washblade.com*) at Lambda Rising (1625 Connecticut Avenue NW; 202–462–6969; *www.lambdarising.com*) for all the current events and listings.

Culture: Washington, DC's cultural scene reflects the diversity of its people through art, music, and theater. Each season 80 professional theaters produce more than 350 productions. The trendy DuPont Circle galleries (*www.artgalleriesdc.com*), showcasing local works, join together monthly to host First Fridays with extended gallery hours and complimentary wines. The National Gallery of Art (National Mall between Third and Seventh streets at Constitution Avenue; 202–737–4215; *www.nga.gov*) contains more than 100,000 works representing the major achievements in painting, sculpture, and graphic arts. The Corcoran Gallery of Art (500 17th Street NW; 202–639–1700; *www.corcoran.org*), the largest non-federal art museum in DC and the first art museum to open in the city, is world-renowned for its permanent collection of 20th-century painting, sculpture, and photography. The Smithsonian Institution (202–357–2020; *www.si.edu*), with its 14 museums and galleries, is recognized as the world's largest complex of art galleries, museums, and research facilities in the world. Music fans will discover a wide range of options from jazz to bluegrass, rock to house, and sophisticated to classical at the many venues ranging from small clubs to the world-renowned Kennedy Center (2700 F Street NW; 202–467–4600/800–444–1324; *www.kennedy-center.org*), home to both the Washington Opera (202–295–2400; *www.dc-opera.org*) and the National Symphony Orchestra (202–416–8100; *www.kennedy-center.org/nso*). The Washington, DC, area is also home to more than 70 choral groups, including the Air Force Singing Sergeants (*www.usafband.com*), National Christian Chorus (301–670–6331; *www.nationalchristianchoir.org*), Gay Men's Chorus of Washington, DC (202–293–1548; *www.gmcw.org*), and the Washington Bach Consort (202–429–2121; *www.bachconsort.com*).

Recreation: There are more than 25 parks and memorials in DC. Visit the Parks and Recreation Website (202–673–7647; *dpr.dc.gov*) for up-to-date information on programs, special events, and facilities. Just minutes from the White House and the thriving commercial center, Washington, DC relaxes into a nature lover's paradise. Fishing, sailing, kayaking, canoeing, and rowing are just a few of the opportunities provided by the majestic Potomac River. Bikers, hikers, and roller bladers use the well-trodden towpath of the C&O Canal from its Georgetown beginnings to Cumberland, MD. Rock Creek Park, home to the Smithsonian National Zoological Park (3001 Connecticut Avenue NW; 202–633–4800; *www.natzoo.si.edu*), is one of the largest and most fervently praised urban parks and offers hiking, biking, skating, horseback riding, golf, tennis, and a host of other fun activities as well as a quiet respite in upper Northwest DC. The National Mall (900 Ohio Drive SW; 202–426–6841; *www.nps.gov/nama*) runs from the Capitol to the banks of the Potomac and hosts softball, flag football, and even rugby leagues near the Washington Monument (900 Ohio Drive SW; 202–426–6841; *www.nps.gov/wamo*). Adjoining the Mall is Potomac Park, which runs south, along the Potomac from the Lincoln Memorial with beach volleyball pits, baseball fields, and soccer fields. Escape to the National Arboretum (3501 New York Avenue NE; 202–245–2726; *www.usna.usda.gov*) and ramble through 400 acres of trees, shrubs, and flowering plants. In the springtime, visitors flock to see the Arboretum's famed azaleas and other seasonal blooms. DC has spectator sports for every taste, including the NHL's Capitals (202–266–2350; *www.washingtoncaps.com*), DC United's men's soccer (202–587–5000; *www.dcunited.com*), and women's soccer team Freedom (763–792–7346; *www.washingtonfreedom.com*), the WNBA's Mystics (202–661–5050; *www.wnba.com/mystics*), the NFL's Redskins (301–276–6050; *www.redskins.com*), and the NBA's Wizards (202–661–5100; *www.nba.com/wizards*).

For the Visitor

Accommodations: As a world destination, Washington, DC, provides luxury, hip, and cozy accommodations all over the city. The William Lewis House (1309 R Street NW; 202–462–7574/800–465–7574; *www.wlewishouse.com*) is a gay bed and breakfast in a beautifully restored historic home located just off Logan Circle.

Jurys Washington Hotel (1500 New Hampshire Avenue NW; 202–483–6000; *www.jurys-washingtondc-hotels.com*) overlooks DuPont Circle. This four-star hotel has a reputation for Irish comfort and hospitality. Jury's Normandy Hotel (2118 Wyoming Avenue NW; 202–483–1350) is just minutes from DuPont Circle in the heart of the embassy district, and all major attractions are within easy reach.

For More Information

Gay & Lesbian Center
The Washington Center for Gay, Lesbian, Bisexual and Transgender People
1111 14th Street NW, Suite 350
Washington, DC 20005
202–518–6100
www.thedccenter.org

Publications
Washington Post
1150 15th Street NW
Washington, DC 20071
703–469–2500
www.washingtonpost.com

Washington Times
3600 New York Avenue NE
Washington, DC 20002-1947
202–636–3000
www.washtimes.com

Convention and Visitors Bureau
Washington, DC Convention and Tourism Corporation
901 7th Street NW, 4th Floor
Washington, DC 20001-3719
202–789–7000
www.washington.org

Chamber of Commerce
DC Chamber of Commerce
1213 K Street NW
Washington, DC 20005
202–347–7201
www.dcchamber.org

Realtor
Mark Meyerdirk, Broker
Urban Brokers, LLC
1601 18th Street NW, Suite 1
Washington, DC 20009
202–319–1303
www.urbanbrokers.com

## 13

Key West, Florida

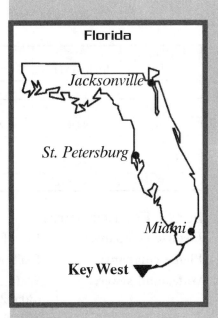

A Look at Key West

Key West, the southernmost city in the continental United States, lies near the end of the chain of islands known as the Florida Keys. First-time visitors to the Florida Keys comment almost immediately on the island chain's laid-back atmosphere, which is unique and a world away from big cities and theme parks. Key West is not just a great place to visit; it is a fabulous place to live. The island, being only a few square miles, has a small town atmosphere with a cosmopolitan flair. The island's balmy climate, historic structures, and anything-goes ambiance have long provided a tropical refuge for writers, artists, and free-spirited folks yearning for a place to unravel the mind, body, and soul. The island population of approximately 28,000 year-round residents continues to support diversity through its live-and-let-live attitude. The unique confluence of history, climate, natural beauty, cultural diversity, architecture, and unabashed romantic appeal cloak the island of Key West in mystery. It is a mystery that captivates the human soul, stealing it away from the hassles of the modern-day world. Residents and visitors to Key West actively participate in sightseeing, outdoor and maritime activities, and shopping by day, then yield to the transition toward evening, when flame-swallowers, tightrope-walkers, and shopping-cart balancers strive to show up a more captivating performer: the fiery sun settling into the Gulf of Mexico.

Possible drawbacks: Key West and surrounding Keys are islands with limited building capacity. Property is extremely expensive, with values rising dramatically on an annual basis.

- Nickname: Paradise
- County: Monroe
- Area code: 305
- Time zone: Eastern
- Population: 25,478
- County population: 79,589
- Region: Southwest Florida
- Closest metro area: Miami
- Average home price: $700,000
- Fabulous reasons to live here:
  Laid-back lifestyle, recreation, nightlife, artist's haven, large GLBT community, excellent weather, some of the world's most dramatic sunsets

Climate

Elevation 8'	Avg. high/low(F°)	Avg. inches rain	snow	Avg. # days precip.	Avg. % humidity
Jan.	75/65	2.2	–	6	75%
April	82/72	2.1	–	5	70%
July	89/80	3.3	–	12	72%
Oct.	85/76	4.3	–	11	75%
YEAR	83/73	39.0	–	109	73%
# days 32° or below: 0			# days 90° or warmer: 50		

Local Connections

Electric company: Keys Energy (305–295–1000; *www.keysenergy.com*)

Phone company: BellSouth (305–780–2355; *www.bellsouth.com*)

Water and sewer: Water: Florida Keys Aqueduct Authority (305–296–2454; *www.fkaa.com*); Sewer: City of Key West Utilities Department (305–292–8129; *www.keywestcity.com*)

Cable company: Comcast (800–266–2278; *www.comcast.com*)

Car registration/License: Florida Department of Highway, Safety and Motor Vehicles (850–922–9000; *www.hsmv.state.fl.us*)

You have 30 days after establishing residency to get your Florida license. Only a vision exam is required when surrendering an out-of-state license. Initial License Fee: $20 (additional fees required for testing). Car registration fee: $100. New license plate issue fee: $10. Annual registration is based on car weight: up to 2,499 pounds $27.60; 2,500–3,499 pounds $35.60; 3,500 pounds and above $45.60.

The Tax Ax

Sales tax: 7.5 percent

State income tax: No state income tax

Property tax: Taxes are based on the just or fair market value of the property. The Property Tax Administration Program (800–352–3671; *www.myflorida.com*) administers the assessment and collection of taxes.

Local Real Estate

Overview: The city's historical area, known as "Old Town," has a very distinctive appearance, combining features of both New England and Bahamian building styles. The basic features that distinguish the local architecture include wood frame construction of one to two-and-a-half story structures set on foundation piers about 3 feet above the ground. Exterior characteristics of the buildings are peaked "tin" roofs, horizontal wood siding, pastel shades of paint, side-hinged louvered shutters, covered porches (or balconies, galleries, or verandas) along the fronts of the structures, and wood lattice screens covering the area elevated by the piers.

Median price for a single-family home: $950,000

Average price for a single-family home: $700,000

Average price for a 2BR condo: $550,000

Rental housing market: The housing market in Key West is tight and expensive. A two-bedroom apartment averages $1,500–2,000.

Gay-friendly neighborhoods: All of Key West is gay-friendly.

Nearby areas to consider: Each small city and town of the Florida Keys is quite gay-friendly, and they all offer something special. Key Largo is the dive capital of the world and provides easy access to America's only living barrier reef. Home to the Dolphin Research Center, Marathon is the heart of the Keys, providing easy access to Key West and the northern Keys, with Booth Key Harbor, a sheltered cove at the center of the island, as a hub to marine and water activities. If deep sea fishing is your passion, Islamorada is the place for you. It's also home to the Windley Key's Theater of the Sea, where you can swim with dolphins.

Earning a Living

Per capita income: $26,316

Median household income: $43,021

Business climate: With an estimated 650,000 annual tourists, tourism and related services are the strong, primary industries of the Florida Keys.

Help in starting a business: The Key West Chamber of Commerce acts as the business advocate, information center, and business promoter for area businesses. Through their many functions and meetings, they provide a platform for members to promote their businesses and to exchange information with other business professionals. In addition, the Key West Business Guild represents the gay business community by providing comprehensive information about gay Key West and promoting the island to a national and international travel market.

Job market: Arts, entertainment, recreation, and accommodation and food services provide more than a quarter of Key West's job opportunities followed by educational, health and social services, and retail trade.

The Community

Overview: Key West has evolved into a melting pot for all types. The locals are as proud of the way everyone gets along as they are of the lush tropical gardens and beautiful sunsets. On any given night, you will find community members and tourists alike enjoying drag shows together or laughing at one of the island's many theater productions.

Community organizations: The Gay & Lesbian Community Center of Key West provides resources and services, a youth outreach program, a lending library, and meeting space to community groups such as PFLAG, AA, and Key West Alternative Community Socials, a local not-for-profit social organization.

Medical care: The Lower Keys Medical Center (305–292–9353; *www.lkmc.com*) is a fully accredited, 167-bed acute healthcare facility that includes the dePoo Building, a 49-bed psychiatric and chemical-dependency unit. It is the area's sole hospital care provider and, with a staff of 500, including 75 physicians and more than 200 nurses, is the largest employer in the City of Key West. The Gay & Lesbian Community Center of Key West (305–292–3223; *www.glcckeywest.org*) offers anonymous HIV testing at the Center twice a week.

Nuptials: Commitment ceremonies are performed virtually every day in Key West. Worth noting is that Key West is the first city, and encompassing Monroe County the first county, in Florida to officially recognize same-sex domestic partnerships.

Getting Around Town

Public transportation: City Bus for Key West and Stock Island (305–292–8165; *www.keywestcity.com*); Park and Ride Shuttle service (305–293–6426) to Key West's Old Town/Historic District with stop-and-board locations along the entire route.

Road: US1

Airport: Key West International Airport (airport code: EYW) (305–296–5439; *www.keywestinternationalairport.com*) and Florida Keys Marathon Airport (airport code: MTH) (305–289–6060; *www.floridakeysairport.com*) are serviced by several major air carriers. These include US Airways, Delta, and American Eagle Airlines.

It's a Gay Life

Annual events: Hardly a weekend goes by in Key West without some kind of special event or festival taking place. Every aspect of the diverse Key West landscape, from its unique cultural heritage to its 1982 secession from the United States, is commemorated with colorful festivals that delight visitors and display residents' penchant for partying. The Gay & Lesbian Community Center of Key West produces three major annual events for the GLBT community: PrideFest Key West (*www.pridefestkeywest.com*), a nine-day celebration in early June that includes Pride Follies, a golf tournament, family picnic, awards ceremonies and contests, a street fair, and a parade; WomanFest (888–324–2996; *www.womenfest.net*); and Fantasy Fest (*www.fantasyfest.net*), a memorable 10-day party with thousands of costumed revelers in October. The Monroe County Development Council (*www.fla-keys.com*) maintains a complete list of other events.

Nightlife: At night, the stars illuminate assorted entertainment opportunities including jazz clubs, piano bars, dance clubs, drag shows, and saloons. The nightlife in Key West can be exciting and diverse. A few of the popular gay clubs are Aqua Nightclub (711 Duval Street; 305–294–0555; *www.aquakeywest.com*), with drag shows, karaoke, and dancing; Atlantic Shores Pool Bar (510 South Street; 305–296–2491/800–526–3559; *www.atlanticshoresresort.com*), Key West's "clothing-optional" pool and bar, with daily drink specials, good food, and Sunday's Famous Tea-by-the-Sea from 7 to 11 p.m.; and Bourbon St. Complex (724–801 Duval Street; 305–296–1992; *www.bourbonstreetcomplex.com*), a complex of a guesthouse, two restaurants, and eight bars. La Te Da (1125 Duval Street; 305–296–6706; *www.lateda.com*) is another favorite on the "Duval Crawl," the popular phrase used to describe fun-seekers' evening jaunts up and down the island's main street to sample numerous taverns and entertainment offerings. Pearl's Patio (525 United Street; 305–292–1450; *www.pearlsrainbow.com*) provides great drinks and Key West ambience just for women.

Culture: It's been said that the idiosyncratic architecture and the laid-back atmosphere of this small, 2- by 4-mile island probably have nurtured the talents of more writers per capita than any other city in the country. More than 100 published authors reside, full- or part-time, in Key West, and the island is noted for its artistic community with a number of galleries exhibiting artwork in varying styles and mediums. Three area playhouses feature Broadway-quality performances November through May and the Key West Symphony (305–292–1774; *www.keywestsymphony.com*) and the Key West Pops (305–295–7501; *www.keywestpops.com*) perform throughout the year. Impromptu concerts and gallery walks showcase the talents of local and visiting musicians and artists. The Key West Aquarium (1 Whitehead Street; 800–868–7482; *www.keywestaquarium.com*) showcases the diverse marine life that inhabit the waters of Key West; the Key West Butterfly & Nature Conservatory (1316 Duval Street; 305–296–2988/866–949–0900; *www.wingsofimagination.com*) features a 5,000-square-foot glass-domed tropical butterfly habitat; and Audubon House & Tropical Gardens (205 Whitehead Street; 305–294–2116; *www.audubonhouse.com*) houses original Audubon engravings from 1832, when the artist and ornithologist visited Key West and sketched 18 new species for his "Birds of America" folio.

Recreation: One of the favorite pastimes on Key West is to do nothing at all. But, when you're ready to do something, you can pet a shark, tour a cemetery, visit the Hemingway Home and Museum (907 Whitehead Street; 305–294–1136; *www.hemingwayhome.com*) and experience the riches of a spectacular salvage expedition. Island beaches offer ample sunning and water sport opportunities, and beneath the surrounding turquoise and cobalt waters, historic shipwrecks, a living coral reef, and myriad marine plants and animals entice those eager to explore. For water lovers, Key West is protected from the seas by the only barrier reef in North America. The reef provides divers and snorkelers with breathtaking sights of corals and a profusion of brilliantly colored tropical fish. Just beyond the reef runs the Gulf Stream, a powerful ocean current that is home to spectacular game fish. For anglers, billfish beyond the reef and permit and tarpon on the flats are just a few of the local game fish that offer spirited and sometimes acrobatic displays of strength.

For the Visitor

Accommodations: For intimate lodging, the island provides a bounty of bed and breakfasts with architectural qualities evoking eras past, as well as lavish resorts that offer modern services and amenities amid grander surroundings. There are lots of gay-friendly and gay-exclusive options on the island. Here's a small sampling: Atlantic Shores Resort (510 South Street; 305–296–2491/800–526–3559; *www.atlanticsshoresresort.com*) is an all-inclusive hotel resort. Banana Bay Resort & Marina (2319 N. Roosevelt Boulevard; 305–296–6925/800–226–2621; *www.bananabay.com*), ideally situated where "Old Town" Key West begins, is the Keys' most romantic destination. Pearl's Rainbow (525 United Street; 305–292–1450/800–749–6696; *www.pearlsrainbow.com*) is Key West's Distinctive Resort for Women. Island House for Men (1129 Fleming Street; 305–294–6284/800–890–6284; *www.islandhousekeywest.com*) is a guesthouse exclusively for gay men, featuring a gym, pool, restaurant, bar, sundeck, sauna, and indoor/outdoor Jacuzzis.

For More Information

Gay & Lesbian Center
Gay & Lesbian
Community Center of
Key West
513 Truman Avenue
Key West, FL 33040
305–292–3223
www.glcckeywest.org

Publications
Celebrate!
524 Eaton Street,
Suite 110
Key West, FL 33040
305–295–8292
www.celebratekeywest.com

Key West Citizen
3420 Northside Drive
Key West, FL 33040
305–294–6641
www.keysnews.com

**Convention and
Visitors Bureau**
Florida Keys & Key
West Monroe County
Tourist Development
Council
Stuart Newman
Associates
2140 S. Dixie Highway,
Suite 203
Miami, FL 33133
www.fla-keys.com

**Chambers of
Commerce**
Key West Chamber of
Commerce
402 Wall Street
Key West, FL 33040
305–294–2587
www.keywestchamber.org

**Key West Business
Guild**
513 Truman Avenue
Key West, FL 33040
305–284–4603/
800–535–7797
www.gaykeywestfl.com

Realtor
Century 21 Keysearch
Property
701 Caroline Street
Key West, FL 33040
305–294–6637
www.c21keysearch.com

## 14

Miami Shores, Florida

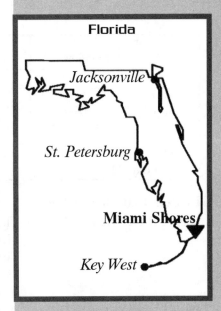

A Look at Miami Shores

Miami Shores is a fabulous city to raise a family and enjoy life. Located in northeast Miami-Dade County, about 20 minutes from downtown Miami, this little village of just more than 10,000 residents combines a high quality of life in a small town atmosphere with all the available amenities the Greater Miami metro area has to offer. Miami Shores is home to Barry University, a fully accredited, four-year coeducational university offering more than 100 programs of undergraduate and graduate study. Miami Shores is a community with interesting shops, an outstanding recreational program, fine schools, and beautiful churches. Many of the residents participate in local clubs and organizations that work to insure the continued quality of the community. Local government is responsive to the concerns of both local residents and businesses. The community boasts several fabulous amenities for such a small town, including the Miami Shores Country Club, the Aquatic Center with two pools, and the Shore's Performing Arts Theater, a restored 1940s movie house that's now home to one of Miami's up-and-coming theater companies. Miami Shore's location, just west of Biscayne Bay and north of Miami, provides easy access to all of southern Florida's natural beauty, culture, and recreation opportunities.

Possible drawbacks: In an ongoing effort to preserve the small village atmosphere and high quality of life, there are strict zoning laws and community rules in Miami Shores. The gay community in Miami, though large and visible, lacks the support and services available in most other large metro areas.

▶ Nickname:
The Village Beautiful

▶ County:
Miami-Dade

▶ Area code: 305

▶ Time zone: Eastern

▶ Population:
10,380

▶ County population:
2,253,362

▶ Region:
Southeast Florida

▶ Closest metro area:
Miami

▶ Average home price:
$300,000

▶ Fabulous reasons to live here:
Excellent weather, ocean views, recreation, culture, arts, large GLBT community, great education and continuing education opportunities, strong economy

Climate

Elevation 10'	Avg. high/low (F°)	Avg. inches rain	snow	Avg. # days precip.	Avg. % humidity
Jan.	75/61	2.3	–	7	72%
April	82/69	3.4	–	6	66%
July	90/77	5.6	–	16	73%
Oct.	85/73	5.8	–	14	74%
YEAR	75/	57.9	–	130	72%
# days 32° or below: 0			# days 90° or warmer: 62		

Local Connections

Gas and electric companies: There are more than 20 gas and electric providers servicing the area due to deregulation. The Florida Public Service Commission (800–342–3552; *www.psc.state.fl.us*) can provide specific details on programs and providers.

Phone companies: Bell South (888–757–6500; *www.bellsouth.com*); Sprint (800–877–7746; *www.sprint.com*); among others

Water and sewer: Water: Miami-Dade County Water and Sewer Department (305–665–7477; *www.miamidade.gov/wasd*); Sewer: Village of Miami Shores Sanitation Division (305–795–2207; *www.miamishoresvillage.com*)

Cable company: Comcast (800–266–2278; *www.comcast.com*)

Car registration/License: Florida Department of Highway, Safety and Motor Vehicles (850–922–9000; *www.hsmv.state.fl.us*)

You have 30 days after establishing residency to get your Florida license. Only a vision exam is required when surrendering an out-of-state license. Initial License Fee: $20 (additional fees required for testing). Car registration fee: $100. New license plate issue fee: $10. Annual registration is based on car weight: up to 2,499 pounds $27.60; 2,500–3,499 pounds $35.60; 3,500 pounds and above $45.60.

The Tax Ax

Sales tax: 6.5 percent

State income tax: No state income tax

Property tax: Dade County Property Appraiser (305–375–1205; *www.miamidade.gov/pa*)

If you purchase a home in Florida, the tax on it is based on the just or fair market value of the property. Ad valorem taxes are assessed and collected annually by the county property appraiser. The current annual rate is 16.4895 per thousand of taxable value.

Local Real Estate

Overview: The Miami area offers many styles and types of urban living. Houses vary from the 1920s art deco to modern contemporary. One-story and two-story houses to mansions, as well as older charming homes, are available, including waterfront. There are many historical neighborhoods throughout Miami preserving and protecting the period of the home. Availability is limited due to the fact that Miami is a hot market, and you need to act fast when you find something.

Median price for a single-family home: $350,000

Average price for a single-family home: $300,000

Average price for a 2BR condo: $300,000

Rental housing market: Rents range from $800 to $2,500 and up. The market includes apartments and houses.

Gay-friendly neighborhoods: All of Miami Shores is gay-friendly.

Nearby areas to consider: There's no shortage of gay-friendly cities and towns in the Miami area. Wynwood, North Bay Village, Normandy Isle, Buena Vista, Biscayne Corridor, Belle Meade, Bayside Shorecrest, Design District, Edgewater, El Portal, Davis Harbor, and South Beach are just a few of the favorites of Miami's many GLBT communities. With so many options to choose from, the decision becomes a personal one based on community size, amenities, housing styles, and costs. If you're considering a move to the Miami area, plan a visit that includes a rental car so you can take your time exploring the region's many wonderful cities and neighborhoods.

Earning a Living

Per capita income: $26,134

Median household income: $64,963

Business climate: Miami-Dade County is the port area for most of America's import and export trade with Latin America. The movement of this growing sector of trade creates a strong foundation for area business. Additionally, tourism is a huge boon to the area and creates a large number of jobs.

Help in starting a business: The Greater Miami Shores Chamber of Commerce provides leadership for the advancement of the economic vitality, civic affairs, and quality of life of the total community. In addition, the nearby Greater Miami Chamber of Commerce, the largest chamber in Florida, provides hundreds of networking events each year, health insurance options for small businesses, and programs to promote and enhance the business of the Greater Miami area. The Miami-Dade Gay Chamber of Commerce promotes networking within the community, business opportunities, and gay and gay-friendly tourist promotion and resources and outreach from the community to other organizations.

Job market: The greater Miami area is home to several Fortune 500 companies. Industries providing employment in the Miami area include educational, health, and social services; professional, scientific, management, administrative, and waste management services; arts, entertainment, recreation, accommodation, and food services; and retail trade and construction.

The Community

Overview: Miami Shores is a quiet respite for the Miami-Dade County area's large gay community. The Village is well maintained and provides a small-town atmosphere for its residents. The area is home to a large, diverse, and visible gay population that is well established in the community's political, cultural, social, and business life. The constant flow of tourists makes for fun nightlife and other social opportunities.

Community organizations: Miami Shores doesn't have any gay-specific organizations, but nearby Miami has a few social, spiritual, and support organizations. Project YES (*www.yesinstitute.org*) works to prevent suicide and ensure the healthy development of gay, lesbian, bisexual, transgender, and all youth by initiating dialogue, providing education, and creating support systems. The Gay Men's Multi-ethnic Association (*www.angelfire.com/fl/ymact*) is South Florida's social group for professional gay men from all ethnic backgrounds. Miami Beach's SoBe Social Club (*www.sobesocialclub.com*) is a group for gay professionals in the metro Miami Beach area.

Medical care: Miami-Dade County is home to a score of hospitals and medical service providers. The two institutions closest to Miami Shores are Miami's 357-bed North Shore Hospital (305–835–6000; *www.northshoremedical.com*), which employs more than 900 employees and more than 400 affiliated physicians offering a broad spectrum of specialties; and St. Catherine's Rehabilitation Hospital (305–357–1735; *www.catholichealthservices.org*) in North Miami, a 60-bed, state-of-the-art medical facility designed for patients who are medically stable and can benefit from intensive rehabilitation in a disciplined hospital setting.

Nuptials: Florida doesn't offer domestic partnership or other committed relationship options, but Miami-Dade County is a popular destination for commitment ceremonies.

Getting Around Town

Public transportation: Miami-Dade Transit (305–770–3131; *www.co.miami-dade.fl.us/transit*) provides Metrobus, Metrorail, Metromover, and Paratransit services for the county. Fares: regular $1.25; express $1.50; shuttle bus 50 cents; Metromover is free.

Roads: I-95, I-195, US1

Airports: Miami International Airport (airport code: MIA) (305–876–7000; *www.miami-airport.com*) is approximately 9 miles away; Ft. Lauderdale/Hollywood International Airport (airport code: FLL) (954–359–6100; *www.fortlauderdaleinternationalairport.com*) is about 15 miles away.

It's a Gay Life

Annual events: Miami Shores Village (*www.miamishoresvillage.com*) has a series of annual, hometown style events including the Mayor's Ball; spring's Marshmallow Drop, Egg Dive, and annual Spring Concert; Fourth of July picnic and events; the Dive In Theater and a Halloween Howl. To the south, the Miami Gay and Lesbian Film Festival (*www.mglff.com*) is an annual spring affair. There are many parties but no gay pride festival or parade. There is a long party season that begins with the Thanksgiving weekend White Party (*www.carersource.org/whiteparty*) and ends in March with the Winter Party (*www.winterparty.org*). In between is a hot Black Pride event (*www.sizzle2005.com*) on Memorial Day weekend. To help navigate and search a variety of up-to-the-minute facilities, events, and activities, both gay and general-interest, the Miami-Dade Gay & Lesbian Chamber of Commerce has set up a helpful Website (*www.gogaymiami.com*).

Nightlife: As the sun sets head over to Miami's South Beach (the locals call it SoBe). A stroll through this art deco haven, with its swaying palm trees and ocean views, provides some of the best people-watching opportunities in the gay world. There are a few dozen gay bars scattered throughout the Miami area. Here are a few of the options: Laundry Bar (721 N. Lincoln; 305–531–7700) is a Laundromat and bar popular with the boys on Thursdays and girls on Saturdays. Cupids Cabaret (1060 NE 79th Street; 305–756–2694; *www.cupidscabaret.com*) has nude dancers. The circuit crowd enjoys Pump (841 Washington Avenue; 305–538–7867), a multi-level after-hours club on the beach, and Twist (1057 Washington Avenue; 305–538–9478; *www.twistsobe.com*) is a popular dance bar. The Cactus Bar & Grill (2041 Biscayne Boulevard; 305–438–0662), though packed on Friday nights, is otherwise a more laid-back, friendly bar. The Loading Zone (1426-A Alton Road; 305–531–5623) draws the leather crowd. Plan to spend Sundays at Crobar (1445 Washington Avenue; 305–531–5027; *www.crobarmiami.com*). Pick up a copy of *Contax Guide* (305–757–6333; *www.contaxguide.com*) or *The Weekly News (TWN)* (*www.twnonline.org*) for current listings, news, and events.

Culture: The Miami Shores Fine Arts Commission plans and organizes fine arts and special events for the community throughout the year. The Greater Miami area is home to quality theaters such as the Coconut Grove Playhouse (3500 Main highway, Miami; 305–442–4000; *www.cgplayhouse.com*), which often features nationally known actors and playwrights, and there are scores of other performing arts venues, from salsa to symphonies and blues to ballet. The abundance of art galleries and institutions can hold its own with those of most major American cities. You could spend the better part of a week just prowling through the likes of Miami Beach's Wolfsonian Museum (1001 Washington Avenue, Miami Beach; 305–531–1001; *www.wolfsonian.org*) and Bass Museum (2121 Park Avenue, Miami Beach; 305–673–7350; *www.bassmuseum.org*), the Lowe Museum of Art in Coral Gables (1301 Stanford Drive, Coral Gables; 305–284–3535; *www.lowemuseum.org*), downtown's Miami Art Museum (101 West Flagler Street, Miami; 305–375–3000; *www.miamiartmuseum.org*), and the Museum of Contemporary Art (770 NE 125th Street, North Miami; 305–893–6211; *www.mocanomi.org*)

off Biscayne Boulevard. Venues such as the Shores Performing Arts Theatre in Miami Shores (9806 NE Second Avenue, Miami Shores; 305–751–0562; *www.shorestheatre.org*) regularly showcase gay-themed works.

Recreation: Facilities provided by the Miami Shores Recreation Department (*www.miamishoresvillage.com*) include the Community Center, Field House, Tennis Center, Tot Lot, a soccer field, a baseball field, and basketball courts. Just a few miles away, Miami caters to action-oriented visitors with some of the world's top golf, tennis, and sporting facilities. The sparkling waters of the Atlantic Ocean and Biscayne Bay are a magnet for boating enthusiasts, fishermen, divers, and water sports aficionados. Twenty minutes north, there's the gay scene and volleyball at SoBe's 12th Street Beach and the gay section of Haulover Beach Park, which has a clothing-optional section. The beach at Bill Baggs State Park is more low-key and romantically picturesque, complete with a lighthouse. Water activities also include windsurfing and snorkeling off Key Biscayne, zooming along the Intracoastal Waterway on wave runners, canoeing near Vizcaya (the elegant mansion that's the site of the White Party itself), plenty of golf and tennis, and of course skimming across the Everglades in an airboat. Take it to the next level with a new series of expert-guided eco-adventure tours, which lets you hike, bike, kayak, and snorkel through the area's top nature sites. For spectators, Miami offers the NFL's Miami Dolphins (888–FINS–TIX; *www.miamidolphins.com*), NBA's Miami Heat (786–777–1000; *www.heat.com*), baseball's 2003 World Series champion Florida Marlins (305–626–7200; *www.flamarlins.com*), and the NHL's Florida Panthers (954–835–7000; *www.floridapanthers.com*). Thoroughbred racing fans can catch the action at Calder Race Course (21001 NW 27th Avenue, Miami; 305–625–1311; *www.calderracecourse.com*) and Gulfstream Park (901 S. Federal Highway, Hallandale Beach; 954–454–7000/800–771–TURF; *www.gulfstreampark.com*).

For the Visitor

Accommodations: The Miami Area is known as "The Gay Riviera" for good reason. There are high-end resorts that cater to your every whim, plus lovely beachfront inns and a wide range of B&Bs. The following are just a few of the many gay-owned and gay-friendly accommodation options in Miami-Dade County. The Cavalier Hotel (1320 Ocean Drive; 305–531–3555; *www.cavaliermiami.com*) is an art deco treasure located on world famous Ocean Drive and is popular with the fashion industry. The Jefferson House (1018 Jefferson Avenue; 305–534–5247; *www.jeffersonhouse.com*) is Miami Beach's fabulous clothing-optional property with sundecks and a nightly cocktail hour in tropical settings. The Miami River Inn (118 S.W. South River Drive; 800–HOTEL89; *www.miamiriverinn.com*) is a beautiful B&B where weddings are a specialty. The Miami-Dade Gay & Lesbian Chamber of Commerce (305–573–4000; *www.gogaymiami.com*) maintains an extensive list of accommodation.

For More Information

Publications

Miami Herald
One Herald Plaza
Miami, FL 33132
305–350–2111
800–437–2535
www.miami.com

TWN: The Weekly News
901 NE 79 Street
Miami, FL 33138
305–757–6333
www.twnonline.org

Contax Guide
901 NE 79 Street
Miami, FL 33138
305–757–6333
www.contaxguide.com

Convention and Visitors Bureau

The Greater Miami Convention and Visitors Bureau
701 Brickell Ave., Suite 2700
Miami, FL 33131
305–539–3000/800–933–8448
www.gmcvb.com

Chambers of Commerce

Greater Miami Shores Chamber of Commerce
9701 NE Second Avenue
Miami Shores, FL 33138
305–754–5466
www.miamishores.com

Miami-Dade Gay & Lesbian Chamber of Commerce
3510 Biscayne Boulevard, Suite 202
Miami, FL 33137
305–573–4000
www.gogaymiami.com

Greater Miami Chamber of Commerce
Omni International Complex
1601 Biscayne Boulevard
Miami, FL 33132-1260
305–350–7700
www.greatermiami.com

Realtor

Kristine Flook, Real Estate Associate
Majestic Properties
5046 Biscayne Boulevard
Miami, FL 33137
305–318–6366
www.miamibiscayneliving.com

## 15

St. Petersburg, Florida

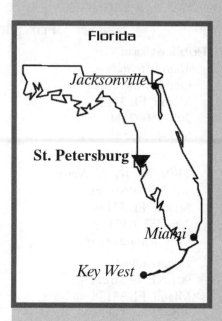

A Look at St. Petersburg

Located on the southern tip of the Pinellas Peninsula, St. Petersburg is Florida's fourth-largest city. The Sunshine City is currently experiencing a renaissance and the transformation is apparent in the revitalization of downtown, the growing gay community, and the area's strengthening economy. Surrounded by the sparkling blue waters of Tampa Bay and the Gulf of Mexico, St. Pete's neighborhoods wind along 234 miles of shoreline, bays, and bayous. Florida's Beach offers 35 miles of white-sand beaches on some 20 barrier islands, also known as keys, that buffer the Pinellas Peninsula from the Gulf of Mexico. The gentle slope and calm surf make area beaches perfect for water activities. The area's 345 miles of shoreline around the peninsula encompass the resort communities. The sun shines an average of 361 days a year in this semi-tropical setting, making the 280 square miles of Florida's Beach a year-round playground, offering unlimited opportunities to take advantage of a stunning outdoor lifestyle, including water sports; golf, outdoor arts, and cultural festivals; world championship, professional sporting events; and more. World-class museums, symphony performances, Broadway shows, rock concerts, ballet, and art festivals are just a few of the cultural offerings presented throughout the year.

Possible drawbacks: The gay community is growing, but there's currently a lack of cohesion in the community—although this is already beginning to improve. The summer months can be quite hot and humid.

▶ Nickname:
The Sunshine City

▶ County:
Pinellas

▶ Area codes:
727; 813

▶ Time zone:
Eastern Standard

▶ Population:
252,246

▶ County population:
939,864

▶ Gay population:
25,000

▶ Region:
Central Florida

▶ Average home price:
$102,600

▶ Fabulous reasons to live here:
Excellent weather, ocean views, nightlife, recreation, culture, arts, growing GLBT community, affordable housing

Climate

Elevation 44'	Avg. high/low(F°)	Avg. inches rain	snow	Avg. # days precip.	Avg. % humidity
Jan.	69/54	2.7	–	7	73%
April	80/64	1.9	–	5	69%
July	90/76	6.7	–	16	75%
Oct.	83/70	2.6	–	7	73%
YEAR	81/66	49.2	–	107	86%
# days 32° or below: 2			# days 90° or warmer: 87		

Local Connections

Gas company: TECO/Peoples Gas (813–228–4111; *www.peoplesgas.com*)

Electric company: Progress Energy (727–820–5151; *www.progress-energy.com*)

Phone company: Verizon (800–483–4000; *www.verizon.com*)

Water and sewer: City of St. Petersburg (727–893–7241; *www.stpete.org*)

Cable companies: Bright House Networks (727–562–5015; *www.cfl.mybrighthouse.com*); Knology (727–217–2600; *www.knology.net*)

Car registration/License: Florida Department of Highway, Safety and Motor Vehicles (850–922–9000; *www.hsmv.state.fl.us*)

You have 30 days after establishing residency to get your Florida license. Only a vision exam is required when surrendering an out-of-state license. Initial License Fee: $20 (additional fees required for testing). Car registration fee: $100. New license plate issue fee: $10. Annual registration is based on car weight: up to 2,499 pounds $27.60; 2,500–3,499 pounds $35.60; 3,500 pounds and above $45.60.

The Tax Ax

Sales tax: 7 percent

State income tax: No state income tax

Property tax: Pinellas County Tax Collector (727–562–3262; *www.taxcollect.com*)

Property taxes are based on approximately 75–80 percent of market value with a levy of 24.306 mils based on a 3 year average. With homestead exemption (your primary residence) you subtract the first $25,000 of assessed value, saving about $600 per year and annual tax increases are capped at 3 percent per year.

Local Real Estate

Overview: St. Petersburg offers many laid-back, gay-friendly, affordable, and charming neighborhoods that value a high quality of life. There are a wide variety of styles and ages from historic 1920s homes of all sizes with architecture ranging from bungalows, Mediterranean revival, American foursquare to 1940s and 1960s ranch-style homes. There's also new construction near downtown with town- and loft-style homes and high-rise condominiums.

Median price for a single-family home: $217,800

Average price for a single-family home: $267,800

Average price for a 2BR condo: $216,000 (includes many that are waterfront)

Rental housing market: A variety of rental options from houses to large apartment complexes. Many of the older neighborhoods have carriage houses (or garage) apartments as well as many apartment buildings with charm and character from the 1920s.

Gay-friendly neighborhoods: 1920s neighborhoods: Historic Old Northeast & Old Southeast, Crescent Lake & Crescent Heights, Historic Kenwood, Historic Round Lake, Historic Roser Park; 1940s neighborhoods: Central Oak Park, Lake Pasadena, and Downtown St. Petersburg, with restored 1910 buildings to brand new construction;1960s and 1970s neighborhoods (include some waterfront): Tropical Shores, Broadwaters, Maximo Moorings, Pinellas Point

Nearby areas to consider: In addition to Tampa-St. Petersburg, gay-friendly communities span Florida's Gulf Coast. To the south, Naples (home to the Florida Symphony), Venice, Sarasota (home to the Aslo State Theater, Florida Studio Theater, and the Sarasota Ballet), and Bradenton offer a wide array of arts and recreation opportunities and slightly higher per-capita income opportunities. To the north, Clearwater, Duneden, Tarpon Springs, Port Richey, and New Port Richey offer all the amenities of waterside resort towns, but at much lower prices Also of note to the east are Temple Terrace, Zephyrhills, and Plant City, with substantial GLBT communities and easy commute.

Earning a Living

Per capita income: $21,107

Median household income: $34,597

Business climate: The St. Petersburg area consistently ranks high for future job growth and as a destination for entrepreneurs and new small businesses. St. Petersburg also has a growing and distinguished center for marine research, with 10 research and educational institutions involved in the oceanographic sciences. As the city is located on a peninsula and is the most densely populated county in Florida, redevelopment, particularly in the housing market, is extremely strong.

Help in starting a business: The St. Petersburg Chamber of Commerce is the largest member organization of Tampa Bay and provides advocacy, advertising, and networking opportunities for its members. Tampa Bay Business

Guild (813–237–3751; *www.tbbg.org*) is the area's gay and lesbian chamber of commerce and offers community networking and advertising opportunities.

Job market: Hospitality and leisure services; manufacturing; health services; technology; financial services; marine sciences; educational, health, and social services; retail trade, professional, scientific, management, administrative, and waste management services; finance, insurance, real estate, and rental and leasing; and manufacturing are all major job market sectors.

The Community

Overview: Partners for Livable Communities (*www.mostlivable.org*), a national, non-profit organization working to restore and renew America's communities, ranks the top 30 "Most Livable Communities" each year. St. Pete was ranked among the top 10 mid-sized cities for 2005. St. Petersburg celebrates its diversity and offers residents a quality of life that integrates a strong economy, historic neighborhoods, strong cultural community, and an active outdoor lifestyle. As this community continues to grow it becomes more organized and vibrant.

Community organizations: The Metro Center is Pinellas County's gay, lesbian, bisexual, and transgender community center and home to many of Tampa Bay's social and support organizations. Metro Charities (*www.metrocharities.org*) provides health and social services to the community and maintains an online list of organizations in the area. In addition to hosting pride, St. Pete Pride sponsors community events throughout the year.

Medical care: Bayfront Medical Center Inc. (727–823–1234; *www.bayfront.org*) is a 502-bed, private, not-for-profit hospital that employs more than 2,100 team members, including nearly 600 physicians with seven Convenient Care Clinics offering minor emergency care; two family health centers offering primary and obstetrical care; two outpatient rehabilitation facilities; family practice and OB/GYN residency programs; and maternal fetal medicine practice specializing in high-risk obstetrics. St. Anthony's Hospital (727–825–1100; *www.stanthonys.com*) is a not-for-profit, 405-bed hospital established in 1931. St. Anthony's is dedicated to improving the health of the community through community-owned healthcare that sets the standard for high-quality, compassionate care and offers a wide array of medical services that provide a continuum of care for our community.

Nuptials: The state of Florida has a law defining marriage as between a man and a woman and purports to not honor marriages between same-sex couples from other states, but St. Petersburg's beach settings are a popular destination for commitment ceremonies.

Getting Around Town

Public transportation: Pinellas Suncoast Transit Authority (PSTA) (727–530–9911; *www.psta.net*) provides area-wide bus service. The county bus hub in St. Petersburg connects the area to downtown. PSTA also operates the Suncoast Beach Trolley with service between beach hotels and downtown's cultural and entertainment district. Fares: $1.25; daily "Unlimited Go" card $3. The Looper Downtown Trolley offers convenient and affordable 25-cent service between all downtown hotels and attractions, connecting with the county's PSTA buses and beach trolley.

Roads: I-275, I-175, I-375, US19

Airports: Tampa International (airport code: TIA) (813–870–8700; *www.tampaairport.com*) is consistently rated the nation's best by the International Passenger Traffic Association; St. Petersburg/Clearwater International (airport code: PIE) (727–453–7800; *www.fly2pie.com*) is centrally located between the metropolitan areas of Clearwater, St. Petersburg, Sarasota, and Tampa.

It's a Gay Life

Annual events: St. Pete Pride (*www.stpetepride.com*) hosts one of Florida's largest and most spirited pride celebrations that include a promenade and street festival. They also host several other annual events and provide a good collection of online links and resources for the community. In addition to the fall event, the Annual Tampa International Gay and Lesbian Film Festival (*www.tiglff.com*) sponsors film series throughout the year.

Nightlife: The second Thursday of each month is The Grand Stroll through downtown St. Petersburg's Grand Central District (727–328–7086; *www.grandcentraldistrict.org*). The city is home to one of the largest gay and lesbian resort properties in the world, the Suncoast Resort Hotel (3000 34th Street S.; 727–867–1111; *www.suncoastresort.com*), with two restaurants, 30,000 square feet of shopping, and 15,000 square feet of bars and lounges. The Suncoast is an impressive and popular center of gay activity. A few of the favorite gay bars include: Georgie's Alibi (3100 3rd Avenue N.; 727–321–2112; *www.georgiesalibi.com*), which includes Video Bar, Sports Bar, and Cafe Mainly Male; the upscale Haymarket Pub (8308 4th Street; 727–577–9621). In addition to the other local bars, nearby Tampa and Clearwater have lists of their own. The Rainbow Shuttle Express Inc. (727–525–2711) provides all-night-long rides between six bars in St. Pete, Tampa, and Clearwater. Pick up a copy of the *Tampa Bay Gazette* (*www.gazettetampabay.com*) or *Contax Guide* (*www.contaxguide.com*) for current news and listings.

Culture: St. Petersburg's Mahaffey Theater for the Performing Arts at the Bayfront Center (400 1st Street S.; 727–892–5710; *www.mahaffeytheater.com*), including an 8,250-seat arena, is the scene for many activities including concerts and touring productions. Ruth Eckerd Hall (1111 N. McCullen-Booth Road, Clearwater; 727–791–7400; *www.rutheckerdhall.com*), the theater in Clearwater's Richard Baumgardner Center for the Performing Arts, offers a wide array of cultural activities. County and community parks are regular sites for art shows and open-air concerts, such as the Clearwater Jazz Holiday (727–461–5200; *www.clearwaterjazz.com*) in October, acclaimed as one of the South's premier jazz festivals. There are 15 community theaters and four professional theaters. Among the 15 museums throughout Florida's Beach are the Salvador Dali Museum (1000 3rd Street S.; 727–823–3767; *www.salvadordalimuseum.org*), Museum of Fine Arts (255 Beach Drive N.E.; 727–896–2667; *www.fine-arts.org*), Florida International Museum (100 2nd Street N.; 800–777–9882; *www.floridamuseum.org*), Florida Holocaust Museum (55 5th Street S.; 727–820–0100/800–960–7448; *www.flholocaustmuseum.org*), and the Sunken Gardens (1825 4th Street N.; 727–551–3100; *www.sunkengardens.com*).

Recreation: The Gulf and Intracoastal waterways offer areas for practically every water activity imaginable, including deep-sea fishing; backwater salt flats fishing; boating, sailing, canoeing and sea kayaking; scuba diving (dive shops offer trips to artificial reefs, wrecks, and area springs and rivers); wind surfing; and shelling. Fort De Soto Park (Mullet Key; *www.fortdesoto.com*) attracts visitors wishing to sample some of Florida's most picturesque beaches and picnicking and camping facilities. The park is located on five islands south of St. Petersburg. Mullet Key is the largest and is the site of Fort De Soto, an artillery installation created during the Spanish-American War. Golf and tennis are played year-round, and facilities for both are plentiful. Top golfers from around the world compete in the PGA Chrysler Championship (36750 US19 N., Palm Harbor; 727–942–5566; *www.chryslerchampionship.com*) in October. Pari-mutuel wagering is available with greyhound and thoroughbred racing. Professional sports fans have Major League Baseball's Tampa Bay Devil Rays (727–825–3137; *www.devilrays.com*), who play in St Petersburg's Tropicana Field (One Tropicana Drive; 888–326–7297), the NFL's Tampa Bay Buccaneers (813–879–2827; *www.buccaneers.com*), NHL's Tampa Bay Lightning (813–301–6600; *www.tampabaylightning.com*), and Arena Football's Tampa Bay Storm (813–276–7300; *www.tampabaystorm.com*). The area is baseball's spring training capital, with nine teams training within an hour's drive. Just 30 minutes away is Busch Gardens in Tampa (Corner of Busch Boulevard and 40th Street; 888–800–5447; *www.buschgardens.com*) and 90 minutes away are Walt DisneyWorld Resort (Lake Buena Vista; 407–939–7639; *www.disneyworld.com*), Sea World (7007 Sea World Drive; 407–363–2200; *www.seaworld.com*), and Universal Studios Orlando (1000 Universal Studios Plaza; 407–363–8000/800–711–0080; *www.universalorlando.com*).

For the Visitor

Accommodations: There are more than 35,000 rooms in the area. Properties range from amenity-filled beachside resorts to cozy B&Bs. The Suncoast Resort (3000 34th Street S.; 727–867–1111; *www.suncoastresort.com*), with 120 hotel rooms and suites, calls itself the world's largest all-gay resort and entertainment complex. Ask for a unit overlooking the pool and courtyard. Weekends are particularly boisterous and active. Don CeSar Beach Resort & Spa (3400 Gulf Boulevard; 727–363–1881; *www.doncesar.com*) is a longtime point of reference on maritime navigation charts. This historic "pink palace" features Mediterranean and Moorish architecture and includes numerous balconies and terraces. The Pier Hotel (253 2nd Avenue N.; 727–822–7500/800–735–6607; *www.thepierhotel.com*) is located in the heart of Florida's premier Waterfront district, within walking distance to many local museums and attractions.

For More Information

Gay & Lesbian Center

The Metro Center
3170 3rd Avenue N.
St. Petersburg, FL
727–321–3854
www.metrocharities.org/
MetroCenter.htm

Publications

St. Petersburg Times
490 First Avenue S.
St. Petersburg, FL 33701
727–893–8111
www.sptimes.com

Tampa Tribune
200 S. Parker Street
Tampa, FL 33606
813–259–7600
www.tampatrib.com

Tampa Bay Gazette
P.O. Box 11987
St. Petersburg, FL 33733
727–821–5009
www.gazettetampabay.com

Contax Guide
901 NE 79 Street
Miami, FL 33138
305–757–6333
www.contaxguide.com

Convention and Visitors Bureau

St. Petersburg/Clearwater Area
Convention & Visitors Bureau
14450 46th Street, Suite 108
Clearwater, FL 33762-2922
727–464–7200/877–352–3224
www.floridasbeach.com

Chambers of Commerce

St. Petersburg Area Chamber of
Commerce
2010 1st Avenue S.
St. Petersburg, FL 33712
727–821–4069
www.stpete.com

Gateway Chamber of Commerce
P.O. Box 20241
St. Petersburg, FL 33742
727–530–9999
www.gatewaychamber.org

Realtor

Brian Longstreth
Broker-Owner
Your Neighborhood Realty, Inc.
2440 Central Avenue
St. Petersburg, FL 33712
727–321–1734
www.sellstpete.com

16

West Palm Beach, Florida

Florida

Jacksonville

St. Petersburg

West Palm Beach ▼

Miami

Key West

A Look at West Palm Beach

West Palm Beach enjoys mild tropical temperatures all year-round. The great weather is celebrated with weekly outdoor greenmarkets, jazz concerts, nature walks and events. From world-class museums and historical sites to performing arts and theater, Palm Beach County is growing as Florida's Cultural Capital. More than 40 museums are located throughout the county and a year-round schedule of exceptional plays, concerts, musicals, and theatrical events are available. World-class shopping and gourmet dining are always an option and available, whatever your tastes. The county is a also a sports paradise, home to the Marathon of the Palm Beaches, two PGA tournaments, 160 private and public golf courses, world-class polo, the nation's best croquet, year-round tennis, and the St. Louis Cardinals and Florida Marlins spring training. With 47 miles of coastline and the second-largest freshwater lake in the country, the area offers a plentitude of aquatic activities including fishing, boating, swimming, and scuba diving at the area's many reefs. Distinctive attractions, an assortment of cultural venues, top-notch festivals, and edge-of-your-seat sporting activities are what you'll call home in this subtropical paradise.

Possible drawbacks: Parts of the city are plagued with high crime rates.

▶ Nickname:
Capital City of the Palm Beaches
▶ County: Palm Beach
▶ Area code: 561
▶ Time zone: Eastern
▶ Population: 97,708
▶ County population: 1,131,184
▶ Region: Southwest Florida
▶ Closest metro area: Palm Beach
▶ Average home price: $341,000
▶ Fabulous reasons to live here:
Tropical weather, ocean views, culture, arts, entertainment, recreation, excellent education, social GLBT community

Climate

Elevation 21'	Avg. high/low(F°)	Avg. inches rain	snow	Avg. # days precip.	Avg. % humidity
Jan.	75/57	3.7	–	8	71%
April	82/65	3.6	–	7	67%
July	90/75	6.0	–	15	74%
Oct.	85/71	5.5	–	13	73%
YEAR	76/67	61.4	–	134	75%
# days 32° or below: 0			# days 90° or warmer: 65		

Local Connections

Gas and electric company: Florida Public Utilities Company (561–832–0872; *www.fpuc.com*)

Phone companies: Bell South (888–757–6500; *www.bellsouth.com*); Sprint (800–877–7746; *www.sprint.com*); among others

Water and sewer: City of West Palm Beach Public Utilities (561-822-1300 *www.wpb.org/utilities*)

Cable company: Comcast (800–266–2278; *www.comcast.com*)

Car registration/License: Florida Department of Highway, Safety and Motor Vehicles (850–922–9000; *www.hsmv.state.fl.us*)

You have 30 days after establishing residency to get your Florida license. Only a vision exam is required when surrendering an out-of-state license. Initial License Fee: $20 (additional fees required for testing). Car registration fee: $100. New license plate issue fee: $10. Annual registration is based on car weight: up to 2,499 pounds $27.60; 2,500–3,499 pounds $35.60; 3,500 pounds and above $45.60.

The Tax Ax

Sales tax: 6.5 percent

State income tax: No state income tax

Property tax: Palm Beach County Property Appraiser (561–355–2883; *www.co.palm-beach.fl.us/papa*)

The current mil rate is $8.417 per $1,000 of taxable value.

Local Real Estate

Overview: West Palm Beach is renowned for its many art deco homes. The city has created 12 historic neighborhood districts to protect this and other housing styles. Historic neighborhoods have a unique character. It may be related to the architecture, method of construction, vegetation, and/or some other special attribute. When an area becomes a historic district, these characteristics are protected along with the architectural characteristics. Property has been appreciating about 10 percent annually for the past few years.

Median price for a single-family home: $271,000

Average price for a single-family home: $341,000

Average price for a 2BR condo: $150,000

Rental housing market: The rental market is seasonally tight (more expensive in winter and more affordable in summer and fall). A two-bedroom apartment rents for $900–1,200.

Gay-friendly neighborhoods: All of West Palm Beach is gay-friendly. The GLBT community is drawn to some of the older, art deco areas and neighborhoods.

Nearby areas to consider: There are many fabulous cities near West Palm Beach that the GLBT community calls home, including Boca Raton, Palm Beach, Riviera Beach, and Northwood. Of special note is Lake Worth. This midsize, beachfront city has a substantial GLBT community. The city prides itself on its excellent public education system, which includes one of Florida's premier high schools. The Street Painting Festival is Lake Worth's signature winter event, when the streets are turned into works of art. The city also boasts 19 acres of public beach, a municipal golf course that spans the Intracoastal Waterway, and a growing arts community.

Earning a Living

Per capita income: $23,188

Median household income: $36,774

Business climate: A strong dedication to its school system creates a well-educated workforce in West Palm Beach. West Palm Beach also has a pro-businesses government. This combination is drawing national companies such as Rexall Sundown and Scott Paper to the area. Recent growth and financial successes, plus the great weather and work environment, will continue to provide momentum for the areas long-term growth.

Help in starting a business: Palm Beach County has several chambers of commerce to assist area businesses. Depending on where in the county you decide to do business there's the Chamber of Commerce of the Palm Beaches, the Women's Chamber of Commerce of Palm Beach County (*www.womenschamber.biz*), Palms West Chamber (561–790–6200; *www.palmswest.com*), and the North Palm Beach County Chamber of Commerce (561–694–2300; *www.npbchamber.com*). All of these organizations provide networking, advertising, and educational opportunities for business owners.

Job market: The largest area employer is the School Board of Palm Beach County. Government, retail services, professional services, retail, and housing and commercial building construction will continue to provide future growth in West Palm Beach.

The Community

Overview: The West Palm Beach and Palm Beach County's GLBT community is social, active, and supportive. The GLBT environment, while catering to thousands of visitors annually, is more grounded and solid than many other tourist-based cities. The many gay-owned businesses, including bars, boutiques, guest houses, and retail stores and large numbers of organizations, are responsible for this strong community foundation.

Community organizations: Compass GLBT Community Center of Palm Beach County (*www.compassglcc.com*) is an integral part of West Palm Beach's community, providing health services, referrals, education, and space for area support and social organizations, while promoting pride and diversity. The Compass Website has listings of the areas many active groups and organizations.

Medical care: Columbia Hospital (561–842–6141; *www.columbiahospital.com*) is a 250-bed, acute-care facility offering a broad spectrum of medical, surgical, and mental health services as well as an outpatient center. Columbia Hospital employs more than 750 people and has a medical staff of more than 400 physicians. Good Samaritan Medical Center (561–655–5511; *www.goodsamaritanmc.com*), a 341-bed, acute-care facility, provides comprehensive cancer services, assists the medical community in caring for patients with known or suspected cardio diseases, and offers a wide range of outpatient services, including outpatient surgery and diagnostic imaging. Saint Mary's Medical Center (561–844–6300; *www.stmarysmc.com*) provides a comprehensive range of health services and medical programs designed to meet the community's healthcare needs. Wellington Regional Medical Center (561–798–8500; *www.wellingtonregional.com*) is a 120-bed, acute-care hospital. As a full service community hospital Wellington Regional prides itself on its commitment to meet the changing needs of patients, physicians, payors, staff, and the community at large.

Nuptials: The State of Florida has a law similar to DOMA that defines marriage as between a man and a woman. Same-sex marriages from other jurisdictions are not recognized. In February 2005, the City Commission adopted legislation that affords certain rights and benefits to qualified committed relationships that have registered with the City of West Palm Beach (*www.cityofwpb.com*). Partners need not be West Palm Beach residents. Fee: $50.

Getting Around Town

Public transportation: Palm Tran Bus Services (561–841–4287/877–930–4287; *www.co.palm-beach.fl.us/palmtran*) have $1.25 per ride or $3 daily unlimited fares; Molly's Trolleys (561–838–9511; *www.mollystrolleys.com*). Tri-Rail (800–TRI–RAIL; *www.tri-rail.com*) is South Florida's premiere commuter railroad, operating seven days a week with service between Miami, Palm Beach and Ft. Lauderdale.

Roads: I-95, SR441, SR7, US1, Coastal Highway A1A

Airport: Palm Beach International Airport (airport code: PBI) (561–471–7420; *www.pbia.org*) is a congestion-free airport plus a state-of-the-art international port facility.

It's a Gay Life

Annual events: In April, Compass (*www.compassglcc.com*) hosts PrideFest in nearby Bryant Park and the Stonewall Ball in May. West Palm Beach is known for many of its annual community festivals including The Palm Beach International Film Festival (*www.pbifilmfest.org*), eight days of independent films and events in April, the Tropical Fruit Festival (*www.mounts.org*), the Bon Festival (*www.morikami.org*), and SunFest (*www.sunfest.com*). Contact the Palm Beach County Convention and Visitors Bureau (*www.palmbeachfl.com*) for the complete list.

Nightlife: With more than 2,000 restaurants, dining is an adventure in Palm Beach County. From the storied cuisine at The Breakers' L'Escalier (*www.thebreakers.com*) to the award-winning French chefs Sebastien Thieffine and Johann Willar at Ritz-Carlton, Palm Beach (*www.ritzcarlton.com*), foodies will be tempted with a barrage of international flavors, distinct settings, and annual culinary festivals that bring the best of the world to Palm Beach County's doorstep. CityPlace (*www.cityplace.com*) is a $600 million shopping, dining, entertainment, and residential complex in the heart of West Palm Beach. West Palm Beach also has a nice mix of GLBT bars and restaurants. Changing Times Bookstore (911 Village Boulevard; 561–640–0496) has a large GLBT section where you can pick up copies of *Hotspots! Magazine, Southern Voice,* or *TLW Magazine* for current listings and events across Florida.

Culture: More than 40 cultural venues are located across Palm Beach County. Here are just a few of the cultural options that reflect the diversity of excellent entertainment and unequaled exhibits that will make you want to leave the beach. The Raymond F. Kravis Center for the Performing Arts (701 Okeechobee Boulevard; 561–832–7469; *www.kravis.org*) hosts a wide range of concerts and tours and performances by the world class Ballet Florida (500 Fern Street; 561–659–2000; *www.balletflorida.com*). The Norton Museum of Art (1451 S. Olive Avenue; 561–832–5196; *www.norton.org*) has an impressive collection of 19th- and 20th-century American art, including many contemporary pieces and photographs, important Chinese works, and a European collection spanning three centuries. The Boca Raton Museum of Art (501 Plaza Real, Boca Raton; 561–392–2500; *www.bocamuseum.org*) hosts traveling exhibitions and an eclectic permanent collection of American, European, and African art. Hailed as "Palm Beach's coolest concert venue," the Colony's Royal Room (155 Harmon Avenue, Palm Beach; 561–655–5430; *www.thecolonypalmbeach.com*) is widely considered to be one of the top five cabarets in the country, spotlighting an impressive roster of jazz legends. The Flagler Museum (1 Whitehall Way, Palm Beach; 561–655–2833; *www.flagler.org*) is the first Beaux Arts–style building constructed in the

United States in the last 60 years; the pavilion will house Flagler's private rail-car. The Palm Beach County Cultural Council (561–471–2901/800–882–2787; *www.pbccc.org*) offers a complete list of cultural events and organizations in the county.

Recreation: With an average annual temperature of 78 degrees, visitors can enjoy the great outdoors year-round at any of the County's 70 parks, 13 of which are beachfront. Adventures await yachters, canoe and kayaking enthusiasts, beachgoers, divers, and pleasure boaters. Anglers will find the best in deep-sea fishing and numerous freshwater spots. For scuba enthusiasts, the waters offer brilliantly colored corals, sea turtles, nurse sharks, and the Western Hemisphere's widest variety of tropical and sport fish. The Florida Everglades provide the perfect setting to watch alligator, fish, and tropical birds via airboat. By canoe, see Florida's wetlands unfold along the State's only nationally designated wild and scenic river (the Loxahatchee). Those who prefer dryer options will enjoy guided tours of the famous Palm Beach coastline and the island of Palm Beach via water taxi, participating in a nighttime walk to observe endangered sea turtles nesting habits at the Jupiter Outdoor Center (1000 Coastal A1A, Jupiter; 561–747–9666; *www.jupiteroutdoorcenter.com*) or Gumbo Limbo Environmental Complex (1801 N. Ocean Boulevard, Boca Raton; 561–338–1473; *www.gumbolimbo.org*) in Delray Beach. Outdoor settings such as Palm Beach Zoo at Dreher Park (1301 Summit Boulevard; 561–547–9453; *www.palmbeachzoo.org*) and Lion Country Safari (2003 Lion Country Safari Road, Loxahatchee; 561–793–1084; *www.lioncountrysafari.com*) provide close encounters with lions, giraffes, and monkeys. Other attractions include the Moroso Motorsports Park (17047 Beeline Highway, Jupiter; 561–622–1400; *www.morosomotorsportspark.com*) racing facility and Loxahatchee Everglades Tours (15490 Loxahatchee Road, Boca Raton; 561–482–6107/800–683–5873; *www.evergladesairboattours.com*).

For the Visitor

Accommodations: Palm Beach County boasts more than 16,000 guestrooms at more than 200 hotels. Luxurious resorts, affordable inns, and bed & breakfasts create an extensive list of accommodations from which to choose. Elegant and casual dining is found at more than 2,300 unique restaurants. A few gay-friendly favorites include Grandview Gardens Bed & Breakfast (1608 Lake Avenue; 561–833–9023; *www.grandview-gardens.net*). Nestled in a tropical garden paradise, directly on Howard Park across from the Armory Art Center, this historical 1923 home has been carefully restored to reflect the original Spanish Mediterranean and offers a luxurious and yet homey atmosphere with private entrances and terraces for all guest suites. Hibiscus House Bed & Breakfast (501 30th Street; 561–863–5633; *www.hibiscushouse.com*) offers elegant surroundings for your comfort both indoors and out; step through French doors onto your private terrace and drink in the beauty of South Florida tropical foliage. Tropical Gardens B&B (419 32nd Street; 800–736–4064; *www.tropicalgardensbandb.com*) is a charming respite offering a tropical garden and private pool.

For More Information

Gay & Lesbian Center

Compass
7600 S. Dixie Highway
West Palm Beach, FL 33405
561–533–5131
www.compassglcc.com

Publications

Palm Beach Post
P.O. Box 24700
West Palm Beach, FL 33416
561–820–4663/
800–926–POST
www.palmbeachpost.com

HOTSPOTS! Magazine
5100 NE 12th Avenue
Fort Lauderdale, FL 33334
954–928–1862
www.hotspotsmagazine.com

Convention and Visitors Bureau

Palm Beach County Convention and Visitors Bureau
1555 Palm Beach Lakes Boulevard, Suite 800
West Palm Beach, FL 33401
561–233–3000
www.palmbeachfl.com

Chamber of Commerce

Chamber of Commerce of the Palm Beaches
401 North Flagler Drive
West Palm Beach, FL 33401
561–833–3711
www.palmbeaches.org

Realtor

Illustrated Properties
12794 Forest Hill Boulevard
Wellington, FL, 33414
561–793–4660
www.ipre.com

Wilton Manors, Florida

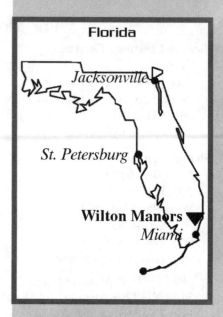

A Look at Wilton Manors

Wilton Manors, referred to as the "Island City" because its boundaries follow the north and south forks of the Middle River, is ideally located within minutes of the beach and downtown Fort Lauderdale. The City embraces the vision of a "sustainable urban village" and has created regulations that promote New Urbanism and Smart Growth principles. The City's signature thoroughfare, Wilton Drive, is home to the Arts and Entertainment District, a pedestrian-oriented environment where residents can shop, dine, and experience the best of what Wilton Manors has to offer. Nearby, Greater Fort Lauderdale's 23 miles of Blue Wave certified beaches provide adventures from parasailing and windsurfing to basketball and badminton. Quiet stretches of beach remain where, protected by tall grasses and seagrape trees, sea turtles lay their precious eggs; where exotic birds congregate in the early morning to feed on sea life left by the tide; and where beach lovers can walk for uninterrupted miles, accompanied only by the surge of the incoming sea.

Possible drawbacks: Ft. Lauderdale is overrun every spring with college students from all over the world. If your livelihood doesn't depend on tens of thousands of annual college visitors, spring might be a good time to take your own vacation. The east coast of Florida is occasionally overrun by hurricanes, too. Living in paradise has its price.

▶ Nickname:
The Island City

▶ County: Broward

▶ Area code: 954

▶ Time zone: Eastern

▶ Population: 12,697

▶ County population:
1,623,018

▶ Region:
East Central Florida

▶ Closest metro area:
Ft. Lauderdale

▶ Average home price:
$392,843

▶ Fabulous reasons to live here:
Small-town charm, near big city amenities, family-oriented GLBT community, significant local political support, excellent weather, recreation

Climate

Elevation 8'	Avg. high/low(F°)	Avg. inches		Avg. # days precip.	Avg. % humidity
		rain	snow		
Jan.	75/59	2.9	–	7	72%
April	82/66	3.9	–	6	66%
July	89/75	6.6	–	15	73%
Oct.	85/71	6.4	–	14	74%
YEAR	81/68	63.7	–	130	72%
# days 32° or below: 0			# days 90° or warmer: 62		

Local Connections

Gas and electric companies: There are more than 20 gas and electric providers servicing the area due to deregulation. The Florida Public Service Commission (800–342–3552; *www.psc.state.fl.us*) can provide specific details on programs and providers.

Phone companies: Bell South (888–757–6500; *www.bellsouth.com*); Sprint (800–877–7746; *www.sprint.com*); among others

Water and sewer: Wilton Manors Utilities (954–390–2100; *www.wiltonmanors.com*)

Cable company: Comcast (800–266–2278; *www.comcast.com*)

Car registration/License: Florida Department of Highway, Safety and Motor Vehicles (850–922–9000; *www.hsmv.state.fl.us*)

You have 30 days after establishing residency to get your Florida license. Only a vision exam is required when surrendering an out-of-state license. Initial License Fee: $20 (additional fees required for testing). Car registration fee: $100. New license plate issue fee: $10. Annual registration is based on car weight: up to 2,499 pounds $27.60; 2,500–3,499 pounds $35.60; 3,500 pounds and above $45.60.

The Tax Ax

Sales tax: 6 percent

State income tax: No state income tax

Property tax: Property taxes are approximately 2 percent of the sale price of the property. There is a homestead exemption for owners who reside in the property for more than six months of the year as their primary residence. This exemption reduces the annual property tax by about $750. The homestead exemption cannot be claimed the first year of ownership.

Local Real Estate

Overview: The housing market includes single-family ranch style, condominiums, and town homes. Estate homes with canal and oceanfront access are also available. Prices are on the rise here in the Wilton Manors/Fort Lauderdale area by as much as 30–35 percent a year. Many new town house developments have sprung up in Wilton Manors in the past two years at prices more reminiscent of New York City and San Francisco.

Median price for a single-family home: $304,000

Average price for a single-family home: $392,843

Average price for a 2BR condo: $198,158

Rental housing market: The rental market is soft. The average two-bedroom apartment rents for about $900; a two-bedroom, single-family home rents for approximately $1,200. Seasonal rentals are usually for oceanfront properties and can cost upwards of $4,000 per month with a four-month minimum for a two-bedroom condominium. The seasonal rental market is much tighter than the annual rental market.

Gay-friendly neighborhoods: All of Wilton Manors is gay-friendly.

Nearby areas to consider: Throughout the Ft. Lauderdale metro area are many gay-friendly neighborhoods and cities. Of particular note is the growing city of Oakland Park. In the fall of 2005, Oakland Park will annex several small surrounding cities, including gay-friendly North Andrews Gardens. The growing Oakland Park is among the highest per-capita gay population cities in the nation and is noted not only for its large GLBT community, but as being a friendly small town. The area boasts safe and attractive neighborhoods, quality schools, outstanding parks, and exceptional recreation programs, with the social, cultural, and business opportunities of a big city.

Earning a Living

Per capita income: $21,770

Median household income: $43,346

Business climate: Fort Lauderdale is home to a growing number of small businesses and technology start-ups and is a popular center for business conferences. Shipping and tourism are flourishing, and the real estate market, driven in part by foreign investment in high-end coastal property, is booming.

Help in starting a business: The goal of the Wilton Manors Business Association (*www.wiltonmanorsbusinessassociation.com*) is to attract and promote business in Wilton Manors. The Greater Fort Lauderdale Chamber of Commerce (*www.ftlchamber.com*) has programs to help businesses of all sizes network and advertise and also offers assistance for business start-ups.

Job market: Top corporate-sector employers are American Express, Motorola, JM Family Enterprises, Nova Southeastern University, Sun-Sentinel, Bank of America, Alamo, University Hospital, Holy Cross Medical Group, and Ed Morse

Automotive Group. The market consists primarily of education and health sector positions, followed by professional and business services, and then retail, leisure, and hospitality.

The Community

Overview: Wilton Manors is unique in that a majority of its elected officials are gay. Until recently it had a gay mayor as well. Wilton Manor's downtown business district is home to many gay-identified businesses, including bars, restaurants, clothing stores, antiques shops, and all the other kinds of establishments that make up small-town America, but with a twist.

Community organizations: Ft. Lauderdale has an active and organized GLBT community. The Gay & Lesbian Community Center of South Florida (*www.glccsf.org*) is an organizing force within the GLBT community, serving as a source for information, education, advocacy, and support. The Center works to foster the personal development and quality of life of the community it serves, as well as to increase understanding and acceptance within the greater South Florida community. Visit the Center's Website for the most current list of community organizations and to sign up for its e-newsletter ("GLCC e-Voice").

Medical care: The 332-bed North Ridge Medical Center (954–776–6000; *www.northridgemedical.com*) is an acute-care facility that opened in 1975 and is a premier cardiac facility in South Florida. North Ridge offers a variety of community educational opportunities and wellness screenings throughout the year. Ft. Lauderdale Hospital (954–463–4321; *www.psysolutions.com/facilities/ftlauderdale*) is a fully licensed, 100-bed private hospital providing inpatient and outpatient care to adults and adolescents suffering from psychiatric and/or chemical dependency.

Nuptials: The State of Florida has a law defining marriage as between a man and a woman and purports to not honor marriages between same-sex couples from other states, but this beach setting is a popular destination for commitment ceremonies.

Getting Around Town

Public transportation: The Broward County Mass Transit (954–357–8400; *www.broward.org/bct*) bus system connects all municipalities and interconnects with Palm Beach and Dade Counties. Fares: regular fare $1; all-day pass $2.50; youth, senior, and disabled discounts offered. Tri-Rail (800–874–7245; *www.tri-rail.com*) provides commuter rail service connecting Ft. Lauderdale with Miami and Palm Beach. Fares based on time of day and zones traveled; one-way fares $1–5.50; round trip $2–9.25. The Water Bus is another way to get around the area with one-way fares $4 and an all-day pass $5.

Roads: I-95, US1, SR5, SR9

Airports: Ft. Lauderdale/Hollywood International Airport (airport code: FLL) (954–359–6100; *www.fortlauderdaleinternationalairport.com*) is about 7 miles from Wilton Manors; Miami International Airport (airport code: MIA) (305–876–7000; *www.miami-airport.com*) is about 28 miles away; Palm Beach International Airport (airport code: PBI) (561–471–7420; *www.pbia.org*) is approximately 36 miles away.

It's a Gay Life

Annual events: Pride South Florida (*www.pridesouthflorida.org*) hosts PrideFest in March. The other festivals in Ft. Lauderdale are frequent and have broad appeal. The McDonald's Air and Sea Show (*www.airseashow.com*) kicks off the summer season in May, and the spectacular Cingular Winterfest Boat Parade (*www.winterfestparade.com*) presented by Nokia caps the monthlong December Winterfest celebration. The Pompano Beach Seafood Festival and Fishing Rodeo (*www.pompanobeachseafoodfestival.com*) in April celebrate the bounty of the sea. Art and food festivals, jazz festivals, the Ft. Lauderdale International Boat Show (*www.flibs.net*), the world's largest boat show, in October, and the Fort Lauderdale International Film Festival (*www.fliff.com*) in November make for special happenings every month of the year.

Nightlife: Wilton Manors is a pretty quiet place by night, but just a few minutes away Ft. Lauderdale tempts with dozens of gay and gay-friendly bars and restaurants, plus there are about another hundred bars and restaurants in the city, many with live music and comedy. Although a jacket and tie are never required, a few upscale clubs and eateries might require long pants. Broward County also hosts four Seminole Indian casinos, including the newly opened Hard Rock Casino (1 Seminole Way, Hollywood; 866–502–7529; *www.seminolehardrock.com*). Pick up a copy of *411, Express*, or *TWN* at the Pride Factory & CyberCafe (845 N. Federal Highway; 954–463–6600) for current area listings and events.

Culture: Wilton Manors' Hagen Park Community Center (2020 Wilton Drive; 954–390–2100; *www.wiltonmanors.com*) hosts small cultural and performing art events. Serving to enhance Wilton Manors' exceptional quality of life, the Wilton Manors Public Library (500 NE 26th Street; 954–390–2195; *www.wiltonmanors.com*) has undergone a major expansion providing for a larger collection and extensive electronic resources. The pedestrian-friendly, tree-lined Riverwalk links Las Olas Boulevard to Fort Lauderdale's cultural and museum zones. With the Broward Center for the Performing Arts (201 SW Fifth Avenue, Fort Lauderdale; 954–522–5334; *www.browardcenter.org*), Greater Fort Lauderdale has become the center for theater, music, and dance in South Florida. The Office Depot Center in Sunrise (One Panther Parkway, Sunrise; 954–835–8000; *www.officedepotcenter.com*) presents popular musical concerts. The Fort Lauderdale Museum of Art (One East Las Olas Boulevard, Fort Lauderdale; 954–525–5500; *www.moafl.org*) is home of one of the world's premier collections of early-20th-century art. The Museum of Discovery and Science, with the Blockbuster 3D IMAX Theater (401 SW

Second Street, Fort Lauderdale; 954–467–6637; *www.mods.org*), is the most visited museum in Florida. Not to be missed is Butterfly World (3600 W. Sample Road, Coconut Creek; 954–977–4400; *www.butterflyworld.com*), featuring a specially designed screened enclosure that lets thousands of butterflies fly free in their native habitats. A hummingbird exhibit and a hatchery complete this unique "world."

Recreation: Wilton Manors has acquired a great deal of park and open space, much of which is located on Florida's Middle River. The riverfront parks provide a host of leisure and recreational opportunities, including a canoe trail, a mangrove preserve, and two nature walks. In addition, Broward County's 288 other parks offer horseback riding, nature trails, picnicking and camping areas, waterskiing, and fresh-water lakes. Racing fans have multiple choices with thoroughbred racing at Gulfstream Park in Hallandale (901 S. Federal Highway, Hallandale; 954–454–7000; *www.gulfstreampark.com*), host of the prestigious Breeders Cup (*www.breederscup.com*) and the annual Florida Derby festival, trotters at the Pompano Park Harness Track (1800 SW 3rd Street ("Race Track Road"), Pompano Beach; 954–972–2000; *www.pompanopark.com*), greyhound racing in Hollywood, and Jai Alai in Dania. There are more than 56 public and private golf courses; the PGA Eagle Trace (1111 Eagle Trace Boulevard E., Coral Springs; 954–753–7222; *www.tpcateagletrace.com*) is perhaps the best known, but others are wonderfully challenging and readily accessible. Public and private tennis courts (550 in all) provide world-class tennis options. Spectator sports include the NFL's Miami Dolphins (888–FINS–TIX; *www.miamidolphins.com*), MLB's Florida Marlins (305–626–7200; *www.flamarlins.com*), the NBA's Miami Heat (786–777–1000; *www.heat.com*), and the NHL's Florida Panthers (954–835–7000; *www.floridapanthers.com*). Broward County is also home to baseball spring training of the Baltimore Orioles (410–685–9800; *www.theorioles.com*) and Miami Dolphins (888–FINS–TIX; *www.miamidolphins.com*) and football training at Nova Southeastern University (3301 College Avenue, Fort Lauderdale–Davie; 954–262–8350; *www.nova.edu*). You can also attend schools for sailing or motor boating, learn boardsailing, deep-sea fish for big sails and marlin, and ride an airboat or swamp buggy in the Everglades at Billie Swamp Safari (6300 Stirling Road, Clewiston; 800–949–6101; *www.seminoletribe.com/safari*). Scuba divers will find clear water and coral formations as elaborate and spectacular as those in the fabled Florida Keys—with one big advantage: The reefs are a lot less crowded with divers and are more accessible. For the last few years, Broward County has made a concerted effort to create an ideal environment for divers through an artificial reef-building process that is essentially "reforesting" the sea and introducing divers to dozens of new and interesting sights.

For the Visitor

Accommodations: Broward County offers more than 612 lodging establishments, with 33,000 hotel rooms ranging from luxurious high-rises to smaller motels. Gorgeous guesthouses and intimate inns provide an array of choices for those looking for the ultimate in charm and privacy. Get closer to nature and a perfect tan at one of several clothing-optional Superior Small Lodging properties or pamper yourself with a getaway to one of the area's spectacular resorts. There are more than 30 gay and gay-friendly places to stay. Nearby is one of the area's award-winning, premier resorts, Pineapple Point Guesthouse (954–527–0094/888–844–7295; *www.pineapplepoint.com*). Also of interest is the award-winning Royal Palms (954–564–6444/800–237–7256; *www.royalpalms.com*).

For More Information

Gay & Lesbian Center

The Gay & Lesbian Community Center of South Florida
1717 N. Andrews Avenue
Fort Lauderdale, FL 33311
954–463–9005
www.glccftl.org

Publications

The Express
5399 NE 14th Avenue,
Suite 1
Fort Lauderdale, FL 33334
954–568–1880
www.expressgaynews.com

411 Magazine
1110 NE 34th Court
 Fort Lauderdale, FL 33334
954–567–1981
www.the411mag.com

HOTSPOTS! Magazine
5100 NE 12 Avenue 33334
Fort Lauderdale, FL
954–928–1862
www.hotspotsmagazine.com

Convention and Visitors Bureau

The Greater Ft. Lauderdale Convention and Visitors Bureau
100 East Broward Boulevard, Suite 200
Fort Lauderdale, FL 33301-3510
954–765–4466/800–22–SUNNY
www.sunny.org

Chambers of Commerce

Wilton Manors Business Association
P.O. Box 24332
Fort Lauderdale, FL 33307
www.wiltonmanorsbusinessassociation.com

Greater Ft. Lauderdale Chamber of Commerce
512 NE 3rd Avenue
Fort Lauderdale, FL 33301
954–462–6000
www.ftlchamber.com

Realtor

Mark Eagle, PA
Realtor
RE/Max Partners
2810 E. Oakland Park Boulevard
Fort Lauderdale, FL 33306
954–895–0141
www.ahomeforyouinfortlauderdale.com

DeKalb County, Georgia

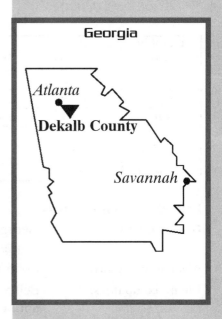

A Look at DeKalb County

DeKalb County, part of the 10-county metro Atlanta region, is home to many gay-friendly cities, including Druid Hills (pop. 12,741), North Druid Hills (pop. 18,852), Decatur (18,147), and North Decatur (pop. 15,270). Additionally, many of Atlanta's neighborhoods, which straddle DeKalb and Fulton Counties, are gay-friendly, including Midtown, Atlanta's first "gay ghetto," Virginia-Highlands, and Little Five Points. The area's extensive art scene and rich history create cultural offerings unmatched in the South. From historic to modern, you can enjoy art, performances, beauty, and education throughout the city. Atlanta has one of the fastest-growing music scenes with recording artists, annual music festivals, and unique venues. Southern gospel, local artists, and national concert tours encourage everyone to enjoy a wide sampling of music. Atlanta has an abundance of trees and green spaces that add natural beauty to metropolitan cityscapes. World-class sporting venues, sports teams, and international events are creating the title "Sports Capital" for Atlanta. The entire area has been growing at a rapid pace. Quality-of-life issues are important to the area's well-educated population, drawing major corporations and creative economy jobs to this flourishing area.

Possible drawbacks: Is every street named "Peachtree"? It sure seems that way at times to new and seasoned residents alike. The metro area's urban sprawl can create dramatic traffic problems.

▸ County:
DeKalb

▸ Area code:
770; 404

▸ Time zone:
Eastern

▸ County population:
665,865

▸ Region:
North Central Georgia

▸ Closest metro area:
Atlanta

▸ Average home price:
$200,000

▸ Fabulous reasons to live here:
Southern charm and style; arts; culture; strong high-tech economy; entertainment; recreation; affordable housing; large, active GLBT community

Climate

Elevation 940'	Avg. high/low(F°)	Avg. inches		Avg. # days precip.	Avg. % humidity
		rain	snow		
Jan.	51/32	5.5	1.0	12	69%
April	73/49	4.0	–	9	64%
July	89/69	4.9	–	12	73%
Oct.	73/51	3.3	–	7	69%
YEAR	72/51	52.5	2.1	116	69%
# days 32° or below: 35			# days 90° or warmer: 35		

Local Connections

Gas company: Georgia Natural Gas (770–850–6200; *www.gasguy.com*)

Electric company: Cobb EMC (770–429–2100; *www.cobbemc.com*)

Phone companies: Bell South (888–757–6500; *www.bellsouth.com*); Sprint (800–877–7746; *www.sprint.com*)

Water and sewer: DeKalb County Water and Sewer (770–621–7200; *www.dekalbwatersewer.com*)

Cable company: Comcast (800–266–2278; *www.comcast.com*)

Car registration/License: Georgia Department of Motor Vehicle Safety (License: 678–413–8400; Registration: 404–362–6500; *www.dmvs.ga.gov*)

New Georgia residents must apply for a Georgia driver's license within 30 days. Only an eye exam is required when surrendering an out-of-state license. Fee: $15. It is recommended that you obtain a Georgia driver's license or Georgia identification card before registering your vehicle in the state. Fees: title $18; registration $20; tag/decal $20.

The Tax Ax

Sales tax: 8 percent; prescription drugs, certain medical devices, and groceries exempt

State income tax: 1–6 percent graduated, based on income

Property tax: DeKalb County Board of Assessors (404–371–2477; *www.co.dekalb.ga.us/propappr*)

Property is appraised at 100 percent of its fair market value and assessed at 40 percent of that value. Unincorporated DeKalb has among the lowest property taxes in the state.

Local Real Estate

Overview: DeKalb County has a very diverse selection of housing styles from historic neighborhoods such as Druid Hills, Decatur, and Brookhaven to farms in east and Southeast DeKalb. Styles in housing include high-rise, lofts, town houses, condominiums, single-family homes, and small farms. The housing market continues to grow due to proximity to Atlanta, Emory, and the Centers for Disease Control and Prevention.

Median price for a single-family home: $200,000

Average price for a single-family home: $200,000

Average price for a 2BR condo: $185,000

Rental housing market: From $750 to $2,400

Gay-friendly neighborhoods: All of DeKalb County's communities are diverse and gay-friendly. In particular, the cities of Decatur, North Decatur, Druid Hills, North Druid Hills, and East Atlanta are home to large sectors of the area's large GLBT population.

Nearby areas to consider: On the edge of Little Five Points is the unique Candler Park (*www.candlerpark.org*), one of Atlanta's first suburbs. This small, historic registry community of only 7,000 residents is home to an eclectic mix of community members where anything goes and everyone is welcomed. This family-friendly neighborhood is known for being a walkable community with an emphasis on positive living conditions. Chandler Park's openness and friendliness provides a setting where folks still sit on their front porches and talk to neighbors and passersby. Additional gay-friendly communities include Emory, Oakhurst, Stone Mountain, Briarcliff, Brookhaven, Tucker, Chamblee, Clarkston, and Lithonia.

Earning a Living

Per capita income: $23,968

Median household income: $49,117

Business climate: With more than 60 million square feet of office and industrial space, thousands of well-educated professionals, more interstate miles than any county in Georgia, thousands of undeveloped acres, a variety of housing options, and an importance placed on a high quality of life, DeKalb County's strong economy should continue well into the future. The Atlanta metro area is home to 13 Fortune 500 and 24 Fortune 1000 headquarters. The area is positioned to continue attracting high-paying industries.

Help in starting a business: The DeKalb County Chamber of Commerce is an active community institution, and its Business Education Program provides education and access for local businesses along with continual networking opportunities for its members. In addition, the Atlanta Metro Chamber of Commerce's Economic Development Division has a business recruitment team actively marketing to and working with corporate executives and relocation experts in a continuing effort to bring new industry to the area. Atlanta Executive Network's (*www.aen.org*) mission is to encourage and educate its members and the Atlanta business community by promoting business contacts and friendships, advocating equality for the GLBT community, and championing diversity.

Job market: Manufacturing industries comprise 9 percent of the jobs in DeKalb, though service industries, with 37 percent of the jobs, provide the majority of employment in the county. The top employers offering service jobs are in business services ranging from data processing to temporary firms, health services, engineering, and management. Retail trade, the arts, and tourism round out this mix.

The Community

Overview: There is a large, active, metropolitan gay community in DeKalb County and the Atlanta metro area. Because of the large GLBT population, there are hundreds of community bars, restaurants, retail shops, and organizations. The community supports several out elected and appointed officials, and the community is in turn supported by the government.

Community organizations: If you want to get involved there's a group for you in the Atlanta metro area. The community has arts, music, and recreational groups, support and health groups, and many social organizations. The Rainbow Center, founded by members of the Atlanta Jewish Community and sponsored by Congregation Bet Haverim, a synagogue founded to serve the needs of Jewish GLBT people, is an Atlanta-based resource and support center for people of all ages and all religions. The Rainbow Center has an excellent online list of community resources.

Medical care: The 20-county metro-Atlanta area is home to approximately 60 hospitals plus many emergency and neighborhood clinics. The metro area also has more than 18,000 physicians. The AIDS Survival Project (404–874–7926; *www.aidssurvivalproject.org*) is committed to providing people living with HIV the most up-to-date information and support they need to lead healthy, productive lives; the organization offers vital tools for living to people throughout Georgia and beyond while maintaining a grassroots, community-based focus.

Nuptials: Georgia's constitution bans gay marriage, but commitment ceremonies are common.

Getting Around Town

Public transportation: The Metropolitan Atlanta Rapid Transit Authority's (MARTA) (404–848–4711; *www.itsmarta.com*) integrated rapid rail and bus system serves the metro Atlanta counties of DeKalb and Fulton. Fares: one-way $1.75; unlimited weekend pass $9; unlimited visitor pass: one-day $7; two-day $8, and so on.

Roads: I-20, I-75, I-85, I-285, I-675, US78

Airport: Hartsfield-Jackson Atlanta International Airport (airport code: ATL) (800–897–1910; *www.atlanta-airport.com*) is only 6 miles from DeKalb and the world's busiest airport.

It's a Gay Life

Annual events: It seems there's always an art, music, culture, or sports festival going on in Atlanta. Just a few of the annual events include the Atlanta Pride Festival (*www.atlantapride.org*), the largest pride festival in the Southeast, celebrated in June at Piedmont Park. Out on Film (*www.outonfilm.com*) is Atlanta's annual GLBT film festival (held in November). The annual Tour de Georgia (*www.tourdegeorgia.com*) in April is quickly becoming America's premier cycling event; a "rolling festival" accompanies the six-day, professional cycling stage race. The Atlanta Dogwood Festival (*www.dogwood.org*), also in April, is a showcase of springtime in Atlanta, featuring local artists, crafters, and musicians. In July, the National Black Arts Festival (*www.nbaf.org*) is a 10-day cultural festival with events around the city. The square at Little Five Points comes to life each October during the Little Five Points Halloween Festival (*www.L5p.com*).

Nightlife: With more than three dozen gay bars in metro Atlanta you'll have no problem finding a favorite or two of your own. You might want to explore the area by neighborhood. Little Five Points is Atlanta's source for eclectic dining, bohemian shopping, and artistic creativity; it's known for its progressive theaters, variety of music venues, and diversity of cuisine as well as scene. Popular music and performing arts venues include 7 Stages Theater (1105 Euclid Avenue, Atlanta; 404–523–7647; *www.7stages.com*), Variety Playhouse (1099 Euclid Avenue, Atlanta; 404–524–7354; *www.variety-playhouse.com*), and the Star Community Bar (437 Moreland Avenue, Atlanta; 404–681–9018; *www.starbar.net*), which converted a former bank vault into a shrine to Elvis. Midtown, just north of downtown, covers a large area radiating from the city's largest green space, Piedmont Park (1071 Piedmont Avenue, Atlanta; 404–876–4024; *www.piedmontpark.org*), on its eastern edge. Piedmont Park is central to Atlanta's gay, lesbian, bisexual, and transgender identity. It is not uncommon to see gay and lesbian couples strolling hand in hand along the park's paths or for groups of friends to gather to enjoy this green respite. Located just east of Midtown's Piedmont Park, the Virginia-Highlands neighborhood was one of the first areas gays began to gentrify outside of Midtown, and a gay sensibility is still entrenched there, as reflected in the election of the second consecutive openly lesbian councilmember. Pick up a free copy of *Out & Active* (*www.outandactive.com*) at Outwrite Bookstore & Coffeehouse (991 Piedmont Avenue NE; 404–607–0082; *www.outwritebooks.com*), Brushstrokes (1510-J Piedmont Avenue NE; 404–876–6567; *www.brushstrokesatlanta.com*), or Charis Books & More (1189 Euclid Avenue NE; 404–524–0304; *www.charisbooksandmore.com*) for current listings and events.

Culture: The pedestrian-friendly Chamblee's International Village District is the heart of the DeKalb International Corridor, a showcase of international cultures and entrepreneurial development. The District is a top Atlanta region destination because of its eclectic collection of shops, bars, and restaurants. One of the nation's finest orchestras, the Grammy Award–winning Atlanta Symphony Orchestra (404–733–4900; *www.atlantasymphony.org*) performs more than 230 times annually. Broadway shows, concerts, operas, ballets, and events are hosted at many venues throughout the region including Chastain Park Amphitheatre (Powers Ferry Road and Stella Drive; 404–733–4955; *www.classicchastain.org*); the Fox Theatre (660 Peachtree Street NE, Atlanta; 404–881–2100; *www.foxtheatre.org*); the Tabernacle (152 Luckie Street NW, Atlanta; 404–659–9022; *www.sgnr.com*), recently named by *Rolling Stone* as the best live music venue in Atlanta; the Rialto Center for the Performing Arts (80 Forsyth Street NW, Atlanta; 404–651–1234; *www.rialtocenter.org*); Centennial Olympic Park (265 Park Avenue NW, Atlanta; 404–222–7275; *www.centennialpark.com*); and HiFi Buys Amphitheatre (2002 Lakewood Way, Atlanta; 404–443–5090; *www.hifibuys.com*). A few miles away the metro area provides the Atlanta Botanical Garden (1345 Piedmont Avenue NE, Atlanta; 404–876–5859; *www.atlantabotanicalgarden.org*), Atlanta History Center (130 West Paces Ferry Road NW, Atlanta; 404–814–4000; *www.atlhist.org*), Center for Puppetry Arts (1404 Spring Street NW, Atlanta; 404–873–3391; *www.puppet.org*), CNN Center Studio Tour (190 Marietta Street NW, Atlanta; 404–827–2300; *www.cnn.com.StudioTour*), Fernbank Museum of Natural History (767 Clifton Road NW, Atlanta; 404–929–6300; *www.fernbank.edu*), High Museum of Art (1280 Peachtree Street NE, Atlanta; 404–733–4400; *www.high.org*), Imagine It! Children's Museum of Atlanta (275 Centennial Olympic Park Drive NW, Atlanta; 404–659–5437; *www.imagineitcma.org*), Martin Luther King, Jr. Historic Site (450 Auburn Avenue NE, Atlanta; 404–331–6922; *www.nps.gov/malu*), Underground Atlanta (50 Upper Alabama Street, Atlanta; 404–523–2311; *www.underground-atlanta.com*), and Woodruff Arts Center (1280 Peachtree Street NE, Atlanta; 404–733–5000; *www.woodruffcenter.org*). Contact the Atlanta Convention and Visitors Bureau for complete details.

Recreation: The 1996 Olympics in Atlanta left a legacy of multi-million-dollar sporting venues, presenting Atlanta with long-term advantages for sports and special events. These venues included Centennial Olympic Stadium, renamed Turner Field (755 Hank Aaron Drive SW, Atlanta; 404–577–9100; *www.atlantabraves.com*) and the permanent home of the Atlanta Braves (404–522–7630; *www.atlantabraves.com*); the Georgia Tech Aquatic Center (Hemphill and Ferst streets; *www.gatech.edu*); Georgia International Horse Park (1996 Centennial Olympic Parkway, Conyers; 770–860–4190; *www.georgiahorsepark.com*), which now hosts traditional equestrian events as well as concerts, conventions, cultural events, trade shows, and other special events; and Stone Mountain Tennis Center (5525 Bermuda Road, Stone Mountain; 770–413–5288; *www.stonemountaintennis.com*), which attracts professional as well as local tennis tournaments. Georgia is home to 450 golf courses, many among the finest in the nation. Freedom Park (651 Dallas Street, Atlanta; *www.artinfreedompark.org*) is a 45-acre park with biking and jogging paths. The famous 180-acre Piedmont Park in midtown Atlanta has become an area for urban recreation, hosting two million visitors each year. Other fun recreational opportunities include Atlanta Cyclorama (800 Cherokee Avenue SE, Atlanta; 404–624–1071; *www.bcaatlanta.com*), Six Flags Over Georgia (275 Riverside Parkway, Austell; 770–948–9290; *www.sixflags.com*), Six Flags White Water (250 Cobb Parkway N., Marietta; 770–948–9290; *www.sixflags.com*), the World of Coca-Cola Atlanta (55 Martin Luther King, Jr. Drive, Atlanta; 404–676–5151; *www.woccatlanta.com*), Turner Field and Braves Museum, and Zoo Atlanta (800 Cherokee Avenue SE, Atlanta; 404–624–5600; *www.zooatlanta.org*). For spectators there's the National League's Atlanta Braves, the NFL's Atlanta Falcons (404–223–8000; *www.atlantafalcons.com*), the NBA's Atlanta Hawks (404–827–DUNK; *www.nba.com/hawks*), the professional men's soccer team Atlanta Silverbacks (404–508–3016; *www.atlantasilverbacks.com*), the NHL's Atlanta Thrashers (404–584–PUCK; *www.atlantathrashers.com*), and the Arena Football League's Georgia Force (770–965–4344; *www.georgiaforce.com*). Road Atlanta (5300 Winder Highway, Braselton; 770–967–6143/800–849–RACE; *www.roadatlanta.com*), located in Braselton, 45 miles north of downtown Atlanta, features International Motor Sports Association and Sports Car Club of America championship road racing, motorcycle racing, vintage car events, and amateur racing.

For the Visitor

Accommodations: The Atlanta metro area has hundreds of hotel, spa, and inn options. These are just a few of the gay-friendly places to stay in the area: Ansley Inn (253 15th Street NE; 404–872–9000/800–446–5416; *www.ansleyinn.com*) is a 1907 historic residence located in the heart of Midtown. Also in Midtown is the Shellmont Inn (821 Piedmont Avenue NE; 404–872–9290; *www.shellmont.com*), a beautifully restored 1891 mansion. Beverly Hills Inn (65 Sheridan Drive NE; 404–233–8520; *www.beverlyhillsinn.com*) is the only bed and breakfast inn to grace the charming and exclusive Buckhead neighborhood. Inman Park Bed & Breakfast – The Woodruff House (100 Waverly Way NE; 404–688–9498; *www.inmanparkbandb.com*) is the former home of Coca Cola magnet Robert W. Woodruff, this historic inn near Little Five Points is located in Inman Park. Visit the Atlanta Gay and Lesbian Travel Guide (*www.gay-atlanta.com*) for a complete list of options.

For More Information

Gay & Lesbian Center

The Rainbow Center
2684 Clairmont Road NE
Atlanta, GA 30329
404–235–6800
www.therainbowcenter.com

Publications

The Atlanta-Journal Constitution
72 Marietta Street NW, # 4
Atlanta, GA 30303
404–522–4141
www.ajc.com

Southern Voice
075 Zonolite Road, Suite 1-D
Atlanta, GA 30306
404–876–1819
www.sovo.com

Convention and Visitors Bureau

Atlanta Convention & Visitors Bureau
233 Peachtree Street NE, Suite 100
Atlanta, GA 30303
404–521–6600
www.atlanta.net

Chambers of Commerce

DeKalb County Chamber of
Commerce
750 Commerce Drive,
Suite 201
Decatur, GA 30030
404–378–8000
www.dekalbchamber.org

Metro Atlanta Chamber of
Commerce
235 Andrew Young
International Boulevard NW
Atlanta, GA 30303
404–880–9000
www.metroatlantachamber.com

Realtor

Terry York
Realtor
REMAX Greater Atlanta
1878 Piedmont Road
Atlanta, GA 30324
404–483–5866
www.terryyork.net

Kihei, Hawaii

19

A Look at Kihei

Kihei shares the sunniest, driest end of Maui with Wailea. One of the most remarkable things about Kihei is the 6-mile-long stretch of sandy beach with views of Kaho'olawe, Molokini, Lana'i and West Maui. The island is a microcosm of the world's climates and terrains. Less than 25 percent of the island's 729 square miles is inhabited and, because much of the terrain is rugged and remote, it remains pristine. The island's beauty is seen on long, sandy beaches, tropical rainforests, rolling green pasture lands, dry land forests, and spectacular rocky cliffs. Maui's average temperature is between 75 and 85 degrees, but in one day you can huddle at the top of Haleakala Crater watching a sunrise in 40-degree weather, sit on the sand at Kihei enjoying the trade winds at noon, and watch the sun set in the west in the cooler evenings. The naturalist can hike Maui's forested trails and view native plant species, watch rare birds in its wetlands, and follow the highways of ancient chiefs. Small shopping malls, a bustling farmer's market, activity centers, and a host of family restaurants and sundown mai tai spots enliven the scene. Everyone eventually ends up at Azeka's Market to buy old-fashioned Maui potato chips and Azeka's famous barbecued ribs. If there is one reason for Maui's enduring popularity it is its diversity. The island dazzles and soothes almost at the same time.

Possible drawbacks: Paradise comes at a price—a high price. Because only a quarter of the island is developed, property is expensive both to rent and purchase. The gay community in this small town is fun and pleasant, but you won't find the services and opportunities of a big city.

▶ Nickname:
The Island of Aloha

▶ County:
Maui

▶ Area code:
808

▶ Time zone:
Hawaii Standard (no DST)

▶ Population:
16,749

▶ County population:
128,094

▶ Region:
Central Western Coast

▶ Closest metro area:
Honolulu, Hawaii

▶ Average home price:
$500,000

▶ Fabulous reasons to live here:
Perfect weather; white sand beaches; laid-back atmosphere; casual, open GLBT community; arts and artists; recreation

Climate

Elevation 7'	Avg. high/low(F°)	Avg. inches		Avg. # days precip.	Avg. % humidity
		rain	snow		
Jan.	76/59	3.4	–	10	72%
April	78/60	0.9	–	10	66%
July	82/65	0.1	–	7	63%
Oct.	82/64	0.7	–	7	65%
YEAR	80/62	13.9	–	96	66%
# days 32° or below: 0			# days 90° or warmer: 24		

Local Connections

Gas company: The Gas Company (808–877–6557; *www.hawaiigas.com*)

Electric company: Maui Electric Co. Ltd. (808–565–6445; *www.mauielectric.com*)

Phone companies: Pacific Lightnet Inc. (808–270–2250; *www.plni.net*); MCI Telecommunciations (808–667–7591; *www.mci.com*)

Water and sewer: County of Maui Department of Water Supply (808–270–7730; *www.mauiwater.org*)

Cable company: Oceanic Time Warner Cable (808–871–7303; *www.oceanic.com*)

Car registration, license: Kihei Department of Motor Vehicles (808–270–7363); Maui District Tax Office (808–984–8500; *www.hawaii.gov*)

New residents must obtain a Hawaii drivers license before their current license expires. A short written exam is required. Road test may be waived. Some bicycles and all mopeds are required to be registered. The permanent registration fee is $15. If you obtain an out-of-state permit (fee: $10) your out-of-state plates are valid until their expiration date or for 12 months, whichever occurs first. The Vehicle Use Tax is waved for transferred out-of-state vehicles older than three months.

The Tax Ax

Sales tax: 4 percent; hotel tax 11.42 percent

State income tax: 1.4–8.25 percent graduated, based on income

Property tax: Property Taxes on Maui are based on the usage, with the highest rate charged on units used for vacation rental. Lowest are for owner-occupied. Homes generally are not zoned for vacation rental, although some condos are. The tax ranges from $3.75 per thousand of value to approximately $8 per thousand. There are exemptions available for seniors and disabled.

Local Real Estate

Overview: The area has beautiful single-family homes near the beaches or with views. Many of the condos in south Maui are vacation rental/resort properties. If planning a move to Maui it is suggested that you rent a short-term vacation rental while shopping for something permanent and schedule your move for spring or summer to avoid the winter season when little if anything is available.

Median price for a single-family home: $600,000

Average price for a single-family home: $500,000

Average price for a 2BR condo: $250,000

Rental housing market: The rental housing market is quite tight. When available, one-bedroom cottages or condos start at $1,000 per month; two bedrooms $1,300. Single-family homes start at $2,000 and up per month.

Gay-friendly neighborhoods: All of Kihei is gay-friendly. Maui is a very friendly island so neighborhood choices will be based on needs such as space, size, and views.

Nearby areas to consider: Lahaina is often called Maui's crown jewel. This small, historic community, once an old whaling port, has provided a home for many cultures over the centuries. It's one of Maui's most visited cities and offers spectacular views of the calm waters of the Auau Channel facing Lana'i Island and the glorious peaks of the West Maui mountain range Mauna Kahalawai. Home to artists and entrepreneurs, the community has frequent special events, festivals, and gallery nights.

Earning a Living

Per capita income: $21,591

Median household income: $50,738

Business climate: Maui is home to a $19.5 million super-computer, now making the island a major center for international business, technology, research, and communication. In addition, the Maui county government has not only rolled out the red carpet for new businesses but streamlined procedures and adopted innovative business support programs.

Help in starting a business: The Maui Economic Developsment Board (808–875–2300; *www.medb.org*) provides information on the islands many programs. The Maui Research and Technology Park (808–539–3806; *www.mrtc.org*) provides services including office support programs, accounting and consulting services, leading edge data and telecommunications capabilities, access to low-interest loans, and a marketing umbrella. Additionally, the Maui Chamber of Commerce offers networking, advertising, and educational opportunities.

Job market: The island has a deep-water harbor, major airport, and superior telecommunication systems, creating a pro-high-tech environment. Additionally, arts, entertainment, recreation, accommodation, and food services; educational, health, and social services; and retail trade provide many opportunities.

The Community

Overview: Maui's GLBT community is friendly and laid back. Although there aren't many formal venues where the community comes together, there are frequent events, dinners, parties, and fundraisers throughout the island, and guests are always encouraged to join in the fun. Pick up a copy of *Odyssey Hawaii* (*www.odysseyhawaii.com*) for listings of events throughout the state.

Community organizations: There is no GLBT community center on Maui. Out In Maui (808–244–4566) and the Women's Hotline (808–573–3077) both present recorded info on current area GLBT events and activities. There are several support organizations, including the Maui AIDS Foundation (808–242–4900); Bridges (808–242–6821), the island's GLBT youth group; PFLAG (808–879–0097); Aloha Metropolitan Community Church (808–283–8483); and, Dignity/Maui (808–874–3950).

Medical care: Maui Memorial Hospital in Wailuku (808–244–9056; *www.mmmc.hhsc.org*) is licensed for 196 beds and employs nearly 700; it's the oldest and largest acute-care facility of the Hawaii Health Systems Corporation-operated facilities. The new hospital was named "Malulani" (Protection of Heaven) by Queen Kapiolani and began operations in 1884. Hana Medical Center (808–248–8924)) provides prevention-oriented health care, acute and chronic care, urgent care, dental care, and limited laboratory testing and x-ray services to East Maui's isolated population of 3,000.

Nuptials: The State of Hawaii has a law similar to DOMA defining marriage as between a man and a woman. Maui is a popular destination for commitment ceremonies. *GayOnMaui.com* and *LesbianOnMaui.com* (800–503–9840) will help you create the ceremony of your dreams either on one of the beautiful beaches or another special island spot.

Getting Around Town

Public transportation: Maui Public Transit System (808–270–7511; *www.co.maui.hi.us/bus*) provides bus service Monday through Saturday on three public routes that connect the major cities of Maui. Fare: one-way $1; all-day pass $10.

Roads: SR30, SR31, SR37, SR350

Airports: There are many airports connecting the island chain; Hawaii's Department of Transportation (808–872–3893; *www.hawaii.gov/dot/airports*) maintains a comprehensive list. Kahului Airport (airport code: OGG), 9 miles from Kihei, is the main airport with facilities for domestic overseas and interisland commercial service; Hana Airport (airport code: HNM) supports commuter, unscheduled air taxi, and general aviation activities.

It's a Gay Life

Annual events: Maui's resident population represents an ethnic mix of Caucasians, Japanese, Filipinos, Hawaiians, and Chinese. This melting pot has created a unique cultural mix that extends to activities open to everyone. Each summer the Japanese population holds colorful lantern-lit Bon Dances. Aloha Week (*www.alohafestivals.com*) in the fall celebrates the first king to unite the islands, Kamehameha, with parades and exhibits. There are Filipino barrio fiestas, and church feasts in the primarily Portuguese communities on the Upcountry slopes. Kaanapali hosts the annual Maui Onion Festival (*www.whalersvillage.com*) at summer's end. A major annual Maui Music Festival (*www.mauimusicfestival.com*) draws acclaimed musicians from around the world, and there are cultural and food festivals throughout the year.

Nightlife: The fun doesn't stop with the setting sun. Kihei's nightlife includes sports bars, karaoke spots, and a comedy club. There are sizzling night clubs all over Lahaina, Kaanapali, Kahului, Wailea, Kihei, and Makawao. They range from the latest LA–style rage to cheek-to-cheek. Check the local *Maui News* (808–244–3981; *www.mauinews.com*) and free tourist publications to see who is playing where. Hapa's Nightclub (41 East Lipoa Street; 800–879–9100; *www.hapas-maui.com*), located in the heart of Kihei, is the area's only gay club. Tuesday night is Gay Hawaii night in this otherwise straight hot spot. It is currently Gay Maui's only club where visitors and locals alike go for drinks and dancing.

Culture: Although it's known for its natural beauty, Maui is also a cultural center of the Islands, a place where music, art, and a spirited international film festival complement the casual Maui lifestyle, providing world-class offerings in both the visual and performing arts. This sun-blessed, breeze-swept island in the middle of the blue Pacific has more than 50 art galleries and a thriving colony of artists, many with international reputations. Friday is Art Night in Lahaina, when gallery browsers are offered music, complimentary wine, and hors d'oeuvres. Even the lusty whalers of Lahaina left their mark on the arts. Lahaina, with more than 40 Maui scrimshanders, is the largest market for scrimshaw in the world, specializing in both antique and contemporary pieces. The Maui Arts & Cultural Center (MACC) (One Cameron Way, Kahului; 808–242–7469; *www.mauiarts.org*) in Kahului hosts performances and events and is home to the Maui Symphony Orchestra (808–244–5439; *www.mauisymphony.com*), an active contributor to the cultural life of the island, performing regularly at the MACC with excellent symphonic musicians from the community. The MACC also hosts regular "First Light" screenings and café theater events for the Maui film community, which goes into rapturous celebration of the film arts with the annual spring Maui Film Festival (808–579–9244; *www.mauifilmfestival.com*) at Wailea. Committed to compassionate and life-affirming storytelling, the festival is highly regarded nationally.

Recreation: In an hour or two, you can travel from the stark beauty of a lava flow to the luxuriant green of a rain forest, from balmy beaches swept by sea foam to the alpine tundra of a dormant volcano. Maui is home to 10 state parks, 94 county parks and community centers (*www.co.maui.hi.us/parks*), Haleakala National Park (*www.halekala.national-park.com*), and 16 golf courses. Players of every handicap will find a challenge at the Silverwood, Kihei's public course.

The quintessential tropical beaches (*www.hawaiiweb.com/maui/beaches*) Memorial Beach Park, Kalepolepo, Waipuilani, and the three beaches of Kamaole are wide, sandy, and sunny. Big Beach and Little Beach, in the Makena District at Maui's southern end, are well worth the drive. The far end of the beach is the gay end and nudity, though officially illegal, is common. Also on the southern coast, in the waters off Grand Wailea Resort (3850 Wailea Alanui, Wailea, Maui; 808–875–1234; *www.grandwailea.com*), lies the marine preserve of Molokini with the exposed rim of a submerged, extinct volcano. Molokini's clear, protected waters attract colorful and curious pelagic fish—and the equally curious divers and snorkelers who sail out to meet them each day. At the north end of Kihei is the national Wildlife Conservation District, Kealia Pond (808–875–1582), a salt-water marsh that is a refuge for the Hawaiian stilt and coot, birds that are on the endangered species list. Nearby Kihei, the harbor at Maalaea is the launching site for an armada of pleasure boats taking visitors on charter fishing excursions, whale-watching expeditions, and snorkel trips to Molokini. The nearby Lana'i Cathedrals is considered to be one of the most beautiful dive sites in the world. Glass-bottom boats and even a pleasure submarine open up the wonders of the Hawaiian reef to non-swimmers.

For the Visitor

Accommodations: There are many condominiums, small hotels, and cottages along Kihei's beach road, as well as luxury resorts throughout the island. Located in lively central Kihei is Bali House (22 Waimahaihai Street; 808–875–8501), a gay guest house within walking distance to beaches, parks, dining, shopping, and nightlife. The Maui Sunseeker Inn (551 S. Kihei Road; 808–879–1261/800–532–6284; *www.mauisunseeker.com*) is a romantic, friendly, and welcoming place for you to drop your bags and to use as your home base while exploring all that the island of Maui has to offer.

For More Information

Publication

Maui News
P.O. Box 550
Wailuku, Maui, HI 96793
808–244–3981
www.mauinews.com

Convention and Visitors Bureau

Maui Visitors Bureau
1727 Wili Pa Loop
Wailuku, Maui, HI 96793
808–244–3530
www.visitmaui.com

Chamber of Commerce

Maui Chamber of Commerce
250 Alamaha Street, Unit N-16A
Kahului, Maui, HI 96732
808–871–7711
www.mauichamber.com

Realtor

Jack St.Germain
Owner, PB
Maui Suncoast Realty and Vacation Rental
2837 Panepoo Street, Suite 220
Kihei, HI 96753
808–874–1048
www.mauisuncoast.com

Chicago, Illinois

A Look at Chicago

Located on the shores of Lake Michigan in the heart of the Midwest, Chicago is a virtual explosion of cultural activity and multicultural expression. As the birthplace of modern building, historic landmarks and contemporary technological masterpieces by genius architects such as Daniel Burnham, Louis Sullivan, and Frank Lloyd Wright, among many others, Chicago's skyline is a living museum of architecture. The city's diverse collections of museums explore a variety of subjects including natural history, art, culture, and astronomy. The theater scene rivals New York in its originality and talent. The "Magnificent Mile" offers hundreds of specialty shops offering goods from around the world. Thousands of restaurants serve a medley of culinary delights; Chinatown, Greektown, West Rogers Park, and Pilsen are among the neighborhoods offering tempting tastes from around the world. Chicago is home to world-championship sports teams, an internationally acclaimed symphony orchestra, and several of the nation's best colleges and universities. A well-educated, diverse workforce helps the city evolve through changing economic times. With so much at their doorstep, it's no surprise that Chicagoans have a great sense of civic pride. Residents love calling Chicago home.

Possible drawbacks: Try as they might, the moniker "The Windy City" remains a title for Chicago. Bitter winds off Lake Michigan are furious in the winter months, often pushing temperatures 40 degrees below zero. High crime rates and violence continue to plague sections of the city.

▶ Nickname:
The City of Big Shoulders

▶ County: Cook

▶ Area codes:
312; 773

▶ Time zone:
Central

▶ Population:
2,896,016

▶ County population:
9,157,540

▶ Region:
Northeast Illinois

▶ Average home price:
$425,000

▶ Fabulous reasons to live here:
Midwest at its finest; amazing architecture; proud, well-supported GLBT community; strong evolving economy; arts, culture, and recreation

Climate

Elevation 596'	Avg. high/low(F°)	Avg. inches		Avg. # days precip.	Avg. % humidity
		rain	snow		
Jan.	30/16	1.9	11.2	11	74%
April	59/39	3.8	1.6	13	67%
July	84/65	3.7	–	10	71%
Oct.	63/44	2.8	0.4	9	70%
YEAR	59/41	37.8	38.5	125	71%
# days 32° or below: 88			# days 90° or warmer: 47		

Local Connections

Gas company: Peoples Energy (866–556–6001; *www.peoplesenergy.com*)

Electric company: Commonwealth Edison (ComEd), a division of Exelon Corp. (800–334–7661; *www.exeloncorp.com/comed*)

Phone company: SBC Communications (800–244–4444; *www.sbc.com*)

Water and sewer: City of Chicago Water and Filtration (312–747–9090; *www.cityofchicago.org/WaterManagement*)

Cable companies: Comcast (800–COMCAST; *www.comcast.com*); RCN (800–RING–RCN; *www.rcn.com*); WideOpenWest (866–496–9669; *www.wowway.com*)

Car registration/License: Driver Services (312–814–2975; *www.sos.state.il.us/departments/drivers*)

Drivers moving to Illinois have 90 days to obtain a license. A vision screening, a written exam, and possibly a driving test are required when surrendering an out-of-state license. License is valid for four years. Fee: $10. Original, duplicate, or corrected title fee: $65. License plates: $78 (vehicle gross weight under 8,000 lbs.).

The Tax Ax

Sales tax: 9 percent

State income tax: 3.5 percent (flat rate)

Property tax: Cook County Treasurer's Office (312–443–5100; *www.cookcountytreasurer.com*)

Chicago property tax is imposed by counties, townships, municipalities, school districts, and special taxing districts, so taxes can vary widely by area. Most property is assessed every two years at a third of the fair market value.

Local Real Estate

Overview: There's a mix of housing styles in Chicago. The older neighborhoods feature many Victorian homes. Along the lakeshore and throughout the city are many high-rise buildings with all of the expected amenities and lake views. Most of the northern city neighborhoods have tree-lined streets, and the further north you go the lots grow larger. One of the charms of Chicago neighborhoods is that they're walkable areas.

Median price for a single-family home: $739,665

Average price for a single-family home: $425,000

Average price for a 2BR condo: $275,000

Rental housing market: Two-bedroom apartments on the gay-friendly north side rent for approximately $1,500.

Gay-friendly neighborhoods: "Boystown" or Lakeview straddling Halstead, Near North, Andersonville, Ravenswood, Old Town, and Lincoln Park are all popular GLBT community neighborhoods.

Nearby areas to consider: The Village of Oak Park is a home-rule suburb just north of Chicago with a large GLBT community. It boasts median household incomes almost 50 percent higher than the national average. The city is the birthplace of Ernest Hemingway, Ray Kroc (founder of McDonald's), astronauts, chemists, and a Miss America. The village was Frank Lloyd Wright's home for 20 years, and its two historic districts contain 25 of his buildings along with excellent examples of Prairie and Victorian architecture. These artistic, business, and scientific influences are still embraced and encouraged with excellent schools, high-quality medical care, well-funded libraries, preservation of historic architecture, and a strong community spirit.

Earning a Living

Per capita income: $20,175

Median household income: $38,625

Business climate: Second only to New York in the number of Fortune 500 companies, the city is a global center of commerce and boasts great overall business strength. High-tech job demand continues to grow, but the city's economy is diverse, with no single sector controlling job demand or creation. This diversity helps Chicago flex with changing times.

Help in starting a business: The Chicago Area Gay & Lesbian Chamber of Commerce (*www.glchamber.org*) provides networking, promotions, and marketing opportunities and works with area businesses to attract tourism. The Chicagoland Chamber of Commerce (*www.chicagolandchamber.org*) has many programs to help business owners, including the Chicagoland Entrepreneurial Center with information, education, and support for new and existing small businesses in Chicago.

Job market: The U.S. government is the area's largest employer. The educational, health, and social services; professional, scientific, management, administrative, and waste management services; and manufacturing, arts, leisure, and tourism sectors all provide jobs in Chicago.

The Community

Overview: One word describes Chicago's GLBT community: pride. It's obvious when you walk through the streets, watch one of the many GLBT league games, attend the rallies, or talk to local community members. Chicago's GLBT community is supported by local government, with both the mayor's office and police department having GLBT liaisons who work closely with the community. Out elected and appointed officials and judges are parts of Chicago's political landscape.

Community organizations: Chicago's large and active community has hundreds of health, support, recreation, and social groups. Under construction and expected to open in 2006, the new Center on Halstead will provide a much-needed physical hub for the city's GLBT community. Center on Halsted (*www.centeronhalsted.org*) currently provides programs designed to address a wide range of needs in GLBT community. Center on Halsted also maintains a comprehensive list of area groups and provides a help line (773–929–4357). The GLBT community honors its biggest contributors and supporters by inducting them into the Chicago Gay and Lesbian Hall of Fame (*www.glhalloffame.org*).

Medical care: More than 40 hospitals offer healthcare in Chicago. Howard Brown Health Center (773–388–1600; *www.howardbrown.org*) is the leading provider of services for meeting the challenges of HIV/AIDS in the Midwest and is on the forefront of medical and psychosocial services to the LGBT community. Howard Brown offers a comprehensive range of services for men and women including: comprehensive medical services for both men and women; laboratory and diagnostic services; reproductive health/family planning (including alternative insemination); nutritional counseling; in-house Walgreen's pharmacy; individual and group counseling; education and outreach; youth services, including the Youth Drop-In Clinic and counseling; research; and HIV/AIDS services, including anonymous HIV and STD testing

Nuptials: The State of Illinois has passed laws defining marriage to the exclusion of same-sex couples. The Cook County Clerk's Office (*www.cookctyclerk.com*) registers same-sex couples as domestic partners, and commitment and union ceremonies are common.

Getting Around Town

Public transportation: Bus and rail services are offered by Chicago Transit Authority (312–836–7000; *www.transitchicago.com*). Fare: one-way $1.75; transfer 25 cents; one-day visitor pass $5. Regional Rail Transit (312–322–6777; *www.metra.com*) connects the city center to the surrounding area. Fares are zone-based and start at $1.85. METRA also offers an unlimited weekend ride pass ($5). Chicago Trolley Service (773–648–5000; *www.chicagotrolley.com*) provides tours and hop-on/hop-off service with unlimited daily ride passes starting at $18.

Roads: I-55, I-90, US41

Airports: O'Hare International Airport (airport code: ORD) (800–832–6352; *www.flychicago.com/ohare*) is one of the busiest airports in the world, servicing 45 commercial, commuter, and cargo airlines. Midway International Airport (airport code: MDW) (773–838–0600; *www.flychicago.com/midway*), with its convenient location and low-cost airfares, is one of the fastest-growing airports in North America.

It's a Gay Life

Annual events: PrideChicago (*www.chicagopridecalendar.org*) is the last Sunday in June, but a month of events lead up to the big day including parties, lectures, fundraising events that include Pride Run, local television programming, and Halsted Tastes Better. The community celebrates Halloween with a parade and costume contest. A sponsor of many of Chicago's GLBT community events, Northalsted Merchants Association (773–883–0500; *www.northalsted.com*) hosts Market Days, a huge Boystown street fair, in August. Lots of other annual events take place around Chicago including the Chicago Improv Festival (*www.cif.com*), Chicago Blues Festival (*www.chicagobluesfestival.org*), Chicago Outdoor Film Festival (*www.chicagoparkdistrict.com*), and much more.

Nightlife: The food is fabulous; live music, comedy, and theater abound; and bars stay open late, making for fun nights on the town. More than a hundred bars, clubs, and restaurants cater to the community in Chicago. N. Halsted, N. Clark, and Belmont form a triangle around the action. Lakeview, called Boystown, is in the center. You'll quickly discover that Chicago is different from other large gay-enclave cities. The community isn't slick and polished, and you won't spend time out on the street hoping to be admitted into the clubs; instead, a friendly Midwest attitude prevails. The community is grounded, friendly, and social. *Gay Chicago Magazine* (*www.gaychicagomagazine.com*) and *Boys Town Chicago* (*www.boystownchicago.com*) are fabulous sources for listings of bars, current events, and gay-Chicago news.

Culture: Chicago is home to 54 museums, more than 200 theaters, the world-class Chicago Symphony Orchestra (312–294–3000; *www.cso.org*), and Ballet Chicago (312–251–8838; *www.balletchicago.org*). Chicago's Museum Campus (*www.museumcampus.org*) is a scenic park with easy access to the Adler Planetarium & Astronomy Museum (1300 S. Lake Shore Drive; 312–922–STAR; *www.adlerplanetarium.org*), the Shedd Aquarium/Oceanarium (1200 S. Lake Shore Drive; 312–939–2438; *www.sheddaquarium.org*), and the Field Museum of Natural History (1400 S. Lake Shore Drive; 312–922–9410; *www.fieldmuseum.org*). The Shedd Aquarium offers the world's largest array of more than 8,000 aquatic mammals, reptiles, amphibians, invertebrates, and fish. After exploring the oceans, attendees can gaze up at the heavens in the nearby Adler Planetarium & Astronomy Museum. The Field Museum offers exciting displays of mummies, Egyptian tombs, Native American artifacts, and dinosaur skeletons. Other Chicago museums include the Chicago Historical Society (Clark Street at North Avenue; 312–642–4600; *www.chicagohs.org*), the city's oldest cultural institution, the Museum of Science and Industry (5700 S. Lake Shore Drive; 773–684–1414; *www.msichicago.org*), the DuSable Museum of African-American History (740 East 56th Place; 773–947–0600; *www.dusablemuseum.org*), the Art Institute of Chicago (111 S. Michigan Avenue; 312–443–3600; *www.artic.edu*), one of the world's leading art museums, the Museum of Contemporary Art (220 E. Chicago Avenue; 312–280–2660; *www.mcachicago.org*), and the Museum of Contemporary Photography (600 S. Michigan Avenue; 312–663–5554; *www.nocp.org*). In addition, Chicago's latest showcase is Millennium Park (Welcome Center at 201 E. Randolph Street; 312–742–1168; *www.millenniumpark.org*). The 24.5-acre park has instantly become a world-class attraction and a Chicago landmark. It contains an outdoor performing arts pavilion, indoor year-round theater, restaurant, ice-skating rink, contemporary garden, public art, fountains, promenade area for special events, and landscaped walkways and green spaces.

Recreation: Chicago's spectacular lakefront and parks provide golf, running, fishing, sailing, bicycling, and many other recreational sports. Navy Pier (600 E. Grand Avenue; 312–595–PIER; *www.navypier.com*) is the city's lakefront playground and the state's most popular attraction. Navy Pier offers visitors a unique blend of family-oriented attractions from the thrilling ride on the Wave Swinger in Pier Park to the 3-D Time Escape ride. The Pier also boasts the 150-foot-high Ferris wheel, a musical carousel, the Chicago Children's Museum (700 E. Grand Avenue; 312–527–1000; *www.chichildrensmuseum.org*), a variety of restaurants and the Chicago Shakespeare Theatre (800 E. Grand Avenue; 312–595–5600; *www.chicagoshakes.com*). Other attractions not to miss include Buckingham Fountain at Grant Park (*www.chicagoparkdistrict.com*), the Hancock Observatory (John Hancock Center; 875 N. Michigan Avenue; 312–751–3681; *www.hancock-observatory.com*), and the Sears Tower Skydeck (233 S. Wacker Drive; 312–875–9696; *www.the-skydeck.com*). One baseball team isn't enough for Chicago, home to MLB's National League Chicago Cubs (773–404–CUBS; *www.cubs.com*) and the American League's Chicago White Sox (312– 674– 1000; *www.chisox.com*). Likewise, there are two hockey teams: the NHL's Chicago Blackhawks (312–455–7000; *www.chiblackhawks.com*) and the AHL's Chicago Wolves (847–724–GOAL; *www.chicagowolves.com*). Chicago spectators also root for the NBA's Chicago Bulls (312–455–4000; *www.nba.com/bulls*), the NFL's Chicago Bears (847–295–6600; *www.chicagobears.com*), Major League Soccer's Chicago Fire (312–705–7200; *www.chicago-fire.com*) and Arena Football League's Chicago Rush (773–243–3434; *www.chicagorush.com*)

For the Visitor

Accommodations: With about 100,000 available rooms in the Chicago metro area it's easy to find something to suit your desires. There's a fine array of gay-friendly accommodations, too. Boystown/Lakeview is among one of the GLBT centers of Chicago. Here are just a few options to help you plan your stay. Best Western Hawthorne Terrace (3434 N. Broadway; 773–244–3434/888–675–2378; *www.hawthorneterrace.com*) is a boutique hotel with 59 rooms and suites featuring the warmth and charm of a vintage hotel combined with modern amenities. Majestic Hotel (528 W. Brompton Avenue; 773–404–3499/800–727–5108; *www.cityinns.com*) is reminiscent of a quaint English inn with Dickensian touches such as poster beds and tapestry furnishings. Villa Toscana B&B (3447 N. Halstead Street; 773–404–2643/800–404–2643; *www.villa-toscana.com*) is a Victorian-style bed and breakfast in the heart of Boystown.

For More Information

Gay & Lesbian Center
Center on Halsted
961 W. Montana, 2nd Floor
Chicago, IL 60614
773–472–6469
www.centeronhalsted.org

Publications
Chicago Tribune
435 N. Michigan Avenue
Chicago, IL 60611
800–874–2863
www.chicagotribune.com

Chicago Free Press
5115 N. Clark Street
Chicago, IL 60640
773–325–0005
www.chicagofreepress.com

Convention and Visitors Bureau
Chicago Convention and Tourism Bureau
2301 S. Lake Shore Drive
Chicago, IL 60616
877–244–2246
www.chicago.il.org

Chambers of Commerce
Chicago Area Gay & Lesbian Chamber of Commerce
1210 W. Rosedale
Chicago, IL 60660
773–303–0167
www.glchamber.org

Chicagoland Chamber of Commerce
One IBM Plaza
330 N. Wabash, Suite 2800
Chicago, IL 60611-3605
312–494–6700
www.chicagolandchamber.org

Realtor
Baird & Warner
120 South Lasalle
Chicago, IL 60603
800–644–1855
bairdwarner.com

## 21

New Orleans, Louisiana

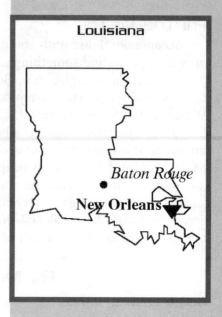

A Look at New Orleans

Jazz streams out into the moonlight, French doors open to the night breezes, sweet olive scents the air. Nearby there is laughter, a cork popping, and café brûlot aflame. Welcome to New Orleans. Here, in this little corner of Europe and the Caribbean in the American South, the history is as colorful as the local architecture; the food is the stuff of legend. Haitian and African Creoles developed an exotic, spicy cuisine. The street names are French and Spanish, and the European and Creole architecture comes in a carnival of tropical colors. The magic is irresistible. New Orleans may be the most fragrant city in the world. The scents are ubiquitous and intoxicating. Sweet olive mingles with gardenias; the magnolias intertwine with honeysuckle and night-blooming jasmine. The air is dense and sweet, drifting as currents do along the river breezes. Fragrance, however, is the only atmospheric excess. True, occasionally it rains with tropical abandon, making music as the drops hit wide banana leaves and palm fronds, but the torrents are short-lived. The original city planners chose high ground for the French Quarter, so it doesn't flood. The climate is mild and pleasant most of the year—a cross between the Mediterranean and the Caribbean.

Possible drawbacks: Although the area's economy is improving, the city still makes a living off tourism, and that translates into service-industry jobs. The summer heat and humidity can be overwhelming.

▶ Nickname:
The Big Easy

▶ County: Orleans

▶ Area code: 504

▶ Time zone:
Central

▶ Population:
484,674

▶ County population:
1,200,000

▶ Region:
Southern Louisiana

▶ Average home price:
$330,000

▶ Fabulous reasons to live here:
Nightlife; music; culture; recreation; excellent food; large, organized GLBT community

Climate

Elevation 11'	Avg. high/low(F°)	Avg. inches		Avg. # days precip.	Avg. % humidity
		rain	snow		
Jan.	63/45	5.7	–	10	76%
April	78/60	4.8	–	7	74%
July	91/75	6.4	–	14	79%
Oct.	80/62	2.8	–	6	74%
YEAR	78/61	62.2	0.1	115	76%
# days 32° or below: 9			# days 90° or warmer: 72		

Local Connections

Gas and electric company: Entergy Louisiana (800–368–3749; *www.entergy-louisiana.com*)

Phone companies: Bell South (888–757–6500; *www.bellsouth.com*); Sprint (800–877–7746; *www.sprint.com*); among others

Water and sewer: Sewage and Water Board of New Orleans (504–529–2837; *www.swbnola.org*)

Cable company: Comcast (800–266–2278; *www.comcast.com*)

Car registration/License: Louisiana Office of Motor Vehicles 877–368–5463; *omv.dps.state.la.us*

New residents have 30 days to get a Louisiana driver's license and transfer auto registration. No written or road tests are required when transferring a valid out-of-state license. Fee: $24.50. Title fee: $18.50. Use tax of 1 percent of vehicle book value (minimum tax $100) is due on all vehicles registered in Louisiana. Credit can be given for up to 4 percent for tax paid in reciprocal agreement states. License plate fees are bi-annual and also based upon the vehicle selling price. Minimum plate fee: $20.

The Tax Ax

Sales tax: 9 percent

State income tax: 2–6 percent graduated, based on income

Property tax: Residential properties are assessed at 10 percent of fair market value and the mileage is $171 per thousand of assessment. A $75,000 homestead exemption is available on the first $75,000 in value to an owner occupant.

Local Real Estate

Overview: The vast majority of the urban architecture hails from the mid-to-late-19th century. Details usually include tall (12+ foot) ceilings and wood floors (heart of pine) but may also contain plaster crown molding, ceiling medallions, wainscoting, and vintage bath fixtures. Most housing is multi-family, so a single-family residence commands a real premium. Whereas there was no need to accommodate an automobile in the 19th century many, if not most, have no off-street parking. Most of the historic districts are located in walking neighborhoods with adequate on-street parking.

Median price for a single-family home: $250,000

Average price for a single-family home: $330,000

Average price for a 2BR condo: $225,000

Rental housing market: From apartments and condos to houses and historic slave quarters, New Orleans provides rentals from $700.

Gay-friendly neighborhoods: All of the historic districts are gay-friendly, including the French Quarter, Lower Garden District, Garden District, Faubourg Marigny, Bywater, Treme, Irish Channel, Faubourg St. John, Carrollton, Uptown, and warehouse district

Nearby areas to consider: Two New Orleans suburbs are popular with the GLBT community. Metaire, at the center of Jefferson Parish on the shores of Lake Pontchartrain and Ellen DeGeneres's hometown, is an early suburb of New Orleans. The community provides all the basics of daily living, including parks, office buildings, and shopping centers, but boasts classic neighborhoods, Mardi Gras, Fat City, the Zephyer Baseball Stadium, the New Orleans Saints training facilities, and great southern people. On the opposite, north shore of the lake, connected by the 24-mile Lake Pontchartrain Causeway, is Slidel, the Camellia City. This family-oriented suburb has the best schools in the state of Louisiana. The city is home to many cultural festivals, community parks, great shopping, and first-class restaurants.

Earning a Living

Per capita income: $17,258

Median household income: $27,133

Business climate: New Orleans is embracing a new business attitude. Business real estate values are attractive, and the Downtown Development District initiatives on Canal Street and the surrounding neighborhood have created an accessible and beautiful environment. The city is known as a top tourist destination, though it's also home to one of the nation's largest and most modern seaports, making it a Latin American gateway. The entrepreneurial spirit is embraced and a good quality of life and tropical climate add to the attractive future of New Orleans.

Help in starting a business: Greater New Orleans Inc. is the Regional Economic Alliance and works to create new jobs in southeast Louisiana and market the parishes to companies seeking to relocate, as well as retain and expand existing businesses in the region. GNO's professional economic development staff is available at all times to work with companies interested in locating operations in the New Orleans region or expanding existing facilities.

Job market: Most of the area's jobs are tourism-related, including arts, entertainment, recreation, accommodation, and food services. Other market sectors include educational, health, and social services.

The Community

Overview: The New Orleans GLBT community is large, friendly, active, and visible. City residents reflect the historic, multi-cultural influences. Visitors usually experience the French Quarter's frenetic, carnival atmosphere during major events such as Mardi Gras and Southern Decadence, though the city actually enjoys a laid-back, live-and-let-live attitude.

Community organizations: The Lesbian and Gay Community Center of New Orleans is an information and referral center that also hosts a variety of local community group meetings and events. The city's large GLBT community is home to dozens of social, spiritual, health, and support groups. Gay New Orleans (*www.gayneworleans.com*), *Ambush Magazine*'s online portal, maintains a comprehensive list of the city's many groups and organizations.

Medical care: There are approximately 20 hospitals and rehabilitation centers in New Orleans. NO/AIDS Task Force (504–821–2601; *www.noaidstaskforce.org*) has been delivering HIV/AIDS services since its inception in 1983. The agency offers a continuum of services, including prevention education (street and community outreach, venue-based outreach, condom distribution, and community mobilization targeting men who have sex with men), HIV antibody testing and counseling, the statewide HIV/AIDS hotline, case management, case finding, housing coordination, early intervention/primary medical care, mental health, support groups, home delivered meals, food bank, peer support services, housing case management, and medication disbursement.

Nuptials: Louisiana has amended its state constitution and bans gay marriage. The city remains a popular destination for commitment ceremonies, and a large number of gay couples call the city and surrounding area home.

Getting Around Town

Public transportation: New Orleans Regional Transit Authority (504–827–7802; *www.regionaltransit.org*) provides bus service throughout the region and streetcar service in New Orleans. Standard fare: $1.25; unlimited rides day pass $5.

Roads: I-10, I-610, US11, US61, US90

Airport: Louis Armstrong New Orleans International Airport (airport code: MSY) (504–464–0831; *www.flymsy.com*) is 20 minutes from the city center.

It's a Gay Life

Annual events: "Laissez les bons temps rouler" ("Let the good times roll") is more than a reminder of New Orleans' French heritage; it's a way of life that began three centuries ago. A cultural gumbo, New Orleans celebrates differences.

In fact, they celebrate almost anything in the Big Easy. The community has several major annual events, including spring's Gay Mardi Gras (*www.gaymardigras.com*) and the Gay Easter Parade (*www.gayeasterparade.com*) and Labor Day Weekend's Southern Decadence (*www.southerndecadence.net*). Gay Pride (*www.gayprideneworleans.com*) is celebrated at Armstrong Park in late September and a circuit party fundraiser for Halloween (*www.gayhalloween.com*). Just a few of the other New Orleans annual events include the Nokia Sugar Bowl (*www.nokiasugarbowl.com*), Jazz and Heritage Festival (*www.nojazzfest.com*), International Arts Festival (*www.internationalartsfestival.com*), and the New Orleans Film Festival (*www.neworleansfilmfest.com*).

Nightlife: The origins of "Big Easy" go back to the turn of the century and a famed dance hall of that name. Eventually, the nickname transferred to the city as a whole, referring to the gentle pace of life and somewhat lax morals for which New Orleans is known. Most bars are open around-the-clock, and the liquor laws are relaxed. Just be sure to ask your bartender for a "go cup," because glass and cans aren't allowed on the French Quarter streets. Of the hundreds of bars in the city, there are dozens of favorites among the GLBT community. One of the nation's oldest gay bars, Café Lafitte in Exile (901 Bourbon Street; 504–522–8397; *www.lafittes.com*) is where everyone eventually spends time. Lafitte's has many themed nights, drink specials, and eclectic music and videos. Upstairs, The Balcony Bar, with excellent views of Bourbon Street, is a great place to work your beads. The Gay New Orleans Guide (*www.gayneworleansguide.com*) has a fabulous list of the city's bars with detailed descriptions.

Culture: New Orleans is a giant, outdoor museum, one big block party, a never-ending concert, and a food lover's paradise. There are glorious parades, brassy bands, haunted houses, historic Streetcars and paddle wheelers, the Audubon Zoo (6500 Magazine Street; 866–ITS–AZOO; *www.auduboninstitute.org/zoo*), a world-class zoo, festivals for every occasion, Aquarium of the Americas (1 Canal Street; 800–774–7394; *www.auduboninstitute.org/aoa*), a top-five aquarium, and nationally recognized children's museum (420 Julia Street; 504–523–1357; *www.lcm.org*), the French Market (1008 N. Peters Street; 504–522–2621; *www.frenchmarket.org*), the National D-Day Museum (945 Magazine Street; 504–527–6012; *www.ddaymuseum.org*), and Jazzland theme park (12301 Six Flags Parkway; 504–253–8100; *www.sixflags.com*). An area highlight is the 42 cemeteries in the metropolitan New Orleans area. Metairie Cemetery (5100 Pontchartrain Boulevard; 504–486–6331) is the most beautiful as well as the most unique not only in New Orleans, but anywhere in the world. If you wish to see the architecture of the world, you need only visit Metairie Cemetery. The New Orleans Museum of Art (1 Collins Diboll Circle; 504–488–2631; *www.noma.org*) hosts touring exhibitions and houses more than 40,000 pieces in its permanent collection. At Jackson Square you'll discover the Louisiana State Museum (701 Chartres Street; 504–568–6968; *lsm.crt.state.la.us*) in the State Capital Complex, St. Louis Cathedral (615 Pere Antoine Alley; 504–525–9585; *www.stlouiscathedral.org*), and the Mardi Gras Museum (504–568–6968; *www.neworleansmuseums.com*).

Recreation: The Louisiana Super Dome (Sugar Bowl Drive; 504–587–3663; *www.superdome.com*) is a frequent stop for the Super Bowl and home to the crescent city's beloved Saints (877–8SAINTS; *www.neworleanssaints.com*) as well as host to the Nokia Sugar Bowl, clearly the premier annual sports event to take place in New Orleans; the 20,000-seat New Orleans Arena hosts major concert tours and is home to the NBA's New Orleans Hornets (504–301–4000; *www.nba.com/hornets*). The AAA affiliate of the Houston Astros, the Zephyrs (504–734–5155; *www.zephyrsbaseball.co*]) play in beautiful Zephyr Field (6000 Airline Drive, Metairie; 504–734–5155; *www.zephyrsbaseball.com*), a new 3,000-seat stadium located in Metairie, about 15 miles from downtown New Orleans. For fishing enthusiasts, offshore adventures and back-bayou flat boat fishing are in store. A license issued by the Department of Wildlife and Fisheries (225–765–2800; *www.wlf.state.la.us*) is required for any outing and is available from most sporting goods stores and marinas. On the bayous and inlets off the Mississippi River, you're likely to find redfish, trout, and bass; lemon fish, tuna, and red snapper can be found around the oil rigs a few miles offshore. Game around Louisiana includes everything from deer and water fowl to rabbit and alligator (all are seasonal). Permits are available from most of the expedition outfits.

For the Visitor

Accommodations: The metropolitan area boasts 30,000 hotel rooms. There are accommodations from high-end spas to local guest houses and antique-filled B&Bs. Most hotels and guest houses in and around the French Quarter are very gay-friendly. Here are just a few of the many options in New Orleans: The Lafitte Guest House (1003 Bourbon Street; 504–581–2678; *www.lafitteguesthouse.com*) is located right on Bourbon Street. St. Peter House (1005 St. Peter; 800–535–7815; *www.stpeterhouse.com*), across from the Corner Pocket, is a great location for exploring the French Quarter. If you're planning on exploring the Marigny, just outside the French Quarter is the Elysian Fields Inn (900 Elysian Fields Avenue; 866–948–9420; *www.elysianfieldsinn.com*).

For More Information

Gay & Lesbian Center
Lesbian and Gay Community Center
of New Orleans
2114 Decatur Street
New Orleans, LA 70116
504–945–1103
www.lgccno.net

Publications
Times-Picayune
3800 Howard Avenue
New Orleans, LA 70125
504–822–6660
www.timespicayune.com

Ambush Magazine
828-A Bourbon Street
New Orleans, LA 70116-3137
504–522–8047
www.ambushmag.com

Convention and Visitors Bureau
New Orleans Metropolitan
Convention and Visitors Bureau
1520 Sugar Bowl Drive
New Orleans, LA 70112
800–672–6124
www.neworleanscvb.com

Chamber of Commerce

Greater New Orleans, Inc.
601 Poydras Street, Suite 1700
New Orleans, LA 70130
504–527–6900
www.norcc.org

Realtor

Michael Baker, President
Realty Resources, Inc.
1022 Orange Street
New Orleans, LA 70130
504–523–5555
www.oldhousebroker.com

## 22

Portland, Maine

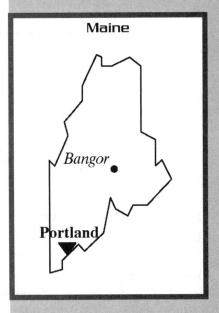

A Look at Portland

Nestled between Maine's forest-covered mountains and spectacular rugged coast, Portland is a rough-hewn gem of New England. Seascapes and cityscapes blend harmoniously in Portland, perched on a peninsula, jutting out into island-studded Casco Bay. Within a 15-mile radius of the city lies a range of countryside and coastal landscapes including ocean, many beautiful freshwater lakes, great mountains for skiing in the winter, and the unsurpassed beauty of Acadia National Park. Portland is Maine's business, financial, and retail capital, and the city's natural deep water port rivals Boston, New York, and Philadelphia for cargo and oil shipments. Historic architecture blends gracefully with the new as you stroll along her working waterfront or the cobblestone streets of the restored Old Port section of the city. The waterfront provides access to the sea for commercial shipping and a host of pleasure activities. Today, from the welcoming beacon of Portland Head Light to the salty lobstermen of Casco Bay, the coast remains an area steeped in nautical history and graced with the beauty of the sea.

Possible drawbacks: The weather is wet and cold a good portion of the year; almost a third of the year sees temperatures below freezing, and it hardly ever gets warm. The gay community is largely coupled, a positive or a negative depending on what's important to you.

▶ County:
Cumberland

▶ Area code:
207

▶ Time zone:
Eastern

▶ Population:
64,249

▶ County population:
265,612

▶ Region:
Southeast Maine

▶ Average home price:
$300,000

▶ Fabulous reasons to live here:
Recreation, spectacular sea harbor views, laid-back atmosphere, excellent education opportunities, family-oriented GLBT community

Climate

Elevation 75'	Avg. high/low(F°)	Avg. inches		Avg. # days precip.	Avg. % humidity
		rain	snow		
Jan.	31/12	4.1	19.3	10	68%
April	53/35	4.3	2.9	12	64%
July	79/59	3.3	–	10	69%
Oct.	58/37	4.4	0.2	9	71%
YEAR	55/36	45.8	70.4	127	69%
# days 32° or below: 109			# days 90° or warmer: 4		

Local Connections

Gas company: Northern Utilities, Inc. (800–552–3047; *www.northernutilities.com*)

Electric company: Maine consumers purchase their electricity services from electricity suppliers who compete to produce or sell the electricity itself and distribution companies that deliver electricity. The Maine Public Utilities Commission (207–287–3831; *www.state.me.us/mpuc*) has lists of current service providers.

Phone company: Verizon (800–483–4000; *www.verizon.com*)

Water and sewer: Portland Water District (207–761–8310; *www.pwd.org*)

Cable company: Time Warner Cable (207–253–2222; *www.timewarnercable.com*)

Car registration/License: Maine Bureau of Motor Vehicles (207–624–9000, ext. 52119; *www.state.me.us/sos/bmv*)

New residents who surrender a valid, out-of-state license pay a $10 application fee plus the $30 photo license fee (six-year license). Age 65 or older: $21 (four-year license with photo). A vehicle is required to have a title in the State of Maine if it is 15 years old or newer. Title application: $23. Registration: 5 percent sales tax based on sticker price for new cars, sale price for used, plus an excise tax paid yearly when you register your vehicle, ranges from $4 to $24 per $1,000 of value.

The Tax Ax

Sales tax: 6.4 percent

State income tax: 2.0–8.5 percent graduated, by income level

Property tax: Assessor (207–874–8486; *www.portlandassessors.com*)

The current property tax levy is $26.53 per $1,000 of valuation. Exemptions include blind, veteran, and homestead.

Local Real Estate

Overview: Portland prides itself as a city with various historical homes of architectural significance. The city's very strong market consists of one-family residential homes and condos with mostly medium to higher-end properties. With its new residential and commercial developments (condos, hotels, etc.), Portland has the feel of a small city with a flair of a big one.

Median price for a single-family home: $250,000

Average price for a single-family home: $300,000

Average price for a 2BR condo: $250,000

Rental housing market: It can be very difficult to find good rentals, depending on location, expect to pay $900 and up.

Gay-friendly neighborhoods: Portland is one of the gay-friendliest cities in the Northeast. GLBT community members will be comfortable throughout the city.

Nearby areas to consider: Things come in threes in nearby Ogunquit (*www.gayogunquit.com*). This small town of about 1,300 residents has three miles of white sandy beach, three theaters, and three GLBT community bars. There's also a performing arts center, an American art museum, and a handful of unique galleries, not to mention a large GLBT community. The small community swells considerably during the summer months with visitors who enjoy the great views and sailing opportunities of Perkins Cove, the 7,000-acre Mount Agamenticus with miles of trails, and the Rachel Carson National Wildlife Refuge.

Earning a Living

Per capita income: $22,698

Median household income: $35,650

Business climate: Portland is an easygoing city with friendly, hardworking people and a strong economy. The city is the metropolitan hub of Maine's south coast region; it's a lively city incorporating the character of yesteryear into a modern urban environment. A diverse, well-educated work force, strong work ethic, and commitment to the community, Greater Portland is the perfect place to start and grow a business.

Help in starting a business: Rainbow Business and Professional Association (207–775–0077) is a non-profit organization dedicated to promoting the vitality, productivity, and growth of the gay, lesbian, bisexual, and transgender business and professional community throughout the State of Maine. The Portland Regional Chamber of Commerce (207–772–2811; *www.portlandregion.com*) maintains active programs of service to members and a vigorous government representation effort and annually produces major events that help make greater Portland an even better place to live and work.

Job market: Portland's strong economy provides jobs in educational, health, and social services; retail trade; professional, scientific, management, administrative, and waste management services; finance, insurance, real estate and rental, and leasing; arts, entertainment, recreation, accommodation, and food services.

The Community

Overview: Many of the community events revolve around living life. Potluck dinners, parties, and family gatherings are common events. As the nation's home to highest concentration of lesbian couples and ranking in the top 10 for the most male couples, domestic gatherings just make sense. There's also a strong youth contingent stemming from the USM campus.

Community organizations: Portland has no formal gay community center, but there's a strong sense of community and the city is home to some fabulous social, political, and support-oriented groups. Just a few of the area's groups include: Equality Maine (*www.equalitymaine.org*); Metropolitan Community Church (888–264–6223); GLBTQIA Resources, USM (*www.usm.maine.edu/glbtqa*); Maine Gay Men's Chorus (*www.mainegaymenschorus.org*); Women in Harmony (*www.wihmaine.org*); Maine Speakout Project Community Counseling Center (207–874–1030); Outright, Portland (*www.outright.org*); Harbor Masters of Maine (*www.harbormastersofmaine.com*); and Seacoast Gay Men (*www.sgmnh.org*).

Medical care: Maine Medical Center (207–662–0111; *www.mmc.org*), the largest hospital in Maine, is the premier referral hospital for Maine and northern New England. The 606-bed facility is both a teaching hospital and an active research center, providing comprehensive services in all medical specialties. MMC prides itself on offering the latest innovations in technology, delivered by dedicated, compassionate caregivers. Mercy Hospital (207–879–3000; *www.mercyhospital.com*) offers a wide range of services, including addiction medicine; the Birthplace, delivering complete obstetrical care for women; an oncology-hematology center; Breast Health Resource & Lymphedema Treatment Center; diagnostic and preventative care; therapeutic outpatient programs; and VNA Home Health Care, offering home and hospice care services.

Nuptials: Although the state has a law similar to DOMA defining marriage as between a man and a woman, the City of Portland established a registry for domestic partnerships and passed a domestic partnership ordinance requiring equal benefits for the domestic partners of city employees.

Getting Around Town

Public transportation: Greater Portland Transit District (The Metro 207–774–0351; *www.gpmetrobus.com*) provides fixed route bus service to the Portland, Westbrook, South Portland (Maine Mall area), and Falmouth Crossing

(Banknorth) areas. Fare: one-way $1; unlimited monthly ride pass $30. The Downeaster (207–780–1000; *www.thedowneaster.com*) provides daily service to Boston for $35 round-trip.

Roads: I-95, US1, US202, US302

Airport: Portland International Jet Port (airport code: PWM) (207–774–7301; *www.portlandjetport.org*)

It's a Gay Life

Annual events: Southern Maine Pride (*www.southernmainepride.org*) hosts a month-long series of pride events in June including an art show, concerts, film festival, rally, parade, and festival. Maine Maple Sugar Sunday, Old Port Festival (*www.portlandmaine.com*), Bar Harbor Music Festival (*www.barharbormusicfestival.com*), Portland Festival of Nations (*www.wini.us*), and the Maine Lobster Festival (*www.mainelobsterfestival.com*) are just a few of the area's annual events.

Nightlife: Known regionally for its thriving local music scene, Portland boasts some of the best eclectic venues with live rock, hip-hop, jazz clubs, reggae, and bluegrass. In the summer, the music moves outdoors and echoes down to the harbor. Portland is home to several gay clubs. Blackstones (6 Pine Street; 207–775–2885; *www.blackstones.com*) is Portland's oldest neighborhood gay bar and sponsors events, pool tournaments, and theme nights. Sisters (45 Danforth Street; 207–774–1505) is a lesbian-owned dance bar and a fine pub. Somewhere (117 Spring Street; 207–871–9169) is a pleasant piano bar. Underground (3 Spring Street; 207–773–3315) is Portland's dance club. There are also some excellent pubs downtown and around the Old Port. Gay in Maine (*www.gayinmaine.com*) has the best list of area gay attractions.

Culture: Portland boasts a thriving arts scene and an exclusive Downtown Arts District. Greater Portland combines the diverse cultural offerings of a major metropolitan area with a charming small-town flavor. From classical to cutting-edge, Portland's professional performing arts organizations Portland Stage Company (25 Forest Avenue; 207–774–0465; *www.portlandstage.com*), PCA Great Performances (207–842–0800; *www.pcagreatperformances.com*), Merrill Auditorium (20 Myrtle Street; 207–874–8200; *www.portlandevents.com*), Cumberland County Civic Center (1 Civic Center Square; 207–775–3458; *www.theciviccenter.com*), and the Portland Symphony (207–773–6128; *www.portlandsymphony.com*) present an exciting array of dance, theater, and musical events. One of the community favorites is the First Friday Art Walk (*www.firstfridayartwalk.com*), a self-guided tour through the Arts District on the first Friday of every month. Located in the heart of the Arts District (207–772–6828; *www.portlandmaine.com*), the Portland Museum of Art (7 Congress Square; 207–775–6148; *www.portlandmuseum.org*) is one of the area's best-known cultural treasures, offering three centuries of art and architecture, including collections of renowned Maine artists Winslow Homer and Andrew Wyeth. Other Portland gems include Victoria Mansion (109 Danforth Street; 207–772–4841; *www.victoriamansion.com*), Tate House (1270 Westbrook Street; 207–774–9781; *www.tatehouse.org*), Wadsworth- Longfellow House (489 Congress Street; 207–774–1822; *www.mainehistory.org*), Children's Museum of Maine (142 Free Street; 207–828–1234; *www.childrensmuseumofme.org*), Maine History Gallery (489 Congress Street; 207–774–1822; *www.mainehistory.org*), Maine Narrow Gauge Railroad Co. & Museum (58 Fore Street; 207–828–0814; *www.mngrr.org*), Portland Harbor Museum (2 Fort Road; 207–799–6337; *www.portlandharbormuseum.org*), and Portland Observatory (138 Congress Street; 207–774–5561; *www.portlandlandmarks.org*). For more information on the diverse art scene of Portland, check out *www.gotoportland.com*.

Recreation: Maine's fresh air ushers the desire to get outdoors to kayak in and around the many islands; to bicycle up and down the beautiful coastline; and to watch the sailboats in Portland Harbor. Greater Portland sits with the sea in her front yard and mountains to her back. In autumn, the countryside is ablaze with classic New England foliage, and four seasons of activities await lovers of the outdoors in Maine. Camping is available at a wide variety of sites, from coastal to inland, mountain to lake, developed to primitive. Golf enthusiasts will find numerous courses situated amid the beauty of Maine's natural landscape. Skiing opportunities, both downhill and cross-country, are plentiful in Maine, with most downhill recreational areas open into late spring. Cross-country skiers will appreciate the almost-unlimited potential for quiet and isolation and the unique opportunity to ski next to the ocean. Greater Portland's intricate network of trails hugs the waterfront, loops through the woods, and runs along pavement, providing plenty of beautiful scenery while walking, hiking, biking, or Nordic skiing. Gilsland Farm in Falmouth, headquarters of the Maine Audubon Society (20 Gilsland Farm Road, Falmouth; 207–781–2300; *www.maineaudubon.org*), is a bird sanctuary on the Presumpscot River estuary. Maine Audubon sponsors naturalist outings for groups, nature slide shows, and easy-terrain guided walks. For spectators there's hockey's Portland Pirates (207–828–4665; *www.portlandpirates.com*) and the Portland Sea Dogs (800–936–3647; *www.portlandseadogs.com*), the Red Sox training team.

For the Visitor

Accommodations: The Inn at St. John (939 Congress Street; 207–773–6481; *www.innatstjohn.com*), Portland's longest continuously operating Inn, offers more than 100 years of outstanding service in the heart of the city. The Percy Inn (15 Pine Street; 207–871–7638/888–417–3729; *www.percyinn.com*) is a beautifully restored 1830 building situated in the heart of Portland's West End Historic District at Longfellow Square. Wild Iris Inn (273 State Street; 207–775–0224/ 800–600–1557; *www.wildirisinn.com*) is a cozy seven-room bed and breakfast conveniently located within walking distance of downtown Portland. Fifteen miles outside Portland is Auberge by the Sea (103 East Grand Avenue, Old Orchard Beach; 207–934–2355; *www.aubergebythesea.com*) with a short private pathway that leads onto the beach.

For More Information

Publications

*Portland Press Herald/Maine
Sunday Telegram*
390 Congress Street
Portland, ME 04101-5009
207–791–6650
www.pressherald.com

Convention and Visitors Bureau

Convention & Visitors
Bureau of Greater Portland
245 Commercial Street
Portland, ME 04101
207–772–5800
www.visitcascobay.com

Chambers of Commerce

The Portland Regional Chamber
60 Pearl Street
Portland, ME 04101
207–772–2811
www.portlandregion.com

Rainbow Business and Professional Association
P.O. Box 11148
Portland, ME 04104-7148
207–775–0077
www.rbpa.org

Realtor

Thomas Schardt, Realtor
Flaherty Realty
113 Pleasant Street
Brunswick, ME 04011
800–536–4079
www.flahertyrealty.com

23 ► Takoma Park, Maryland

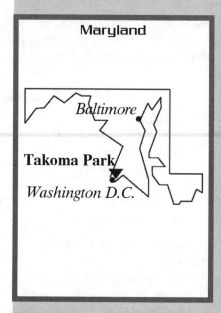

A Look at Takoma Park

Takoma Park is a sanctuary city with Victorian homes, tree-lined streets, and lush green parks. Its citizens are unusually diverse in age, ethnicity, language, economic condition, and length of residence. Founded in 1883 by Benjamin Franklin Gilbert along the Metropolitan Branch of the Baltimore and Ohio Railroad, Takoma Park was the first planned commuter suburb in Montgomery County, Maryland. The city now lies completely within Montgomery County and borders the upper northwest/northeast boundary of Washington, DC. It is less than 5 miles from the center of DC, but a world away in style and attitudes. Takoma Park strives to retain a small-town feel, the residents taking pride in many churches, neighborhood associations, civic groups, and arts organizations. The Sunday Farmer's Market (held April–Nov) is a community gathering place. An interesting facet of the city is that residents who are not yet U.S. citizens may vote in local elections and hold local elected office. In addition to the large city-wide celebrations throughout the year, there are also concerts, exhibits, political crusades, dances, neighborhood parties, quilting bees, and volunteer action projects. The city boasts several parks, an extensive recycling program, a municipal library, an economic and community development program, a tool-lending library, and two colleges: Columbia Union College and Montgomery College-Takoma Park.

Possible drawbacks: The population density is extreme, with more than 17,000 residents in just more than 2 square miles. Crime levels are also above the national average.

► Nickname:
Azalea City

► County:
Montgomery

► Area code:
301

► Time zone:
Eastern

► Population:
17,299

► County population:
873,341

► Region:
Central Maryland

► Closest metro area:
Washington, DC

► Average home price:
$420,000

► Fabulous reasons to live here:
Small-town charm; large GLBT community; city pride; good education; artist enclave; excellent location near arts, culture, and recreation

Climate

Elevation 250'	Avg. high/low(F°)	Avg. inches		Avg. # days precip.	Avg. % humidity
		rain	snow		
Jan.	42/23	3.5	5.6	10	63%
April	66/42	3.4	–	10	59%
July	88/66	4.2	–	10	65%
Oct.	68/44	3.5	–	7	67%
YEAR	66/44	44	16.9	112	64%
# days 32° or below: 65			# days 90° or warmer: 31		

Local Connections

Gas company: Washington Gas (703–750–1000/800–752–7520; *www.washgas.com*)

Electric company: Potomac Electric Power Company (202–833–7500/ 800–424–8028; *www.pepco.com*)

Phone company: Verizon (800–275–2355; *www.verizon.com*)

Water and sewer: Washington Suburban Sanitary Commission (301–206–8000/800–828–6439; *www.wssc.dst.md.us*)

Cable company: Comcast (800–266–2278; *www.comcast.com*)

Car registration/License: Maryland Department of Transportation Motor Vehicle Administration (301–729–4550; *www.marylandmva.com*)

New residents have 60 days to obtain a Maryland driver's license and registration. Vision test required; driving and written tests waived when surrendering a valid, out-of-state license. Fee: $45 new residents, $30 renewal. New residents receive a tax credit for annual fees paid in another state. Title fee: $23. Maryland Excise Titling Tax is 5 percent of minimum book value. Registration fee: $100 (minimum).

The Tax Ax

Sales tax: 5 percent

City tax: 3.2 percent "piggybacked" on state income tax

State income tax: 2–4.75 percent graduated, based on income

Property tax: Director of Assessments and Taxation (410–767–1199; *www.dat.state.md.us*)

Real property is reassessed on a three-year cycle by reviewing one-third of all property in Maryland every year. The review includes an exterior physical inspection of the property. The current mil rate for Takoma Park is .734 per $100 of value.

Local Real Estate

Overview: Takoma Park is an eclectic community in personality and housing styles. Along the tree-lined streets are Colonials, Victorians, bungalows, and contemporary structures that blend together just as the community members who call this city home do.

Median price for a single-family home: $250,000

Average price for a single-family home: $420,000

Average price for a 2BR condo: $350,000

Rental housing market: The rental market is very tight, but the rents are reasonable: approximately $875 for a two-bedroom.

Gay-friendly neighborhoods: All of Takoma Park is gay-friendly.

Nearby areas to consider: Silver Spring, with a population of 76,000, is one of nation's fastest-growing commercial centers. The city's large GLBT community gets the best of all worlds in this community centrally located between Baltimore and Washington, DC, with easy access to Annapolis and Northern Virginia. Housing costs are lower than the nearby metropolitan areas and fabulous public transportation makes for easy commuting and provides access to a wide range of community services, nightlife, culture, and recreation options. The area is drawing both small, creative, and artistic firms as well as large corporations, making for excellent career opportunities and a high quality of living standard.

Earning a Living

Per capita income: $26,437

Median household income: $63,434

Business climate: More than 700 businesses and non-profit organizations are located in Takoma Park, most of them small. This is a community of entrepreneurs, including many writers, musicians, and artists.

Help in starting a business: Takoma Park features two area business organizations. The Takoma/Langley Crossroads Development Authority actively promotes the Maryland International Corridor, the area's multi-cultural section of businesses and services. Old Takoma Business Association actively promotes the Old Takoma section of town, home to unique shops, boutiques, and restaurants. Both organizations create marketing and networking opportunities for area businesses.

Job market: Educational, health, and social services; professional, scientific, management, administrative, and waste management services; and the entrepreneurial arts all provide jobs in the city.

The Community

Overview: Takoma Park has a long history of openly gay elected officials beginning with Bruce Williams winning a city council seat in the early '90s. The community at large is supportive of the local GLBT community to the point of sexual orientation being a non-issue.

Community organizations: Being just a few miles away from Washington, DC, Takoma Park residents have hundreds of social, support, health, and spiritual organizations available. The Washington Center for Gay, Lesbian, Bisexual and Transgender People, known as The Center, celebrates, strengthens, and supports the GLBT residents and organizations of Metropolitan Washington, DC. Gay Washington (*www.gaywdc.com*) is a one-stop online resource for all the community organizations and businesses in the DC metro area.

Medical care: Washington Adventist Hospital (301–891–7600; *www.adventisthealthcare.com/WAH*) is a 300-bed, state-of-the-art, acute-care facility and Montgomery County's only complete cardiac center, performing 800 open-heart surgeries and more than 6,000 heart catheterizations each year. A fast-paced emergency department provides round-the-clock, high-volume medical and nursing care throughout the year. The hospital employs nearly 2,000 people, has a medical staff of 750 physicians, and is part of the Adventist HealthCare system. Holy Cross Hospital (301–754–7000; *www.holycrosshealth.org*), about 3 miles away in Silver Spring, Maryland, is a 380-bed hospital with more than 1,400 affiliated physicians, many among the most renowned specialists and general practitioners in the area. Specialties include cancer treatment, women's health, senior services, and minimally invasive surgery. The hospital is a member of Trinity Health of Novi, Michigan, the nation's third-largest Catholic healthcare system.

Nuptials: The State of Maryland has a law defining marriage as between a man and a woman. Takoma Park has four times the national average of GLBT domestic couples.

Getting Around Town

Public transportation: Washington Metropolitan Area Transit Authority (202–637–7000; *www.wmata.com*) operates buses and subway lines that service Takoma Park. Metrobus fare: $1.25; unlimited day pass $3. Metrorail one-way fare: $1.35–3.90.

Roads: I-495

Airports: Three major airports serve the area: Ronald Reagan Washington National Airport (airport code: DCA) (703–417–8000; *www.mwaa.com*) is about 7 miles south; Dulles International Airport (airport code: IAD) (703–572–2700; *www.mwaa.com*) is 30 miles southwest; and Baltimore-Washington International Airport (airport code: BWI) (410–859–7992; *www.bwiairport.com*) is 30 miles north.

It's a Gay Life

Annual events: There are many events that fill up the calendars of Takoma Park residents. Just a few include: the Takoma Park Jazz Festival (*www.tpjazzfest.org*) and the House & Garden Tour (*www.historictakoma.org*), both in May; the Arbor Day Tree Give-Away (*www.takomagov.org*) in April; summer concerts from June to August; Fourth of July, honored with a parade, concert, and fireworks (*www.takomapark4th.org*); Takoma Park Folk Festival (*www.tpff.org*) in early September; Takoma Old Town Street Festival (*www.takomafestival.com*) on the first Sunday in October; and Solstice Celebration in December.

Nightlife: Takoma Park has an eclectic community, providing varied options for nighttime entertainment. The many area restaurants serve as meeting places and the city's diverse ethnic mix creates a plethora of available tastes. Mark's Kitchen (7006 Carroll Avenue; 301–270–1884) and Savory Café (7071 Carroll Avenue; 301–270–2233; *www.savorycafe.com*) are popular gay restaurants. Traditionally a haven for artists and musicians, live music is common in the evenings. Because Takoma Park is home to two colleges, there are several fun small bars and pubs in the area. Additionally, the Washington Metro area is home to dozens of gay bars, clubs, and restaurants. *Metro Weekly,* Washington, DC's gay and lesbian magazine, has current listings; you'll find it at Mark's Kitchen.

Culture: Historic Takoma (*www.historictakoma.org*) works diligently to preserve the area's past. The historic Thomas-Siegler House & Garden (corner of Tulip and Cedar avenues; 301–270–2831; *www.historictakoma.org*), set on an acre of white oak, magnolia, and azaleas, is one of the organization's jewels. Built in 1884, it was the first completed house in Takoma Park. The main house remains a private residence; the gardens and outbuildings are maintained by Historic Takoma. In 1995, Historic Takoma opened the Thomas-Siegler Carriage House Museum. The museum retains the carriage house in its original configuration and also includes exhibits from the entire spectrum of Takoma Park's history. Historic Takoma offers walking tours and other educational events that join Takoma Park's present and past. The Takoma Park Theater (6833 4th Street NW, Washington, DC; *www.takomatheatre.org*), a movie house built in 1924, is now a center for arts, cultural events, and performances. This quaint space, available for rental, is a common showcase for local performers and groups. The Takoma Park Singers (301–270–4048) and Takoma Park Symphony Orchestra (507 Philadelphia Avenue; 301–589–4433) perform throughout the year. Both Columbia Union College (760 Flower Avenue; 301–891–4000; *www.cuc.edu*) and Montgomery College-Takoma Park (7600 Takoma Avenue; 301–891–3000; *www.mc.cc.md.us*), with its Performing Arts Center (*www.montgomerycollege.edu*), have arts and music programs providing the area with many cultural opportunities. Being located just a few miles from Washington, DC, there are other countless regional opportunities, including some of the world's finest museums, galleries, opera, symphony, and historic sites. The Washington, DC Convention and Tourism Corporation (202–789–7000; *www.washington.org*) is a fabulous source for information on all that the Washington metro area has to offer.

Recreation: The City of Takoma Park Recreation Department (301–891–7101; *www.collabitat.com/TPRecreation*) offers a collection of programs and events for the entire Takoma Park community. Takoma Park is home to Hodges Field, Ed Wilhelm Field, and Jequie Park, where leagues play baseball, basketball, tennis, and soccer. The Recreation Department provides classes in a diverse range of opportunities including fitness, quilting, message, music theory, and art. The new, state-of-the art Community Center includes a gym, meeting rooms for local organizations, a game room, quiet lounges, and a host of planned activities. For additional activities, the Washington metro area is home to more than 25 parks and memorials. Visit the DC Department of Parks and Recreation (202–673–7647; *dpr.dc.gov*) for up-to-date information on programs, special events, and facilities. The Potomac River provides fishing, sailing kayaking, canoeing, and rowing. The well-trodden towpath of the C&O Canal is frequented by bikers, hikers, and in-line skaters. Rock Creek Park to the west is one of the largest and most fervently praised urban parks and offers hiking, biking, skating, horseback riding, golf, tennis, and a host of other fun activities.

For the Visitor

Accommodations: There are several pleasant places to stay in Takoma Park. Built in about 1855, the Davis Warner Inn (8114 Carroll Avenue; 301–408–3989/888–683–3984; *www.daviswarnerinn.com*) is a 6,400-square-foot historic Stick Style house mansion with a history as a veterans hospital, brothel, speakeasy, and gambling house. The fabulous inn has relaxing gardens with two lily ponds. Built in 1919 in the Victorian resort style, Eden Park Guest House (7063 Carroll Avenue; 301–270–8210; *www.edenparkguesthouse.com*) is a modern and charming bed and breakfast with luxury rooms at affordable rates. The recently renovated Quality Inn (7411 New Hampshire Avenue; 301–439–3000/877–424–6423; *www.comfortinn.com*) has 168 guest rooms, a beautiful outdoor pool, and a sundeck.

For More Information

Gay & Lesbian Center
The Washington Center for
Gay, Lesbian, Bisexual and
Transgender People
1111 14th Street NW, Suite 350
Washington, DC 20005
202–518–6100
www.thedccenter.org

Publications
The Takoma Voice
6935 Laurel Avenue, #207
Takoma Park, MD 20912
301–891–6744
www.takoma.com

Washington Post
1150 15th Street NW
Washington, DC 20071
703–469–2500
www.washingtonpost.com

Metro Weekly
1012 14th Street NW, #209
Washington, DC 20005
202–638–6830
www.metroweekly.com

Chambers of Commerce
Takoma/Langley Crossroads
Development Authority
7676 New Hampshire Avenue, Suite 101
Mailbox 142
Takoma Park, MD 20912
301–445–7910

Old Takoma Business Association
P.O. Box 5440
Takoma Park, MD 20913
www.takomaonline.com

Realtor
Lydia Vine, Realtor
Coldwell Banker Residential Brokerage
10244 River Road
Potomac, MD 20854
301–980–8111

## 24

Boston, Massachusetts

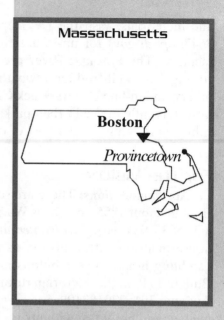

Massachusetts

Boston

Provincetown

A look at Boston

Harbor-lined cityscapes, thousands of college students, world-renowned and nationally beloved orchestras, and American Revolution battlefields are just a part of Boston. When you walk the city's tree-lined streets, home to more historic buildings than any other American city, you're following in the footsteps of our founding fathers. Boston is a rich tapestry of history, culture, recreation, and a strong economy. Steeped in living history, this city is continually changing and reinventing itself. World-class education at 20 area colleges creates a well-educated workforce sought after by America's leading corporations. Boston is also home to many innovative hospitals. The city boasts world-class museums, orchestras, theaters, and opera and ballet companies. Thousands root for their award-winning sports teams. With miles of shoreline and islands dotting a deep bay, the Paul Revere City is a recreation haven with rowing, biking, swimming, sailing, and golfing just a few of the many options.

Possible drawbacks: Property rates continue to rise quickly as America's smallest big city continues to grow. Traffic can be unbearable because the narrow, curved streets were designed for horses, not SUVs.

Local Connections

Gas company: KeySpan Energy Delivery
(781–684–5200;
www.keyspanenergy.com)

▶ Nickname:
The Walking City

▶ County: Suffolk

▶ Area code: 617

▶ Time zone: Eastern

▶ Population:
589,141

▶ County population:
5,819,100

▶ Region:
Eastern Massachusetts

▶ Average home price:
$399,000

▶ Fabulous reasons to live here:
Historic architecture; good education; strong high-tech economy; large GLBT community; history, arts, culture, recreation, and style

Climate

Elevation 20'	Avg. high/low(F°)	Avg. inches		Avg. # days precip.	Avg. % humidity
		rain	snow		
Jan.	36/21	4.3	12.9	12	63%
April	56/39	3.9	0.9	11	62%
July	82/64	3.3	–	9	65%
Oct.	72/45	4.1	–	9	67%
YEAR	59/42	46.3	42.2	128	65%
# days 32° or below: 67			# days 90° or warmer: 13		

Electric company: NSTAR (800–592–2000; *www.nstaronline.com*)

Phone company: Verizon (800–483–4000; *www.verizon.com*)

Water and sewer: Boston Water and Sewer Commission (617–989–7800; *www.bwsc.org*)

Cable companies: Comcast (800–266–2278; *www.comcast.com*); RCN (800–RING–RCN; *www.rcn.com*)

Car registration/License: Executive Office of Transportation (617–351–4500; *www.mass.gov/rmv*)

You must obtain a valid Massachusetts license upon becoming a resident. You must provide the RMV with your current out-of-state photo license and proof of your current Massachusetts residency. Your current license gets you out of the written and road test. An eye test will be required. Licenses are good for five years and fees range from $40 to $60. Normal passenger registration is for two years. Fee: $36. The registration transfer fee is $15.

The Tax Ax

Sales tax: 5 percent; food and prescription drugs exempt

State income tax: 5.3 percent (flat rate for all residents); 9.5 percent on all corporate income

Property tax: Tax information (617–626–2300)

Boston is considered expensive when it comes to property taxes. Massachusetts does not provide for a general homestead exemption. However, Boston allows a 30 percent exemption for the principal residence. Taxes are based on a set amount up to 11 cents per $1,000 of assessed value. A building assessed for $500,000 would pay property tax of $5,500.

Local Real Estate

Overview: Greater Boston is a thriving and very active real estate market. The type of housing is generally limited to older style Victorian homes and brownstones to modern high- and mid-rise buildings. There is also a large selection of townhouses and single-family houses outside of Boston.

Median price for a single-family home: $449,000

Average price for a single-family home: $399,000

Average price for a 2BR condo: $359,000

Rental housing market: The rental market has been the one of the strongest in the country; however, due to over-development and a surge in purchasing, that market is now more a renter's market. Landlords are now willing to pay the entire rental fee, but prices are still relatively high (two-bedroom apartments approximately $1,650).

Gay-friendly neighborhoods: Most of Greater Boston is gay-friendly, with the South End being a popular gay community. Other gay-friendly neighborhoods include Back Bay, Beacon Hill, Central Square, Inman Square, South End, and Davis and Porter Squares.

Nearby areas to consider: Cambridge, just across the river from Boston, is renowned for its colleges and universities and is popular with the GLBT community because of the city's liberal politics. Cambridge was the first city in the state to issue gay marriage licenses, and there are dozens of well-funded support and social service organizations for the city's GLBT community. Another nearby suburb to consider is Somerville. The arts are well represented in this mid-size city of 78,000 that's 3 miles northwest of Boston. This lively arts community is home to hundreds of musicians, artists, and writers and an active city arts council.

Earning a Living

Per capita income: $23,353

Median household income: $39,629

Business climate: The influence of the areas many colleges and excellent school system gives Greater Boston a highly educated and desirable work force. The city is known for its cutting-edge healthcare, growing biotechnology sector, and strong financial markets. Businesses continue to grow and change with the times, maintaining an ongoing, healthy economy.

Help in starting a business: The Greater Boston Business Council promotes a positive image of the diversity of GLBT citizens and strengthens their position in society by providing opportunities and an environment for the personal, professional, and social growth of its members and by networking with other GLBT professional organizations, both locally and nationally. The Greater Boston Chamber of Commerce provides its members advocacy, information, and marketing exposure that enhances their business success. The Chamber also works for legislative changes that are critical to economic growth in the city. Both organizations provide networking, advertising, and educational opportunities for their members.

Job market: Educational, health, and social services; professional, scientific, management, administrative, and waste management services; finance; insurance; real estate; and rental and leasing are sectors providing many jobs in the Boston area.

The Community

Overview: With 20 institutions of higher learning in the area, a large section of Boston's community maintains a youthful air, and this is reflected in the many youth-oriented organizations. As a cultural and historic center, there's also an organized and sophisticated gay community. When combined, the group is large, diverse, visible, and well supported by the city. This support is most obvious in the number of publications and radio and television broadcasts dedicated to Greater Boston's GLBT community.

Community organizations: It's impossible to actually list all of the community organizations in the Boston area. There's literally a group for every need, from healthcare and HIV services to spirituality, social, and recreational. Boston Glass Community Center (*www.bostonglass.org*) is a drop-in center for gay, lesbian, bisexual, transgender, and questioning young people between the ages of 13 and 25. BAGLEY, The Boston Alliance of Gay, Lesbian, Bisexual, & Transgender youth, is a youth-led, adult-supported organization offering weekly social gatherings, fabulous events, plus myriad resources and referrals. The Women's Center (*www.cambridgewomenscenter.org*) is an anti-racist community center for women fighting for women's rights and against all forms of oppression. *Bay Windows*, New England's largest gay and lesbian newspaper, *In Newsweekly*, and *EDGE* are Boston GLBT publications with the latest community information. The South End's Cuttyhunk, formerly We Think The World of You (*www.wethinktheworldofyou.com*), is a busy bookstore in the heart of Boston and a good place to pick up copies of area magazines, guides, and free maps.

Medical care: Boston is home to 18 hospitals, many of which are teaching hospitals connected to the areas many colleges and universities. The services provided by Fenway Community Health (617–267–0900; *www.fenwayhealth.org*) include primary healthcare, specialty care (HIV/AIDS, obstetrics, gynecology, gerontology, podiatry, and nutritional counseling), mental health and addictions services, complementary therapies (chiropractic, massage, and acupuncture), health promotion, violence prevention and recovery, and family and parenting services, including alternative insemination. AIDS Action Committee (617–437–6200; *www.aac.org*), New England's first and largest AIDS organization, is dedicated to stopping the spread of HIV/AIDS by preventing new infections and optimizing the health of those already infected. The Committee provides free confidential services to men and women already living with HIV/AIDS, conducts extensive educational and prevention outreach to those at risk of infection, runs Massachusetts' only statewide AIDS Hotline (800–235–2331), and advocates for effective science-based prevention programs. The Boston Living Center (617–236–1012; *www.bostonlivingcenter.org*) is a non-profit community and resource center whose mission is to foster the wellness of all HIV-positive people and respond to the changing needs of the HIV/AIDS community. The BLC provides programs and services, free of charge, to members in the context of an exceptionally welcoming, drug-free, safe, confidential, and culturally diverse environment.

Nuptials: The State of Massachusetts issues marriage licenses to resident same-sex couples, and many area businesses provide wedding planning services.

Getting Around Town

Public transportation: Massachusetts Bay Transportation Authority (617–222–3200; *www.mbta.com*) operates bus, subway, commuter rail, and water shuttle services. Fares are zone-based. The standard inner harbor and subway fares are $1.25; most bus fares range from 90 cents to $1.25; commuter rail fares $1.25–$6. The one-day visitor pass at $7.50 is a fabulous deal.

Roads: I-90, I-93, US1, US128

Airport: Logan International Airport (airport code: BOS) (617–561–1800; *www.massport.com/logan*) is only 2 miles outside the city center, with several convenient public transportation options to the airport from downtown and suburban locations.

It's a Gay Life

Annual events: Boston Pride (617–262–9405; *www.bostonpride.org*) hosts New England's largest gay pride event in June. This weeklong celebration includes block parties, contests, including Boston Gay Idol, a festival, and a parade. There are many other annual events in Boston. A few of the largest are the Dragon Boat Festival (*www.bostondragonboat.org*) in June, Harborfest (*www.bostonharborfest.co*) in June and July, the Saint Patrick's Day Parade (*www.irishmassachusetts.com*) in March, and the Seaport Festival (*www.bostonseaportfestival.com*) in July. Contact the Greater Boston Convention and Visitors Bureau for a complete list of annual events.

Nightlife: With more than 25 gay bars and clubs, plus a vast array of restaurants, cafés, coffee shops, and bookstores, you'll want to make a habit of picking up the area rags to keep up with all the events, specials, and theme nights around Boston. For newcomers, start your city exploration in the South End and Theater District. A few of the clubs in those areas include: Boston Eagle (520 Tremont Street; 617–542–4494), which attracts a fun Levi and leather crowd; Club Café (209 Columbus Avenue; 617–422–0862; *www.clubcafe.com*), a trendy restaurant that includes the video bar Moonshine; Chaps (100 Warrenton Street; 617–695–9500), which has theme nights and hosts Sunday T-dance; Jacques (79 Broadway; 617–426–8902), a fabulous drag cabaret; Buzz (67 Stuart Street; 617–267–8969; *www.buzzboston.com*), with two dance floors, go-go boys, and a great Saturday night party; and Dedo's (69 Church Street; 617–338–9999; *www.dedo.biz*).

Culture: History and culture are Boston's foundation. Boston is home to the phenomenal Boston Symphony Orchestra (617–266–1492; *www.bso.org*), Boston Pops (617–266–1492; *www.bostonpops.org*), Boston Lyric Opera (617–542–4912; *www.blo.org*), and Boston Ballet (617–695–6954; *www.bostonballet.org*). There are galleries and museums that trace the history of world art, including the Museum of Fine Arts (465 Huntington Avenue; 617–267–9300; *www.mfa.org*) and

Boston Tea Party Ship and Museum (380 Dorchester Street; 617–269–7150; *www.bostonteapartyship.com*). The Isabella Stewart Gardner Museum (280 The Fenway; 617–566–1401; *www.gardnermuseum.org*) is home to more than 2,500 objects and includes works of Rembrandt, Botticelli, Raphael, Titan, and Matisse. The Museum of Science (Science Park; 617–723–2500; *www.mos.org*) remains on the cutting edge of science education, with hands-on exhibits and an IMAX theater. The area's other theaters range from classic to modern and include Commonwealth Shakespeare (270 Tremont Street; 617–532–1252; *www.freeshakespeare.org*), the Boston Conservatory Theatre (8 The Fenway; 617–536–6340; *www.costonconservatory.edu*), Shubert Theatre (265 Tremont Street; 617–482–9393; *www.wangcenter.org*), Cutler Majestic Theatre (219 Tremont Street; 617–824–8000; *www.maj.org*), and American Repertory Theatre (64 Brattle Street, Cambridge; 617–547–8300; *www.amrep.org*), among others. The city boasts two world-class zoos: Stone Park Zoo (149 Pond Street, Stoneham; 781–438–5100; *www.zoonewengland.com*) and Franklin Park Zoo (1 Franklin Park Road; 617–541–LION; *www.zoonewengland.com*). There are fabulous parks (City of Boston Parks and Recreation; 617–635–PARK; *www.cityofboston.gov/parks*), including the Boston Commons and Adams National Historic Park and Spectacle Island and famous trails including Irish Heritage Trail (*www.irishheritagetrail.com*), Black Heritage Trail (*www.afroammuseum.org*), and Women's Heritage Trail (*www.bwht.org*). The Freedom Trail (*www.thefreedomtrail.org*) is a 3-mile outdoor walking tour of 16 sites and structures of historic importance in downtown Boston and Charlestown. The trail is always open; you can explore it on your own or take a 90-minute tour that begins at the Visitor Center at 15 State Street and covers the heart of the Freedom Trail from the Old South Meeting House (310 Washington Street; 617–482–6439; *www.oldsouthmeetinghouse.org*) to the Old North Church (193 Salem Street; 617–523–6676; *www.oldnorth.com*).

Recreation: The City of Boston is home to 215 parks and playgrounds, 65 squares, urban woodlands, 16 historic burying grounds, and two golf courses. The Boston Harbor Islands National Recreation Area (*www.BostonIslands.com*) is a combination of 34 islands off the Boston coast. Each island is unique and offers visitors a different collection of amenities and experiences. The combination of green spaces and shorefront create a great wealth of recreational opportunities including golfing, hiking, biking, sailing, fishing, swimming, sunbathing, and relaxing. For spectators, Fenway Park (4 Yawkey Way; 617–267–1700; *www.bostonredsox.com*), TD Banknorth Garden (1 FleetCenter Place; 617–624–1331; *www.fleetcenter.com*), and Gillette Stadium (1 Patriot Place; 508–543–1776; *www.gillettestadium.com*) are home to Boston's professional sports teams: Revolution Soccer (877–GET–REVS; *www.revolutionsoccer.net*); the Boston Celtics (617–854–8000; *www.nba.com/Celtics*); the New England Patriots (800–543–1776; *www.patriots.com*); the Boston Redsox (617–267–9440; *www.bostonredsox.com*); and the Boston Bruins (*www.bostonbruins.com*).

For the Visitor

Accommodations: The Greater Boston area holds 33,064 rooms in 161 hotels and inns. In the historic South End, Chandler Inn (26 Chandler Street; 617–482–3450; *www.chandlerinn.com*) offers 56 refurbished contemporary rooms. The Encore B&B (116 West Newton Street; 617–247–3425; *www.encorebandb.com*) provides 21st-century comfort in a 19th-century town house. A warm kitchen welcomes you to an early or late breakfast at Rutland Square House B&B (56 Rutland Square; 617–247–0018; *www.rutlandsquarebandb.com*), an elegant yet relaxed bed and breakfast in a beautiful South End brownstone row house.

For More Information

Publications

Boston Globe
135 Morrissey Boulevard
Boston, MA 02109
617–929–2000
www.boston.com/globe

Boston Herald
1 Herald Square
Boston, MA 02106
617–426–3000
www.bostonherald.com

Bay Windows
637 Tremont Street
Boston, MA 02118
617–266–6670
www.baywindows.com

EDGE
EDGE Publications, LLC
398 Columbus Avenue, #353
Boston, MA 02116
www.edgeboston.com

In Newsweekly
450 Harrison Avenue,
Suite 414
Boston, MA 02118
617–426–8246
www.innewsweekly.com

Convention and Visitors Bureau

Greater Boston Convention and
Visitors Bureau
Two Copley Place, Suite 105
Boston, MA 02116-6501
888–SEE–BOSTON
www.bostonusa.com

Chambers of Commerce

Greater Boston Business Council
P.O. Box 1059
Boston, MA 02117-1059
866–594–4222
www.gbbc.org

Greater Boston Chamber of
Commerce
75 State Street, 2nd Floor
Boston, MA 02109
617–227–4500
www.bostonchamber.com

Realtor

Alex Haidar
CEO
Skyline Realty
10 Magazine Street
Cambridge, MA 02139
617–547–8700
www.skylinerealty.com

Provincetown, Massachusetts

25

A Look at Provincetown

Provincetown is captivating. Remarkable ocean views, wide dune fields, and sandy bluffs edge the Cape Cod National Seashore. The unique lure of Provincetown are those charming harbors, quaint villages, and forests that smell of the sea. Days at the beach are kissed by ocean breezes. Fresh-caught seafood is a plan for dinner. Luxuriant seaside inns provide escape or employment. Swimming, sailing, fishing, whale watching, walking and bicycling along miles of trails, and more miles of woods and pristine beaches provide recreation. When a need for history calls, visit the sites of the Pilgrims' landing or travel back in time to the days of whaling. Art galleries and museums from Falmouth to Provincetown display the works of local and world-renowned artists. Theaters and concerts add fantasy, whimsy, and classics to the mix. You can dance the night away at one of the local clubs or walk the moonlit beaches—all in a small-town setting that creates friends from neighbors.

Possible drawbacks: Provincetown is a tourist town, dependent on weekend and summer travelers. When travel is slow, incomes are lowered; when travel is high, P-town can be overcrowded and overwhelming. But, at least you can always turn and look out over lovely dunes at the water.

Local Connections

Gas and electric company: Nstar (800–592–2000; *www.nstaronline.com*)

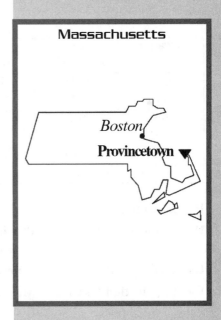

Massachusetts

▶ Nickname:
P-town

▶ County: Barnstable

▶ Area code: 508

▶ Time zone: Eastern

▶ Population: 3,431

▶ County population:
222,230

▶ Region:
Southeast Massachusetts

▶ Closest metro area:
Boston

▶ Average home price:
$895,000

▶ Fabulous reasons to live here:
Beautiful setting, beaches, laid-back atmosphere, excellent location, nightlife, recreation, social GLBT community

Climate

Elevation 40'	Avg. high/low(F°)	Avg. inches		Avg. # days precip.	Avg. % humidity
		rain	snow		
Jan.	37/23	3.8	12.9	12	58%
April	52/37	3.5	–	11	55%
July	79/63	2.8	–	9	57%
Oct.	60/45	3.6	–	9	58%
YEAR	57/42	41.9	42.2	128	58%
# days 32° or below: 34			# days 90° or warmer: 0		

Phone company: Sprint (800–877–7746; *www.sprint.com*)

Water and sewer: Provincetown Water Department (508–487–9560; *www.provincetowngov.org/works.html*)

Cable company: Comcast (800–266–2278; *www.comcast.com*)

Car registration/License: Massachusetts Registry of Motor Vehicles (617–351–4500; *www.mass.gov/rmv*)

You must obtain a valid Massachusetts license upon becoming a resident. You must provide the RMV with your current out-of-state photo license and proof of your current Massachusetts residency. Your current license gets you out of the written and road test. An eye test will be required. Licenses are good for five years and fees range from $40 to $60. Normal passenger registration is for two years. Fee: $36. The registration transfer fee is $15.

The Tax Ax

Sales tax: 5 percent; food and prescription drugs exempt

State income tax: 5.3 percent (flat rate for all residents); 9.5 percent on all corporate income

Property tax: Provincetown Board of Assessors (508–487–7017; *www.provincetowngov.org/assessor.html*)

Property is assessed at 100 percent of market value and taxed based on class of use. The Fiscal 2004 tax rate is $5.45 per $1,000 of valuation.

Local Real Estate

Overview: Charming and historic Provincetown has many single-family and duplex homes. Properties ages range from 19th-century historic to modern construction, but the housing styles remain traditional. A few of those styles include the familiar Cape Cod and saltbox. Many of the "antique" homes include wide board floors, lovely porches, and clapboard paneling.

Median price for a single-family home: $750,000

Average price for a single-family home: $895,000

Average price for a 2BR condo: $483,000

Rental housing market: Two-bedroom rentals start at approximately $1,200 a month.

Gay-friendly neighborhoods: All of Provincetown is gay-friendly.

Nearby areas to consider: Barnstable County is also home to the cities of Barnstable, Harwich, Hyannis, and Chatham. These small communities along the peninsula are all popular with the GLBT community because of the weather, views, and small-town, friendly atmosphere. Though each city offers its own unique charms, there are also some general similarities such as historic, New England shore housing styles, a wide array of artists and art galleries, excellent dining, and fabulous recreation opportunities such as sailing, swimming, and hiking.

Earning a Living

Per capita income: $26,878

Median household income: $39,786

Business climate: Provincetown's economic interests rest in a service and tourism foundation. The city's focus on gay and lesbian travel has proved a profitable one. Small businesses and entrepreneurial interests make up the business base.

Help in starting a business: Provincetown Business Guild and the Provincetown Chamber of Commerce provide networking and promotional opportunities for local businesses.

Job market: Small businesses, boutique retail, lodging, arts, and other customer services create the area's job market base.

The Community

Overview: Visitors swell this small Cape Cod city during the summer months, creating the impression of a crowded place. It's only those visitors who call it P-town. Provincetown is home to the largest concentration of gay and lesbian couples in the country. The permanent community in this seaside whaling village is very small. This is a city where you can know all of your neighbors, and they can know you. There's a small-town sense of community pride. Successes for one person, couple, or business are successes for the community.

Community organizations: All the cities in Barnstable County are small, and there aren't many area support groups, but small-town friends and neighbors lend support and social stimuli. Two important area groups include AIDS Support Group of Cape Cod (800–905–1170), providing services to people with HIV and AIDS and educating the community at large about the disease and those affected, and Helping Our Women (HOW) (508–487–4357) a non-profit agency providing services to women with chronic and life-threatening and disabling illness. HOW provides case management, weekly support groups, financial assistance, and transportation.

Medical care: Cape Cod Hospital (508–771–1800/877–227–3263; *www.capecodhealth.org*) is a 218-bed community hospital serving residents of and visitors to Cape Cod, particularly those living and visiting the towns surrounding Hyannis and as far east as Provincetown. Falmouth Hospital (508–548–5300; *www.capecodhealth.org*) is an 83-bed facility located on a beautiful hilltop campus that it shares with the JML Care Center, Heritage at Falmouth, the VNA of Cape Cod, and a physician office complex. Jordan Hospital (508–746–2000; *www.jordanhospital.org*) is an acute-care, 139-bed, not-for-profit community hospital with more than 30 departments, programs, and services serving 12 towns in Plymouth and Barnstable counties. Rehabilitation Hospital of The Cape and Islands (508–833–4000; *www.rhci.org*) is the only facility providing comprehensive, hospital-level rehabilitation on Cape Cod with physicians and staff uniquely qualified to help people with disabling illness and injury regain function and independence, return home, and improve quality of life.

Nuptials: The State of Massachusetts issues marriage licenses to resident same-sex couples; weddings and commitment ceremonies are common in Provincetown, and many area businesses provide wedding services.

Getting Around Town

Public transportation: Provincetown is a member of the Cape Cod Regional Transit Authority (CCRTA) (800–352–7155; *capecodtransit.org*), which operates a b-bus demand response service. (B-bus picks you up, takes you where you want to go, and returns you home.) Fares are based on length of trip and paid for via a prepaid account system. The Breeze connects the entire Cape Cod peninsula. Fares start at $1 and increase based on the length of ride; one-day shuttle pass $3. The Plymouth and Brockton Street Railway Company (508–746–0378; *www.p-b.com*) provides two trips daily between Provincetown and Boston (one-way $26; round trip $47). The seasonal Provincetown Trolley (508–487–9483; *www.provincetowntrolley.com*) offers hop on/hop off service for $9. Passenger Ferries to Boston begin in May and run through October for Bay State Cruise Co. (617–748–1428; *www.boston-ptown.com*) and through September for Boston Harbor Cruises (617–227–4321; *www.bostonharborcruises.com*). Both charge $59 round trip (car and bike fees also apply).

Roads: US6, US6A

Airports: Provincetown Municipal Airport (airport ode: PVC) (508–487–0241; *www.massairports.com*); Logan International Airport (airport code: BOS) (617–561–1800; *www.massport.com/logan*) is approximately a two-and-a-half hour drive or a 25-minute flight on Cape Air (800–352–0714; *www.flycapeair.com*).

It's a Gay Life

Annual events: A score of annual events fill the Provincetown calendar. The big events in May are the Monumental Yard Sale (*www.ptown.org*) and Women's Singles Weekend (*www.womeninnkeepers.com*). Couples Weekend, the Annual

By the Sea Bike Trek Helping Our Women Fundraiser (*www.helpingourwomen.org*), International Birdman Competition (*www.GMDVP.org*), Annual Tennis for Life Tournament (508–487–1930), and Provincetown International Film Festival (*www.ptownfilmfest.org*) are just a few of the June events. Provincetown Carnival (*www.ptown.org*), a full week of festivities and a world famous parade, heats up August. Women's Week (*www.womeninnkeepers.com*) and later Fantasia Fair (*www.fantasiafair.org*) fill October. Holly Follies (*www.hollyfolly.com*) is a major GLBT holiday celebration. Contact Provincetown Business Guild (*www.ptown.org*) for the entire annual calendar of events.

Nightlife: Just about every establishment in Provincetown is gay-friendly. This fabulous resort town offers lots of restaurants and cafés, many with terrific views. The night comes alive at the excellent mix of bars clubs. The Boatslip Beach Resort (161 Commercial Street; 800–451–SLIP; *www.glrestorts.com*) is the spot for the afternoon Tea Dance. PiedBar (193A Commercial Street; 508–487–1527; *www.piedbar.com*) is mostly a women's bar, but the boys join in for the world-famous After Tea T-Dance. Atlantic House (8 Masonic Place; 508–487–3821; *www.ahouse.com*), known as the "A-House," is where most of the evening action takes place; it has weekly theme parties and is home to The Little Bar and the Macho Room. Bars close pretty early (1 a.m.) and "last call" happens at the legendary Spiritus Pizza (190 Commercial Street) until 2 a.m. Visit Provincetown Bookshop (246 Commercial Street; 508–487–0964) or Now, Voyager (357 Commercial Street; 508–487–0848; *www.nowvoyagerbooks.com*) to pick up a copy of *Cape Cod and Islands Pride Pages* for current listings and news.

Culture: Provincetown Theater Company (PTC) (238 Bradford Street; 508–487–7487; *www.provincetowntheater.org*) and the Provincetown Repertory Theatre (REP) (238 Bradford Street; 508–487–0600; *www.ptownrep.org*) present a season of works. The Provincetown Art Association and Museum (460 Commercial Street; 508–487–1750; *www.paam.org*), founded in 1914, has the works of its masters: Hawthorne (who founded the Cape Cod School of Art in 1899), Henry Hensche (who founded the Cape School of Art in 1935), Hans Hofmann, Edward Hopper, Robert Motherwell, and many contemporary artists. The Fine Arts Work Center (*www.fawc.org*), a converted lumberyard, houses 20 emerging writers and artists in the same studios inhabited by indigent artists before the FAWC was founded in 1968, when the lumberyard owners patronized starving artists by renting out disused lofts to them for a pittance. Truro Center for the Arts at Castle Hill (10 Meetinghouse Road, Turo; 508–349–7511; *www.castlehill.org*) holds exhibitions, lectures, forums, concerts, and other similar activities in order to promote social interaction among artists, craftsmen, laymen, and the community at large. The works of artists, past and present, is displayed extensively in Provincetown. Gallery owners promote the art of unrecognized artists alongside the work of successful artists. Pilgrim Monument & Provincetown Museum (High Pole Hill Road; 508–487–1310; *www.pilgrim-monument.org*) commemorates the landing of the Mayflower Pilgrims in 1620. The 252-foot granite structure has been admired and climbed by millions. The annual lighting of the monument every November, which celebrates the Pilgrims' stay in Provincetown before moving on to Plymouth, has become a much-loved tradition. The current museum, built in 1961, offers permanent exhibits on Provincetown history highlighting the arrival of the Mayflower pilgrims, the town's rich maritime history, the early days of modern American theater in Provincetown, and the building of the monument.

Recreation: Lying beachside while ocean breezes blow is one of the more popular summer daytime activities in Provincetown. The Cape is a fabulous place to explore, and walking, hiking, jogging, and biking are a few of the best ways to get around. Bike rentals are available and open up the many miles of paths for exploration. Also worth exploring is the Expedition Whydah Sea Lab (16 MacMillan Wharf; 508–487–8899; *www.whydah.com*), a Pirate Museum with the world's only display of pirate shipwreck treasure. Several area companies provide dune tours and whale and dolphin watching sea excursions. Heading out of town by car to explore the many galleries throughout Cape Cod is popular. Wineries are scattered throughout the Cape and Bay area, and tasting trips and tours make for a pleasant day on the Cape.

For the Visitor

Accommodations: There's no shortage of guest houses, inns, and bed and breakfast accommodations in Provincetown. There's a wide selection of styles, price ranges, and amenities available from more than 70 gay-owned and most gay-friendly establishments. The Boatslip Resort (161 Commercial Street; 508–487–1669/800–451–7547; *www.glresorts.com*), home to the daily Tea Dance, has 45 rooms, many with private balconies overlooking the sea (and pool deck). The Fairbanks Inn (90 Bradford Street; 508–487–0386/800–324–7265; *www.fairbanksinn.com*), built in 1776 as a sea captain's home, is renowned for its unique blend of historic charm and guest amenities. The White Wind Inn (174 Commercial Street; 508–487–1526/888–449–WIND; *www.whitewindinn.com*), a stately 1845 Victorian mansion built by a prosperous shipbuilder, has 12 guest rooms and a "great" room with fireplace and grand piano.

For More Information

Publications

Cape Cod and Islands Pride Pages
P.O. Box 929
Brewster, MA 02631
508–896–8088
www.capecodandislandspridepages.com

Cape Cod Times
319 Main Street
Box 550
Hyannis, MA 02601
508–487–1602
www.capecodonline.com

Convention and Visitors Bureau

Massachusetts Office of Travel &
Tourism
10 Park Plaza, Suite 4510
Boston, MA 02116
617–973–8500/800–227–MASS
www.massvacation.com

Chambers of Commerce

Provincetown Business Guild
3 Freeman Street, #2
P.O. Box 421-94
Provincetown, MA 02657
508–487–2313/800–637–8696
www.ptown.org

Provincetown Chamber of
Commerce
307 Commercial Street
P.O. Box 1017
Provincetown, MA 02657-1017
508–487–3424
www.ptownchamber.com

Realtor

Harbor Side Realty
162 Commercial Street
Provincetown, MA 02657
508–487–4005
www.harborside-realty.com

## 26

Ferndale, Michigan

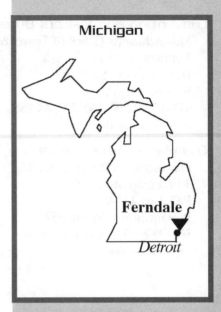

A Look at Ferndale

Founded in 1890 with the name Urbanrest, Ferndale was then and is now one of the handsomest Detroit suburbs. The tree-lined streets, summer little league and adult softball games, and a community involved in local organizations and city government are reminiscent of historic small-town America. Community pride is at the center of this city's success. Hundreds of Ferndale citizens volunteer on city government committees and the many social and support groups in the area. Individuality and entrepreneurship are encouraged. Neighbors know one another and support the local shops and businesses. Education is held in esteem, the city is home to Ferndale Montessori Center, and a majority of city residents hold college degrees. With 10 city parks, there's plenty of public green space for sports, picnics, and events. As a Detroit suburb, Ferndale enjoys the availability of attractions and events afforded a metropolitan center such as museums, concerts, sporting events, and the area's other recreational opportunities.

Possible drawbacks: Public transportation is limited in this Motor City suburb, so a car is a must. Although Ferndale continually enjoys low unemployment rates, the metro Detroit area has suffered a long period of hard economic times and crime rates for the area tend to be above the national average.

Local Connections

Gas company: Consumers Energy
(800–477–5050;
www.consumersenergy.com)

▶ County: Oakland

▶ Area code: 248

▶ Time zone: Eastern

▶ Population: 22,105

▶ County population: 1,194,156

▶ Region: Southeast Michigan

▶ Closest metro area: Detroit

▶ Average home price: $159,000

▶ Fabulous reasons to live here:
Excellent location, small-town charm, affordable housing, recreation, well-organized GLBT community, supportive local government, community pride

Climate

Elevation 649'	Avg. high/low(F°)	Avg. inches		Avg. # days precip.	Avg. % humidity
		rain	snow		
Jan.	31/16	1.8	10.6	13	75%
April	58/36	3.1	1.2	13	66%
July	84/62	3.1	–	10	68%
Oct.	66/35	2.6	0.2	10	70%
YEAR	59/39	32.5	41.1	136	70%
# days 32° or below: 92			# days 90° or warmer: 12		

Electric company: DTE Energy (800–477–4747; *www.dteenergy.com*)

Phone company: SBC Communications (800–244–4444; *www.sbc.com*)

Water and sewer: Detroit Metro Sewer, Water & Solid Waste (DWSD) (313–964–9090; *www.dwsd.org*)

Cable companies: Comcast Cable (248–549–2100; *www.comcast.com*); Wide Open West (866–496–9669; *www.wowway.com*)

Car registration/License: Michigan Department of State (517–322–1460; *www.michigan.gov/sos*)

New Michigan residents must obtain a Michigan driver's license immediately upon establishing a permanent domicile (home) within the state and/or obtaining employment with the intent of remaining in the state. Vision test required. A valid out-of-state license may waive other exams. License Fee: $25. Vehicle Title Fee: $15. Vehicle registration includes plates; fees are an *ad valorem* tax based on the MSR. Minimum fee: $200 annually.

The Tax Ax

Sales tax: 6 percent

State income tax: 3.95 percent (flat rate)

Property tax: Michigan Department of Treasury (800–487–7000; *www.treas.state.mi.us*)

Assessed at the local level, property taxes are determined based on the city's assessment of taxable value, and that value can rise yearly only by a percent of the cost of living. Homeowners who live in their property pay a significantly lower tax rate.

Local Real Estate

Overview: Ferndale boasts a wide range of housing from 1920s bungalows and brick two-family homes to newly constructed brick and vinyl Colonials and ranches. In the past 10 years, the city has experienced an enormous number of neighborhoods that have been dramatically changed by homeowners and landlords updating their properties. As a result, the housing market is strong and prices are climbing.

Median price for a single-family home: $120,000

Average price for a single-family home: $159,000

Average price for a 2BR condo: $153,000

Rental housing market: In the past 10 years, the city has tightened its requirements for rental certificates. As a result, the majority of rental properties have been improved and there is a wide range of rentals available.

Gay-friendly neighborhoods: The entire city of Ferndale is gay-friendly.

Nearby areas to consider: The Detroit suburbs of Royal Oak, Pleasant Ridge, Huntington Woods, and Birmingham all boast large GLBT communities. Each offers a different atmosphere and style and varied housing prices and commute times. The fabulous thing about so many places in the Detroit metro area welcoming GLBT community members is that the choice becomes about which amenities such as housing styles and prices, shopping, neighborhood comfort zones, city services, parks, and school districts will meet your individual needs while making you comfortable and happy. There are a lot of options in Detroit.

Earning a Living

Per capita income: $23,133

Median household income: $51,687

Business climate: Ferndale maintains a keen emphasis on economic development, attracting a strong, diverse business cadre. Centrally located in metro Detroit, Downtown Ferndale businesses offer unique, convenient, and personalized service. The Detroit Metro area ranks as a leader in the production of paints, non-electrical machinery, and automation equipment, as well as pharmaceutical, rubber products, synthetic resins, and garden seed.

Help in starting a business: The Ferndale Chamber of Commerce provides a variety of services for its members including site location and new business assistance, consultation and referrals, education, and networking and business opportunities. The Ferndale Downtown Development Authority helps companies grow and expand into the local, national, and international markets and find new trade and business opportunities.

Job market: City government, manufacturing, and professional services are major employment sectors. Ferndale supports its small businesses and continually enjoys one of the area's lowest unemployment rates. Entrepreneurs and small businesses do well in Ferndale's stable economy.

The Community

Overview: Ferndale is at the center of GLBT life in the metro area. This small, upscale neighborhood has a strong sense of community and pride. The annual Gay Pride celebration closes down the main street and a number of adjoining streets on a summer Sunday for thousands of visitors. Affirmations, the area's GLBT community center, is on the main street of the city and is now building a multi-million-dollar center in the heart of town. The main street also boasts two GLBT bookstores; a nightclub/dance bar; and many gay-friendly restaurants, coffee shops, and boutiques, as well as several other gay-owned and -operated businesses.

Community organizations: Affirmations Lesbian/Gay Community Center is the hub of the community celebrating wellness, personal growth, and development. The state-of-the-art, multi-use facility is financially secure and provides the community with meeting space, resources and referrals, a game room and library, and a host of social, recreational, educational, and support events. Affirmations hosts a number of the area support and social group and organization meetings, including One Voice, metro Detroit's GLBT chorus.

Medical care: William Beaumont Hospital Clinic (248–898–5000; *www.beaumonthospitals.com*) is a 929-bed tertiary hospital, complete with inpatient and outpatient services and several other buildings, including Imaging Center, housing X-ray and other radiology testing, and the Comprehensive Breast Center, the Beaumont Cancer Center, Renal Center, Vascular Services Center, Research Institute, the Beaumont Heart Center, and medical office building, housing physicians' private practices and several other Beaumont services. Henry Ford–Kingswood Hospital (248–398–3200; *www.henryfordhealth.org*), offering a seamless array of acute, primary, tertiary, quaternary, and preventive care, was founded in 1915 by auto pioneer Henry Ford in Detroit. Today 2,800 Henry Ford physicians work throughout southeast Michigan, delivering high-quality care to more than 2.5 million patients.

Nuptials: The State of Michigan's constitution defines marriage as between a man and a woman. Commitment ceremonies are an annual event at Motor City Pride.

Getting Around Town

Public transportation: The Detroit Metro area does not have a comprehensive public transportation system. Suburban Mobility Authority for Regional Transportation (SMART) (313–962–5515/866–962–5515; *www.smartbus.org*) provides limited fixed-route services and door-to-door services with advance reservations. Fare: $2; transfer 25 cents.

Roads: I-75, I-696

Airport: Detroit Metropolitan Airport (airport code: DTW) (734–AIRPORT; *www.metroairport.com*) has undergone a dramatic transformation, adding a new Northwest Airlines Hub terminal and runway.

It's a Gay Life

Annual events: Motor City Pride (*www.pridefest.net*) takes over the streets of Ferndale in early June with a parade, street festival, beer garden, and events. In January, Reel Pride Michigan (*www.reelpridemichigan.com*) hosts the GLBT

Film Festival. The Ferndale Metro Blues Festival (*www.aidsprevention.org*) in February is five days of music and special events all over the city. In August, the Dream Cruise Car Show (*www.ferndalecruise.com*) hosts 500 classic cars. The Detroit area has a full calendar of annual events including the North American International Auto Show (*www.naias.com*) and the Budweiser Downtown Hoedown (313–877–8077; *www.wattsupinc.com*), widely recognized as the largest free country music festival in the world. The Detroit Metro Convention & Visitors Bureau has a complete list of events.

Nightlife: For a small town, Ferndale provides lots of nighttime opportunities. Ferndale is home to several fabulous dinner and jazz clubs. Two area gay restaurants include Como's (22812 Woodward; 248–548–5005; *www.comospizza.com*) and Sweet Lorraine's (29101 Greenfield Road; 248–559–5985). Ferndale also has several gay clubs, including Cobalt (22061 Woodward Avenue; 248–591–0106), a neighborhood bar with an eclectic house music mix on the dance floor upstairs and a quieter space downstairs; Soho (205 W. 9 Mile Road; 248–542–7646; *www.qferndale.com*), an intimate video bar; and Q (141 W. 9 Mile Road; 248–582–7227; *www.qferndale.com*), which hosts theme nights, special events, and tends to be packed Wednesdays, Fridays, and Saturdays (the only nights it's open). Additionally, the Detroit metro area has about 30 gay bars and clubs and another half-dozen gay restaurants and cafés. *Between the Lines* (*www.pridesource.com*) and *Cruise Magazine* (*www.cruisemagazineonline.com*) are statewide rags with all the current listings; you'll find copies at Ferndale's gay bookstores: A Woman's Perspective (175 W. 9 Mile Road; 248–545–5703; *www.awpbooks.com*) and Just 4 Us (211 W. 9 Mile Road; 248–547–5878).

Culture: One of Ferndale's gems is Magic Bag Theatre (22920 Woodward Avenue; 248–544–3030; *www.themagicbag.com*), home of View & Brew movie nights, a full line-up of concerts and parties, and a rentable space for special events. The Ferndale Arts and Cultural Commission (*www.ferndalearts.org*) hosts art fairs, concerts, and community events throughout the year. Metro Detroit has a unique assortment of attractions and collections not found anywhere in the world. The Detroit Symphony Orchestra (313–576–1111; *www.detroitsymphony.com*) performs in Orchestra Hall (3711 Woodward Avenue, Detroit; 313–576–5111; *www.detroitsymphony.com*), a national historic landmark. The orchestra is heard live by more than 450,000 people annually in a year-round performance schedule that includes 26 weeks of classical subscription concerts. The area is home to more than 20 theaters and concert halls, bringing a wide range of live theater, concerts, and touring shows to the area. Isamu Noguchi–designed Hart Plaza (Woodward at Jefferson, Detroit; 313–877–8077; *www.cobocenter.com*), in the heart of the Detroit, is the site of Detroit's summer-long riverfront festivals and the Ford Detroit International Jazz Festival. Some of the most-visited Detroit attractions include the Henry Ford (20900 Oakwood Boulevard, Dearborn; 313–271–2455; *www.hfmgv.org*) with its museum, Greenfield Village, IMAX theater, and factory tour; Detroit Zoo (8450 W. 10 Mile Road, Royal Oak; 248–398–0900; *www.detroitzoo.org*), located in Royal Oak, which has 125 acres of naturalistic exhibits, fine and performing arts, educational opportunities, and exciting animals; Charles H. Wright Museum of African American History (315 E. Warren Avenue, Detroit; 313–494–5800; *www.maah-detroit.org*), anchored by a permanent exhibit that examines the richness of African civilization from the "Middle Passage" to the Underground Railroad in the escape to freedom; and the Detroit Institute of Arts (5200 Woodward Avenue, Detroit; 313–833–7900; *www.dia.org*), with a collection of more than 65,000 works that range from classic to cutting edge.

Recreation: Ferndale is home to 10 city parks (and Oakland County has another 11) offering natural landscapes for year-round recreation with five golf courses and two water parks and nature centers. Unique recreation opportunities include the Fridge toboggan run. Bowling and baseball are two of the area's favorite pastimes, and there are plenty of fields and lanes throughout the area. Detroit's 1,000-acre Belle Isle Park (313–852–4075; *www.ci.detroit.mu.us/recreation*), with original landscaping by the dean of American landscape architects, Frederick Law Olmstead, features a zoo, aquarium, conservatory, Great Lakes museum, and plenty of room to hike, barbecue, watch boats, bicycle, and more. Spectators will enjoy the NHL's Detroit Red Wings (313–983–6606; *www.detroitredwings.com*), the NBA's Detroit Pistons (248–377–0100; *www.nba.com/pistons*), the NFL's Detroit Lions (313–262–2003; *www.detroitlions.com*), MLB's Detroit Tigers (313–962–4000; *www.detroittigers.com*), and the WNBA's Detroit Shock (248–377–0100; *www.wnba.com/shock*).

For the Visitor

Accommodations: Several gay-friendly accommodations are located in the heart of Detroit. A National Registered Historic Site, Woodbridge Star B&B (3985 Trumbull Avenue; 313–831–9668; *www.woodbridgestar.com*) is an 1891 Victorian home with stained-glass windows, marble and mahogany fireplaces, inlaid parquet floors, ornate plasterwork, 10-foot ceilings, and oak woodwork. The Atheneum Suite Hotel (1000 Brush Street; 313–962–2323/800–772–2323; *www.atheneumsuites.com*), located across from Lafayette Park, is the city's only AAA Four-Diamond hotel.

For More Information

Gay & Lesbian Center
Affirmations Lesbian & Gay
Community Center
195 W. 9 Mile Road
Ferndale, MI 48220
248–398–7105/800–398–GAYS
www.goaffirmations.org

Publications
Between the Lines
20793 Farmington, Suite 25
Farmington, MI 48336
888–615–7003
www.pridesource.com

Publications

Daily Tribune
210 E 3rd Street
Royal Oak, MI 48067
248–541–3000
www.dailytribune.com

Detroit Free Press
600 W. Fort Street
Detroit, MI 48226
313–222–6400
www.freep.com

Convention and Visitors Bureau

Detroit Metro Convention & Visitors
Bureau
211 W. Fort Street, Suite 1000
Detroit, MI 48226
800–338–7648
www.visitdetroit.com

Chambers of Commerce

Ferndale Chamber of Commerce
415 East 9 Mile Road
Ferndale, MI 48220
248–542–2160
www.ferndale-mi.com

Ferndale Downtown Development
Authority
149 W. 9 Mile Road
Ferndale, MI 48220
248–546–1632
www.downtownferndale.com

Realtor

Gerry Banister
Realtor
RE/MAX Showcase Homes
912 S. Old Woodward
Birmingham, MI 48009
248–645–1589
www.GerryBanister.com

Minneapolis, Minnesota

27

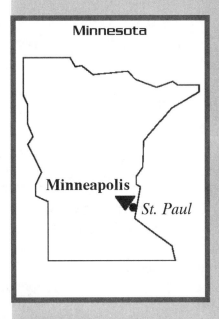

Minnesota

Minneapolis

St. Paul

A Look at Minneapolis

Minneapolis is a city for all seasons. Fall is visually striking. The air is crisp and the trees turn brilliant shades of red, yellow, and orange, making the miles of trails along the Mississippi River, area lakes, and Minnesota River Valley a picturesque playground. Winter brings ice skating, cross country and downhill skiing, ice fishing, and more. The city's 7 miles of enclosed above-ground walkways, called the skyway system, link theaters, hotels, nightlife, and restaurants that stay vibrant and alive all winter long. Spring returns with a vengeance and the city bursts into green, warm life. During this beautiful time of year residents return to sidewalk cafes, lakeshores, and outdoor trails, and golfers flock to urban courses. The many lakes and parks provide summer activity options including boating, running, fishing, hiking, and swimming. Festivals and neighborhood events pack the summer months. The city boasts a vibrant art scene with fabulous museums, award-winning theaters, world-renowned orchestras and choirs, and one of the nation's best jazz scenes. Hundreds of parks create outdoor recreation options beyond compare, and Minneapolis enjoys a stable economy with an ongoing low unemployment rate.

Possible drawbacks: With annual snowfall close to 50 inches and nearly three months of below-freezing temperatures, even the hardiest soul will probably be talking to the furniture come February.

▶ Nickname:
City of Lakes

▶ County:
Hennepin

▶ Area code: 612

▶ Time zone: Central

▶ Population: 382,618

▶ County population:
1,116,200

▶ Region:
Southeastern Minnesota

▶ Average home price:
$250,000

▶ Fabulous reasons to live here:
Beautiful setting; recreation, arts, culture, and music; progressive local politics; large, active GLBT community; excellent education; strong economy

Climate

Elevation 815'	Avg. high/low(F°)	Avg. inches		Avg. # days precip.	Avg. % humidity
		rain	snow		
Jan.	21/4	1.1	10.7	9	72%
April	57/36	2.4	2.8	10	64%
July	83/62	4.2	–	10	70%
Oct.	58/38	2.2	0.5	8	70%
YEAR	54/35	30.5	49.9	113	70%
# days 32° or below: 102			# days 90° or warmer: 14		

Local Connections

Gas and electric company: Xcel Energy (electric: 800–895–4999; gas: 800–481–4700; *www.xcelenergy.com*)

Phone companies: More than 32 long distance carriers provide local phone service in the Twin Cities region. Qwest (800–491–0118; *www.qwest.com*); AT&T (800–222–0300; *www.att.com*)

Water and sewer: Minneapolis Public Works Department (612–673–2352; *www.ci.minneapolis.mn.us/public-works*)

Cable company: Time Warner Cable (612–522–2000; *www.timewarnercable.com/Minnesota*)

Car registration/License: Minnesota Department of Public Safety (651–296–6911; *www.dps.state.mn.us/dvs*)

You have 60 days after becoming a resident in Minnesota to register your vehicle and obtain your Minnesota license. Driving test may be waived when surrendering a valid, out-of-state license. Applicants still need to take the vision and written exams. Fee: $37.50. Title fee: $3 (an additional $2 is due to record a lien). Public Safety Vehicle fee: $3.50. Filing fee: $7. License plate fee: $4.25. In addition, the vehicle registration fee is based on year of car and manufacturer's suggested price (between $35 and $189).

The Tax Ax

Sales tax: 7 percent

State income tax: 5.35–8.5 percent graduated, based on income

Property tax: Hennepin County (612–348–3011; *www.co.hennepin.mn.us*)

Property taxes vary by location and are determined by many government levies (State, county, and local), estimated assessed value, and property type of use.

Local Real Estate

Overview: The local market in Minneapolis consists of town houses, condos, single-family, and investment properties. Styles range from contemporary to Tudor, saltbox to Victorian, ranch to modern.

Median price for a single-family home: $250,000

Average price for a single-family home: $250,000

Average price for a 2BR condo: $190,000

Rental housing market: There's a wide variety of rental possibilities, from apartment buildings to homes. A two-bedroom rental ranges from $600 to $1,200.

Gay-friendly neighborhoods: There's no gay "ghetto" or single gay neighborhood; the GLBT community is wonderfully integrated into the Minneapolis scene.

Nearby areas to consider: Five miles west of Downtown Minneapolis, Golden Valley, a small city of just more than 20,000 residents, with summer concerts in the park, adult and youth sports leagues, a skating park, excellent schools, higher than average median household incomes, and a low crime rate, is a popular Minneapolis first-ring suburb of choice for the GLBT community, especially those raising families. This is a city in which to own a home, with prices about half that of Minneapolis, and to work. Several major corporations are headquartered in Golden Valley, among them General Mills, US Health Care, and Honeywell. (In fact, the city boasts more jobs than residents.)

Earning a Living

Per capita income: $22,685

Median household income: $37,974

Business climate: The metropolitan area has a strong and diversified business base, including companies involved in manufacturing super-computers, electronics, medical instruments, milling, machine manufacturing, food processing, and graphic arts. These businesses, and others, have helped to make the Twin Cities one of the largest commercial centers between the East and West coasts.

Help in starting a business: The Minneapolis Regional Chamber represents all area businesses, including home-based. The Chamber is focused on the development of existing businesses and the global recruitment of new business to the metropolitan area and provides networking, advocacy, and educational programs to assist existing and new businesses.

Job market: The region is home to 16 Fortune 500 and 30 Fortune 1000 companies and consistently enjoys one of the nation's lowest unemployment rates. Educational, health, and social services; professional, scientific, management, administrative, and waste management services; arts, entertainment, recreation, accommodation, and food services; and manufacturing and retail trade are all strong market sectors.

The Community

Overview: Minneapolis has an expressed goal of becoming America's most gay-friendly city and, based on the GLBT population, the large number of organizations, and the outward local government support, it's well on its way. The city's most striking asset is its sense of inclusiveness. The community is active and well supported by local government with several top elected and appointed positions held by out GLBT community members.

Community organizations: There are well in excess of a hundred GLBT organizations in Minneapolis and the Twin City area, truly places and groups for everyone's needs. OutFront Minnesota (612–822–0127; *www.outfront.org*), Minnesota's leading GLBT organization, provides resources and programs to improve the quality of life for all GLBT Minnesotans. There are dozens of support, spiritual, social, and recreational groups and organizations in the Twin Cities area. OutFront maintains an extensive list of organizations and community resources.

Medical care: In the Twin Cities area Abbott Northwestern Hospital (612–863–4000; *www.abbottnorthwestern.com*) is the largest not-for-profit hospital. Each year, the hospital provides comprehensive healthcare for more than 200,000 patients and their families from the Twin Cities area and throughout the Upper Midwest. More than 5,000 employees, 1,600 physicians, and 550 volunteers work as a team for the benefit of each patient served. Abbott Northwestern Hospital is a part of Allina Hospitals & Clinics (612–775–5000; *www.allina.com*), a non-profit network of hospitals, clinics, and other healthcare services providing care throughout Minnesota and western Wisconsin. Allina offer a vast array of services and programs through a dedicated workforce of more than 22,000 employees. Allina owns and operates 11 hospitals, 42 clinics, hospice services, pharmacies, medical equipment, and emergency medical transportation services and provides a continuum of care, from disease prevention programs to technically advanced inpatient and outpatient care to medical transportation, pharmacy, and hospice services.

Nuptials: The State of Minnesota has a law similar to DOMA that defines marriage as between a man and a woman and doesn't recognize same-sex marriages from other jurisdictions. The City of Minneapolis offers domestic partner registration that provides visitation privileges in healthcare facilities. Some employers also provide benefits to registered partners. Applications must be filed with the City of Minneapolis Clerk's Office (612–673–3947; *www.ci.minneapolis.mn.us/clerk*).

Getting Around Town

Public transportation: Metro Transit (612–373–3333; *www.metrotransit.org*) provides light-rail and bus services to the Minneapolis–St. Paul area. Bus fares: local $1.25 (rush hours $1.75); express $1.75 (rush hours $2.50), Downtown Zone at all times is 50 cents. Transfers are free. Day Pass: $6. The Hiawatha Line is a light-rail service with 17 stops between Downtown and Mall of America at the same fares as the local bus.

Roads: I-494, I-694, US10, US52, US169, SR8, SR47, SR56, SR110, SR118

Airport: Minneapolis–St. Paul International Airport (airport code: MSP) (612–726–5800; *www.mspairport.com*) is a hub for Northwest, the nation's fourth-largest airline. The airport is also served by every other major airline but Southwest.

It's a Gay Life

Annual events: GLBT Pride/Twin Cities (*www.tcpride.org*) sponsors the annual Gay Pride Festival and Parade in June. Flaming Film Festival at Intermedia Arts (612–871–4444; *www.intermediaarts.org*) is in May. The city is also known for its many arts and music festivals, including one of the nation's largest Fringe Festivals, the Minnesota Fringe Festival (*www.fringefestival.com*), with 750 performances in August.

Nightlife: The gay-friendly Twin Cities' many bars, nightclubs, and concert halls feature a wide range of live music nightly. If you like jazz, the Dakota Bar and Grill (1010 Nicollet Avenue S.; 612–322–1010; *www.dakotacooks.com*), the Artists Quarter (408 St. Peter Street, St. Paul; 651–292–1359; *www.mnjazz.com*), and Famous Dave's - BBQ and Blues (3001 Hennepin Avenue S.; 612–822–9900; *www.famousdaves.com*) are three excellent choices. The area is home to about 20 gay bars and clubs and another 20 restaurants and cafes. You'll quickly discover that gay-friendly Minnesota doesn't have a gay section of town, instead, most of the bars are literally scattered throughout the area. A few clubs have clustered together in the Warehouse District. Here you'll find Boom and Oddfellows Restaurant (401 E. Hennepin Avenue; 612–378–3188; *www.oddfellowsrestaurant.com*), Brass Rail (422 E. Hennepin Avenue; 612–233–3016; *www.gaympls.com*), Times Bar/Jitters (201 and 205 E. Hennepin Avenue; 612–617–8089; *www.timesbarandcafe.com*), Ground Zero/the Front (15 NE 4th Street; 612–378–5115), and, close by, Margarita Bella (1032 3rd Avenue NE; 612–231–7955). Pick up a copy of *Lavender Magazine* (612–871–2237; *www.lavendermagazine.com*) at the bookstore A Brother's Touch (2327 Hennepin Avenue; 612–377–6279; *www.brotherstouch.com*) for current listings, events, and news.

Culture: The Twin Cities have a community tradition of supporting the arts. Minneapolis is home to more than 57 museums, private art galleries, music and arts festivals, and historic theaters that offer drama, comedy, and music. Minneapolis is a theater-loving city with more than 100 theater companies and 30 theater venues including two Tony Award–winning theaters: the Children's Theatre Company (2400 3rd Avenue S.; 612–874–0400; *www.childrenstheatre.org*) and the Guthrie Theater (725 Vineland Place; 612–377–2224; *www.guthrietheater.org*). In fact, the area boasts more theater per capita than any other U.S. city outside New York. An illuminated area of downtown Minneapolis called the Hennepin Avenue Theater District includes four impressive theater venues within walking distance of an array of restaurants. Minneapolis is abuzz in August with the 750 indoor performances during the Minnesota Fringe Festival and three unique outdoor art festivals: Metris Uptown Art Fair (612–823–4581; *www.uptownminneapolis.com*), Loring Park Art Festival (612–203–9911), and Powderhorn Art Fair (612–729–0111; *www.powderhornartfair.org*). The level of musical artistry in the Twin Cities is extraordinary, featuring more than 18 professional music organizations and 25 community music groups. Minneapolis is a top jazz destination and home to one of the largest civic jazz festivals in the nation: Twin Cities Hot Summer Jazz Festival (Peavy Plaza; 612–343–5943; *www.hotsummerjazz.com*). Minneapolis Arts Explosion (*www.arts.minneapolis.org*) has a complete list of the area's many venues and concert and show schedules.

Recreation: Twin Cities' parks and lakes are extensive, with 136,900 acres of parkland and 950 lakes in the metro area alone. No resident lives more than six blocks from a park. Hiking, fishing, swimming, golfing, snow shoeing, boating, or evening walks around Lake Harriet are all popular and accessible activities. Outwoods (612–825–1953; *www.outwoods.org*), a local non-profit organization, provides non-competitive outdoor recreational activities by and for the GLBT community. With more golfers per capita than any other U.S. state, Minnesota has 175 area golf courses. Mall of America (8100 24th Avenue S., Bloomington; 952–883–8800; *www.mallofamerica.com*) has an indoor amusement park that enjoys perfect weather all year round. You can also hang with the sharks at Underwater Adventures and shop at more than 500 stores. If spectator sports are your preferred form of recreation there are a variety of options, including four professional sports teams to cheer on: the NFL's Vikings (612–338–4538; *www.vikings.com*), the NHL's Wild (651–602–6000; *www.wild.com*), the NBA's Timberwolves (612–673–1600; *www.nba.com/ timberwolves*), and MLB's Twins (612–375–1366; *minnesota.twins.mlb.com*). And when they're not playing, the Xcel Energy Center (199 West Kellogg Boulevard, St. Paul; 651–265–4800; *www.rivercentre.org*) and Target Center (600 1st Avenue N.; 612–673–0900; *www.targetcenter.com*) are active concert venues. The University of Minnesota (*www.umn.edu*) teams and the St. Paul Saints (651–644–6659; *www.saintsbaseball.com*), a minor league baseball team that is a local favorite for a summer evening of fun, are additional possibilities.

For the Visitor

Accommodations: The Greater Minneapolis Convention and Visitors Bureau has created a Website for gay travelers (*www.glbtminneapolis.org*) full of customized content that highlights all the amenities that Minneapolis offers for gay travelers and their families. Many of the city's large chain hotels offer frequent GLBT specials and packages. Here are just a few of the more intimate options available in Minneapolis. The only downtown gay hotel is Hotel Amsterdam (828 Hennepin Avenue; 612–288–0459/800–649–9500; *www.gaympls.com*), self-described as a basic, clean, and reasonably priced hotel. Steps away from the Guthrie Theater, the Minneapolis Institute of Arts, and the Walker Art Center, Nan's B&B (2304 Fremont Avenue S.; 612–377–5118) is an 1890s Victorian family home comfortably furnished with antiques. The gay-friendly Millennium Hotel Minneapolis

(1313 Nicollet Mall; 612–332–6000/ 866–866–8086; *www.millenniumhotels.com*) offers convenient access to commercial districts, dining, vibrant nightlife and cultural activities.

For More Information

Gay & Lesbian Center

OutFront Minnesota
310 38th Street E., #204
Minneapolis, MN 55409-1337
612–822–0127
www.outfront.org

Publications

Lavender Magazine
3715 Chicago Avenue S.
Minneapolis, MN 55407
612–436–4660
www.lavendermagazine.com

Minneapolis Star Tribune
425 Portland Avenue
Minneapolis, MN 55488
612–673–4000
www.startribune.com

Minneapolis-St. Paul Magazine
220 S. Sixth Street, Suite 500
Minneapolis, MN 55402-4500
612–339–7571
www.mspmag.com

Convention and Visitors Bureau

The Greater Minneapolis Convention & Visitors Association
250 Marquette Avenue S., Suite 1300
Minneapolis, MN 55401
888–676–6757
www.minneapolis.org

Chambers of Commerce

Minneapolis Regional Chamber of Commerce
81 South Ninth Street, Suite 200
Minneapolis, MN 55402
612–370–9100
www.minneapolischamber.org

Twin Cities GLBTA Chamber of Commerce (QUARUM)
3010 Hennepin Avenue South, #179
Minneapolis, MN 55408
www.twincitiesquorum.com

Realtor

Mary Keogh, Realtor
Coldwell Banker Burnet
8170 Old Carriage Court, Suite 100
Shakopee, MN 55379
612–708–8898
www.mrkrealty.com

28 ▶ St. Louis, Missouri

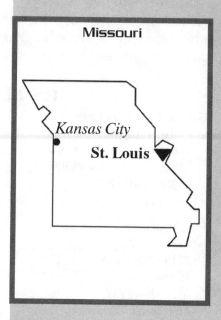

Missouri

Kansas City

St. Louis ▼

A Look at St. Louis

St. Louis has a look that's all its own: red brick buildings, cobblestone streets, terra-cotta friezes, and stained glass are part of the tapestry of St. Louis's amazing architectural heritage. The focal point of St. Louis's skyline is America's tallest man-made national monument: the 630-foot-tall Gateway Arch (*www.gatewayarch.com*), built in 1965 as a monument to President Thomas Jefferson. How did this monumental city of stone and brick spring up in the middle of the country? The wealth of St. Louis's merchant class and a massive fire are two of the answers. The great fire, which started on the levee aboard the steamboat White Cloud in 1849, left one-third of the growing city in ruins and created an ordinance that ensured future buildings would be constructed of brick, iron, and other non-flammable materials. St. Louisans who had been growing rich from the fur trade, commerce of the Mississippi River, and the outfitting of westward travelers for decades rebuilt their city with style, class, and an eye for beauty. These trends continue today both in restoration and new construction projects.

Possible drawbacks: The progressive city of St. Louis is located in a highly conservative state. Crime rates in the city are consistently above the national average, and the public school system is pretty rough; parents will want to consider sending their kids to private schools.

▶ Nickname:
Gateway City

▶ County:
St. Louis City

▶ Area code:
314

▶ Time zone:
Central

▶ Population:
348,189

▶ County population:
348,189

▶ Region:
Eastern Central Missouri

▶ Average home price:
$145,000

▶ Fabulous reasons to live here:
Strong economy; arts; museums; music; large, active GLBT community; affordable housing; historic architecture

Climate

Elevation 465'	Avg. high/low(F°)	Avg. inches		Avg. # days precip.	Avg. % humidity
		rain	snow		
Jan.	38/21	2.0	5.4	9	74%
April	66/47	3.8	0.5	11	67%
July	90/71	3.8	–	9	71%
Oct.	69/49	2.8	–	8	70%
YEAR	66/47	38.8	19.6	110	71%
# days 32° or below: 62			# days 90° or warmer: 40		

Local Connections

Gas company: Laclede Gas (314–621–6960/800–887–4173; *www.lacledegas.com*)

Electric company: Ameren (314–342–1000/800–552–7583; *www.ameren.com*)

Phone company: SBC Communications (800–244–4444; *www.sbc.com*)

Water and sewer: Water: St. Louis Water Division (314–771–2255; *www.stlwater.com*);
Sewer: Metropolitan St. Louis Sewer District (314–768–6200; *www.msd.st-louis.mo.us*)

Cable company: Charter Communications (314–965–0555; *www.charter.com*)

Car registration/License: Missouri Department of Revenue (573–751–4509 *www.dor.mo.gov/mvdl*)

New Missouri residents must surrender their out-of-state license and take the written, vision, and road sign tests (driving test may be waived). Driver's licenses (ages 21–69) are good for six years. Fee: $20. Other-aged drivers receive a three-year license; fee: $10. Title fee: $11. Sales tax: If the vehicle has been owned and operated in another state for at least ninety (90) days prior to the Missouri registration date, no sales tax is due; otherwise, drivers pay both state tax (4.225 percent) and local tax (7.62 percent). Owners who have paid sales tax to another state, less than the amount of Missouri state and local taxes, will be required to show proof of payment of those taxes and also pay the difference of the two amounts. In addition, motor vehicle license fees are based on the taxable horsepower of the motor vehicle plus a $3.50 processing fee for a one-year registration. Sales tax, registration, and title fees for a new $25,000 vehicle would be $1,918.

The Tax Ax

Sales tax: 10.55 percent

State income tax: 1.5–6 percent graduated, based on income

Property tax: Collector of Revenue (314–622–4101)

The local assessor determines a property's assessed value and tax rates are set by several governing bodies of local government, plus the three cent (per $100 valuation) state tax rate.

Local Real Estate

Overview: Homes range from the historic, renovated to retain their historic integrity, to the newest designs in family living. Depending upon your budget there are homes of all shapes and sizes. Spring and summer are always the best times to find homes in St. Louis, however there are plenty available all year long, ready for you whenever you are ready to make that move.

Median price for a single-family home: $140,000

Average price for a single-family home: $145,000

Average price for a 2BR condo: $175,000

Rental housing market: Rental property consists mainly of duplexes, four-family flats, and some larger apartment buildings with no special amenities. Rental rates range from $300 to $1,000.

Gay-friendly neighborhoods: The large St. Louis GLBT population lives throughout the city. The most popular areas are the eastern and northern portions of the Forrest Park neighborhood; the Central West End, a village-esque neighborhood; the South Grand neighborhood district; Tower Grove South and the Shaw neighborhood east of the park; and Soulard, one of St. Louis's oldest neighborhoods, hugging the Mississippi River just south of Downtown.

Nearby areas to consider: Many of the small towns, villages, and communities of St. Charles County to the north of St. Louis and Jefferson County to the south are called home by the metro area's GLBT community. Once you leave the city, housing lots grow larger and areas are generally more rural. If you're planning on raising a family in the St. Louis area, it's worth exploring the smaller communities in these counties because they offer more space and much better schools.

Earning a Living

Per capita income: $16,108

Median household income: $27,156

Business climate: St. Louis is forging new ground in high-technology industries, particularly in plant and life sciences, information technologies, and advanced manufacturing. Low property and living costs and government incentives are drawing large and small firms to the area, stimulating a healthy economy in a 16-county region.

Help in starting a business: The St. Louis Regional Chamber and Growth Association aggressively markets the region nationally and internationally to attract targeted industries to the area. It further spurs economic development by aiding the expansion of companies located within the region through networking, member discount opportunities, and speaker and educational events.

Job market: St. Louis has a higher-than-average concentration of jobs in fields such as computer systems analysis, hardware engineering, software applications engineering, medicinals, and industrial chemicals. Other areas of strength include educational, health, and social services; and manufacturing, arts, entertainment, recreation, accommodation, and food services.

The Community

Overview: The St. Louis GLBT community is large, active, and social. It takes credit for a revitalization of several of the city's neighborhoods. Among them, the Central West End, with tree-lined streets and a village-like atmosphere, is a popular community neighborhood with many shops, restaurants, clubs, and residences.

Community organizations: St. Louis's GLBT community lacks the focus of a community center, but Pride St. Louis (*www.pridestl.org*) hosts, organizes, and supports special events and programs throughout the year, including the area GLBT hotline (Gay and Lesbian City HotLine: 314–367–0084). The city has hundreds of support, social, recreational, health, and spiritual organizations. The St. Louis Community Pride Pages Telephone Directory (*www.thepridepages.com*) maintains a long list of groups (with contact information) as well as area GLBT gay and gay-friendly businesses.

Medical care: Barnes-Jewish Hospital (314–747–3000; *www.barnesjewish.org*) at Washington University Medical Center is the largest hospital in Missouri and the largest private employer in the St. Louis region. An affiliated teaching hospital of Washington University School of Medicine, Barnes-Jewish Hospital has 904 staffed beds and a 1,700-member medical staff, many of whom are recognized in the "Best Doctors in America" list (*www.bestdoctors.com*), one of the most prestigious and credible tools available to consumers for selecting a doctor. That staff is supported by residents, interns, and fellows, in addition to nurses, technicians, and other healthcare professionals. Kindred Hospital St. Louis (314–361–8700; *www.kindredstlouis.com*) is an acute-care specialty hospital with 60 beds, including a five-bed ICU and a four-bed hemodialysis unit, offering 24-hour in-house physician coverage, as well as specialty consults as needed (for infectious disease, pulmonology, nephrology, psychiatry, and others).

Nuptials: City of St. Louis Register (314–622–4145; *www.stlouis.missouri.org*)

The State of Missouri has an amended state constitution defining marriage as between a man and a woman and not recognizing same-sex marriages from other jurisdictions. The City of St. Louis offers a Domestic Partner Registry for city residents providing limited rights.

Getting Around Town

Public transportation: Metrolink (314–231–2345; *www.metrostlouis.org*) provides subway and bus service throughout the St. Louis area. Base fare: $1.50; one-time transfer 25 cents; one-day multi-ride pass: $4.

Roads: I-44, I-55, I-64, I-70, US50, US61, US67

Airport: Lambert-St. Louis International Airport (airport code: ALN) (314–426–8000; *www.lambert-stlouis.com*) has 83 gates serving 10 major airlines.

It's a Gay Life

Annual events: Pride St. Louis (*www.pridestl.org*) hosts PrideFest the last weekend in June. The Central West End Business Association (*www.thecwe.com*) sponsors an adults-only Halloween Street Party & Costume Contest. Cinema St. Louis (*www.cinemastlouis.org*) hosts the St. Louis International Film Festival in November. In addition to hosting a Mardi Gras parade on Fat Tuesday, Mardi Gras, Inc. (*www.stlmardigras.org*) has a series of annual neighborhood events throughout the year. There are many festivals, home and garden tours, and other annual events throughout St. Louis.

Nightlife: Laclede's Landing (314–241–5875; *www.lacledeslanding.org*), listed on the National Register of Historic Places, is a unique shopping and entertainment district. Its cobblestone streets are lined with cast-iron street lamps, and its restored warehouses are home to small shops, unusual restaurants, and live music clubs. Music lovers will hear live bands at the more than 30 restaurants, taverns, and music clubs scattered among Soulard's red brick townhouses and ornate churches. Soulard, Central West End, South City, South Grand District, and the Manchester Gay Strip are home to dozens of gay and gay-friendly clubs, restaurants, and retail outlets. Pick up a copy of *EXP Magazine* (*www.expmagazine.com*) at the GLBT bookshop Left Bank Books (310 N. Euclid Avenue; 314–367–6731; *www.left-bank.com*) for listings of all the clubs and current events around the city.

Culture: All genres of musical sound fill performance venues in St. Louis's Grand Center arts and entertainment district. The world-renowned Saint Louis Symphony Orchestra (314–533–2500; *www.slso.org*) stages performances at historic Powell Symphony Hall (718 N. Grand Boulevard; 314–534–1700; *www.slso.org*); top jazz artists entertain in the intimate atmosphere of Jazz at the Bistro (3536 Washington Avenue; 314–531–1013; *www.jatb.org*); noted international singers and musicians appear at the acoustically pure Sheldon Concert Hall (3648 Washington Boulevard; 314–533–9900; *www.sheldonconcerthall.org*); and touring Broadway shows and major dance company performances rival the over-the-top architecture at the Fabulous Fox Theatre (527 N. Grand Boulevard; 314–534–1678; *www.fabulousfox.com*). Artifacts, memorabilia, and recordings of musical and entertainment icons from St. Louis are featured at the Currents

Gallery at the Missouri History Museum (5700 Lindell Boulevard; 314–454–3150; *www.mohistory.org*). The St. Louis Walk of Fame (*www.stlouiswalkoffame.org*) commemorates music legends with bronze stars in the sidewalk along Delmar Boulevard in the lively Loop neighborhood. Blueberry Hill (6504 Delmar Boulevard; 314–727–4444; *www.blueberryhill.com*) is chock full of rock 'n' roll memorabilia and an entire room devoted to Elvis paraphernalia. Stroll the newly revitalized Washington Avenue and visit Downtown's cutting-edge galleries with offerings of paintings, sculpture, stylized photography, and mixed media along with the sidewalk cafe atmosphere of Washington Avenue restaurants during the First Friday Gallery Walk (*www.downtownnow.org*).

Recreation: Forest Park, home to the 1904 Worlds Fair and Olympic Park, has more free attractions than any other city in America. Here you can visit the St. Louis Zoo (1 Government Drive; 314–781–0900), Jewel Box gardens (Wells and McKinley drives; 314–535–1503), Korean Memorial, Jefferson Memorial, History Museum (5700 Lindell Boulevard; 314–454–3150; *www.mohistory.com*), St. Louis Art Museum (1 Fine Arts Drive; 314–721–0072; *www.slam.org*), St. Louis Science Center and planetarium (5050 Oakland Avenue; 314–289–4444; *www.slsc.org*), Muny Opera Theatre (Hamden Avenue and Government Drive; 314–361–1900; *www.muny.com*), and Worlds fair sites or take a guided gondola boat ride through the canals. Plan time to relax and watch the barges as they make their way up and down the Mississippi, the country's longest river. Anheuser Busch (1 Busch Place; 314–577–2626; *www.budweisertours.com*), the world's largest brewery, offers free tours that include beer tasting. St. Louis is recognized as one of the most active sports centers in the country, and local fans are noted for their enthusiastic support of their professional athletes with the NHL's Blues (314–622–2500; *www.stlouisblues.com*), MLB's Cardinals (314–421–3060; *www.stlcardinals.com*), and the NFL's Rams (314–982–7267; *www.stlouisrams.com*) taking center stage. Other popular teams, Team Tennis Aces (314–726–2237; *www.stlouisaces.com*), the Frontier Baseball League's River City Rascals (636–240–2287; *www.rivercityrascals.com*), United Hockey League's River Otters (636–896–4200; *www.riverotters.com*), and the Major Indoor Soccer League's Steamers (314–613–1880; *www.stlsteamers.com*) draw crowds from a great regional base of fans, earning St. Louis the well-deserved nickname of "Championship City."

For the Visitor

Accommodations: With approximately 35,000 hotel rooms, ranging from luxury to budget accommodations, St. Louis has something for everyone. The St. Louis Guest House (1032 Allen Avenue; 314–773–1016; *www.stlouisguesthouse.com*) in historical Soulard is tucked between Busch Stadium, the Gateway Arch, Anheuser's Busch Brewery, and the Soulard Farmer's Market. (Two gay bars and two gay restaurants are in the same block.) Napoleon's Retreat (1815 Lafayette Avenue; 314–772–6979/800–700–9980; *www.napoleonsretreat.com*) is a restored Victorian townhouse in Lafayette Square. Located in the Central

West End, Chase Park Plaza (212–232 N. Kingshighway Boulevard; 877–587–2427; *www.chaseparkplaza.com*) is a million-square-feet of suites, restaurants, shopping, and entertainment venues providing distinctive charm and upscale sophistication.

For More Information

Gay & Lesbian Center
Pride St. Louis
2256 S. Grand Boulevard
St. Louis, MO 63104
Gay and Lesbian City HotLine:
314–367–0084
www.pridestl.org

Publications
St. Louis Post-Dispatch
900 N. Tucker Boulevard
St. Louis, MO 63101
314–340–8000
www.stltoday.com

Vital Voice Newspaper
P.O. Box 170138
St. Louis, MO 63117
314–865–3787
www.thevitalvoice.com

Convention and Visitors Bureau
St. Louis Convention and Visitors
Commission
One Metropolitan Square, Suite 1100
St. Louis, MO 63102
800–916–8938
www.explorestlouis.com

Chamber of Commerce
St. Louis Regional Chamber & Growth
Association (RCGA)
One Metropolitan Square, Suite 1300
St. Louis, MO 63102
314–231–5555
www.stlrcga.org

Realtor
Carolyn Mantia
The Mantia Team
Re/Max Results
7850 Lemay Ferry Road
St. Louis, MO 63129
314–378–7869
www.themantiateam.com

## 29

Las Vegas, Nevada

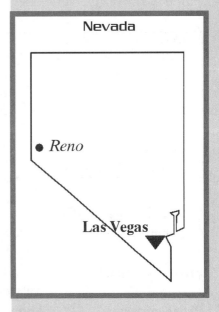

A Look at Las Vegas

"Welcome to Fabulous Las Vegas," the sign proclaims. Kitsch museums, drag queens, showgirls, roller coasters, neon, gambling, high art, and an abundance of jobs are the backdrop of this desert oasis. There's never a shortage of entertainment or fun in Las Vegas, the true city that never sleeps. Casinos glitter and shine 24 hours a day. Visions of Venice, Paris, New York, Egypt, and medieval England greet you as you travel the famed, American Scenic Highway: the Las Vegas Strip. Just as the casinos are, bars and clubs are also open around the clock and provide something for every taste and desire. They don't call this the Wild West for nothing. True to the moniker, "What Happens Here Stays Here," Sin City is quite tolerant and diverse. With more than 26 million annual visitors from around the world and a local population that increases by the thousands monthly, Las Vegas caters to a cross section of cultures and attitudes. A live-and-let-live attitude is most prominent. Those staying, playing, and living in this gay-friendly city will find the locals and businesses exceptionally tolerant.

Possible drawbacks: The summers swelter, and more than a third of the year has temperatures hotter than 90 degrees. The city is young and transient, with more than 4,000 new residents arriving monthly. It can be difficult to make long-term friends. Education is not a priority, and that shows.

▶ Nickname:
Sin City

▶ County:
Clark

▶ Area code:
702

▶ Time zone:
Pacific

▶ Population:
508,604

▶ County population:
1,375,765

▶ Region:
Southwest Nevada

▶ Average home price:
$300,000

▶ Fabulous reasons to live here:
Scenic desert beauty; entertainment; nightlife; strong, growing economy; no state income tax; growing GLBT community; dry climate

Climate

Elevation 2000'	Avg. high/low(F°)	Avg. inches		Avg. # days precip.	Avg. % humidity
		rain	snow		
Jan.	56/34	0.8	0.9	3	43%
April	76/50	0.2	–	2	25%
July	102/78	0.5	–	3	21%
Oct.	79/53	0.3	–	2	28%
YEAR	78/53	5.9	1.2	28	30%
# days 32° or below: 16			# days 90° or warmer: 133		

Local Connections

Gas company: Southwest Gas Corp. (702–365–1555/800–748–5539; *www.swgas.com*)

Electric company: Nevada Power Company (702–367–5555; *www.nevadapower.com*)

Phone company: Sprint (888–723–8010; *www.sprint.com*)

Water and sewer: Las Vegas Valley Water District (702–870–4194; *www.lvvwd.com*)

Cable company: Cox Communications (702–933–9849; *www.cox.com*)

Car registration/License: Nevada Department of Motor Vehicles (702–486–4368; *www.dmvstat.com*)

New residents have 30 days to register their vehicles and obtain a Nevada license. You must complete an application and surrender your out-of-state license. Driving test required for expired, revoked, or suspended out-of-state licenses. License fee: $21.75; $16.75 for those 65 and older. There's no grace period for vehicle plates. The basic registration fee is determined by the manufacturer's suggested retail price and the age and weight of the vehicle. The fee for passenger cars less than 8,500 pounds is $27 plus $6 for the support of the Nevada Highway Patrol and a road tax. Title Fee: $20.

The Tax Ax

Sales tax: 7.5 percent

State tax: No personal income tax in Nevada

Property tax: The property tax formula is strange and convoluted. Homes are assessed for value every five years, the value of the building is depreciated, so that the older the home, the cheaper the taxes. New homes have a start tax rate annually of .9 percent of the purchase price. A new condo might therefore have higher taxes than a 30-year-old, 3,000-square-foot custom home on a large lot.

Local Real Estate

Overview: An extremely old home in Las Vegas dates from 1950. More than half of all homes here have been built since 1993. Styles range from traditional ranch to modern, Spanish hacienda. The newest trend in Las Vegas is vertical living in luxurious high-rise complexes. There are currently more than 50 towers planned for the valley and more on the way. Home prices are projected to double again within the next decade.

Median price for a single-family home: $300,000

Average price for a single-family home: $300,000

Average price for a 2BR condo: $200,000

Rental housing market: The average 1,500-square-foot, three-bedroom home in a good neighborhood rents for $1,200/month. An average two-bedroom in an apartment complex will run $800–900.

Gay-friendly neighborhoods: One of the fabulous reasons for living in Las Vegas is that the GLBT population is spread out into every area, neighborhood, and housing style.

Nearby areas to consider: Clark County is an isolated valley community made up of several cities, including Las Vegas, North Las Vegas, Paradise, Henderson, Summerlin, and a dozen other smaller townships. Each city and township throughout the valley offers a different style and atmosphere. The master-planned cities of Henderson and Summerlin provide modern amenities and well-planned living and shopping districts. You'll find a lot of gated communities and homeowner associations in these cities. The cities of North Las Vegas and Las Vegas offer slightly older homes and established landscaping.

Earning a Living

Per capita income: $22,060

Median household income: $44,069

Business climate: No other city in the United States creates more new jobs every year than Las Vegas, a city that continually enjoys the lowest unemployment rate in the nation. The resort and tourism industry dominates the local market, but new companies, factories, and entrepreneur start-ups are all part of the business landscape. If you've always wanted to start your own business, Las Vegas is an excellent choice. The city can't keep up with its own growth, so there's plenty of room for everything here.

Help in starting a business: The Las Vegas Lambda Business Association (*www.lambdalv.com*) is a GLBT community networking, support, and development organization. The Las Vegas Chamber of Commerce prides itself in serving large and small businesses as the "ultimate business resource." The Chamber offers services and programs that include networking, education, and advertising opportunities.

Job market: Food and service industry jobs abound. Arts, entertainment, recreation, accommodation, and food services provide more than a quarter of available jobs. Educational, health, and social services; retail trade; and construction are also large employment sectors.

The Community

Overview: As a young, transient city, the Las Vegas GLBT community hasn't yet come into its own. There isn't a sense of community pride in the valley, but several groups and organizations are beginning to create a foundation. Las Vegas remains a place where you can come and reinvent yourself.

Community organizations: The Gay and Lesbian Community Center of Las Vegas (702–733–9800; *www.thecenter-lasvegas.com*) provides a home for local group meetings and is a fabulous source for gay-friendly health service and business contacts in Las Vegas. The city has several political, social, and health organizations that support the community, and the Center maintains a current list. Also helpful are the free city directories of gay businesses and services: the bi-annual *Results Pages* (*www.resultspages.com*), published by the *Las Vegas Bugle*, and the *Preferred Directory* published by Lambda (*www.lambdalv.com*).

Medical care: More than a dozen hospitals service valley residents. University Medical Center (702–383–2000; *www.umc-cares.org*), affiliated with the University of Nevada School of Medicine, is the state-designated Level I Trauma Center for Southern Nevada, as well as the only advanced facility to offer a specialized team of medical professionals prepared to respond to the needs of the severely injured 24 hours a day. UMC operates a comprehensive, freestanding unit devoted solely to physical medicine and rehabilitation, operates UMC Quick Care Centers around the valley, and also houses the state's only burn-care facility, the Lions Burn Care Center.

Nuptials: The State of Nevada has a constitutional amendment similar to DOMA defining marriage as between a man and a women and not recognizing same-sex marriages from other jurisdictions. Civil unions and commitment ceremonies are popular in the wedding capital of the world.

Getting Around Town

Public transportation: The Regional Transportation Commission of Southern Nevada's CAT system (800–228–3911; *www.rtcsouthernnevada.com*) has intersecting bus lines that will get you all over the city, but connection times can be long. The 301/302 line runs the Las Vegas Strip 24 hours a day. Fare: $2. The Las Vegas Monorail (702–699–8200; *www.lvmonorail.com*) runs just east of the Strip from Sahara to the MGM Grand. Fare: one-way $3; one-day pass $10. Taxis are plentiful, but don't try to hail one on the street. Your best bet is to grab a cab at any casino's taxi stand or call for service: Western (702–382–7100) or Desert Cab Co. (702–386–9102).

Roads: I-15, I-215, I-515, US95

Airport: McCarran International Airport (airport code: LAS) (702–261–5211; *www.mccarran.com*) is located minutes south of the Las Vegas Strip.

It's a Gay Life

Annual events: The GLBT social events planning organization in Las Vegas, Southern Nevada Association of Pride, Inc. (*www.lasvegaspride.org*), hosts Pride in May and other community events throughout the year. The number of annual events and festivals in Las Vegas is growing. A few perennial favorites include the World Series of Poker (*www.worldseriesofpoker.com*) in April, Jazz/Music Fest (*www.yourjazz.com*) in July, Oktoberfest (*www.lasvegasoktoberfest.com*) in September, Valley Book Festival in October (*www.vegasvalleybookfest.org*), the National Rodeo Finals (Nevada Gay Rodeo Association; *www.ngra.com*) in December, and New Year's Eve.

Nightlife: New clubs and bars open frequently around the city. The two gay epicenters in Las Vegas are the Fruit Loop and the Commercial Center. The Fruit Loop, at Paradise Road between Harmon Avenue and East Naples, is an easy shuffle. Park at Hamburger Mary's (4503 Paradise Road; 702–735–4400; *www.hamburgermaryslv.com*), renowned for the best burgers in town, and walk the loop, including: the Gipsy (4605 Paradise Road; 702–731–1919; *gipsylv.com*), Icon (4633 Paradise Road; 702–791–0100), the Buffalo (4640 Paradise Road; 702–733–8355), and Freezone (610 Naples; 702–794–2300; *www.freezonelasvegas.com*). The Village Square Commercial Center (953 East Sahara Avenue) is a large strip mall with several bars: the Spotlight Lounge (957 E. Sahara; 702–696–0202; *www.spotlightlv.com*), Badlands Saloon (953 E. Sahara, #22; 702–792–9262), and Rainbow Lounge (900 E. Karen Avenue, #H; 702–696–0226; *www.rainbowloungelv.com*). Several other gay clubs are scattered around town. Pick up a free copy of *Q Vegas* (*www.QVegas.com*), *Out Las Vegas* (*www.OutLasVegas.com*), or *Las Vegas Night Beat* (*www.lvnightbeat.com*) at Get Booked (4640 Paradise Road; 702–737–7780; *www.getbooked.com*) for current listings of clubs and events.

Culture: Las Vegas is the Entertainment Capital of the World. Dozens of shows, both permanent and touring, grace the stages of Las Vegas showrooms nightly. The female impersonators, headed by Frank Marino, take center stage every night at the Riviera Hotel and Casino (2901 S. Las Vegas Boulevard; 800–634–3420; *www.rivierahotel.com*) in the long-running and critically acclaimed An Evening at La Cage. Las Vegas runs the gamut from high art to kitsch. The city is home to the Las Vegas Philharmonic (702–258–5438; *www.lasvegasphilharmonic.com*) and Nevada Ballet Theater (702–243–2623; *nevadaballet.com*). Both have October–May seasons. If art's your thing, the Bellagio Fine Arts Museum (3600 S. Las Vegas Boulevard; 888–987–3456; *www.bellagiolasvegas.com*) has a small permanent collection and hosts touring shows. The Guggenheim Hermitage at the Venetian (3355 S. Las Vegas Boulevard; 702–414–2440; *www.guggenheimlasvegas.org*) also mounts touring shows. Steve Wynn's private collection of Masters is at Wynn Las Vegas (3131 S. Las Vegas Boulevard; 702–770–7100; *www.wynnlasvegas.com*),

The Las Vegas Art Museum (9600 W. Sahara Avenue; 702–360–8000; *www.lasvegasartmuseum.org*) mounts Smithsonian touring shows. If you're looking for classic Vegas you'll find it preserved at Elvis-a-Rama (3401 Industrial Road; 702–309–7200; *www.elvisarama.com*) and the Casino Legends Hall of Fame at the Tropicana Hotel and Casino (3801 S. Las Vegas Boulevard; 888–826–8767; *www.tropicanalv.com*), featuring the largest collection of gaming, casino, and entertainment memorabilia ever assembled. For classic neon visit the Neon Museum downtown at Neonopolis (450 Fremont Street; 702–477–0470; *www.neonopolis.com*). Las Vegas began as an outpost, and you can visit the original fort at Old Vegas Mormon State Historic Park (500 E. Washington Avenue; 702–486–3511; *www.parks.nv.gov/olvmf.htm*). Also of interest are the Las Vegas Natural History Museum (900 N. Las Vegas Boulevard; 702–384–3466; *www.lvnhm.org*), the Nevada State Museum (700 Twin Lakes Drive; 702–486–5205; *dmla.clan.lib.nv.us*), and Southern Nevada Zoo (1775 N. Rancho Drive; 702–647–4685; *www.lasvegaszoo.org*).

Recreation: The Las Vegas Valley is more than the Strip. Four major recreation areas—Red Rock National Conservation area (*www.redrockcanyon.blm.gov*), Lake Mead National Recreation area (*www.nps.gov/lame*), the Valley of Fire State Park (*www.parks.nv.gov/vf.htm*), and Mount Charleston—provide fabulous hiking, rock climbing, and skiing opportunities, as well as boating and fishing. But one needn't be a thrill-seeker to enjoy these national treasures. Paved roads and scenic loops offer panoramic views for the Kodak traveler, too. Helicopter and plane charters allow bird's-eye views of the strip, Grand Canyon, and surrounding desert mountains and valleys. When you're ready to hit the links, Las Vegas is home to more than 60 public and private golf courses (*www.golflv.com*). For spectators, Las Vegas Motor Speedway (7000 N. Las Vegas Boulevard; 800–644–4444; *www.lvms.com*) is a great way to spend a NASCAR evening. The Las Vegas 51s (702–386–7200; *www.lv51.com*) are the AAA Affiliate of the LA Dodgers. The Las Vegas Wranglers (702–471–7825; *www.lasvegaswranglers.com*) are a member team of the premier developmental East Coast Hockey League.

For the Visitor

Accommodations: Las Vegas is a resort town with more than 130,000 hotel rooms. There's no shortage of luxury spas, classic casinos, and chain accommodations to fit any budget. A few of the gay-friendly options include: Viva Las Vegas Villas (1205 Las Vegas Boulevard; 800–574–4450; *www.vivalasvegasvillas.com*), catering to romance and fantasy with themed rooms such as "Blue Hawaii" and "Camelot" (Elvis can officiate at your commitment ceremony, too.); on the steamy side is the clothing-optional (male) Blue Moon Resort (2651 Westwood Drive; 866–798–9194; *www.bluemoonlv.com*) with a state-of-the-art steam room, the Jacuzzi Grotto, and a 24-hour coffee shop. Las Vegas Rainbow (1800 Chapman Drive; 866–DORTHY); Lucky You B&B (1248 S. 8th Street; 702–384–1129); and Oasis Guesthouse (662 Rolling Green Drive; 702–369–1396) provide gay-friendly bed and breakfast accommodations.

For More Information

Gay & Lesbian Center

The Gay and Lesbian Community
Center of Las Vegas
953 East Sahara
Las Vegas, NV 89104
702–896–3236
www.thecenter-lasvegas.com

Publications

Las Vegas Review Journal
1111 W Bonanza Road
Las Vegas, NV 89106
702–383–0211
www.reviewjournal.com

Q-Vegas/Out In Las Vegas
Stonewall Publishing, Inc.
2408 Pardee Place
Las Vegas, NV 89104
702–650–0636
www.QVegas.com

Las Vegas Night Beat
1140 Almond Tree Lane, Suite 304
Las Vegas, NV 89104
702–369–8441
www.lvnightbeat.com

Convention and Visitors Bureau

Las Vegas Convention and Visitors
Authority
3150 Paradise Road
Las Vegas, NV 89109
702–892–0711
www.vegasfreedom.com

Chamber of Commerce

Las Vegas Chamber of Commerce
3720 Howard Hughes Parkway, # 100
Las Vegas, NV 89109
702–735–1616
www.lvchamber.com

Realtor

Jack LeVine
Realtor
Keller Williams Realty
2230 Corporate Circle, #250
Henderson, NV 89074
702–378–7055
www.move-to-vegas.com

## 30

Collingswood, New Jersey

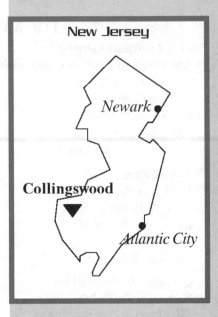

New Jersey

Newark

Collingswood

Atlantic City

A look at Collingswood

The small, inner-ring suburb of Collingswood is the poster-child success story of modern urban development. Through the actions of a community of concerned citizens and local government leaders, led by three-time mayor Jim Maley, Collingswood has been reclaimed from approaching urban blight. The goal of the city is to build its future by restoring its past. Through providing excellent city services, master-planned redevelopment of both downtown businesses and surrounding neighborhoods, and encouragement of the arts and education, Collingswood is not only building that strong future, but is flourishing in the process. At the city center is 60-acre Knight's Park. This lush oasis is used by the public schools and sports leagues and as a location for many of the city's festivals and events. Spreading out from this hub are neighborhoods filled with a mix of longtime residents and newcomers. With solid incentive programs and city investment in property and residents, the circle around that lush oasis is growing larger. There's still more to accomplish and, if you're interested in being part of the urban pioneering spirit in a supportive and open community, Collingswood will provide an excellent hometown with neighbors considered to be the friendliest in New Jersey.

Possible drawbacks: Collingswood is surrounded by Camden, one of the most dangerous cities in the country, and urban pioneering can offer a supreme challenge.

▶ Nickname: Friendliest City in New Jersey

▶ County: Camden

▶ Area code: 856

▶ Time zone: Eastern

▶ Population: 14,326

▶ County population: 516,282

▶ Region: Southwest New Jersey

▶ Closest metro area: Philadelphia, Pennsylvania

▶ Average home price: $238,400

▶ Fabulous reasons to live here:
Family-oriented small-town charm; excellent location; growing GLBT community; fabulous schools; welcoming to small businesses and entrepreneurs

Climate

Elevation 20'	Avg. high/low(F°)	Avg. inches rain	snow	Avg. # days precip.	Avg. % humidity
Jan.	40/24	3.8	6.1	11	67%
April	63/42	3.8	0.3	11	60%
July	82/61	4.6	–	9	67%
Oct.	66/45	3.3	–	8	68%
YEAR	64/44	46.0	20.5	116	65%
# days 32° or below: 63			# days 90° or warmer: 25		

Local Connections

Gas, electric, phone, and cable companies: Because of deregulation, gas, electric, phone and cable services in New Jersey are offered by many different companies. The New Jersey Board of Public Utilities (800–624–0241; *www.state.nj.us/bpu*) provides current lists and comparative rates for all companies offering services in New Jersey.

Water and sewer: New Jersey American Water (800–652–6987; *www.njawater.com*); Camden County Municipal Utilities Authority (856–541–3700; *www.ccmua.org*).

Car registration/License: New Jersey Motor Vehicle Commission (609–292–6500; *www.state.nj.us/mvc*)

You must purchase an examination permit within 60 days of becoming a New Jersey resident. Fees: examination $10; license $24. Vision and knowledge tests required; driving test may be waived when surrendering a valid, out-of-state license. When transferring an out-of-state title to New Jersey, fill out a sales tax form. No tax will be charged, but the form must be filed. Title transfer fee: $20. Registration fees are based on vehicle age and weight. Fees: $29.50–81. Plate fees start at $15.

The Tax Ax

Sales tax: 6 percent; some food items, medicine, clothing, footwear, and disposable paper products for use in the home exempt

State income tax: 1.4–6.37 percent graduated, based on income

Property tax: Collingswood Tax Assessor (856–854–0720, ext. 117; *www.collingswood.com*)

The assessed valuation of real property is based on 94 percent of the fair market value, and property taxes are then calculated by multiplying the general tax rate, currently $3.41/$100. Rates vary by districts and there are many property tax exemptions in New Jersey.

Local Real Estate

Overview: Collingswood has many Victorian, Arts & Crafts, and vintage (pre-1940s) style homes. Also available are many quaint brick row homes. The Borough of Collingswood is offering loan aid, assistance, and incentives for hundreds of city homes requiring renovation.

Median price for a single-family home: $242,000

Average price for a single-family home: $238,400

Average price for a 2BR condo: $195,000 (row home)

Rental housing market: A few apartments available over the business district rent for $900/month average. Other rentals include twin homes and a few small apartment complexes.

Gay-friendly neighborhoods: There are no specific GLBT neighborhoods in Collingswood. All of Collingswood is gay-friendly and the GLBT community is wonderfully integrated.

Nearby areas to consider: There are three gay-friendly New Jersey cities worth exploring: New Brunswick, Asbury Park, and Cape May. New Brunswick, home of Rutgers University, is about an hour northeast of Collingswood. This growing college town, as are so many New Jersey cities, is experiencing redevelopment. Asbury Park, a shore city 70 miles to the northeast, has a large GLBT community. The city is currently undergoing a renaissance that includes infrastructure investments exceeding $2 billion. Cape May, 90 miles southwest at the southern tip of the Jersey Shore, is a quaint town of restored Victorian homes with a large arts and GLBT community.

Earning a Living

Per capita income: $24,358

Median household income: $43,175

Business climate: Large-scale, downtown business improvement districts are calling out to businesses of all sizes. This is a great time for entrepreneurs to relocate or start businesses in this up-and-coming city.

Help in starting a business: Collingswood Partners (856–858–9275) is a non-profit management corporation that oversees the three business improvement districts in Collingswood. The corporation is designed to help new and existing area businesses and also actively promotes local businesses and the city to attract further development.

Job market: Collingswood provides service, retail trade, and education-oriented opportunities. The older Camden County market includes industry, service, education, and healthcare, and nearby Philadelphia provides job sectors including educational, health, and social services; professional, scientific, management, administrative, and waste management services; and retail trade.

The Community

Overview: There's a growing, family-oriented GLBT community in Collingswood. But the community in Collingswood isn't separated from the rest of the city by labels. Yet another success for Collingswood is that there's a sense of community integration in this small town where neighbors are judged and included based on their actions and deeds, rather than labels.

Community organizations: Out in the Neighborhood, a volunteer organization started specifically to provide a social outlet and support system for the growing GLBT community in Collingswood and the surrounding South Jersey communities, sponsors monthly parties at neighborhood homes, coffee house get-togethers, and other social, recreational, and volunteer activities. The William Way Community Center in Philadelphia is a full-service GLBT community center providing meeting space for more than 70 groups and hosting a variety of events and art exhibitions throughout the year. The Collingswood Community Directory is filled with local civic organizations that provide social, recreation, and volunteer opportunities for most tastes.

Medical care: In addition to the private medical services available in Collingswood, nearby Camden provides three major hospitals. Virtua Health Camden (VHC) (856–246–3000; *www.virtua.org*) offers a wide range of outpatient services, including the Kyle W. Will Family Health Center, and provides comprehensive primary care and specialty services for infants, children, teens, and adults. Through the Family Health Center, patients can access specialty care including dentistry, podiatry, ophthamology, gastroenterology, cardiology, and wound care. Evening and weekend hours are offered, and most major insurance plans are accepted. The Cooper Health System's (609–342–2000; *www.cooperhealth.org*) five Centers of Excellence bring together an interdisciplinary team of physicians, nurses, and healthcare professionals with the skills to address the most complex and difficult medical problems. With specific focus areas, the Centers offer access to the best medical technology and clinical expertise to provide world-class care from the premier healthcare providers in their respective fields. The Centers include Cooper Level Trauma Center, Cooper Heart Institute, Cooper Bone & Joint Institute, Cooper Critical Care Medicine, and The Cancer Institute of New Jersey. Our Lady of Lourdes Medical Center (856–757–3500; *www.lourdesnet.org*) is a 377-bed, tertiary-care teaching hospital specializing in cardiac diagnostic and surgical services, high-risk obstetrics and neonatology, kidney dialysis, organ transplantation, and physical rehabilitation sponsored by the Franciscan Sisters of Allegany, New York.

Nuptials: The State of New Jersey currently has no explicit provisions prohibiting same-sex marriages.

Getting Around Town

Public transportation: New Jersey Transit (800–772–2222; *www.njtransit.com*) operates a fleet of 2,027 buses, 711 trains, and 45 light-rail vehicles on 236 bus routes and 11 rail lines statewide. Fares are zone-based: local bus (one zone) $1.25; light-rail (one-zone) $1.75. As a "Transit Village," Collingswood is centered around a train station. The Delaware River Port Authority of Pennsylvania and New Jersey (856–968–2001; *www.drpa.org*) is a regional transportation agency serving southeastern Pennsylvania and southern New Jersey. DRPA provides quality transportation services including the PATCO Speedline from South Jersey to Center City Philadelphia. Fares: $1.15–2.45, based on zones.

Roads: I-76, I-295, US30 (nearby I-95, I-676)

Airport: Philadelphia International Airport (airport code: PHI) (215–937–6937; *www.phl.org*), only 12 miles from the center of Collingswood, is served by all major domestic carriers.

It's a Gay Life

Annual events: Some events sponsored by Collingswood Partners, Inc. and local government (*www.Collingswood.com*) are: the Easter Egg Hunt, May Fair & 5k Run, Second Saturday, Tree Lighting Ceremony, Holiday Parade, Halloween/Valentine Day Promotions, and Sidewalk Sale Days. For gay-themed and gay pride events, head across the river to Philadelphia where Philly Pride (*www.phillypride.org*) hosts Pride Day in June, Outfest in October, and Winter Pride. Philadelphia's GLBT community hosts a series of annual and special events including the Blue Ball Weekend (*www.blueballphilly.com*) in January, Gay Black Pride (*www.phillyblackpride.org*) in April, and the Philadelphia International Gay & Lesbian Film Festival (*www.phillyfests.com*) and Sportsweek (*www.phillysportsweek.org*) in June.

Nightlife: There's a growing selection of dining and entertainment options throughout Collingswood's three businesses improvement districts. Haddon Avenue offers some fabulous dining choices, including Water Lily Bistro (655 Haddon Avenue; 856–833–0098; *www.waterlilybistro.com*), Tortilla Press (701–703 Haddon Avenue; 856–869–3345; *www.thetortillapress.com*), Nunzio's Italian Grill (706–708 Haddon Avenue; 856–858–9840;), and Bistro di Marino (492 Haddon Avenue; 856–858–1700). For GLBT-specific nightlife head over to Philadelphia. Two blocks from the Pennsylvania Convention Center and one block from the Avenue of the Arts is the Gayborhood. This center of gay activity, commerce, and nightlife is located between 11th and Broad streets, from Chestnut to Pine streets. Here you'll discover a vast selection of shops, restaurants, galleries, and bars catering to the GLBT community. Visit Giovanni's Room (345 12th Street; 215–923–2960; *www.giovannisroom.com*), one of the oldest LGBT bookstores in the nation, to pick up the *Philadelphia Gay News* (*www.epgn.com*) for current listings.

Culture: The Collingswood Community Theater (609–617–2220; *www.collingswoodtheater.com*) and the Scottish Rite Auditorium and Grand Ballroom (315 White Horse Pike; 856–338–9000) offer live performances of both touring companies and local talent throughout the year. Hamden Avenue, with an eclectic collection of specialty shops, antiques stores, and art galleries, comes alive during "2nd Saturday" art and entertainment nights. Camden County provides several cultural opportunities. The Tweeter Center (1 Harbour Boulevard, Camden; 856–365–1300; *www.tweetercenter.com*), an indoor/outdoor amphitheater, hosts events throughout the year. Just next door is the New Jersey State Aquarium (1 Riverside Drive, Camden; 856–365–3000; *www.njaquarium.org*), home to more than 5,000 fish and aquatic animals representing more than 800 species, and overlooks the Philadelphia skyline from the vantage of the Delaware River shore. Gay history is also represented at the Walt Whitman Center (2nd and Cooper streets, Camden; 856–964–8300; *www.waltwhitmancenter.org*) a non-profit, multi-cultural literary, performing and visual arts center and at the Walt Whitman House (328 Mickle Boulevard; 856–964–5383; *www.njht.org*), which is open to the public for tours. The Rutgers Camden Center for the Arts presents art exhibits and live performances by some of the country's leading performers. Plus, the countless theater, art, dance, and music opportunities provided by Philadelphia are only moments away.

Recreation: Knight Park, Cooper River Park and Newton Lake Park (856–216–2170; *www.ccparks.com*) combined provide more than 400 acres of outdoor sport, recreation, and relaxation opportunities that include boating, swimming, golfing, hiking, biking, ball fields, stadiums, and more. Home to the city schools, Knight Park is used for many area events/festivals as well as little league sports. Cooper River Park runs through Collingswood and offers scenic views and a wide range of relaxation opportunities. Newton Lake Park has miles of biking and walking trails, the Matrimony Garden, and several picnic areas. The most decorated U.S. battleship, the *USS New Jersey* (Mickle Avenue and the riverfront; *www.battleshipnewjersey.org*), resides majestically in her home port in the Delaware River. Along the Delaware Waterfront, the Independence Seaport Museum (Penn's Landing, Philadelphia; 215–925–5439; *www.phillyseaport.org*) is a family-oriented, interactive museum with magnificent ship models, artifacts, and art that include Admiral Dewey's 1892 cruiser *Olympia* and the WWII submarine *Becuna*; both of these National Historic Landmarks can be toured. For spectators, the Camden Riversharks (856–963–2600; *www.riversharks.com*) is America's newest baseball team of the independent Atlantic League. Catch the games at Campbell's Field (Cooper and Market streets; 856–963–2600), located next to the Benjamin Franklin Bridge; the stadium also hosts the Rutgers' Raptors (856–225–6197; *www.camden.rutgers.edu*). Philadelphia is home to MLB's Phillies (215–463–1000; *www.phillies.com*), the NFL's Eagles (215–463–2500; *www.philadelphiaeagles.com*), the NBA's 76ers (215–339–7676; *www.nba.com/sixers*), the NHL's Flyers (215–218–7825; *www.philadelphiaflyers.com*), National Professional Soccer's KiXX (888–888–5499; *www.kixxonline.com*), National Lacrosse League's Wings (215–389–WING; *www.wingslax.com*), and the Women's United Soccer Association's Charge (215–467–GOAL; *www.philadelphiacharge.com*).

For the Visitor

Accommodations: The small town of Collingswood doesn't offer much in the way of accommodations, but less than 5 miles away, Philadelphia provides many options, including Alexander Inn (12th & Spruce streets; 215–923–3535; *www.alexanderinn.com*), a boutique hotel located in Center City; DoubleTree Hotel (237 South Broad Street; 215–893–1600; *www.doubletree.com*), located in the heart of Philadelphia on the Avenue of the Arts, across the street from the Kimmel Center, the Academy of Music, and the Merriam Theater; Hotel Windsor (1700 Benjamin Franklin Parkway; 215–981–5678; *www.windsorhotel.com*), an all-suite hotel located in the heart of Philadelphia's business and cultural district; Sheraton Rittenhouse Square Hotel (18th & Locust streets; 215–546–9400; *www.sheraton.com*), the first "ecosmart" hotel in the United States, showcasing an environmentally responsible combination of high-tech features.

For More Information

Gay & Lesbian Center

The William Way Community Center
1315 Spruce Street
Philadelphia, PA 19107
215–732–2220
www.waygay.org

Publications

Out in New Jersey
743 Hamilton Avenue
Trenton, NJ 08629
609–213–9310
www.outinjersey.net

Collingswood Town Crier
678 Haddon Avenue
Collingswood, NJ 08108
856–854–0720, ext. 126

Convention and Visitors Bureau

Camden Waterfront Marketing Bureau
One Port Center
2 Riverside Drive, Suite 102
Camden, NJ 08103
856–757–9400
www.camdenwaterfront.com

Chamber of Commerce

Collingswood Partners, Inc.
P.O. Box 9000
Collingswood, NJ 08108
856–858–9275

Realtor

Nancy McCauley
Realtor, Feng Shui Consultant
Main Street Realty
730 Haddon Avenue
Collingswood, NJ 08108
856–858–2200
www.mainstrealty.com

Santa Fe, New Mexico

31

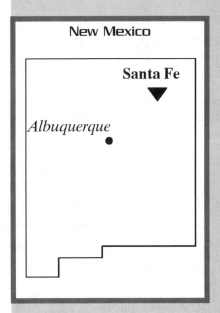

New Mexico

Santa Fe ▼

Albuquerque •

A Look at Santa Fe

Known as the "City Different," Santa Fe supports both historic culture and modern technology, all while offering an outstanding quality of life for both young and old. Founded in 1610, Santa Fe is the oldest state capital in the country. Nestled in the foothills, at the southern tip of the Rocky Mountains at an altitude of 7,000 feet, the city is near the Rio Grande River, Cochiti Lake, and the Sangre de Cristo mountains and surrounded by thousands of acres of national forest and wilderness. Beyond all of the special art events and tours, the city's art galleries, more than 230 of them, embrace an art scene built over the last 100 years on the backs of many of America's most noted artists. In combination with the area's long history of Native American and Spanish art forms, the city has earned a well-deserved reputation as one of the most important art destinations in the country. For outdoor adventures, Santa Fe is only a short distance away from multiple national parks, including Bandelier National Monument, with its ancestral Pueblo dwellings, and Carlsbad Caverns, with its magnificent underground caves. If you are a golfer, hiker, fisher, camper, or skier, you will find exceptional locales nearby for all these activities and more.

Possible drawbacks: If cruising bars is your scene you won't have much opportunity in Santa Fe. The traditional gay nightlife isn't part of the Santa Fe culture. The housing market in Santa Fe is expensive.

▶ Nickname:
The City Different

▶ County:
Santa Fe County

▶ Area code: 505

▶ Time zone:
Mountain

▶ Population:
62,203

▶ County population:
129,292

▶ Region:
Northeast New Mexico

▶ Average home price:
$432,883

▶ Fabulous reasons to live here:
Scenic beauty; dry climate; small-town charm; excellent education; arts and artists; recreation; large, integrated GLBT community; strong, high-tech economy

Climate

Elevation 6989'	Avg. high/low(F°)	Avg. inches		Avg. # days precip.	Avg. % humidity
		rain	snow		
Jan.	43/15	0.6	2.7	4	54%
April	64/31	0.7	0.9	3	35%
July	86/54	2.3	–	9	44%
Oct.	66/35	1.3	0.3	5	45%
YEAR	65/34	14.3	12.7	62	45%
# days 32° or below: 69			# days 90° or warmer: 63		

Local Connections

Gas and electric company: PNM (505–950–1997; *www.pnm.com*)

Phone company: Qwest (800–244–1111; *www.qwest.com*)

Water and sewer: Sangre de Cristo Water Division (505–955–4333; *www.santafenm.gov/public-utilities*)

Cable company: Comcast (505–438–2600; *www.comcast.com*)

Car registration/License: State of New Mexico Tax and Revenue (888–683–4636; *www.state.nm.us/tax/mvd*)

You have 30 days after establishing residency to get your New Mexico license. Licenses are valid for either four ($16 fee) or eight years ($32 fee). Only an eye test is required if you surrender a valid license from another state with the exception that all residents aged 18–24 are required to take a self-study DWI prevention and awareness course ("None for the Road") before getting a license. Drivers age 74 and older must renew annually, but there are no renewal fees. Registration fees are based on vehicle weight and range from $25.50 to $205.50.

The Tax Ax

Sales tax: 7.3125 percent; most food purchases exempt

State income tax: 1.7–8.2% graduated, based on income

Property tax: Assessor (505–986–6300; *www.co.santa-fe.nm.us*)

The tax rate ranges from $8 to $48 per $1,000 of net taxable value after exemptions are taken. Residences are assessed at market value by the sales-comparison approach, which matches a property's value to that of similar properties. One-third of that amount is the taxable value.

Local Real Estate

Overview: Santa Fe is an active real estate market with continued strong appreciation rates. Housing styles are Southwest pueblo and territorial styles, primarily constructed of adobe, or frame and stucco. Availability is strong in Santa Fe, with plenty of new construction in outlying county regions of the downtown area.

Median price for a single-family home: $321,000

Average price for a single-family home: $432,883

Average price for a 2BR condo: $266,000

Rental housing market: Today's rental market is strongly opportunistic for the renter. With low mortgage rates prevailing, first-time buyers continue to leave the rental market with the first-home purchase, causing a glut of rental properties. Two-bedroom in-town units range from $1,100 to $2,000, depending on location and condition. As well, there are numerous short-term vacation properties available, primarily in the more desirable East and North Side areas.

Gay-friendly neighborhoods: Being the small town that it is, Santa Fe does not have a gay ghetto. The entire city is quite gay-friendly, with many gay-owned and gay-friendly businesses throughout the area.

Nearby areas to consider: Eldorado at Santa Fe is a bedroom community a few miles to the south of Santa Fe with a large GLBT population. The area offers modern housing on larger lots and an easy commute into Santa Fe. Twenty-five miles to the north of Santa Fe on the Rio Grande River is Española, the "Jewel of Northern New Mexico." With a history dating back to 1598, early American, Spanish, and Native American historic sites blend with recreation resources, tourism, and affordable housing. Española is what Santa Fe was before it became today's Santa Fe. The areas physical attractions, small-town style, entrepreneurial opportunities, growing arts community, and local pride are drawing the GLBT community to this up-and-coming city.

Earning a Living

Per capita income: $25,454

Median household income: $40,392

Business climate: Santa Fe is an arts and cultural center, with more than 250 art galleries. It has evolved as a center for high-tech businesses of various kinds. The city is the sate capital, with many of the state's offices located in town. Tourism is the second-largest employer within the city encompassing many service and retail businesses. The city is also a major supplier of employees to Los Alamos National Labs, located about 25 miles from Santa Fe.

Help in starting a business: The New Mexico Economic Development Department (800–374–3061; *www.edd.state.nm.us*) facilitates business opportunities and growth throughout the state by providing services for New Mexico businesses and communities as well as information for corporations considering a relocation or expansion.

Job market: High-tech businesses have been choosing Santa Fe for the last 10 years. Santa Fe will continue to develop as a creative community focused on the arts and culture as well. Educational, health, and social services; arts, entertainment, recreation, accommodation, and food services; retail trade; public administration; and professional, scientific, management, administrative, and waste management services are all active market sectors.

The Community

Overview: Santa Fe has an active gay and lesbian community including a large GLBT retirement community. There is no one area or neighborhood that forms a gay district. The GLBT community is active throughout the city's businesses and government.

Community organizations: Although there's no formal gay and lesbian community center, Santa Fe is a GLBT community success story unlike any other in the country. The GLBT community is so well integrated into the Santa Fe community as a whole that there aren't many special community groups and organizations. Instead, GLBT community members participate and find services, support, and social and recreation opportunities through Santa Fe's many offerings.

Medical care: St. Vincent's Regional Medical Center (505–983–3361; *www.stvin.org*) is a non-profit, non-affiliated hospital with 268 licensed beds and 250 staff physicians representing 22 medical specialties that provides the only public Level III Trauma Center in northern New Mexico. Santa Fe Indian Hospital (505-988-9821), located in Northern New Mexico, is an acute-care hospital with 39 licensed beds and a Level III urgent care room and serves about 30,000 patients from eleven pueblos as well as urban Native Americans. Alternative healthcare, including acupuncture, chiropractic services, and traditional Native American medicines, are also popular.

Nuptials: The State of New Mexico currently has no laws prohibiting marriages between same-sex couples. A bill is being considered to define marriage similar to DOMA, but also create a domestic partnership law that will provide same-sex couples the same rights as marriage. The State of New Mexico and many businesses offer domestic partner benefits.

Getting Around Town

Public transportation: City bus service (505–955–2001; *www.santafenm.gov/public-works*) is offered by Santa Fe Trails (505–955–2002; *www.santafenm.gov*). Fare: single ride $1; unlimited daily ride $2; unlimited ride monthly passes $20.

Roads: I-25, US84, US285

Airport: The Santa Fe Municipal Airport (airport code: SAF) (505–955–2908; *www.santafenm.gov*) is a non-hub airport. Albuquerque International Sunport (airport code: ABQ) (505–244–7780; *www.cabq.gov/airport*), 72 miles away, is the closest sub-hub airport.

It's a Gay Life

Annual events: Put enough artists, writers, musicians, and theater people together in a beautiful place shaped by enduring cultural traditions and there are bound to be activities and events all year. These include annual music, art, and theater festivals, Carnival (*www.carnivalsantafe.com*), wine festivals and fairs, and a wide array of feast days. In addition to Albuquerque's Gay-Lesbian Film Festival and June Pride festival and parade, Albuquerque Pride (*www.abqpride.com*) hosts GLBT events and fundraisers throughout the year.

Nightlife: Santa Fe is known for excellent restaurants, and spending an evening lingering over a fabulous dinner makes for a pleasant evening. The gay bar culture isn't a way of life for Santa Fe's GLBT community. Drama Club (125 N. Guadalupe; 505–988–4374) provides dancing and entertainment. Santa Fe also has two gay-friendly nightclubs that offer dancing and food: The Paramount/Bar B Lounge (331 Sandoval; 505–982–8999) and Swing (135 W. Palace Avenue, 3rd Floor; 505–955–0400). Another friendly spot is Applewoods, with a restaurant and lounge. If you feel the need to do a gay bar crawl you'll need to head down to Albuquerque, with its half-dozen clubs along Central Avenue.

Culture: The arts are everywhere in the Santa Fe area. In combination with the area's long history of Native American and Spanish art forms, the city has earned a well-deserved reputation as one of the most important art destinations in the country. In addition to the galleries there are 12 museums and 16 performing arts groups, along with festivals and specialty markets throughout the year. Highlights include the Museum of Fine Arts (107 W. Palace Avenue; 505–476–5072; *www.mfasantafe.org*), featuring more than 20,000 works of art from the Southwest; the Museum of New Mexico (107 W. Palace Avenue; 505–476–5041; *www.museumofnewmexico.org*), which runs four museums and five monuments throughout the region; and the Georgia O'Keefe Museum (217 Johnson Street; 505–946–1000; *www.okeefemuseum.org*), dedicated to her own art, as well as other American Modernist artists. Performing arts of all types are offered throughout the year from such groups as the Santa Fe Opera (505–986–5955; *www.santafeopera.org*) and the New Mexico Ballet (505–292–4245; *www.nmballet.org*) and by worldwide jazz musicians at the annual Santa Fe Jazz Festival (505–989–8442; *www.santafejazzfestival.com*).

Recreation: There are centuries-old Anasazi villages to explore around Santa Fe that are home to the world's largest collection of folk art and relics of the Old West. Santa Fe's setting and amazing parks provide sweeping dramatic landscapes for walkers, hikers, and bikers. The Randall Davey Audubon Center (1800 Upper Canyon Road; 505–983–4609; *www.audubon.org*) is located next to a wonderful old house on Upper Canyon Road. There are 100 acres of gentle hiking and interpretive trails through this preserved old property. The Santa Fe National Forest (1474 Rodeo Road; 505–438–7840; *www.fs.fed.us/r3/sf*), just 7 miles from downtown, opens into more than 300,000 acres of public land covered in trails. El Rancho de Las Golondrinas (334 Los Pinos Road; 505–471–2261; *www.golondrinas.org*) is a living museum of Spanish Colonial life located on the old Camino Real. The museum is on 200 acres filled with 18th-century buildings, a mill pond, plenty of animals, and lots of hands-on demonstrations such as rope making and yarn spinning by folks dressed in period clothes. Bandelier National Monument (15 Entrance Road; 505–672–0343; *www.nps.gov/band*) is home to Anasazi cliff dwellings with a 1-mile interpretive trail that wanders in and out of the carved-out rooms, ceremonial caves, and kivas. There is also a long trail system through this 32,000-acre archeological site. The Santa Fe Southern Railroad (410 S. Guadalupe Street; 505–989–8600; *www.sfsr.com*) does three-hour excursion trips through the scenic New Mexico countryside with period cars including a dome car and an outdoors flat car.

For the Visitor

Accommodations: Both historic and comfortable, the Inn of the Turquoise Bear (342 East Buena Vista Street; 505–983–0798/800–396–4104; *www.turquoisebear.com*) occupies the home of Witter Bynner (1881–1968), who for decades was a prominent citizen in Santa Fe, actively participating in the cultural and political life of the city. Bynner was a staunch advocate of human rights, especially of Native Americans and other minorities. The Arius Compound (1018 Canyon Road; 505–310–3527/800–735–8453; *www.ariuscompound.com*) has three adobe guest houses surrounded by gardens and fruit trees, patios, and fountains and offers an outdoor hot tub, tile floors, and corner fireplaces with one or two bedrooms and fully equipped kitchens. The Marriott Residence Inn (1698 Galisteo Street; 505–988–7300/800–331–3131; *www.marriott.com*) is a gay-friendly option with a pool, Sport Court, and residential-like grounds.

For More Information

Gay & Lesbian Hotline
AA Gay & Lesbian Hotline
505–982–8932

Publications
Santa Fe New Mexican
202 E. Marcy Street
Santa Fe, NM 87501
505–983–3303
www.santafenewmexican.com

Santa Fe Reporter
132 E. Marcy Street
Santa Fe, NM 87501
505–988–5541
www.sfreporter.com

Convention and Visitors Bureau
Santa Fe Convention & Visitors
Bureau
Box 909
Santa Fe, NM 87504-0909
505–955–6200/800–777–2489
www.santafe.org

Chamber of Commerce
Santa Fe Chamber of Commerce
P.O. Box 1928
Santa Fe, NM 87504-8380
505–988–3279
www.santafechamber.com

Realtor
Grace Berge
Fine Homes Specialist
Prudential Santa Fe Real Estate
510 N. Guadalupe Street, Suite K
Santa Fe, NM 87501
505–577–1087
www.prudentialsantafe.com

32 ▶ Ithaca, New York

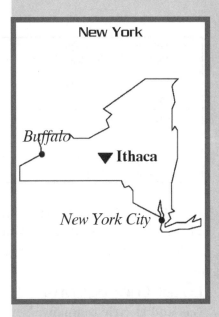

A Look at Ithaca

Ithaca is surrounded by ice-age, deep-cut gorges and 150 spectacular waterfalls that flow out of the wooded glens into Cayuga Lake, the largest of New York's famous Finger Lakes. Brilliant sunrises and sunsets of spectacular colors take your breath away. The city offers the invigorating richness of four full seasons: flowering springs give Ithaca the title Forsythia City, balmy summers, unmatched fall colors, and winters direct from Currier and Ives. The lifestyle is culturally rich, engagingly diverse, and refreshingly laid back; nobody is in a hurry. Founded in the late 1700s as a trading post with easy access to water transport, eventually including the Erie Canal, Ithaca grew to become a bustling port city of colorful characters and a bawdy reputation. Education grew into a major industry after Ezra Cornell founded Cornell University in 1868, followed by Ithaca College and Tompkins Cortland Community College. The largest concentration of shops, galleries, and restaurants are found at the Ithaca Commons on State Street. Restricted from car traffic and lined with galleries and shops, the Commons is a great place to stroll or people-watch. One example of the city's continuing innovation is Ithaca Hours (*www.ithacahours.org*), a local paper currency exchange that has set standards worldwide and brings important visitors to Ithaca and community development specialists from every continent.

Possible drawbacks: As a college town, many of Ithaca's residents are transient. Fortunately, the abundance of affordable housing doesn't create a major price war during the

▶ Nickname:
Ithaca is Gorges
▶ County:
Tompkins
▶ Area code: 607
▶ Time zone:
Eastern
▶ Population:
29,541
▶ County population:
101,411
▶ Region:
Upstate New York
▶ Closest metro areas:
Buffalo, New York
▶ Average home price:
$191,914
▶ Fabulous reasons to live here:
Liberal, college-town atmosphere; fabulous natural beauty; recreation; affordable housing; arts; excellent education; strong economy; large, active GLBT community

Climate

Elevation 1099'	Avg. high/low(F°)	Avg. inches		Avg. # days precip.	Avg. % humidity
		rain	snow		
Jan.	31/14	2.1	24.5	18	74%
April	55/33	3.3	4.3	14	65%
July	80/57	3.6	0.0	11	70%
Oct.	59/37	3.3	0.6	12	73%
YEAR	56/36	37.0	96.6	167	71%
# days 32° or below: 94			# days 90° or warmer: 6		

school year. Summer temperatures remain moderate because of the Finger Lakes, but winters can get downright nasty with weeks on end of below-freezing temperatures.

Local Connections

Gas and electric company: New York State Electric and Gas (800–572–1111; *www.nyseg.com*)

Phone company: Sprint (800–877–774; *www.sprint.com*)

Water and sewer: City of Ithaca Water and Sewer Division (607–272–1717; *www.ci.ithaca.ny.us*)

Cable company: Time Warner Cable (315–634–6000; *www.timewarnercable.com*)

Car registration/License: New York Department of Motor Vehicles (518–473–5595; *www.nydmv.state.ny.us*)

New residents of New York State have 30 days to obtain a driver's license and register their vehicles. Surrender your out-of-state license to waive exams. Fees: $10 application fee; driver's license fee based on age: $50–80. Sales tax is charged for new car purchases only. Vehicle registration fee is based on vehicle weight and ranges from $20.50 to $112 annually. Vehicle plates fee: $15. Title certificate fee: $10. Vehicle Use Tax based on vehicle weight and county of residence: $5–10 per year.

The Tax Ax

Sales tax: 8.25 percent

State income tax: 4.0–7.7 percent graduated, based on income

Property tax: Tompkins County Department of Assessment (607–274–5517; *www.tompkins-co.org/assessment*)

The property tax comes in two parts. The first is the school tax at $19.92 per $1,000; the second is the city and county tax at $20.256500 per $1,000.

Local Real Estate

Overview: Downtown Ithaca is filled with huge 1900s Victorian homes, brownstones, and contemporary houses. Outside the city limits you will find more ranch-style and newer-built homes. To-be-built homes are becoming very popular in the North East, Cayuga Heights, and South Hill areas.

Median price for a single-family home: $170,000

Average price for a single-family home: $191,914

Average price for a 2BR condo: $116,000

Rental housing market: Student housing rents from $500 to $800 per month; upscale rentals $700 to $1,800.

Gay-friendly neighborhoods: All of Ithaca's neighborhoods are gay-friendly.

Nearby areas to consider: Tompkins County, in the area along Cayuga Lake to the north of Ithaca, has a collection of small villages that are popular with the GLBT community. These are classic, small-town America, Main Street–centered communities with affordable housing, good public schools, history, pride, and tradition; small communities where you know your neighbors. With the Finger Lakes and mountains, the area provides fabulous outdoor recreation opportunities, and the arts are well represented, too. Towns of note for the GLBT community are Trumansburg, Lansing, Groton, Dryden, Newfield, Endfield, and Cortland.

Earning a Living

Per capita income: $13,408

Median household income: $21,441

Business climate: Tompkins County boasts one of the strongest economies in the northeastern United States. This robust economy can be accredited to durable goods manufacturers and new technology-oriented enterprises and the research activities conducted in the Center of Excellence at Cornell University. A relatively prosperous private sector and very strong education market have kept unemployment rates consistently low, generally under 3%.

Help in starting a business: Agencies such as Tompkins County Area Development (*www.tcad.org*), the Ithaca Downtown Partnership (*www.downtownithaca.com*), and the Tompkins Chamber of Commerce (*www.tompkinschamber.org*) play a facilitative role in promoting business growth and helping businesses in the Ithaca area through advice, education, networking, and advertising opportunities.

Job market: Cornell University is Ithaca's largest employer. The vibrant commerce calls for the skills of nuclear physicists and physical therapists, auto techs and computer techs, farmers and framers, machinists and marketers, thespians and theologians. Manufacturing has always been a prominent part of the Tompkins County landscape, and current products include computer chips, jet engine and automotive parts, satellite guidance systems, and computer software.

The Community

Overview: The GLBT community in Ithaca is active and out. Being a college town, politics and ideals are in general liberal. Ithaca and Tompkins County thrive on the creative resources brought to the community by its GLBT members in both the arts and business. There aren't any gay ghetto sections of Ithaca; instead, the gay community is home throughout the city.

Community organizations: The Ithaca Lesbian, Gay, Bisexual, and Transgender Task Force (607–387–8252; *www.ilgbttf.org*) is an advocate for the creation of a social and cultural environment that nurtures a wide range of gender, sexuality, and family arrangements. It's an advocate for the elimination of sexual exploitation and gender inequality as well as institutionalized homophobia and heterosexism. The Task Force maintains the most complete list of groups and organizations in Ithaca.

Medical care: Cayuga Medical Center at Ithaca (607–274–4011; *www.cayugamed.org*) has been providing healthcare to the citizens of Ithaca and the greater Finger Lakes region for more than 100 years. The fifth-largest employer in Tompkins County, Cayuga Medical Center employs 800 healthcare professionals and has an affiliated medical staff of 180 physicians. A 204-bed, acute-care facility that offers state-of-the-art diagnosis and treatment services, Cayuga Medical Center at Ithaca is a highly accredited, not-for-profit regional healthcare organization, and one of only nine rural referral centers in the state. Each year more than 150,000 patients use the comprehensive acute-care and outpatient services.

Getting Around Town

Public transportation: Tompkins Consolidated Area Transit (607–277–RIDE; *www.tcatbus.com*) provides local bus transportation 360 days a year. Fares are based on zone: one-way, multiple zones, Monday–Friday $3; one-way, zone one (all of Ithaca) and all zones on weekends $1.50. Discounted rates for youths and seniors. Cornell faculty and staff with ID ride free Monday–Friday; Cornell students with ID ride routes 92 and 93 free.

Roads: SR13, SR89, SR 96 (nearby I-81, I-86)

Airports: Ithaca Tompkins Regional Airport (airport code: ITH) (607–257–0456; *www.ithaca-airport.com*) provides commuter and shuttle services; Syracuse-Hancock International Airport (airport code: SYR) (315–454–4330; *www.syrairport.org*), about 60 miles north, is a full-service facility.

It's a Gay Life

Annual events: In June, Southern Tier Pride New York (*www.stnypride.com*) hosts a three-day pride festival spread over three cities. The events include a kick-off party and dance in Binghamton and a pride parade and rally in Elmira, and conclude with a barbecue, tea dance, and bonfire in Ithaca. The Ithaca Women's Music Festival (*www.ithacacommonground.com*) is in July. Two other major annual events include the Ithaca Festival (*www.ithacafestival.com*), a family-oriented celebration of the arts showcasing more than 1,000 local musicians, ensembles, community groups, visual and performance artists, craftspeople, actors, dancers, storytellers, poets, and writers, and the Finger Lakes GrassRoots Festival of Music and Dance (*www.grassrootsfest.org*), featuring more than 60 bands playing on four stages for four days and nights. It is a community event that encompasses performers from all over the world, a music lover's paradise.

Nightlife: Home to a major university and a number of small colleges, there's no shortage of nighttime activities. Common Ground (1230 Danby Road; 607–273–1505; *www.ithacacommonground.com*) is Ithaca's only gay bar, with music, dancing, food, and friendly clientele. It provides a weekly line-up of events including live bands, comics, and jazz night and hosts other social activities. Felicia's Atomic Lounge (508 West State Street; 607–273–2219; *www.atomicloungeithaca.com*) has a large gay following; it's the perfect bar in which to find a spot on the velvet couch and enjoy the daily drink creation or excellent pizza. College Avenue and State Street both have many bars and restaurants that are active day or night. A few favorites include Stella's Bar & Restaurant (403 College Avenue; 607–277–1490), with a fabulous gourmet menu, cocktails, jazz lounge, and extensive wine, scotch, and martini lists, and Chapter House Brewpub (400 Stewart Avenue; 607–277–9782; *www.chapterhouseithaca.com*) in Collegetown with 51 taps of microbrews and imports.

Culture: Theater productions at the colleges rival Broadway, from musicals to Shakespeare, and several community groups provide intimate and offbeat offerings. Of special interest are the historic State Theater (107 W. State Street; 607–277–7477; *www.statetheatreofithaca.com*), which hosts the Ithaca Ballet and touring productions; The Center for the Arts at Ithaca, Inc., also known as the Hangar Theatre (116 N. Cayuga Street; 607–273–4497; *www.hangartheatre.org*), providing exceptional theater experiences of high professional quality for the diverse audience in the Finger Lakes region; and Kitchen Theatre (116 N. Cayuga Street; 607–273–4497; *www.kitchentheatre.com*), a year-round professional theater offering an engaging mix of regional and world premiere plays in an intimate 73-seat theater. If music is your preference, Ithaca College's Dillingham Performing Arts Center (953 Danby Road; 607–274–3224; *www.ithaca.edu/theatre*) and Cornell's Schwartz Center for the Performing Arts (430 College Avenue; 607–254–2700; *www.arts.cornell.edu/theatrearts*) shine, with performance groups that regularly perform at New York's Lincoln Center and other top concert halls. The Sciencenter (601 First Street; 607–272–0600; *www.sciencenter.org*) provides hands-on experience to delight both young and old. The Johnson Museum at Cornell (Central and University avenues; 607–255–6464; *www.museum.cornell.edu*) has a fine collection of Asian art in addition to hosting many traveling exhibits. There are also some excellent galleries, many of which literally spill out onto State Street.

Recreation: With the abundance of lakes, streams, forests, parks and trails in and around Ithaca there are excellent outdoor recreation activities all year round. With more than 128 different species of fish in the Finger Lakes region, it's not surprising that Cayuga Lake was selected one of the top 10 bass-fishing lakes by *Sports Afield* magazine. Then there's swimming, boating, hiking, running, biking, camping, baseball, softball, lacrosse, soccer, and football. In the winter there's skiing (cross-country and downhill), ice skating (hockey is a major passion), snow shoeing, and hiking. The Finger Lakes Land Trust (*www.fllt.org*) has several preserves in and around Ithaca with public hiking trails. Footprint Press, Inc. (*www.footprintpress.com*) provides comprehensive information on all the area's outdoor activities. The Cayuga Nature Center (1420 Taughannock Boulevard; 607–273–6260; *www.cayuganaturecenter.org*) offers interpretive exhibits, 5 miles of nature trails, and regular programs year-round for every age group. For dinosaur lovers, the Paleontological Research Institution (1259 Trumansburg Road; 607–273–6623; *www.priweb.org*) has one of the largest collections of research fossils in North America (two million!). Cornell's Sapsucker Woods Bird Sanctuary (159 Sapsucker Woods Road; 607–254–2473; *birds.cornell.edu*) combines education and recreation. Sports fans will discover that Cornell University (607–254–4636; *www.cornell.edu*), Ithaca College (*www.ithaca.edu*), and Tompkins Cortland Community College (607–844–8211; *www.sunytccc.edu*) field a number of athletic teams in virtually every intercollegiate sport.

For the Visitor

Accommodations: The gay-friendly William Henry Miller Inn (303 North Aurora Street; 607–256–4553; *www.millerinn.com*) was built as a private home in 1880 by Cornell University's first student of architecture. It's rich in architectural detail, with stained-glass windows, American chestnut woodwork, working fireplaces, seven spacious bedrooms, and large common areas. The Carriage House, located directly behind the inn, provides additional accommodations in a setting that is both private and luxurious. La Tourelle Country Inn (1150 Danby Road; 607–273–2734/800–765–1492; *www.latourelleinn.com*) is a small, 35-room hotel that blends European elegance and old-world charm with contemporary comfort and beauty. La Tourelle is located on 70 acres of rolling hills in the heart of Upstate New York Wine Country. The Frog Haven Women's Bed and Breakfast (578 West King Road; 607–272–3238; *www.froghavenbb.com*), a contemporary log-sided home on 4 acres with cathedral ceiling living room and cozy rooms, is located 2 miles off Route 96B South. The quiet country setting, pond, and homey atmosphere make this a great place to relax (women only).

For More Information

Gay & Lesbian Center

Ithaca Lesbian Gay Bisexual
Transgender Task Force
P.O. Box 283
Ithaca, NY 14851-0283
607–387–8252
www.ilgbttf.org

Publication

The Ithaca Journal
123–127 W. State Street
Ithaca, NY 14850
607–272–2321
www.theithacajournal.com

Convention and Visitors Bureau

Ithaca/Tompkins County Convention
& Visitors Bureau
904 East Shore Drive
Ithaca, NY 14850
607–272–1313800–28–ITHACA
www.VisitIthaca.com

Chamber of Commerce

Tompkins County Chamber of
Commerce
904 E. Shore Drive
Ithaca, NY 14850-1026
607–273–7080
www.tompkinschamber.org

Realtor

Mary Stoe
RE/MAX In Motion
531 Esty Street, Suite 200
Ithaca, NY 14850
607–277–1500, ext. 225
www.ithaca-realestate.com

Manhattan, New York

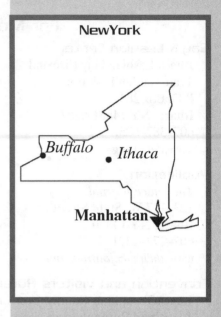

New York

Buffalo   Ithaca

Manhattan

A Look at Manhattan

What are you looking for: music, theater, museums, high culture, high finance, a sense of anonymity or a sense of community? It's all here, bundled into a mere 22.7 square miles known as Manhattan. What appears from the outside as a chaos of traffic, people, and buildings, is from the inside a collection of close-knit neighborhoods. New Yorkers, often seen as rude, cold, and uninvolved, love their city and are proud to show it off. If you stop any residents on the street, they'll gladly give you directions and probably recommend their favorite city spots. The city is built on traditions, history, and gold. The vaults of the Federal Reserve Bank on Maiden Lane store more than one-quarter of the world's gold bullion and, around the corner, Alexander Hamilton and Robert Fulton are buried in the Trinity Church graveyard. In 1969, the Stonewall riots in Manhattan's Greenwich Village changed the course of GLBT history, starting a movement toward equality that continues to be fought around the world today.

Possible drawbacks: Manhattan is one of the most expensive cities in the world. It's not unheard of for renters to pay $2,000 for a one-room studio apartment, and combined city and state taxes will set you back about 13 percent of your income. The city is a clearinghouse rather than a manufacturer of wealth; the city's economy is intimately tied to world events.

▶ Nickname:
The Big Apple

▶ County:
New York

▶ Area codes:
212; 646

▶ Time zone: Eastern

▶ Population:
1,537,195

▶ County population:
1,537,195

▶ Region:
Southeast New York

▶ Average home price:
$900,000

▶ Fabulous reasons to live here:
Arts; culture; music; theater; entertainment; large, politically active GLBT community; strong economy; fabulous public transportation; excellent location

Climate

Elevation 55'	Avg. high/low(F°)	Avg. inches		Avg. # days precip.	Avg. % humidity
		rain	snow		
Jan.	38/26	3.8	7.1	11	63%
April	60/44	3.9	0.7	11	59%
July	84/69	4.5	–	9	63%
Oct.	64/50	3.5	–	8	65%
YEAR	61/47	46.5	26.5	119	63%
# days 32° or below: 55			# days 90° or warmer: 17		

Local Connections

Gas and electric companies: You can choose your energy providers in New York. Power Your Way (800–33–SWITCH; *www.poweryourway.com*), provided by Consolidated Edison (212–460–4600/800–752–6633; *coned.com*), details service providers and costs.

Phone companies: AT&T (212–760–8589; *www.att.com*); MCI (212–826–7090; *www.mci.com*); Sprint (212–619–4008; *www.sprint.com*); among others

Water and sewer: New York City Water Board (718–595–7000; *www.nyc.gov*)

Cable company: Time Warner Cable (212–358–0900; *www.timewarnercable.com*)

Car registration/License: New York Department of Motor Vehicles (518–473–5595; *www.nydmv.state.ny.us*)

New residents of New York State have 30 days to obtain a driver's license and register their vehicles. Surrender your out-of-state license to waive exams. Fees: $10 application fee; driver's license fee based on age: $50–80. Sales tax is charged for new car purchases only. Vehicle registration fee is based on vehicle weight and ranges from $20.50 to $112 annually. Vehicle plates fee: $15. Title certificate fee: $10. Vehicle Use Tax based on vehicle weight and county of residence: $5–10 per year.

The Tax Ax

Sales tax: 8.25 percent; some food and clothing purchases exempt

City tax: Up to 6 percent graduated, based on income

State income tax: 4–6.85 percent graduated, based on income

Property tax: The property tax in New York State provides money for local services in counties, cities, towns, villages, school districts, and special districts. Property is assessed at a percentage of fair market value and based on property use and class; .75 is the current effective rate per $100 for most of Manhattan.

Local Real Estate

Overview: There are very few single-family homes in Manhattan. Eighty percent of the housing market for purchase consists of co-ops, with the balance condos. Downtown offers loft apartments. Rental apartments, from studios to two-bedrooms, are the bulk of Manhattan's housing. Three-bedrooms do exists but at a premium. Pre-war buildings offer details such as hardwood floors, high ceilings, wood burning or decorative fireplaces, and moldings. Post-war buildings offer more modern conveniences and some include concierge services, valet parking, central heating, and air.

Median price for a single-family home: Very rare, $3 million.

Average price for a single-family home: $900,000

Average price for a 2BR condo: $975 price per square foot ($850K–1.2 million and up)

Rental housing market: There are many more options for renters in Manhattan. Several luxury post-war doorman buildings exist with brand new renovated kitchens, great closet space, workout rooms, roof decks, and valet laundry services. Some buildings help their tenants with contacts for dog walkers, maid services, and so on, and have ATMs and postal facilities in the building. Studio rents start at $1,000; two-bedrooms start at $1,500.

Gay-friendly neighborhoods: All of Manhattan is gay-friendly. Some of the more popular neighborhoods are downtown's Greenwich Village, East Village, and Chelsea; midtown's Hell's Kitchen; the Upper West Side; and, uptown's Ft. Washington and Inwood.

Nearby areas to consider: The search for affordable housing in and around New York City draws the GLBT community into many different areas. Urban pioneering is popular in the region, turning once undesirable neighborhoods and even whole cities into trendy communities. A few of these examples include Brooklyn's Park Slope, where artists began converging to take advantage of more affordable, large warehouse, loft, and studio spaces. Long Island City and Astoria, Queens, provide affordable apartments and an easy commute into Manhattan. In New Jersey, Hoboken and Jersey City are enjoying a renaissance initially fuelled by the GLBT community. Bergenfield, New Jersey, with its affordable, single-family homes and easy commute into Manhattan, is attracting a family-oriented GLBT community.

Earning a Living

Per capita income: $42,922

Median household income: $47,030

Business climate: The New York Stock Exchange began in 1792 when 24 brokers met under a buttonwood tree facing 68 Wall Street. The New York Stock Exchange is now the world's largest exchange and provides the financial barometer for the city. Manhattan has the largest collection of national, international, and world headquarters in the United States. As the crossroads of the world, the city also has a large tourism industry.

Help in starting a business: Greenwich Village – Chelsea Chamber of Commerce has hundreds of members and focuses on government policy, small business concerns, economic development, and tourism promotion. The Manhattan Chamber of Commerce provides networking, advertising, and educational opportunities for new businesses of all sizes in Manhattan. New York City Department of Small Business Services (212–513–6300; *nyc.gov/html/sbs*) caters to helping area small business.

Job market: Major market employment sectors include educational, health, and social services; professional, scientific, management, administrative, and waste management services; finance; insurance; real estate; and rental and leasing.

The Community

Overview: New York City is home to one of the largest, collective GLBT communities in the world. Manhattan is divided into more than a dozen neighborhoods, and, although Greenwich Village remains both the historic and modern community epicenter, members of the gay community call all city neighborhoods home. Manhattan's large GLBT population is social, organized, and vocal.

Community organizations: New York City is home to hundreds of GLBT social, recreational, spiritual, and support organizations. Every week more than 300 groups meet at the Lesbian, Gay, Bisexual & Transgender Community Center. The Center is the birthplace of organizations such as ACT UP and the Gay & Lesbian Alliance Against Defamation (GLAAD). The Center maintains an extensive database of groups and organizations in the city and provides Center Orientation, an introduction to the Center and the greater New York City area, an enjoyable and informative way to help navigate you through the jungle of New York City.

Medical care: There's no shortage of quality healthcare in New York City. There are 81 hospitals, five of them academic medical centers. Gay Men's Health Crisis (GMHC) (212–367–1000; *www.gmhc.org*) is a not-for-profit, volunteer-supported, and community-based organization committed to national leadership in the fight against AIDS. GMHC's mission is to reduce the spread of HIV disease, help people with HIV maintain and improve their health and independence, and keep the prevention, treatment, and cure of HIV an urgent national and local priority. In fulfilling this mission, GMHC will remain true to its heritage by fighting homophobia and affirming the individual dignity of all gay men and lesbians.

Nuptials: The State of New York has no law or provision prohibiting same-sex marriage; the state currently acknowledges legal, same-sex marriages and unions performed in other jurisdictions. Most large employers, including city government, provide domestic partner benefits.

Getting Around Town

Public transportation: The Metropolitan Transportation Authority (MTA) (718–330–1234; *www.mta.nyc.ny.us*) provides Metro-North Railroad and Long Island Railroad and oversees New York City Transit bus and subway services. Bus and Subway Fares: one-way, system-wide $2; 1-Day Fun Pass (unlimited rides) $7. Hopstop (*www.hopstop.com*) is a free service that provides door-to-door subway and walking directions.

Roads: I-80, I-95, I-278, I-295, I-495, I-678, US9A

Airports: La Guardia International Airport (airport code: LGA) (212–435–7000; *www.laguardiaairport.com*) is about 6 miles from the city. JFK International Airport (airport code: JFK) (718–244–4444; *www.kennedyairport.com*) is about 12 miles from the city; Newark Liberty International Airport (airport code: EWR) (973–961–6000; *www.newarkairport.com*) is about 13 miles from the city.

It's a Gay Life

Annual events: Heritage of Pride (*www.hopinc.org*) hosts Gay Pride in June. The weeklong event includes rallies, concerts, and social events, culminating with one of the country's largest gay pride parades and a huge street fair. There are several major circuit parties each year, including the Saint-at-Large White Party (*www.saintatlarge.com*) in February and the Saint-at-Large Black Party (*www.saintatlarge.com*) in March. AIDS Walk (*www.aidswalk.net*) in May is a major annual social event. Wigstock (*www.wigstock.nu*) in September is the end-of-summer dragfest. GMHC hosts an annual dance-a-thon fundraiser (*www.gmhc.org*) in November. The city hosts Gay Expo (*www.rdpgroup.com*) in April, Gay Wedding Expo (*www.samesexweddingexpo.com*) in February, and Gay Life Expo (*www.gaylifeexpo.com*) in November. The nation's largest public Halloween parade is the Greenwich Village Halloween Parade (914–758–5519; *www.halloween-nyc.com*). Additionally, every holiday and culture is celebrated with a parade, festival, or street fair in New York.

Nightlife: With more than 100 gay bars and another 100 gay restaurants in Manhattan, there's no shortage of places to go or things to do day or night. Most of the bars have themes that attract certain "types" and their admirers. Themes range from quiet, neighborhood places to Levi and leather to trendy dance clubs and ultimate fetish bars. No matter what you're looking for, a good place to begin a bar crawl is at the intersection of Seventh Avenue, Greenwich Avenue, and Christopher Street. Just past the Duplex (61 Christopher Street; 212–255–5438; *www.theduplex.com*) on Christopher is the Stonewall Inn (53 Christopher Street; 212–463–0950). It's not the original home of the Stonewall Riots (a few doors away), but it remains a historic GLBT center. *HX Magazine* (*www.hx.com*) and *Next* (*www.nextmagazine.net*) are the best sources for up-to-date bar and event listings. In addition to the bars, you'll find them at Oscar Wilde Bookshop (15 Christopher Street; 212–255–8097; *www.oscarwildebooks.com*) or Creative Visions Books (548 Hudson Street; 212–645–7573; *www.creativevisionsbooks.com*).

Culture: Museums to theaters, botanical gardens to zoos, the City's cultural life is brimming with imagination, beauty, excitement, and surprise. No matter what you want to do, it's just around the corner or a quick subway ride away. The New York Botanical Garden (Bronx River Parkway and Fordham Road; 718–817–8700; *www.nybg.org*) is home to the nation's largest Victorian glasshouse: the Enid A. Haupt Conservatory, a New York City landmark that has showcased NYBG's Center for the Performing Arts (between W. 62nd and 65th streets and Columbus and Amsterdam avenues; 212–875–5456; *www.lincolncenter.org*), America's first performing arts center, held its first performance on September 23, 1962, and continues to draw crowds to theater, opera, and orchestra concerts. The Cloisters, a branch of the Metropolitan Museum of Art (Fort Tryon Park; 212–923–3700; *www.metmuseum.org*), is the only museum in America dedicated exclusively to medieval art. Along 5th Avenue are the Metropolitan Museum of Art (1000 Fifth Avenue; 212–535–7710; *www.metmuseum.org*) and Guggenheim Museum of Art (1071 Fifth Avenue; 212–423–3500; *www.guggenheim.org*). The Theater District, from 42nd Street to 57th Street, is home to dozens of Broadway theaters presenting classic, modern, and musical theater productions nightly.

Recreation: New York City is America's greenest city, with more than a quarter of its acreage set aside as parks and open space. The crown jewel, though not the largest park in the city, was created 150 years ago by designers Frederick Law Olmsted and Calvert Vaux, who turned 843 acres of swamp in the middle of Manhattan into Central Park (*www.centralpark.org*), one of the urban wonders of the world. This green oasis in the middle of New York City's concrete jungle is so naturally part of the Manhattan environment that many people may not realize it is entirely man-made. New Yorkers jog, walk, bike, in-line skate, horseback ride, ice skate, rent row boats, play basketball, softball, soccer, and tennis, and enjoy special events and festivals in more than 1,700 parks, playgrounds, and open spaces. Spectator sports enthusiasts will love New York City, where professional sports are played at some of the world's best venues, including Yankee Stadium (161st Street and River Avenue, Bronx; 718–293–4300; *www.yankees.com*) and Shea Stadium (123–01 Roosevelt Avenue, Flushing; 718–507–METS; *www.mets.com*), Madison Square Garden (4 Pennsylvania Plaza; 212–465–MSG1; *www.thegarden.com*), the Meadowlands Sports Complex (50 SR120, East Rutherford, NJ; 201–935–8500; *www.meadowlands.com*), Arthur Ashe Stadium (Flushing Meadows, Corona Park, Flushing; 866–OPEN–TIX; *www.usopen.org*), and the world-famous Aqueduct (110–00 Rockaway Boulevard, Jamaica; 718–641–4700; *www.aqueduct-racetrack.com*) and Belmont (2150 Hempstead Turnpike, Elmont; 516–488–6000; *www.nyra.com/belmont*) racetracks.

For the Visitor

Accommodations: With more than 70,000 hotel rooms in New York City there's something for most budgets. Along with the usual chain hotels there are B&Bs, penthouse suites, boutique hotels, and youth hostels. Downtown, the award-winning Chelsea Pines Inn (317 West 14th Street; 212–929–1023;

www.chelseapinesinn.com) is located between Chelsea and Greenwich Village. Belvedere Hotel (319 W. 48th Street; 212–245–7000; *www.newyorkhotel.com*) is in the heart of midtown and the theater district, and the Lucerne (201 W. 79th Street; 212–875–1000) is the perfect Upper West Side hotel, providing easy access to Central Park, Lincoln Center, and the Natural History Museum.

For More Information

Gay & Lesbian Center
The Lesbian, Gay, Bisexual &
Transgender Community Center
208 West 13th Street
New York, NY 10011
212–620–7310
www.gaycenter.org

Publications
New York Times
229 W. 43rd Street
New York, NY 10036
212–556–1234
www.nytimes.com

New York Daily News
450 W. 33rd Street
New York, NY 10001
212–210–2100
www.nydailynews.com

The New York Post
1211 Avenue of the Americas
New York, NY 10036
212–930–8000
www.nypostonline.com

Gay City News
487 Greenwich Street
New York, NY 10013
646–452–2500
www.gaycitynews.com

Convention and Visitors Bureau
NYC & Company, Inc.—the
Convention & Visitors Bureau
810 Seventh Avenue
New York, NY 10019
212–484–1222
www.nycvisit.com

Chambers of Commerce
Greenwich Village—Chelsea
Chamber of Commerce
80 Eighth Avenue, Suite 412
New York, NY 10011
212–255–5811
www.gvccc.com

Manhattan Chamber of Commerce
1375 Broadway, Third Floor
New York, NY 10018
212–479–7772
www.manhattancc.org

Realtor
Anna Milat-Meyer
Sales Associate
Halstead Property LLC
784 Broadway
New York, NY 10003
212–381–2296
www.halstead.com

34 ▶ Asheville, North Carolina

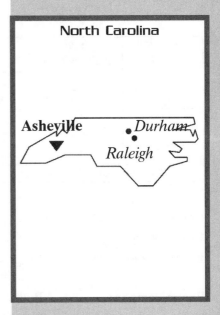

North Carolina

Asheville ▼ · Durham · Raleigh

A Look at Asheville

Nestled in the Blue Ridge Mountains of western North Carolina, Asheville offers the charm of a small city along with a stimulating urban environment. Watch the mountains awaken as spring blankets the hillsides with wildflowers. Glorious summer brings warm days for outdoor adventures and cool nights for enjoying the hours after dark. Autumn cloaks the Blue Ridge Mountains with every shade of red, orange, and yellow imaginable. Then, enjoy mild winter days in Asheville, with easy access to the higher elevations that are dusted in snow. The city has a strong historic preservation program and a fabulous collection of art deco architecture. This assistance in the preservation of downtown housing and historic structures has created a truly unique and vibrant urban atmosphere in downtown with restaurants, galleries, craft and antique shops, and performance venues. The Blue Ridge Parkway through the mountains creates endless opportunities for recreation and day trips. Asheville's natural and architectural beauty, moderate climate, strong job market, and outstanding educational and healthcare facilities make it one of the most attractive locations in the United States.

Possible drawbacks: Though the city provides many activities, there's a sense of isolation in the Asheville region. If mountain seclusion isn't your idea of a good time, you might want to pass through on the Blue Ridge Parkway and head for a larger destination.

▶ County:
Buncombe

▶ Area code:
828

▶ Time zone:
Eastern

▶ Population:
70,070

▶ County population:
206,330

▶ Region:
Western North Carolina

▶ Closest metro area:
Charlotte

▶ Average home price:
$180,000

▶ Fabulous reasons to live here:
Small-town charm; fabulous scenic beauty; culture, music, arts, and artists; affordable housing; temperate year-round climate; active GLBT community

Climate

Elevation 2134'	Avg. high/low(F°)	Avg. inches		Avg. # days precip.	Avg. % humidity
		rain	snow		
Jan.	47/25	3.2	4.8	11	72%
April	68/43	3.2	0.6	10	67%
July	83/63	3.1	–	12	78%
Oct.	68/44	2.5	–	8	74%
YEAR	73/45	46.9	14.9	126	71%
# days 32° or below: 63			# days 90° or warmer: 6		

Local Connections

Gas company: PSNC Energy (828–253–1821; *www.scana.com*)

Electric company: Progress Energy (800–452–2777; *www.progress-energy.com*)

Phone company: BellSouth (828–780–2355; *www.bellsouth.com*)

Water and sewer: Asheville Department of Water Resources (828–258–0161; *www.ci.asheville.nc.us*)

Cable company: Comcast (800–266–2278; *www.comcast.com*)

Car registration/License: North Carolina Department of Transportation Division of Motor Vehicles (919–715–7000; *www.ncdot.org/DMV*)

Auto licenses must be purchased within 30 days of relocating in the state. Fee: $3/year, renewed for four to eight years. Certificate of Title: $36; Instant Title: $51. License Plate Registration Fee for Private Passenger Vehicles: $20; License Plate Registration Fee for Private Truck Under 4,000 lbs.: $21.50. Highway Use Tax: 3 percent, based on vehicle's purchase price or value.

The Tax Ax

Sales tax: 7.5 percent

State income tax: 6–7.75 percent; bracketed based on income

Property tax: Buncombe County Tax Office (828–250–4910; *www.buncombecounty.org*)

The present property tax rate is approximately $1.35 per $100 in the city and around $.85 per $100 in the county. Rates change each three–four years when the tax rate is altered based on new assessments.

Local Real Estate

Overview: The Asheville housing market remains stable. New construction keeps pace with the growing population. Housing styles range from traditional to unique, including round houses, log homes, Victorian, and contemporary. New home construction is averaging $120–150 a square foot. There are also many condos being built.

Median price for a single-family home: $200,000

Average price for a single-family home: $180,000

Average price for a 2BR condo: $140,000

Rental housing market: There are many rentals, as investors have come in, bought, and renovated many older houses. The average price for a two-bedroom rental is around $600–800. For a three-bedroom, two-bath expect to pay $900–1,200.

Gay-friendly neighborhoods: There are many gay-friendly neighborhoods, and the GLBT community is home in every part of Asheville.

Nearby areas to consider: The GLBT community is spread throughout the small towns and cities surrounding Asheville. As the city's popularity continues to accelerate, the nearby areas' attractions will increase because of natural beauty and real estate affordability. When considering the communities surrounding Asheville, it's not an issue of them being gay-friendly, because the area *is* gay-friendly, but rather how remote you want to live. There are many rural and mountain areas the GLBT community calls home, including Weaverville, Skyland, Fletcher, Arden, Leicester, Black Mountain, Enka, Candler, Barnardsville, and Fairview.

Earning a Living

Per capita income: $20,024

Median household income: $32,772

Business climate: Asheville is a regional center for manufacturing, transportation, healthcare, banking, professional services, and tourism. The city currently enjoys a growing entrepreneurial services sector, but the local economy remains connected to a tourism base.

Help in starting a business: The Business and Industry Services Program is a high-priority part of the Asheville Area Chamber of Commerce Economic Development efforts. In addition to acting as the local business advocate, the Chamber provides a first point of contact for existing industry with local government, trade, professional, and community organizations.

Job market: Job growth in Asheville is being led by a strong healthcare industry, tourism, professional services, a strong housing market, and stable population growth. This is reflected by Ashville's top employers including Mission/St. Joseph's Health System and the VA hospital, Community Care Partners, Buncombe County Board of Education and County Government, G.E. Lighting Systems, and Blue Ridge Paper Products, Inc.

The Community

Overview: The GLBT community comprises a large percentage of the local population and continues to grow exponentially. The community is active in all aspects of Asheville life. Many local businesses are gay-owned, and local government is supportive.

Community organizations: Asheville lacks a formal GLBT community center, but there are many well-supported GLBT groups and organizations in the city and surrounding areas, including social, recreational, support, and spiritual groups. Visit Downtown Books & News (67 N. Lexington; 828–253–8654) or Malaprops Bookstore & Café (55 Haywood; 828–254–6734) and pick up *Community Connections* and *The Front Page* for listings of events, groups, and current news.

Medical care: Memorial Mission Hospitals (828–213–1111; *missionhospitals.org*) is the regional medical referral center for the western quarter of North Carolina and parts of several adjoining states. The area's "safety net" hospital, located on a 90-acre hilltop campus, has 800 beds and a medical staff of more than 600 physicians, who represent virtually every specialty and sub-specialty. Thoms Rehabilitation Hospital (828–274–2400; *www.thoms.org*) is a 100-bed, private, not-for-profit regional referral center with comprehensive inpatient and outpatient programs for all ages. Thoms also provides aquatic therapy services and Satellite Outpatient Physical Therapy Clinics.

Nuptials: North Carolina's constitution bans recognition of same-sex marriage. There are no other forms of relationship recognition for same-sex couples in state law or policies. However, the beauty of Asheville draws many couples, and commitment ceremonies are common.

Getting Around Town

Public transportation: The Asheville Transit System (828–253–5691; *www.ci.asheville.nc.us/transit*) provides transportation to all parts of the City of Asheville and the surrounding area; portions of the central downtown area are a "Free Fare Zone." You may ride any bus in the system within the Free Zone free of charge. Regular fare: $0.75; transfers $0.10.

Roads: I-26, I-40, I-240, US19, US23, US25, US25A, US70, US74

Airports: Asheville Regional Airport (airport code: AVL) (828–684–2226; *www.flyavl.com*) is served by the commercial carriers Continental Airlines, Delta Air Lines, Northwest Airlines, and US Airways; travelers can reach any destination in the world. Greenville-Spartanburg International Airport (airport code: GSP) (864–877–7426; *www.gspairport.com*), about 54 miles from Asheville, is a full-service international airport.

It's a Gay Life

Annual events: There are fun annual events throughout the year in Asheville, including the Annual Mountain Sports Festival (*www.mountainsportsfestival.com*)

in May and Bele Chere (*www.belechere.com*), the Southeast's largest outdoor street festival, in July. In August, the Annual Mountain Dance and Folk Festival (*www.folkheritage.org*) brings the rich musical traditions of Southern Appalachian Mountains to life and the annual Goombay! Festival (*www.ymicc.org*) celebrates African and West Indian traditional dance. Traditional mountain musicians converge on City/County Plaza Saturday evenings during the summer for Shindig on the Green (*www.folkheritage.org*), one of the longest-running jam sessions in the Southeast. The Buncombe County Tourism Development Authority (*www.exploreasheville.com*) maintains a complete list of annual events.

Nightlife: Asheville is home to lively nightspots, music venues, and theaters. The Diana Wortham Theatre presents more than 170 events each year, and live comedy, drama, and music are all presented at local playhouses. Live music of all genres spills out of a delicious mix of clubs and venues. Every third Friday, June through September, the Asheville Downtown Association (828–251–9973; *www.ashevilledowntown.org*) presents Downtown After Five, a free outdoor concert series on Pack Square. Asheville is also home to several lively GLBT nightspots, including O Henry's (59 Haywood Street; 828–254–1891), North Carolina's oldest gay bar; Scandals (11 Grove Street; 828–252–2838; *www.scandalsclub.com*), a high energy dance club that also features regular drag shows; the dance club the Hairspray Café (38 N. French Broad; 828–256–2027) with drag shows and occasional live music; the jazz club Tressa's (28 Broadway; 828–254–7072; *www.tressasdowntownjazzandblues.com*), and Tracks II (828–258–8729), a fabulous disco bar.

Culture: Experience the arts, crafts, and drama of this vibrant cultural center and you'll discover why artisans of all types find their inspiration in the mountains of western North Carolina. Asheville's favorite native sons include writers Thomas Wolfe and O. Henry. Asheville features theater, film, and entertainment of every kind: Shakespeare and rock 'n' roll, fine film and mellow jazz, experimental theater and country music, African rhythms and Broadway musicals, symphony and ballet. Traditional crafts are flanked by contemporary arts, and many artisans open their studios to demonstrate their trade to visitors. Ongoing events such as the River District Artist Studio Strolls (*www.riverdistrictartists.com*), City Center Art Walks (828–258–0710; *www.ashevillearts.com*), and Art Safari Tours (828–258–9994; *www.artsafaritours.com*) keep artists and art connoisseurs busy. The Folk Art Center (382 Blue Ridge Vista; 828–298–7928), located 10 minutes from downtown Asheville on the Blue Ridge Parkway, is a haven for admirers of mountain crafts with works on display and for sale by members of the Southern Highland Craft Guild (828–298–7928; *www.southernhighlandguild.org*). The Pack Place Education, Arts and Science Center (2 S. Pack Square; 828–257–4500; *www.packplace.org*) in downtown Asheville is home to the Asheville Art Museum (828–253–3227; *www.ashevilleart.org*), Colburn Earth Science Museum (828–254–7162; *www.colburnmuseum.org*), the Diana Wortham Theatre (828–257–4530; *www.dwtheatre.com*), the Health Adventure (828–254–6373; *www.thehealthadventure.org*), and the YMI Cultural Center (828–252–4614;

www.ymicc.org). One of the area's most famous attractions is the Biltmore Estate (1 Approach Road; 800–624–1575; *www.biltmore.com*), America's largest home, with beautiful gardens, restaurants, shops, and an award-winning winery.

Recreation: Recreational opportunities abound in and around Asheville. Considered the nation's most scenic highway, the 470-mile Blue Ridge Parkway (828–298–0398; *www.blueridgeparkway.org*) winds through the Blue Ridge Mountains into the entrance of the Great Smoky Mountains National Park. Numerous overlooks, roadside exhibits, and hiking trails make a trip along the Parkway a delight year-round. Asheville's newest facility, by renowned skate park designer Team Pain, the 17,000 square foot Food Lion SkatePark (Flint and Cherry streets; 828–259–5800; *www.foodlionskatepark.com*), is located just north of downtown in the Montford Neighborhood. There's league play for adults in the sports of basketball, flag football, softball, and volleyball, and youth leagues include youth baseball and softball, basketball, and tennis. The Asheville Botanical Gardens (151 W. T. Beaver Boulevard; 828–252–5190; *www.ashevillebotanicalgardens.org*) is a 10-acre garden featuring native plants. Cradle of Forestry (Pisgah National Forest US276, Transylvania County; 828–877–3130; *www.cradleofforestry.com*) allows you to travel back in time with historic cabins, crafters, old logging equipment, and much more. Experience the natural beauty of western North Carolina through miles of nature trails at the North Carolina Arboretum (100 Frederick Law Olmstead Way; 828–665–2492; *www.ncarboretum.org*). WNC Nature Center (75 Gashes Creek Road; 828–298–5600; *www.wildwnc.org*) offers environmental education with lots of fun on 42 acres home to native Southern Appalachian Region wildlife. WNC Farmers Market, operated by the North Carolina Department of Agriculture (570 Brevard Road; 828–253–1691; *www.ncagr.com*), has several retail and wholesale buildings, a restaurant, and a garden center.

For the Visitor

Accommodations: 1889 White Gate Inn & Cottage (173 E. Chestnut Street; 800–485–3045; *www.whitegate.net*) is a short walk from downtown. The house has amazing gardens (be sure to ask for a tour of the greenhouse) and is filled with antiques and original works of art. Biltmore Village Inn (119 Dodge Street; 866–274–8779; *www.biltmorevillageinn.com*) is an 1892 Queen Anne Victorian mansion located just steps away from the Biltmore Estate gates. Plan to spend some time on the fabulous porches. Compassionate Expressions Mountain Inn, Cabins & Spa (207 Robinson Cove Road, Leicester; 828–683–6633; *www.compassionatexpression.com*), located 30 minutes outside Asheville in the secluded mountains of Leicester, is a 40-acre private mountain retreat providing spectacular mountain views from your choice of inn rooms, cabins, or RV sites. Quality spa and healing services are available to soothe your soul. The retreat is a great spot for commitment ceremonies, retreats, and workshops.

For More Information

Gay & Lesbian Center
GLBT Community Hotline
828–253–2971

Publications
Asheville Citizen-Times
P.O. Box 2090
Asheville, NC 28802
828–252–5610
www.citizen-times.com

The Front Page
P.O. Box 27928
Raleigh, NC 27611
919–829–0181
www.frontpagenews.com

Community Connections
P.O. Box 18088
Asheville, NC 28814
828–251–2449

Out in Asheville
P.O. Box 1545
Skyland, NC 28776
848–687–7237
www.outinasheville.com

Convention and Visitors Bureau
Asheville Convention and Visitors Bureau
P.O. Box 1010
Asheville, NC 28802
888–247–9811
www.exploreasheville.com

Chamber of Commerce
Asheville Area Chamber of Commerce
151 Haywood Street
Asheville, NC 28801
828–258–6101
www.ashevillechamber.org

Realtor
Lyssa Cross, Realtor
C21 Mountain Lifestyles
1280 Hendersonville Road
Asheville, NC 28730
828–712–6289
www.mountainlaurelbnb.com

## 35

Durham, North Carolina

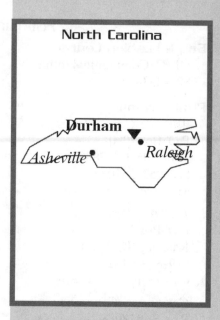

North Carolina

Durham

Asheville

Raleigh

A Look at Durham

Durham's landscape is characterized by 98,000 acres of hardwood and evergreen forests, including the only remaining old-growth Piedmont bottomland forests, hills and dales, meandering rivers and streams, and several lakes. The landscape creates endless recreation possibilities from hiking and biking to swimming and boating. Located at the pinnacle of the 3,000-square-mile "Triangle Region" in the northeast Piedmont of North Carolina, the city is home to Research Triangle Park, Duke, and North Carolina Central universities and a $1.5 billion healthcare industry with 300 related companies and practices. The arts are well represented with galleries, museums, theaters, and music. Downtown Durham is the historic birthplace and geographic heart of this compact 299-quare-mile single-city county. The community has fascinating and varied architecture from the art deco of downtown to the neo-Romanesque tobacco warehouses to Gothic Duke West Campus and Georgian Duke East Campus to the futuristic designs in Research Triangle Park to the funkiness of the Ninth Street District. The small city size mixes well with the creative, high-tech environment creating a home-town feel embraced by Durham's residents.

Possible drawbacks: Although the GLBT community is well supported by the local government, Durham lacks the central focus of a GLBT community center. The university environment creates an often-transient feel to the younger community population.

▶ Nickname: City of Medicine

▶ County: Durham

▶ Area code: 919

▶ Time zone: Eastern

▶ Population: 187,035

▶ County population: 223,314

▶ Region: North Central North Carolina

▶ Average home price: $223,000

▶ Fabulous reasons to live here: Scenic beauty, culture, music, arts, history, excellent education, affordable housing, temperate year-round climate, active GLBT community, strong economy

Climate

Elevation 394'	Avg. high/low(F°)	Avg. inches		Avg. # days precip.	Avg. % humidity
		rain	snow		
Jan.	49/28	4.4	2.8	10	67%
April	71/46	3.3	–	9	63%
July	89/70	4.0	–	11	73%
Oct.	71/47	3.7	–	7	71%
YEAR	70/48	47.6	7.5	112	69%
# days 32° or below: 48			# days 90° or warmer: 39		

Local Connections

Gas company: PSNC Energy (877–776–2427; *www.scana.com*)

Electric companies: Duke Power (800–827–5114; *www.dukepower.com*); Progress Energy (919–878–5300; *www.progress-energy.com*)

Phone company: Verizon (800–483–3000; *www.verizon.com*)

Water and sewer: The Department of Water Management, City of Durham (919–560–4326; *www.ci.durham.nc.us*)

Cable company: Time Warner Cable (919–220–2281; *www.timewarnercable.com*)

Car registration/License: North Carolina Department of Transportation Division of Motor Vehicles (919–715–7000; *www.ncdot.org/DMV*)

Auto licenses must be purchased within 30 days of relocating in the state. Fee: $3/year, renewed for four to eight years. Certificate of Title: $36; Instant Title: $51. License Plate Registration Fee for Private Passenger Vehicles: $20; License Plate Registration Fee for Private Truck Under 4,000 lbs.: $21.50. Highway Use Tax: 3 percent, based on vehicle's purchase price or value.

The Tax Ax

Sales tax: 7 percent

State income tax: 6 percent to $12,750; $765 plus 7 percent between $12,750 and $60,000; $4,072.50 plus 7.75 percent over $60,000 for people filing as singles

Property tax: Durham County Tax Administration (919–560–0300 *www.co.durham.nc.us*)

Property is assessed every eight years at 100 percent of market value. Tax rates are determined by each county, and most areas have a combination of the county rate plus city tax and any special tax or fire district that may apply. Current levy is $1.37 per $100 of home value.

Local Real Estate

Overview: Building has been nonstop for many years now. Planned new home communities are being built all over the Triangle with a strong mix of detached single-family homes and townhouses. In the downtown areas several old tobacco warehouses are being converted into loft-style condos. New home communities trend towards an emphasis on community amenities such as walking trails, pools, lakes, and golf courses. Several have an independent village concept with added shops and schools plus lots of sidewalks. Bungalows and Arts and Crafts styles are always favorites. Many builders are opting for transitional styles that offer a blend of some of the best older exterior styles while making the interiors common living spaces more open. Lots of desirable older home neighborhoods may require a little more patience to find the right home.

Median price for a single-family home: $186,000

Average price for a single-family home: $223,000

Average price for a 2BR condo: $153,000

Rental housing market: Luxury-style complexes with garages and various amenities are competing for tenants by offering incentives such as free washers and dryers or a free month with minimum one-year leases. Average rents for newer apartments are around $900; homes are slightly higher.

Gay-friendly neighborhoods: Watts Hospital, Trinity Park, Forest Hills, Duke Park, and Northgate Park are popular, GLBT communities.

Nearby areas to consider: A location just 11 miles southwest of Durham and home of the Carolina Jazz Fest, quality education, scenic beauty, and liberal politics have drawn a considerable GLBT population to Chapel Hill. Chapel Hill is also worth a visit in August for Sleazefest, a music festival and event like no other in the country. The Town of Carrboro, another mile west, takes pride in being known as a community rich in cultural and economic diversity. This growing community, called "Paris of the Piedmont," provides a small-town atmosphere with a focus on arts and culture and an easy commute to the Raleigh-Durham metro area. Even if you don't decide to move to Carrboro, its fabulous farmer's market is worth a visit.

Earning a Living

Per capita income: $22,526

Median household income: $41,160

Business climate: The Research Triangle Region is the world's largest and most successful university-related research and development business park. Approximately 140 major research and development companies employ more than 45,000. Healthcare, biotechnology, and pharmaceutical companies thrive in the Greater Durham area and are anchored by one of America's top healthcare providers: Duke University Medical Center.

Help in starting a business: The Greater Durham Chamber of Commerce is actively involved in programs of economic development, community promotion, government affairs, and business assistance. The Chamber's Economic Development Division is designed to help business relocate, expand, and operate in Durham. The Triangle Business & Professional Guild (*www.tbpg.org*) provides the area GLBT business community with positive role models, networking opportunities, and business and professional development opportunities.

Job market: Durham's largest employers are Duke University and Medical System. Primary industries include educational services; industrial machinery and equipment; local government; travel and tourism; health services; business services; engineering and management services; electronic and electric equipment; federal government; social services; retail and wholesale trade; and special trade contractors.

The Community

Overview: The Raleigh-Durham-Chapel Hill region in North Carolina is a prime example of the emergence of the new creative class. The area's combination of universities, colleges, and the Research Park Triangle draws scores of creative GLBT community members. The large and vibrant community is active and well supported by local government.

Community organizations: The Durham area lacks the central focus of a GLBT community center, but the needs of the community, from social and recreational to health, support, and political advocacy are met by the many formal groups and organizations in the Research Triangle area. *TriangleLocalEvents.com* and *The Front Page* (*www.frontpagenews.com*) are the Carolina's source for news and information, and they maintain current listings for the many groups, organizations, and businesses serving both North and South Carolina.

Medical care: Duke University Medical Center (888–275–3853; *www.mc.duke.edu*), the centerpiece of Duke's wide-ranging medical programs, is located on the Duke University campus in Durham. The youngest of the nation's leading medical centers, it has grown in just the past three decades from a hospital and single research building into one of the country's largest clinical and biomedical research institutions. The Private Diagnostic Clinic, PLLC, is a separate but integrated organization through which faculty physicians provide specialty, subspecialty, and primary care to more than 100,000 patients per year. Durham Regional Hospital (919–403–4DRH; *www.durhamregional.org*), a 369-bed, acute-care hospital, provides inpatient, outpatient, and emergency care and features a level II nursery, Durham Regional Rehabilitation Institute, and the Davis Ambulatory Surgery Center.

Nuptials: North Carolina's constitution bans recognition of same-sex marriage. There are no other forms of relationship recognition for same-sex couples in state law or policies. However, Durham County and many area employers provide domestic partner benefits to employees.

Getting Around Town

Public transportation: Durham Area Transit Authority, operated by the City of Durham (DATA) (919–683–DATA; *www.ci.durham.nc.us*) provides bus and van service throughout the city. Fares: one-way $1 (free for seniors).

Roads: I-40, I-85, US15, US70, US501

Airport: Raleigh-Durham International (airport code: RDU) (919–840–2100; *www.rdu.com*) is located in the heart of the Research Triangle Region: 10 miles southeast of Durham and 10 miles northwest of Raleigh.

It's a Gay Life

Annual events: The Pride Committee of North Carolina (NC Pride; *www.ncpride.org*) sponsors Pride Fest in late September. The North Carolina Gay and Lesbian Film Festival (*www.carolinatheatre.org*) in August is one of the nation's premier gay and lesbian film festivals, with more than 100 films screened. A few of the other major annual Durham events are February's Native American Powwow (*www.ncssm.edu/Powwow*), the American Dance Festival (*www.americandancefestival.org*) in June, September's Bull Durham Blues Festival (*www.hayti.org/blues*), and the World Beer Festival (*www.allaboutbeer.com*), featuring more than 300 beer vendors from all over the country as well as great music by local and regional artists, in October.

Nightlife: More than 41 nightclubs and venues offer live entertainment throughout the city, many with a focus on South Carolina Blues. One of the South's great musical traditions, the Blues found a special home in Durham in the 1930s. Since then, the Bull City has become the center for Piedmont Blues, a sensitive and delicate form of the Blues. The major renovations of the American Tobacco Historic District/Lucky Strike Cigarette Factory (324 Blackwell Street; 919–433–1560; *www.americantobaccohistoricdistrict.com*) is one of the most ambitious, largest, and farthest-reaching historic preservation and renovation projects in the history of North Carolina. Phase One is complete and includes restaurants, shops, and an amphitheatre. The Raleigh-Durham area has a small collection of GLBT bars and restaurants. Visions (711 Rigsbee Avenue; 919–688–3002; *www.clubvisions.bigstep.com*) is Durham's only GLBT bar, with monthly drag-king shows. Visit Regulator Bookshop (720 9th Street; 919–286–2700; *www.regbook.com*) and pick up a copy of *The Front Page* (*www.frontpagenews.com*) for the area's latest listings, news, and events.

Culture: Durham is home to 100 working visual artists, scores of studios, 41 galleries, two major art museums with unique collections, nine performance arts venues, 74 murals and pieces of outdoor art and sculpture, as well as funereal art, and the city hosts more than 20 major festivals and events including nine signature events with national or regional recognition. Each December, the Durham Art Walk hosts a walking tour of artists' studios in historic downtown Durham. North Carolina Central University Art Museum's (NCCU campus; 919–530–6211; *www.nccu.edu/artmuseum*) collection features the works of various

African-American artists from both the 19th and 20th centuries as well as a selection of objects from the African continent. Replacing the Duke University Museum of Art (DUMA), the new Nasher Museum of Art at Duke University (Duke University Campus; 919–684–5135; *www.nasher.duke.edu*) features an increased focus on modern and contemporary art. The Museum of Life and Science (433 Murray Avenue; 919–220–5429; *www.ncmls.org*) is an interactive museum showcasing aerospace, weather, geology, Carolina wildlife, farmyard, train rides, traveling exhibits, gift shops, café, and more, culminating with the tropical Magic Wings Butterfly House and Bayer CropScience Insectarium.

Recreation: Durham offers more than 60 parks, four major river ways/ greenways, a state park, a state recreation area, several major lakes, and a budding series of greenbelts with walking, hiking, and biking trails. Durham is home to the Sarah P. Duke Gardens (426 Anderson Street; 919–684–3698; *www.hr.duke.edu/ dukegardens*), one of the signature formal gardens in the nation, as well as some of the few scenic byways found within a major urban community, several forests, and a series of lakes and rivers. Durham is also home to flora and fauna very rare in the Piedmont region, a major rails-to-trails, and a host of other greenways and trails. Bird-watching, boating/sailing, boat launches, camping, concessions, fishing, hiking, marina, picnic shelter, playground, swimming, swimming beaches, water skiing, and windsurfing are just a few of the activities available at Rollingview State Recreation Area at Falls Lake (13304 Creedmoor Road, Wake Forest; 919–676–1027; *www.ncsparks.net*). Owned by the U.S. Army Corps of Engineers and managed by the N.C. Botanical Garden, Penny's Bend Nature Preserve (UNC campus, Chapel Hill; 919–962–0522; *www.ncbg.unc.edu*), an 84-acre peninsula bounded on three sides by the Eno River as it flows toward Falls Lake, is best known for its unusual wildflowers and rock formations. For spectators, the Durham Bulls Baseball Club (919–687–6500; *www.durhambulls.com*) is credited with the revival of minor league baseball and a return to its roots in Americana. Durham is also home to four national collegiate basketball championships, 10 golf courses (several with national reputations), and championship high school sports.

For the Visitor

Accommodations: There are more than 60 lodging properties and more than 7,000 rooms available ranging from bed and breakfasts to extended-stay hotels in Durham. There are several gay-friendly options in the area. Originally built for the CEO of Liggett and Meyers, Morehead Manor B&B (914 Vickers Avenue; 919–942–5621; *www.moreheadmanor.com*), a Colonial Revival–style home, is located within walking distance to the Downtown area, the Durham Bulls Athletic Park, and historic Brightleaf Square. Morehead Manor is just moments away from Duke University, North Carolina Central University, Research Triangle Park, and RDU International Airport. In nearby Raleigh and listed on the National Register of Historic Places as the Raynor-Stronach House, The Oakwood Inn B&B (411 N. Bloodworth Street; 919–832–9712/800–267–9712;

www.oakwoodinnbb.com), built in 1871 and nestled in the beautiful Historic Oakwood neighborhood, is an antiques-decorated inn and was Durham's first B&B.

For More Information

Publications

Durham Herald-Sun
2828 Pickett Road
Durham, NC 27705
800–672–0061
www.herald-sun.com

The Front Page
P.O. Box 27928
Raleigh, NC 27611
919–829–0181
www.frontpagenews.com

Q-Notes
P.O. Box 221841
Charlotte, NC 28222
704–531–9988
www.q-notes.com

The Raleigh Hatchet
110 Glascock Street
Raleigh, NC 27604
913–332–2912
www.raleighhatchet.com

Convention and Visitors Bureau

Durham Convention and Visitors Bureau
101 East Morgan Street
Durham, NC 27701
919–687–0288/800–446–8604
www.durham-nc.com

Chamber of Commerce

Greater Durham Chamber of Commerce
300 W. Morgan Street
Durham, NC 27701
919–682–2133
www.durhamchamber.org

Realtor

Julie Parrish
REALTOR
Julie Parrish Realty
229 Forestwood Drive
Durham, NC 27707
919–489–9694
www.julieparrishrealty.com

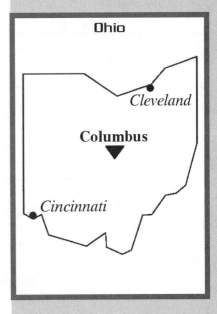

Columbus, Ohio

36

A Look at Columbus

Columbus is a city of variety. It's a patchwork of communities with distinct character and offerings. Sample the historic, the artsy, the sports-oriented, the high fashion, and the college life, all in one easy-to-manage, friendly Midwestern city. German Village (*www.germanvillage.com*) is Columbus's premiere downtown neighborhood and one of the preeminent historic districts in the United States. This charming community is a mix of the old world and the new, creating a vibrant mix. The Short North district has become the gay community's center. The neighborhood has an eclectic mix of shops, art galleries, restaurants, and bars. In between these districts is a vibrant downtown core with theaters, museums, the Cultural Arts Center, the Arena District, and Ohio State University. The city boasts one of the most stable city economies in the nation, and *Popular Science* recently ranked Columbus as one of the top 10 high-tech cities in the country. Columbus's combination of historic and modern architecture and industry, arts and culture, sports, and education create a high and desirable quality of life.

Possible drawbacks: Columbus has an up-to-date and progressive attitude, but the politics in Ohio are dramatically conservative. The Columbus GLBT community, outwardly supported by local government, is continually denied equal rights by the Buckeye State's legislature.

▶ Nickname:
Cowtown

▶ County:
Franklin

▶ Area code:
614

▶ Time zone:
Eastern

▶ Population:
711,470

▶ County population:
1,068,978

▶ Region:
Central Ohio

▶ Average home price:
$185,000

▶ Fabulous reasons to live here:
Excellent education, nightlife, culture, music, arts, affordable housing, politically supported GLBT community, strong economy

Climate

Elevation 800'	Avg. high/low (F°)	Avg. inches		Avg. # days precip.	Avg. % humidity
		rain	snow		
Jan.	36/20	2.5	8.8	13	73%
April	64/41	3.5	0.9	13	64%
July	85/64	4.4	–	11	70%
Oct.	66/43	2.5	0.1	9	68%
YEAR	63/46	39.4	27.7	135	69%
# days 32° or below: 77			# days 90° or warmer: 16		

Local Connections

Gas company: American Electric Power (614–716–1000; *www.aep.com*)

Electric companies: Department of Public Utilities Division of Electricity (614–645–7360; *www.utilities.ci.columbus.oh.us*); American Electric Power (614–716–1000; *www.aep.com*)

Phone company: SBC (800–660–1000; *www.sbc.com*)

Water and sewer: City of Columbus Department of Water (614–645–8270; sewer: 614–645–8164; *www.columbuswater.com*

Cable companies: Time Warner Cable (614–481–5320/800–934–4181; *www.timewarnercable.com*); Wide Open West (866–496–9669; *www.wowway.com*)

Car registration/License: Ohio Bureau of Motor Vehicles (614–752–7500; *www.bmv.ohio.gov*)

New residents have 30 days to obtain a license. If you hold a valid out-of-state driver's license you'll need to take both a vision and written exam. The road test is generally waived. Fee: $23 (renewal $24). Title fee: $5–15 plus notarization fee and inspection fee of $3.50. Registration and plates: $34.50–54.50.

The Tax Ax

Sales tax: 6.75% percent

State income tax: 0.743–7.5 percent graduated, by income bracket

Property tax: Franklin County Auditor (614–462–3247; *www.co.franklin.oh.us/auditor*)

The tax rates vary among Ohio's counties, as the total tax rate includes levies from all the state's taxing jurisdictions, such as county, township, municipal, corporation, and school district.

Local Real Estate

Overview: Columbus has an eclectic mix of housing styles from the old world charms of German Village, the new loft-style buildings downtown, and traditional Colonial and ranch style houses mixed with contemporary construction throughout the area. There are also large estate properties on the outskirts of greater Columbus.

Median price for a single-family home: $225,000

Average price for a single-family home: $185,000

Average price for a 2BR condo: $113,000

Rental housing market: The rental market in Columbus is cyclical because of the large influx of college students every fall. Rents are affordable. A two-bedroom apartment rents for approximately $600–750.

Gay-friendly neighborhoods: Most of the greater Columbus area is gay-friendly. A few of the popular neighborhoods include the Short North Arts district and German Village.

Nearby areas to consider: Travel a few miles outside the Greater Columbus area and you're in the country. There are several small towns dotting the countryside, and many of these offer larger, more affordable homes on bigger lots, quality schools, and low crime rates. With good amenities and easy commutes, the little towns, villages, and cities surrounding Columbus attract a large portion of the area's GLBT community. Of special note, 7 miles north of Columbus, is Worthington. Home to the American Whistle Factory, Worthington boasts highly-ranked schools, a new community center with two pools and a fitness center, an easy commute, and the vital and active Olde Worthington Business District that embraces both entrepreneurial spirit and civic pride.

Earning a Living

Per capita income: $20,450

Median household income: $37,897

Business climate: Columbus is among the more economically stable metropolitan areas in the United States and is one of just a handful of cities in the northeastern quadrant of the country whose economy and population both grew steadily through the last three decades of the 20th century. This trend is expected to continue.

Help in starting a business: The Columbus Chamber of Commerce is the local business advocate and provides networking and advertising opportunities. The Chamber's Economic Development Team is the region's contact point for research, analysis, and resources. Additionally, Stonewall Columbus Business and Professionals Council (SCBC) (*www.stonewallcolumbus.org*) works to educate on the importance of supporting community businesses and to establish a network—a GLBT "chamber of commerce"—for businesses and professionals.

Job market: About half of the jobs in the eight-county Columbus metropolitan region are concentrated between service businesses and retail. Other top employment sectors include government, manufacturing, finance, insurance and real estate, wholesale trade, transportation, utilities, and construction.

The Community

Overview: The Columbus GLBT community is among the best in the nation when it comes to size and organization. The Short North Arts District (*www.shortnorth.org*), featuring eclectic galleries, bookstores, vintage clothing shops, and bars, is the GLBT community hub in Columbus.

Community organizations: Stonewall Columbus is a human rights organization serving central Ohio through advocacy, community building, and education. Stonewall Columbus operates The Center, providing space for meetings, a lending library, and an array of support, education, and social services for the community. Additionally, Columbus has several hundred social, spiritual, support, and recreational groups and organizations. Stonewall Columbus publishes the annual *Lavender Listings*, an area directory of GLBT-owned and supportive businesses and organizations.

Medical care: More than a dozen hospitals serve the Columbus metro area. The Stonewall Columbus Hotline (614-299-7764) provides referrals to the area's gay-friendly service providers. The Columbus Health Department (614–645–7417; *www.publichealth.columbus.gov*) is the local public health agency for the City of Columbus. The department is made up of a range of programs providing clinical, environmental, health promotion, and population-based services. Among these programs is the Sexually Transmitted Diseases (STD) Clinic, which provides a range of quality services, including prevention, education, testing, diagnosis, treatment, and control of sexually transmitted diseases. In addition to the clinic, the Sexual Health Program provides community outreach, education and prevention programs, and support services for people with HIV.

Nuptials: The state of Ohio's constitution defines marriage as between a man and a woman and doesn't honor same-sex marriages from other jurisdictions. At this time there is no domestic partner registry in Columbus, but many area businesses provide domestic partner benefits.

Getting Around Town

Public transportation: Central Ohio Transit Authority (614–228–1776; *www.cota.com*) offers regular bus service throughout the city. Fares: one-way local $1.25; transfer 10 cents; unlimited ride $3; express $1.75.

Roads: I-70, I-71, I-270, I-670, US23, US62, US315

Airports: Columbus Regional Airport Authority (*www.columbusairports.com*). Eleven major carriers and many regional airline partners combine to offer 350 daily departures and arrivals at Port Columbus International Airport (airport code:

CMH) (614–239–4000), 10 minutes from downtown; Rickenbacker International Airport (airport code: LCK) (614–491–1401) is 20 minutes from downtown.

It's a Gay Life

Annual events: Stonewall Columbus (*www.stonewallcolumbus.org*) hosts the local pride celebration at the end of June; the event includes a march, festival, and rally. In September, the Ohio Lesbian Festival (*www.ohiolba.org*), in nearby Pataskala, provides a progressive, diverse, multi-cultural experience for women of all ages with art, music, and educational seminars. Other annual events include the Columbus Arts Festival (*www.gcac.org*), German Village Oktoberfest (*www.germanvillage.com*), Jazz & RibFest (*www.musicintheair.org*), Festival Latino (*www.musicintheair.org*), Red, White & Boom! (*www.nbc4i.com*), Dublin Irish Festival (*www.dublinirishfestival.com*), Ohio State Fair(*www.ohioexpocenter.com*), and First Night Columbus (*www.firstnightcols.com*). Each of these festivals offers great live entertainment, games, food, and fun. Experience Columbus (*www.experiencecolumbus.com*) has up-to-date listing information for all area events.

Nightlife: From the breweries of German Village to theaters and music halls throughout downtown, to the restaurants, discos, and bars lining High Street, there's never a dull evening in Columbus. The Reality Theater (117 High Street; 614–221–6339; *www.realitytheater.com*) presents GLBT stage plays among its offerings. Of special interest is the Arena District (*www.arena-district.com*), featuring restaurants, nightclubs, and office space, as well as the Arena Grand Theatre (175 W. Nationwide Boulevard; 614–470–9900; *www.arenagrand.com*) and the PromoWest Pavilion (405 Neil Avenue; 614–461–5483; *www.promowestlive.com*), an indoor/outdoor music hall styled after the House of Blues. Columbus boasts more than 20 gay bars and clubs, many in the Short North district along High Street. Visit the bookstores An Open Book (685 N. High Street; 614–221–6339) or The Book Loft of German Village (631 S. 3rd Street; 614-464-1774; *www.bookloft.com*) to pick up *Outlines Magazine, Outlook News, Spotlight Magazine*, and *The Stonewall Journal* for current listings and events.

Culture: Downtown Columbus features three historic theaters: the Ohio (55 E. State Street; 614–469–1045; *www.capa.com*), Palace (34 W. Broad Street; 614–469–9850; *www.capa.com*), and Southern (21 E. Main Street; 614–340–9698; *www.capa.com*), all of which host a variety of performing arts. They are homes to the Columbus Symphony Orchestra (614–228–9600; *www.columbussymphony.com*), Ballet Met (614–229–4860; *www.balletmet.org*), Broadway in Columbus (614–224–7654), and the city's many other performing arts groups. The Columbus Museum of Art (48 E. Broad Street; 614–221–6801; *www.columbusmuseum.org*) features works from an outstanding collection of impressionists, German expressionists, cubists, American modernists, and contemporary artists. The Short North Arts District (614–228–8050; *www.shortnorth.org*) contains an eclectic concentration of art galleries. Most galleries stay open late the first Saturday of each month for the popular "Gallery Hop" events. The district also has a variety of restaurants, pubs, and specialty shops. COSI Columbus (333 W. Broad Street; 614–228–COSI; *www.cosi.org*), the city's 300,000-square-foot interactive science center, features eight "Learning Worlds" where visitors can experience hands-on activities that make science understandable and fun. The Wexner Center for the Arts (1871 N. High Street; 614–292–3535; *www.wexarts.org*), a landmark of postmodern architecture, houses galleries, performance spaces, a film video theater, a bookshop, and a café. Along with honoring the memory of Dr. Martin Luther King, Jr., the King Arts Complex (867 Mt. Vernon Avenue; 614–645–5464; *www.thekingartscomplex.com*) provides a place to celebrate the influential contributions of Africa- Americans throughout history by offering performing, cultural, and educational programs. The Franklin Park Conservatory and Botanical Garden (1777 E. Broad Street; 614–645–8733; *www.fpconservatory.org*) features horticulture from a wide variety of climate zones, as well as large bonsai and orchid collections. Special exhibits include an annual living butterfly display.

Recreation: The Columbus Department of Recreation (614–645–3300; *recparks.columbus.gov*) manages more than a hundred city parks and sponsors 28 Neighborhood Recreation Centers, municipal golf course, and several pools, plus a variety of summer camp experiences and adult and seniors sports leagues, including volleyball, basketball, and softball. Wyandot Lake (10101 Riverside Drive, Powell; 614–889–9283; *www.sixflags.com*) is a Six Flags park featuring more than 45 wet and dry attractions, including nine towering, twisting slides, a wave pool and a 36,000-square-foot innovative, interactive water play area. The Columbus Zoo and Aquarium (9990 Riverside Drive; 614–645–3550; *www.colszoo.org*), located adjacent to Wyandot Lake, has received national recognition for its success in breeding cheetahs and lowland gorillas and for having the country's largest collection of reptiles. The Manatee Coast, a $10 million mangrove waterway habitat, holds 190,000 gallons of water, various fish and turtle species, and three manatees. Sixty miles east of Columbus, The Wilds (14000 International Road; 740–638–5030; *www.thewilds.org*) is a 14-mile tract of reclaimed strip-mined land where giraffes, zebras, camels, rhinos, and other exotic creatures roam free. The Jack Nicklaus Museum (2355 Olentangy River Road; 614–247–5959; *www.nicklausmuseum.org*) includes interactive exhibits and memorabilia. Highlights include a series of exhibits that chronicle Nicklaus's playing career through his performance in the sport's five major championships. For spectators there's the NHL franchise Columbus Blue Jackets (614–246–4156; *www.bluejackets.com*), the New York Yankees' AAA team, the Columbus Clippers (614–462–5250; *www.clippersbaseball.com*), Women's Professional Football's Columbus Comets (614–322–0568; *www.columbuscomets.com*), and major league soccer's Columbus Crew (614–447–CREW; *www.thecrew.com*). For race fans there's the NHRA championship drag racing at National Trail Raceway (2650 National Road S.W., Hebron; 740–928–5706; *www.nationaltrailraceway.com*), exciting live harness racing May–September at Scioto Downs, Inc. (6000 S. High Street; 614–491–2515; *www.sciotodowns.com*), and the horse-racing and entertainment facility Beulah Park (3664 Grant Avenue, Grove City; 614–871–9600; *www.beulahpark.com*).

For the Visitor

Accommodations: Columbus style is being able to choose from more than 20,000 hotel and motel rooms, plus bed & breakfasts, resorts, and campgrounds; it's the depth and breadth of selection in and around the city. So it's easy to find the right accommodations for you—in terms of convenience, cost, and comfort—no matter how you plan to experience Columbus. These are a few of the gay-owned and gay-friendly favorites. 50 Lincoln Inn (50 E. Lincoln Street; 888–299–5051; *www.50lincoln.com*) is ideally situated in the heart of the fabulous Short North. From the Inn, guests may stroll to the finest restaurants, art galleries, shops, pubs, and parks in Columbus. A landmark German Village bed and breakfast, Brewmaster's House (1083 S. High Street; 614–449–8298; *www.damron.com/homepages/BrewmastersHouse*), is a grand 1909 house within walking distance to German Village bars and attractions. Westin Great Southern Hotel (310 S. High Street; 614–220–7043; *www.greatsouthernhotel.com*), the city's most-renowned hotel, is ideally situated in the heart of the downtown business district and offers guests the utmost in gracious service and luxurious surroundings.

For More Information

Gay & Lesbian Center
Stonewall Columbus
1160 N. High Street
P.O. Box 10814
Columbus, OH 43201-2411
614–299–7764
www.stonewallcolumbus.org

Publications
The Columbus Dispatch
34 S. Third Street
Columbus, OH 43215
614–461–5000
www.dispatch.com

The Daily Reporter
580 S. High Street
Columbus, OH 43215
614–228–6397
www.sourcenews.com

Outlook News
406 E. Wilson Bridge Road
Columbus, OH 43085
614–268–8525/866–452–6397
www.outlooknews.com

Convention and Visitors Bureau
Experience Columbus
90 N. High Street
Columbus, OH 43215
614–221–6623/800–354–2657
www.experiencecolumbus.com

Chamber of Commerce
Columbus Chamber of Commerce
37 N. High Street
Columbus, OH 43215
614–221–1321
www.columbus-chamber.org

Realtor
Keller Williams Capital Partners
500 W. Wilson Bridge Road,
Suite 260
Worthington, OH 43085
614–832–2121
www.kw.com

Lakewood, Ohio

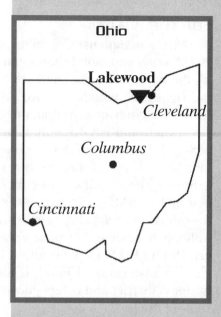

A Look at Lakewood

Widely known as a "City of Homes," Lakewood offers both the amenities of city living and the charm of a small town. Located along Lake Erie's shore, just west of Cleveland, Lakewood is an older, inner-ring suburb. As a mature community with high-density development, it has not contributed to the broader, regional problems attributed to urban sprawl. Tree-lined streets and solidly built one- and two-family homes, many with comfortable front porches, are Lakewood's charm. The construction of a municipal light plant in 1896 and a streetcar line in 1903 facilitated the village's growth. In 1917 the Detroit-Superior Bridge opened connecting Lakewood and Cleveland, causing a real-estate boom that brought the city close to its current population. The Cleveland metro area boasts leading cultural and educational centers, internationally acclaimed health institutions, and world-class sports and entertainment facilities combined with the community's rich traditions and unique, ethnic flavor. Lakewood remains a stable, welcoming community with a rich past, a vibrant present, and a promising future.

Possible drawbacks: The weather. You've got to love the change of seasons to make northeastern Ohio your home. Lake Erie creates hot, humid summers and cold, snowy winters. Lake effect snows can dump 2 to 4 feet of the white stuff in a 24-hour period. On average, there are only 70 clear, sunny days a year.

▶ Nickname:
City of Homes

▶ County:
Cuyahoga

▶ Area codes:
216; 440

▶ Time zone:
Eastern

▶ Population:
56,646

▶ County population:
1,393,978

▶ Region:
Northeast Ohio

▶ Closest metro area:
Cleveland, Ohio

▶ Average home price:
$150,000

▶ Fabulous reasons to live here:
Culture; music; arts; recreation; lake views; affordable housing; large GLBT community; strong, evolving economy

Climate

Elevation 710'	Avg. high/low(F°)	Avg. inches		Avg. # days precip.	Avg. % humidity
		rain	snow		
Jan.	33/19	2.5	13.5	16	74%
April	58/39	3.4	2.4	15	67%
July	82/62	3.5	–	10	69%
Oct.	61/44	2.7	0.6	11	70%
YEAR	58/41	38.6	56.9	155	71%
# days 32° or below: 85			# days 90° or warmer: 9		

Local Connections

Gas company: Dominion East Ohio (800–362–7557; *www.dom.com*)

Electric company: Cleveland Public Power (216–664–4600; *www.cpp.org*)

Phone companies: Qwest (216–623–0924; *www.qwest.com*); SBC (440–942–9979; *www.sbc.com*)

Water and sewer: Division of Water and Wastewater Collection (City of Lakewood) (216–529–6820; *www.ci.lakewood.oh.us/pw_water.html*)

Cable company: Cox Communications (216–676–8100; *www.cox.com*)

Car registration/License: Ohio Bureau of Motor Vehicles (614–752–7500; *www.bmv.ohio.gov*)

New residents have 30 days to obtain a license. If you hold a valid out-of-state driver's license you'll need to take both a vision and written exam. The road test is generally waived. Fee: $23 (renewal $24). Title fee: $5–15 plus notarization fee and inspection fee of $3.50. Registration and plates: $34.50–54.50.

The Tax Ax

Sales tax: 7 percent

City tax: The city has both an employment tax and a residence tax, ranging from 1 to 1.5 percent. All residents with earned income are required to file a Municipal Income Tax Return with the Regional Income tax Agency (440–526–0900; *www.ritaohio.com*).

State income tax: 0.743–7.5 percent, graduated by income bracket

Property tax: Cuyahoga County Auditor (216–443–7010; *auditor.cuyahogacounty.us*)

Real estate taxes, commonly referred to as "property taxes," are collected by the county treasurer twice a year, based on the assessment of value made by the county auditor. Tax rates vary because the total includes levies from all the state's taxing jurisdictions, such as county, township, municipal, corporation, and school district.

Local Real Estate

Overview: Lakewood is a city loaded with charm. Most of the homes are Colonials built in the first half of the 20th century. There are homes available ranging from $100,000 to $1,000,000 (along the lakefront). Lakewood is a very desirable city, being easily accessible to the downtown area as well as shopping and restaurants, Lakewood is a widely diverse community and has a very large gay population.

Median price for a single-family home: $160,000

Average price for a single-family home: $150,000

Average price for a 2BR condo: $100,000

Rental housing market: There are several doubles and duplexes in Lakewood, making it a prime area for rentals.

Gay-friendly neighborhoods: All of Lakewood is gay-friendly, as are the bordering communities of Tremont, Cleveland Heights, and Ohio City.

Nearby areas to consider: The western Cleveland suburbs of Euclid, Willowick, Eastlake, and Wickliffe are also considered home by the area's GLBT community. These little suburbs of largely two- to three-bedroom tract housing were created during the steel boom years of the 1960s–70s. They offer an easy commute into downtown, good schools, and affordable housing on many tree-lined streets. Urban pioneers will find east Cleveland's Collinwood area of interest. The blocks from East 156th Street to East 180th Street that straddle Grovewood Avenue are filled with turn-of-the-20th century, double, brick homes featuring classic hardwood floors and woodwork. The local businesses have seen better days, and the area is ripe for GLBT community conversion.

Earning a Living

Per capita income: $23,945

Median household income: $40,527

Business climate: With more than 1,000 small businesses, the entrepreneurial spirit is welcomed in Lakewood. No longer dominated by heavy manufacturing, Cleveland's stable and balanced economy has entered a new era. More than a dozen Fortune 500 companies and 150 international companies call Cleveland home.

Help in starting a business: An independent nonpartisan citizens group, Lakewood Alive! (216–226–8418; *www.lakewoodalive.com*) is devoted to promoting economic development in Lakewood and enhancing how Lakewood is perceived inside and outside its borders. Members of the Greater Cleveland Partnership's (*www.clevelandgrowth.com*) nationally recognized small business division, the Council of Smaller Enterprises (COSE), benefit from business counseling, mentoring, resources, training and education programs, and networking opportunities, as well as the power of group purchasing for vital business services.

Job market: Top job sectors include educational, health, and social services; professional, scientific, management, administrative, and waste management services; manufacturing; and retail trade, arts, entertainment, recreation, accommodation, and food services.

The Community

Overview: In Lakewood and the surrounding Cleveland metro region, people are nice and easy to talk to. There's no pretension, and everyone is welcome. The large GLBT community here is a community, where neighbors are open, friendly, and helpful. Strangely, in this supportive environment, local and state politics are conservative when it comes to GLBT community issues.

Community organizations: Founded in 1975, the Cleveland Lesbian and Gay Community Service Center is a community-based, non-profit agency working toward a society free of homophobia and gender oppression by advancing the respect, human rights, and dignity of the lesbian, gay, bisexual, and transgender communities. In addition to providing education, culture, and wellness programs, the Center's reference/help desk (216–651–LGBT/888–GAY–8761) pairs GLBT community members with GLBT-affirming doctors, lawyers, therapists, support groups, and more. Many local groups and organizations use the Center space for meetings and events.

Medical care: Founded in 1907, Lakewood Hospital (216–521–4200; *www.lakewoodhospital.org*) is a 400-bed, acute-care, community-oriented hospital located in the city of Lakewood on Cleveland's west side. Lakewood Hospital, which is part of the Cleveland Clinic Health System (CCHS) (*www.cchs.net*), continues to be a leader in northeastern Ohio's healthcare community and each year provides high-quality and innovative patient care for more than 130,000 patients. Not only is Lakewood Hospital a vital community resource for treating illnesses and injuries, but it also helps keep individuals healthy through educational wellness programs, public health screenings, and other community outreach programs. The hospital's affiliation with the Cleveland Clinic Foundation and other hospitals that are a part of the CCHS offers individuals access to state-of- the-art-technology and care throughout all of Cuyahoga County.

Nuptials: The state of Ohio's constitution defines marriage as between a man and a woman and doesn't honor same-sex marriages from other jurisdictions. At this time there is no domestic partner registry in Lakewood, but many area businesses provide domestic partner benefits.

Getting Around Town

Public transportation: Regional Transit Authority (RTA) (216–621–9500; *www.gcrta.org*) offers both bus and light-rail service. Fares currently range from 50 cents for loop buses to $1.50 for a rapid transit trip from downtown to the airport.

Roads: I-90, I-71, I-77, I-271, I-480, I-490, US2

Airport: Cleveland-Hopkins International Airport (airport code: CLE)(216–265–6090; *www.clevelandairport.com*) serves 16 counties in the Greater Cleveland Area and accommodates more than 10 million passengers annually.

It's a Gay Life

Annual events: The Cleveland Gay Pride Festival (*www.clevelandpride.org*) is celebrated in mid-June with performances, a parade, and a street fair. Lakewood Arts Festival (*www.lkwdpl.org/city/artsfest*) is a free August event featuring a juried exhibition of all media in fine arts and crafts, artists from all over the country, and live music and activities. During Labor Day weekend, the Cleveland National Air Show (Burke Lakefront Airport; 1501 N. Marginal Road; 216–781–0747; *www.clevelandairshow.com*) draws large crowds.

Nightlife: A bustling, riverfront entertainment district like no other, the Flats is located along the banks of the Cuyahoga River, housing more than 50 restaurants, nightclubs, and bars; a 5,000-seat amphitheater; and a waterfront boardwalk. The upscale Historic Warehouse District (614 Superior Avenue; 216–344–3937; *www.warehousedistrict.org*) is home to live jazz and Blues, great restaurants, trendy nightclubs, and an improvisational theater. The Historic Gateway Neighborhood (216–771–1994; *www.historicgateway.org*) is a diverse area comprised of neighborhood, commercial, retail, restaurants, bars, and live entertainment. The city is home to more than 20 gay bars, restaurants, and cafes. For current listings and events, pick up a copy of Ohio's largest club magazine, *OUTlines* (*www.outlinesmagazine.com*), at Bookstore (1921 W. 25th Street; 216–566–8897).

Culture: Culture enthusiasts and afficionados enjoy stellar performances at Cleveland's Playhouse Square Center (216–771–4444; *www.playhousesquare.com*), which includes five beautifully restored, circa 1920s State (1519 Euclid Avenue), Palace (1615 Euclid Avenue), Ohio (1511 Euclid Avenue), Allen (1407 Euclid Avenue), and Hanna (207 E. 14th Street) theaters, making Playhouse Square Center the nation's largest performing arts center outside of New York City. These architectural theater gems are home to the Cleveland Opera (216–575–0903; *www.clevelandopera.org*), Ohio Ballet (216–861–5545; *www.ohioballet.org*), Great Lakes Theater Festival (216–241–6590 *www.greatlakestheater.org*), and many Broadway performances. Cleveland is also home to the world's only Rock and Roll Hall of Fame and Museum (One Key Plaza; 751 Erieside Avenue; 216–781–ROCK; *www.rockhall.com*); the Great Lakes Science Center (601 Erieside Avenue; 216–694–2000; *www.greatscience.com*), with 340 interactive exhibits and a six-story Omnimax theater; and the Cleveland Metroparks Zoo and RainForest (3900 Wildlife Way; 216–661–6500; *www.clemetzoo.com*). University Circle, the nation's largest concentration of cultural arts, medical, and educational institutions within 1 square mile, is home to many world-class treasures, including the renowned Cleveland Museum of Art (11150 E. Boulevard; 216–421–7350; *www.clevelandart.org*) and the Cleveland Orchestra (216–231–7300;

www.clevelandorch.com), the world's most recorded orchestra, whose grand winter home, Severance Hall (11001 Euclid Avenue; 216–231–1111; *www.clevelandorch.com*), recently underwent a massive renovation. There's also HealthSpace Cleveland (8911 Euclid Avenue; 216–231–5010; *www.healthmuseum.org*), the Cleveland Children's Museum (10730 Euclid Avenue; 216–791–7114; *www.clevelandchildrensmuseum.org*), the Western Reserve Historical Society (10825 E. Boulevard; 216–721–5722; *www.wrhs.org*), the nation's largest privately funded historical society, the Crawford Auto and Aviation Museum, the Cleveland Museum of Natural History (1 Wade Oval Drive; 216–231–4600; *www.cmnh.org*), the Cleveland Botanical Garden (11030 E. Boulevard; 216–721–1600; *www.cbgarden.org*), and the Cleveland Play House (8500 Euclid Avenue; 216–795–7000; *www.clevelandplayhouse.com*), to name a few.

Recreation: With the 31-acre, lakefront Lakewood Park as its crown jewel, the Lakewood Parks system (303–987–7000; *www.ci.lakewood.oh.u*) consists of 15 dedicated parks and approximately 75 acres of green space. A Lakewood landmark, Winterhurst Ice Rink (14740 Lakewood Hts. Boulevard; 216–529–4400; *www.ci.lakewood.oh.u*) is northeast Ohio's premier ice-skating facility, offering a wide variety of ice sports and leisure activities from figure skating to hockey, broomball to short-track speed skating. Greater Cleveland offers thrilling sports action and outdoor recreation for year-round activities and excitement. The 14 Cleveland Metroparks Reservations (216–635–3200) and the Cuyahoga Valley National Park (15610 Vaughn Road, Brecksville; 216–524–1497; *www.nps.gov/cuva*) offer a combined 52,000 acres for rest and relaxation. There are also more than 275 miles of bike-riding trails in Northeast Ohio. During winter, try tobogganing, sledding, and cross country and downhill skiing. No matter what the season, you can experience thrills and adventure throughout Greater Cleveland. Swing the clubs at one of 300 golf courses throughout northeast Ohio. Enjoy Lake Erie, one of the five Great Lakes, with sport fishing (Lake Erie has some of the best walleye, perch, and bass fishing in the world), swimming, boating, parasailing, jet skiing, scuba diving, and canoeing. Fly fisherman can cast for steelhead trout, salmon, and bass in the Chagrin, Rocky, and Cuyahoga rivers. Cheer on the NFL's Cleveland Browns (440–891–5050; *www.clevelandbrowns.com*), MLB's Cleveland Indians (216–420–4636; *www.indians.com*), the NBA's Cleveland Cavaliers (216–420–2000; *www.nba.com/cavs*), the AHL's Cleveland Barons (216–420–0000; *www.clevelandbarons.net*), and the MISL's Cleveland Force (216–896–1140; *www.clevelandforce.com*).

For the Visitor

Accommodations: There are 22,000 hotel rooms in the Greater Cleveland area, including elegant, luxury hotels, nationally recognized mid-range to economy chains, independent hotels and motels, and quaint bed and breakfasts and inns. A few of the area's gay-friendly options include Edgewater Estates (9803 Edgewater Drive; 216–961–1764; *www.edgewaterestatesbedandbreakfast.com*), a spacious 1900s English Tudor with views of Lake Erie and Stone Gables B&B

(3806 Franklin Boulevard; 216–961–4654/877–215–4326; *www.stonegables.net*), within walking distance to the West Side Market and featuring original artwork from artists such as M. Chagall, Picasso, Durer, Rockwell Kent, and many other masters. Radisson Hotel-Cleveland Gateway (651 Huron Road; 216–377–9000/ 800–333–3333; *www.radisson.com/clevelandoh_gateway*) is located in the heart of the business and entertainment district, directly across from Gund Arena and Jacobs Field and within walking distance to many theaters and attractions.

For More Information

Gay & Lesbian Center

Cleveland Lesbian and Gay
Community Service Center (LGCSC)
1418 W. 29th Street
Cleveland, OH 44113-2905
216–781–6736
www.lgcsc.org

Publications

Lakewood Sun Post
28895 Lorain Road
North Olmsted, OH 44070-4042
440–777–3800/216–986–6070
www.sunnews.com

The Plain Dealer
1801 Superior Avenue
Cleveland, OH 44114
216–999–4870
www.plaindealer.com

Gay People's Chronicle
P.O. Box 5426
Cleveland, OH 44101
216–631–8646/800–426–5947
www.gaypeopleschronicle.com

Convention and Visitors Bureau

Convention & Visitors Bureau of
Greater Cleveland
50 Public Square
3100 Terminal Tower
Cleveland, OH 44113-2290
216–621–4110/800–321–1001
www.travelcleveland.com

Chamber of Commerce

Lakewood Chamber of Commerce
14701 Detroit Avenue, Suite 130
Lakewood, OH 44107
216–226–2900
www.lakewoodchamber.org

Realtor

John Oskowski
Realtor
Realty One
28364 Lorain Road
North Olmsted, OH 44070
440–785–4999
www.john-o.com

Portland, Oregon

A Look at Portland

Portland is known for its green spaces and proximity to natural wonders such as the Columbia River Gorge and Mount Hood. The city is also known as an incubator for progressive urban planning, environmentally conscious public policy, and the sustainable development movement. Portland's Metropolitan Area Express light-rail system, new streetcar line, pedestrian-friendly downtown, half-size city blocks, and cycling-centric commuters are as much a part of the city's identity as the roses and bridges. Portland is a city of bridges. The world's only telescoping double-deck vertical lift bridge (Steel), the world's oldest lift bridge (Hawthorne), and America's longest tied-arch bridge (Fremont) are all in Portland. Fountains dance, sidewalks talk, and weathervanes trumpet. Public art plays an important role in Portland's urban landscape. Funding much of this art abundance are city and county ordinances requiring that 1 percent of major capital construction budgets be set aside for public art. Works commissioned through this program, known as "Percent for Public Art," include Portlandia, a 36-foot hammered copper sculpture set above the entrance to the Portland Building, and the "talking sidewalk," a block of city sidewalk inscribed with famous quotes and colloquialisms.

Possible drawbacks: High humidity, lots of rain, and cool temperatures keep Portland feeling damp throughout the year; of course, this also keeps the area lush and green.

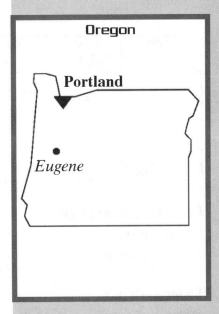

▶ Nickname:
City of Roses

▶ County:
Multnomah

▶ Area code:
503

▶ Time zone:
Pacific

▶ Population:
529,121

▶ County population:
660,486

▶ Region:
Northwest

▶ Average home price:
$255,000

▶ Fabulous reasons to live here:
Progressive environmentally and politically; scenic beauty; recreation; culture; arts; affordable housing; large, active GLBT community

Climate

Elevation 50'	Avg. high/low(F°)	Avg. inches		Avg. # days precip.	Avg. % humidity
		rain	snow		
Jan.	46/36	5.9	3.2	18	80%
April	61/43	3	–	15	70%
July	78/57	0.8	–	4	63%
Oct.	63/47	3.3	–	12	76%
YEAR	62/46	41.7	6.5	152	72%
# days 32° or below: 26			# days 90° or warmer: 11		

Local Connections

Gas company: NW Natural (800–422–4012; *www.nwnatural.com*)

Electric company: Portland General Electric (503–228–6322/ 800–542–8818; *www.portlandgeneral.com*)

Phone company: Qwest (800–491–0118; *www.qwest.com*)

Water and sewer: City of Portland (503–823–7770; *www.portlandonline.com/water*)

Cable company: Comcast (503–295–0123; *www.comcast.com*)

Car registration/License: Oregon Department of Transportation (888–275–6368; *www.oregon.gov/ODOT*)

Surrender any valid driver license or permit issued by another state to avoid written and driving tests. Fee: $54.50. Licenses are good for eight years. Regular Title Fee: $55. Vehicle Registration Fee: $54. Plate Fee: $3 for one plate; $5 for two plates.

The Tax Ax

Sales tax: No sales tax

State income tax: 5–9 percent of adjusted gross income

Property tax: Oregon Department of Revenue (503–378–4988; *egov.oregon.gov/DOR*)

All privately owned real property and personal property used in a business are taxed. The current rate is $73 per $1,000 of value.

Local Real Estate

Overview: As in most areas of the country, Portland home prices have appreciated in recent years, but new home construction is on the rise to meet the area's growing housing demands. This is helping to keep the prices low. Housing styles include palatial estates, traditional Colonial and ranch styles, and a selection of Victorian and even historic properties. Condominium construction and conversion are also increasing.

Median price for a single-family home: $183,000

Average price for a single-family home: $255,000

Average price for a 2BR condo: $225,000

Rental housing market: The rental market includes homes and apartment buildings. The average two-bedroom apartment rents for $500–950 in the Portland area.

Gay-friendly neighborhoods: Southeast Hawthorne, Belmont, Sellwood, Northeast Broadway, Nob Hill/Northwest (Northwest 21st and 23rd avenues), Southwest Stark Street/Burnside Triangle, Pearl District

Nearby areas to consider: Located in the evergreen forests and rolling hills of Willamette Valley wine country, Forest Grove is a beautiful, small town to consider. This city of just less than 20,000 residents and home to Pacific University boasts affordable housing, low crime rates, and high-tech jobs. Located near the base of Mt. Hood, Sandy, a city of just 5,000 residents, combines a mild climate, clean air, good water, and beautiful scenic views in a country setting with an easy commute and progressive government. Volcanoes aside, on the Columbia River at the Washington/Idaho border is beautiful Mt. St. Helens. Fabulous recreation and mountain-filled scenic views are the daily order. Downtown, a 10-block Nationally Registered Historic District includes residences and civic buildings dating back nearly a century

Earning a Living

Per capita income: $22,643

Median household income: $40,146

Business climate: At the time of writing, unemployment is high, but Portland is seen as a city geared to young, extremely bright, and creative people. In recent years, the local economy has made a transition to high technology, and the city's potential for economic growth is extremely good.

Help in starting a business: The Portland Business Alliance is Greater Portland's Chamber of Commerce, providing strong leadership, advocacy and education, partnership, and programs that encourage business growth and vitality. The Portland Area Businesses Association, Portland's GLBT chamber of commerce, provides its members a variety of services, including hosting after-hours receptions, sponsoring special networking events, publishing the quarterly newsletter, *The PABA Advantage*, and offering the chance to participate in various community activities.

Job market: Portland's largest employer is Intel. More than half of the city's employment comes from the following sectors: educational, health, and social services; manufacturing, professional, scientific, management, administrative, and waste management services; and retail trade.

The Community

Overview: Portland offers domestic partner registration and government non-discrimination policies at the local and state levels, and a vast majority of private businesses in the city offer domestic partner benefits. This inclusive environment has welcomed a large, progressive GLBT community.

Community organizations: Portland is a socially conscious and recreationally inviting area. The city is home to a long list of community groups and organizations ranging from HIV/AIDS support and service organizations to choirs and hiking groups. The city lacks a central hub of a community center, but the city is not lacking in social services or community events. The Portland Area Business Association (*www.paba.com*), Portland's GLBT Chamber of Commerce, maintains an extensive list of the city's many community social, support, and health organizations and hundreds of gay and gay-friendly businesses. PABA has an online contact list and publishes the area's Gay Yellow Pages.

Medical care: There are eight hospitals servicing the greater Portland area. Founded in 1983, Cascade AIDS Project (CAP) (503–223–AIDS/800–777–AIDS; *www.cascadeaids.org*) is the oldest and largest community-based provider of HIV/AIDS services, housing, education, and advocacy in Oregon and southwest Washington. With a staff of almost 50, CAP operates 10 programs from its main service site and receives support from more than 600 volunteers. Among CAP's programs is the HIV/AIDS hotline, connecting people with resources including healthcare referrals.

Nuptials: Multnomah County was the first county to legally issue marriage licenses to gay couples, although in 2004 the state's constitution was amended and those marriages were voided. According to the 2000 U.S. census, one out of every seven unmarried couples in Multnomah County is a same-sex couple.

Getting Around Town

Public transportation: Tri-Met (503–238–7433; *www.trimet.org*) provides bus, light-rail, and streetcar service. All public transportation is free within the downtown core area. Fares outside the core are zone-based: $1.35 for one and two zones; $1.65 for all three zones; all-day ticket $3.50.

Roads: I-5, I-84, I-205, I-405, US10, US14, US 26, US30, US213

Airport: Portland International Airport (airport code: PDX) (503–460–4234/877–739–4636; *www.portlandairportpdx.com*) has earned awards for demonstrating that large-scale airports can be both functional and aesthetically pleasing.

It's a Gay Life

Annual events: Pride Northwest (*www.pridenw.org*) hosts the two-day Portland Pride Festival in June with local and national speakers, entertainers, and a parade. Also in June, Peacock in the Park (*www.peacockinthepark.com*) is an annual fundraising picnic where Portland's most glamorous drag queens strut their stuff. The Portland Lesbian and Gay Film Festival (*www.sensoryperceptions.org*) screens some 100 films during its nine-day October run. The Imperial Sovereign Rose Court's Coronation Ball (*www.rosecourt.org*) is an October drag extravaganza and fundraiser for the local GLBT organizations. The Portland Oregon Visitors Association (877–678–5263; *www.travelportland.com*) has details on the area's other exciting annual events, including the Portland Rose Festival (*www.rosefestival.org*), Oregon Brewers Festival (*www.oregonbrewfest.com*), Mount Hood Jazz Festival (*www.mthoodjazz.com*), and Waterfront Blues Festival (*www.waterfrontbluesfest.com*).

Nightlife: When it comes to beverages, Portlanders don't mind if they're served hot or cold; they simply want them to be the best. That's why you can't walk more than a few blocks in any direction without bumping into a specialty coffee shop or a local brewpub, where craft brewers are busily creating some of the country's most distinctive beers. Portland is home to more microbreweries and brewpubs than any other city in the world. Often referred to as the "epicenter of America's craft brewing movement," some 28 microbreweries thrive in Portland. Add in all the pubs offering local microbrews on tap and the number of outlets climbs to 46. The city is home to more than 20 bars, restaurants, and cafés catering to the GLBT community with the largest concentrations in the Pearl District and between China Town and Old Town. Finding a copy of *Just Out* (*www.justout.com*), Portland's source for GLBT news, politics, and entertainment, is no problem in this city, with more bookstores per capita than any city in the nation. Most famous is Powell's Books (1005 W. Burnside Street; 503–228–0540; *www.powells.com*), but community favorites also include Gai-Pied (2544 N.E. Broadway; 503–331–1125) and In Other Words (3734 S.E. Hawthorne Boulevard; 503–232–6003; *www.inotherwords.org*).

Culture: Portland offers a selection of urbane cultural offerings one would expect to find in a city twice its size: an established regional theater, Portland Center Stage (1111 SW Broadway; 503–248–6309; *www.pcs.org*); a resident symphony, Oregon Symphony (503–228–1353; *www.orsymphony.org*), an opera company, Portland Opera (503–241–1802; *www.portlandopera.org*); touring Broadway shows; and a vibrant collection of smaller organizations. Fortunately, Portland also delights anyone willing to scratch below the surface by revealing an impressive range of progressive, smaller-scale programming. With its ever-expanding list of galleries, public artworks, and venues, Portland's visual arts scene is definitely a work in progress. It's this continuous infusion of fresh talent, artistic style, and creative energy that has landed Portland on *AmericanStyle* magazine's list of the country's "Top 25 Arts Destinations" for six years running. One of the best times to explore Portland's galleries is on the first Thursday of every month, during the aptly named First Thursday Gallery Walk (*www.firstthursday.org*). On these nights, the streets are abuzz with performers, sidewalk artists, and enthusiastic crowds, when galleries and shops in Portland's Old Town, Pearl District, and downtown neighborhoods stay open late. Other attractions of note include Oregon Zoo – Portland (4001 SW Canyon Road; 503–226–1561; *www.oregonzoo.org),* Oregon

History Center (1200 SW Park Avenue; 503–222–1741; *www.ohs.org*), World Forestry Center (4033 SW Canyon Road; 503–228–1367; *www.worldforestry.org*), Oregon Maritime Center & Museum (115 SW Ash Street; 503–224–7724; *www.oregonmaritimemuseum.org*), Oregon Museum of Science and Industry (1945 SE Water Avenue; 503–797–6674; *www.omsi.edu*), and Portland Art Museum (1219 SW Park Avenue; 503–226–2811; *www.portlandartmuseum.org*).

Recreation: Portland is home to both the nation's largest urban wilderness—the 5,000-acre Forest Park—and the world's smallest dedicated park: Mill Ends Park (24 inches in size). The Portland metro area boasts 37,000 acres of parkland with 278 public parks, 150 miles of trails, and 246 miles of developed bikeways (*www.portlandparks.org*). Portland's GLBT community is active; a few of the area organizations include the Adventure Group (*www.adventuregroup.org*), with hiking, skiing, camping, and house-boating activities; Rose City Softball Association (503–552–4769; *www.portlandgaysoftball.com*), an adult softball league; Portland Gay and Lesbian Community Bowling Association (PCBA) (503–649–1310; *www.pdxbowl.com*), the oldest organized gay sporting group in Portland; and Portland Frontrunners (*www.portlandfrontrunners.org*), which has weekly runs open to runners of all experience levels. For spectators, there's the NBA's Portland Trail Blazers (503–234–9291; *www.nba.com/blazers*), AAA baseball affiliate of the San Diego Padres Portland Beavers (503–553–5400; *www.pgepark.com/beavers*), the Western Hockey League's Portland Winter Hawks (503–236–4295; *www.winterhawks.com*), and Portland Timbers (503–553–5400; *www.pgepark.com/timbers*), an expansion franchise of the United Soccer Leagues' A-League (*www.pgepark.com/timbers*). Home of the famous "Festival Curves," Portland International Raceway (West Delta Park; 1940 North Victory Boulevard; 503–823–RACE; *www.portlandraceway.com*) has more than 500 events each year, including the Champ Car World Series event during the Portland Rose Festival in June.

For the Visitor

Accommodations: A few of the gay-friendly options in this popular travel destination include Benson Hotel (309 S.W. Broadway; 503–523–6766; *www.bensonhotel.com*), listed on the National Register of Historic Places and a Portland landmark, a stately hotel that retains the opulence for which it is world-famous; Heathman Hotel (1001 S.W. Broadway; 503–241–4100; *www.heathmanhotel.com*), located in the heart of downtown Portland and where many of the 150 luxuriously appointed rooms and suites include original artwork by noted Pacific Northwest artists; and the Paramount Hotel (808 S.W. Taylor Street; 503–223–9900; *www.portlandparamount.com*), a one-of-a-kind boutique hotel offering traditional elegance in the perfect downtown Portland city-center location. Just outside of Portland, at Forest Springs B&B (3680 S.W. Towle Avenue, Gresham; 877–674–9282; *www.forestspring.com*), nestled at the base of more than 1,000 acres of forested open space, there is almost always something in bloom in this restored, 1907 English cottage-style home's terraced gardens.

For More Information

Publications

Just Out
P.O. Box 14400
Portland, OR 97293
503–236–1252
www.justout.com

The Oregonian
1320 S.W. Broadway
Portland, OR 97201
503–221–8100
www.oregonian.com

Convention and Visitors Bureau

Portland Oregon's Visitor Authority
1000 S.W. Broadway, Suite 2300
Portland, OR 97205
503–275–9750/800–962–3700
www.travelportland.com

Chambers of Commerce

Portland Business Alliance
520 S.W. Yamhill Street, Suite 1000
Portland, OR 97204
503–224–8684
www.portlandalliance.com

Portland Area Business Association
(PABA)
P.O. Box 6344
Portland, OR 97228
503–241–2222
www.paba.com

Realtor

RE/MAX Equity Group, Inc.
7886 S.E. 13th Avenue
Portland, OR 97202
888–958–6789
www.equitygroup.com

Harrisburg, Pennsylvania

39

A Look at Harrisburg

Once a modest ferry outpost, Harrisburg is now the largest city on the main course of the Susquehanna River. The rolling Blue Ridge Mountains are the backdrop to a magnificent skyline. This capital city is the hub of a metropolitan region that includes Gettysburg, Hershey, and Lancaster, Pennsylvania. Harrisburg's setting and physical appearance are stunning, blending the best of Pennsylvania history, natural parkland beauty, and urban design. The city's geographic location with river, mountains, and expansive hills creates countless recreation opportunities from hiking and biking to swimming and sailing. Recent years have seen a financial renaissance in Harrisburg's picturesque setting. Economic investment and a well-honed vision for the city's future have combined to form a growing high-tech business base. The infrastructure investment in Harrisburg has resulted in a creative and progressive political landscape. The city is also nurturing its burgeoning arts community with visual and performance arts taking center stage throughout the new downtown landscape of galleries, restaurants, museums, and night spots.

Possible drawbacks: Harrisburg is becoming more politically progressive as shown by the area's new hate-crime legislation and recent political campaigns by openly gay community members. But the city remains without discrimination protection laws for the GLBT community.

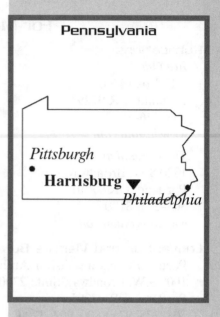

- Nickname:
  Heart of PA
- County:
  Dauphin
- Area code: 717
- Time zone: Eastern
- Population:
  48,950
- County population:
  251,798
- Region:
  Southeast Pennsylvania
- Closest metro area:
  Philadelphia
- Average home price:
  $150,000
- Fabulous reasons to live here:
  Scenic beauty, history, recreation, culture, arts, affordable housing, active GLBT community, strong economy

Climate

Elevation 310'	Avg. high/low	Avg. inches		Avg. # days precip.	Avg. % humidity
		rain	snow		
Jan.	37/19	3.3	9.7	10	65%
April	63/38	3.3	0.5	13	59%
July	84/62	3.6	–	10	65%
Oct.	64/41	3.1	–	9	68%
YEAR	62/40	41.2	34.3	126	65%
# days 32° or below: 72			# days 90° or warmer: 23		

Local Connections

Gas, electric, and phone companies: Pennsylvania takes deregulation of utilities seriously, and Harrisburg residents have choices for natural gas, electric, phone, and water suppliers. For the most up-to-date lists of resources, contact the Pennsylvania Public Utilities Commission (717–783–1740; *www.puc.state.pa.us*).

Water and sewer: Harrisburg Department of Public Works (717–236–4802; *www.harrisburgpa.gov*)

Cable company: Comcast (800–266–2278; *www.comcast.com*)

Car registration/License: Pennsylvania Department of Motor Vehicles (717–391–6190; *www.dmv.state.pa.us*)

All new residents with out-of-state non-commercial driver's licenses must obtain a Pennsylvania driver's license within 60 days of establishing Pennsylvania residency. You will be required to surrender your out-of-state driver's license (valid or expired six months or less) and take a vision-screening test. Initial permit and four-year license fee: $31 (age 65+ two-year license: $20.50). Original Title Issuance: $22.50. Passenger vehicle registration: $36.

The Tax Ax

Sales tax: 6 percent; exemptions: food (not ready-to-eat), most wearing apparel, drugs, textbooks, sales for resale, and residential heating fuels

State income tax: 3.07 percent, flat tax

Property tax: Pennsylvania does not levy or collect taxes on real estate or personal property. Those taxes are reserved for the local governments: counties, municipalities, and school districts. Usually, all three districts levy real estate or property taxes, so you will need to know what county, school district, and municipality you live in.

Local Real Estate

Overview: Downtown Harrisburg offers many housing styles, including row houses, single-family homes, condominiums, and apartment buildings. Many of the downtown homes in Harrisburg are historic.

Median price for a single-family home: $150,000

Average price for a single-family home: $150,000

Average price for a 2BR condo: 110,000

Rental housing market: The Harrisburg rental market is affordable, with the average two-bedroom rent around $500–600.

Gay-friendly neighborhoods: Most neighborhoods in Harrisburg are gay-friendly.

Nearby areas to consider: The boroughs surrounding Harrisburg are attracting the GLBT community because of their historic charm, easy commutes, rural settings, and extremely affordable housing. At about 10,000 residents, the borough of Mechanicsburg provides the small-town American experience. Downtown Mechanicsburg is currently going through redevelopment, and entrepreneurs and start-up businesses are the wave of the future. The country setting, affordable housing, low crime rates, and good schools are attracting the GLBT community. Carlisle, a borough evolving with the times, has historic charm, low crime, good schools, a new, vibrant downtown business center with some of the best restaurants in Pennsylvania, and a strong sense of community pride.

Earning a Living

Per capita income: $20,880

Median household income: $40,106

Business climate: Over the past decade, Harrisburg has invested more than $2.65 billion in infrastructure improvement, allowing for affordable, accessible, and reliable services to business, industry, and residents. Harrisburg is now the region's center for finance, transportation, commerce, recreation, special events, entertainment, history, arts, and government.

Help in starting a business: The Harrisburg Regional Chamber and Capital Region Economic Development Corporation (CREDC) is the lead organization for promoting and implementing business and economic development. The CREDC, the economic development arm of the Chamber, provides assistance to businesses by offering services including business financing, workforce development, site location, and entrepreneurial assistance.

Job market: As the state capital of Pennsylvania, government is the area's largest employer. Other market sectors providing employment include educational, health, and social services; public administration; and retail trade.

The Community

Overview: The progressive, capital city environment is a strong foundation for the Harrisburg GLBT community. The community is socially and politically active and enjoys the support of local government. As the city experiences its renaissance, active community members participate in political change and openness. Through this change the community maintains a small-town feel while being open to newcomers.

Community organizations: The Gay and Lesbian Switchboard of Harrisburg (*www.askglsh.org*) is a non-profit organization that operates an information resource center for the GLBT communities of central Pennsylvania. The Switchboard, through telephone and Internet information services, provides information for the area's communities and co-publishes the annual PRIDE and Resource Guide for the central Pennsylvania GLBT community. Additionally, there are many area support, health, social, and recreational community organizations in and around Harrisburg. Forever Books (41 N. Front Street; 717–939–5507; *www.foreverbooks.biz*), the community GLBT bookstore in nearby Steelton, serves as a community center, providing meeting space for area groups and planned community events. Pick up a copy of *Alternatives Central*, the local GLBT newspaper, for area news and listings.

Medical care: PinnacleHealth (717–782–5678; *www.pinnaclehealth.org*), the principal heathcare provider headquartered in Harrisburg, operates the city's two main hospitals (Harrisburg and Polyclinic) as well as two additional hospitals in the metropolitan area. Both Harrisburg Hospital (at Front and Chestnut streets, downtown), and Polyclinic Hospital (2600 N. Third Street, uptown) are excellent teaching hospitals with a combined count of 884 inpatient beds. PinnacleHealth also includes family practice and urgent care centers, home health and hospice care agencies, managed care entities, and an array of healthcare services.

Nuptials: The State of Pennsylvania has a law similar to DOMA defining marriage as between a man and a woman and purports to not honor marriages between same-sex couples from other states. Some area employers do offer domestic partner benefits.

Getting Around Town

Public transportation: Capitol Area Transit (CAT) (717–238–8304; *www.cattransit.com*) provides a mass-transit bus system. Fare: $1.25; express $1.35; transfers 35 cents.

Roads: I-81, I-83, I-78, I-76, US11, US15, US22

Airport: Harrisburg International Airport (airport code: MDT) (717–948–3900; *www.flyhia.com*) has eight major airlines offering about 120 daily flights.

It's a Gay Life

Annual events: The Pride Festival of Harrisburg (*www.harrisburgpride.org*) sponsors PrideFest in late July, as well as several other community events and fundraisers through the year. PrideFest includes a mass commitment ceremony, live entertainment, and a festival in beautiful Riverfront Park. The City of Harrisburg hosts several annual events and festivals including the Greater Harrisburg ArtsFest (*www.artsfest.harrisburgpa.com*), Susquehanna River Celebration (*www.pacd.org*), Harrisburg Shakespeare Festival (*www.gamutplays.org/hsf*), African Family Festival (717–232–8803), July 4th weekend's American MusicFest (*www.harrisburgpa.gov*), and the Kipona Festival (*www.harrisburgpa.gov*).

Nightlife: Downtown Harrisburg has gone through a renaissance. At the core is Restaurant Row, a collection of more than 30 bars and restaurants. Harrisburg Hello, the Downtown Improvement District Authority (717–236–9762; *www.harrisburghello.com*), provides information and links to Downtown Harrisburg restaurants, attractions, and businesses. Be sure to check out its interactive area map. Also downtown are several GLBT community bars, including Strawberry Cafe (704 N. Third Street; 717–234–4228), a neighborhood bar with a good jukebox; Stallions (706 N. Third Street; 717–232–3060; *www.stallionsinc.com*), the only gay nightclub in town; Neptune Lounge (268 North Street; 717–233–3078), a popular weekend, last-call bar; and Mary's Brownstone (412 Forster Street; 717–234–7009), a country-western bar. Harrisburg is also home to the Pink Lizard (891 Eisenhower Boulevard; 717–939–1123), a lesbian-owned sports bar with regular events and a gallery showcasing the works of local artists.

Culture: The City of Harrisburg is host to many world-class and unique attractions, including the Whitaker Center for Science and the Arts (222 Market Street; 717–214–ARTS; *www.whitakercenter.org*)—the first-of-its-kind complex in the country to use science as an entry to the arts, housing science, the performing arts, and large-format cinema arts under one roof. Susquehanna Art Museum (301 Market Street; 717–233–8668; *www.sqart.org*) is known as the "Museum without Walls." Internationally recognized artists are presented in three galleries, and the Doshi Gallery for Contemporary Art (301 Market Street; 717–233–8668; *www.sqart.org/doshi*) features the works of regional artists. The Art Association of Harrisburg (21 N. Front Street; 717–236–1432; *www.artassocofhbg.com*) is a hub of cultural events in central Pennsylvania. The galleries in the historic Governor Findlay Mansion, across from Riverfront Park, provide exhibition opportunities for artists nationwide, as well as regionally. The Art Association of Harrisburg is the oldest Harrisburg gallery, offering art classes for children and adults, as well as exhibition opportunities for artists. The Design Museum @ Fathom (302 2nd Street; 717–260–9502; *www.thedesignmuseum.com*) curates two shows each year. The National Civil War Museum (One Lincoln Circle; 717–260–1861; *www.nationalcivilwarmuseum.org*) is the only museum in the United States that portrays the entire story of the American Civil War. Equally balanced presentations are humanistic in nature without bias to Union or Confederate causes.

The Pennsylvania National Fire Museum (1820 N. 4th Street; 717–232–8915) preserves the rich history and heritage of fire service in the restored fire station Reily Hose Company No. 10.

Recreation: The City of Harrisburg's Department of Parks and Recreation (717–255–3020; *www.harrisburgpa.gov*) provides summer programming at 17 recreational sites and maintains two city pools, a beach facility, and 27 parks and playgrounds that total more than 450 acres. The Department also plans and produces 200 annual special events. City Island, a family-oriented park, is Harrisburg's crown jewel. A ride on "The General," a Civil War–era steam train, provides a view of all of City Island's sites and facilities, which include Mengels Carousel with its 24 antique horses, the arcade and batting cages, City Island Beach, Harrisburg Seaplane Base Marina, and RiverSide Marina (333 S. Front Street, Wormleysburg; 717–763–7654; *www.bowersbarine.com*). The Skyline Sports Complex features sand volleyball courts; a multi-purpose field for softball, football, and soccer; and Water Golf, a beautifully landscaped, 18-hole miniature golf course. RiverSide Village Park provides great food and a great view. Spectators can venture out to RiverSide Stadium and catch the Harrisburg Senators (717–231–4444; *www.senatorsbaseball.com*), central Pennsylvania's only AA baseball team and affiliate of the Montreal Expos. Catch a ride back in time on Harrisburg's authentic paddlewheel riverboat, the *Pride of the Susquehanna* (717–234–6500), which is docked on City Island. Harrisburg Carriage Company (*www.harrisburgcarriagecompany.com*) provides horse-drawn carriage ride tours of City Island and downtown Harrisburg.

For the Visitor

Accommodations: Canna Country Inn (393 Valley Road, Etters; 717–938–6077; *www.cannainnbandb.com*) is an expertly converted 1840s classic Sweitzer Barn. The combination of a classic 19th-century stone and wood barn with modern interior space creates a simple relaxing environment of style and charm. Battlefield Bed & Breakfast (2264 Emmitsburg Road, Gettysburg; 717–334–8804; *www.gettysburgbattlefield.com*) is an 1809 Civil War home on the Gettysburg Battlefield with daily history programs and Friday night ghost stories. Centrally located in Downtown Harrisburg, the Crowne Plaza Hotel (23 S. Second Street; 717–234–5021; *www.crowneplaza.com*) is the gateway to Restaurant Row and within walking distance to downtown attractions, the picturesque Susquehanna River waterfront, and City Island.

For More Information

Gay & Lesbian Center
Gay & Lesbian Switchboard
P.O. Box 872
Harrisburg, PA 17108
717–234–0328
www.askglsh.org

Publication
The Patriot News
812 Market Street
Harrisburg, PA 17105
717–255–8203
www.pennlive.com

Convention and Visitors Bureau
Hershey-Capital Region Visitors Bureau
Harrisburg Transportation Center
4th & Chestnut Streets, Suite 208
Harrisburg, PA 17101
717–231–7788
www.hersheycapitalregion.com

Chamber of Commerce
Harrisburg Regional Chamber
3211 North Front Street, Suite 201
Harrisburg, PA 17110-1342
717–232–4099
www.harrisburgregionalchamber.org

Realtor
Marsha Wood
Jack Gaughen Realtor Era
(*www.jgr.com*)
101 Schoolhouse Lane
Mechanicsburg, PA 17055
717–903–4537
www.marshawood.com

Philadelphia, Pennsylvania

40

A Look at Philadelphia

The fifth-largest city in the country, Philadelphia is a welcoming place, a city based on freedom of expression and rich in history and culture. The birthplace of American democracy, the Constitution, medicine, and publishing, the Philadelphia area has more than 88 colleges and universities, world-famous art and science museums, and magnificent gardens. Philadelphia is home to America's most historic square mile, Independence National Historical Park, which includes the Liberty Bell, Independence Hall, Lights of Liberty Show, National Constitution Center, Betsy Ross House, and more. Around every corner you'll discover eclectic streets and neighborhoods that combine old-world charm, history, and architecture with friendly, modern life. A stroll down Philadelphia's Benjamin Franklin Parkway, reminiscent of the Champs Elysées, or along the Avenue of the Arts, the city's premier arts district, reveals a wealth of cultural treasures. In the richly historic Philadelphia region, William Penn's horticultural legacy is celebrated and perpetuated at dozens of wonderful historic estates, arboretums, botanic gardens, museums, and parks.

Possible drawbacks: The property tax rate is currently being overhauled, as the present system has little rhyme or reason. Currently, there can be wide discrepancies of taxation on the same street. This is partly due to the rapid increase of home values added to the lack of methodology currently being applied to the tax base.

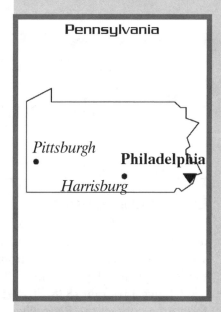

- Nickname:
  City of Brotherly Love and Sisterly Affection
- County: Philadelphia
- Area code: 215
- Time zone: Eastern
- Population:
  1,517,550
- County population:
  1,517,550
- Region:
  Eastern Pennsylvania
- Average home price:
  $448,000
- Fabulous reasons to live here:
  History, culture, arts, museums, recreation, active and politically supported GLBT community, fabulous healthcare, strong economy, excellent education

Climate

Elevation 40'	Avg. high/low(F°)	Avg. inches		Avg. # days precip.	Avg. % humidity
		rain	snow		
Jan.	40/24	3.8	6.1	11	67%
April	64/43	3.8	0.3	11	60%
July	87/67	4.6	–	9	66%
Oct.	67/46	3.2	–	8	68%
YEAR	64/45	45.7	20.5	116	65%
# days 32° or below: 63			# days 90° or warmer: 25		

Local Connections

Overview: Pennsylvania takes deregulation of utilities seriously, and Philadelphia residents have dozens of choices for natural gas, electric, and local phone service suppliers. For descriptions of the many options and programs contact the Pennsylvania Utility Choice (800–782–1110; *www.utilitychoice.org*) and Electric Choice Program (888–782–3228; *www.electrichoice.com*). For additional information contact the Pennsylvania Public Utilities Commission (717–783–1740; *www.puc.state.pa.us*).

Water and sewer: City of Philadelphia Water Revenue Bureau (215–685–6300; *www.phila.gov*)

Cable company: Comcast (800–COMCAST; *www.comcast.com*)

Car registration/License: Pennsylvania Department of Motor Vehicles (717–391–6190; *www.dmv.state.pa.us*)

All new residents with out-of-state non-commercial driver's licenses must obtain a Pennsylvania driver's license within 60 days of establishing Pennsylvania residency. You will be required to surrender your out-of-state driver's license (valid or expired six months or less) and take a vision-screening test. Initial permit and four-year license fee: $31 (age 65+ two-year license: $20.50). Original Title Issuance: $22.50. Passenger vehicle registration: $36.

The Tax Ax

Sales tax: 7 percent; some food purchases, most wearing apparel, drugs, textbooks, sales for resale, and residential heating fuels exempt

State income tax: 3.07 percent, flat tax

Property tax: Board of Revision of Taxes (215–686–9270; brtweb.phila.gov)

The present property tax system has little rhyme or reason to it. Wide discrepancies of taxation on the same street are possible, with counties, municipalities, and school districts all creating a separate levy. You will need to know what county, school district, and municipality you live in.

Local Real Estate

Overview: Housing consists primarily of brick row houses, townhouses, and condominiums. Philadelphia, being a colonial city, has many quaint streets with terrific row houses. Condominiums are a popular trend. Many are converted from older homes, and others are new construction.

Median price for a single-family home: $339,000

Average price for a single-family home: $448,000

Average price for a 2BR condo: $450,000

Rental housing market: Rents have climbed steadily in recent years. The average two-bedroom apartment ranges from $1,300 to $2,000 in Center City Philadelphia.

Gay-friendly neighborhoods: The Gayborhood has traditionally been Washington Square West but, as the "City of Brotherly Love," you will find the city generally very accepting of gays and lesbians. Other gay-friendly neighborhoods are Rittenhouse Square, Art Museum, Italian Market, Bella Vista, Queen Village, Olde City, Graduate Hospital, and Chinatown.

Nearby areas to consider: The Pennsylvania countryside near Philadelphia is dotted with many towns, boroughs, and cities that welcome the GLBT community. One of these communities is New Hope, about 40 miles north. At the turn of the 20th century, the "New Hope School of Impressionists" called the area home. This gave way to the nonobjective and abstract styles of the "New School." This artist's colony of just more than 2,000 residents, with a large GLBT community, is home to the famed Bucks County Playhouse and dozens of GLBT bars, restaurants, and businesses.

Earning a Living

Per capita income: $16,509

Median household income: $30,746

Business climate: The Greater Philadelphia area has more than 150,000 businesses. Nationally, it has the highest concentration of pharmaceutical companies, is the sixth-largest high-tech employment center, and ranks sixth in the number of corporate headquarters. *Greater Philadelphia Business* magazine (*www.gp-biz.com*) provides current area businesses and market information.

Help in starting a business: The Mayor's Business Action Team (MBAT) (*www.phila.gov/mbat*) is a direct connection to the assistance, services, and programs that Philadelphia and its economic development agencies offer businesses. The Greater Philadelphia Chamber of Commerce provides books, guides, networking and educational meetings, and a host of resources for area businesses.

Job market: The largest employment sectors include educational, health, and social services; professional, scientific, management, administrative, and waste management services; and retail trade.

The Community

Overview: Philadelphia's gay community is active and influential in business, politics, and social circles. The community is represented in both state and city government, and Philadelphia's gay media provide a voice within and for the community. *The Philadelphia Gay News*, one of the oldest and most respected gay newspapers in the United States, can be found in purple newspaper boxes on many downtown street corners. Two long-running gay and lesbian programs, Amazon Country and Q'zine, appear on public radio's WXPN 88.5 FM. Barbara Gittings Gay & Lesbian Collection at the Free Library of Philadelphia, Independence Branch (18 S. Seventh Street; 215–685–1633) is the second-largest public library collection of LGBT-themed books, movies, and magazines in the country.

Community organizations: William Way Lesbian, Gay, Bisexual and Transgender Community Center is the focal point of Philadelphia's GLBT community. The Center provides meeting space for more than 70 groups and hosts a variety of events and art exhibitions throughout the year. The city boasts a long list of active GLBT athletic, social, cultural, service, and religious organizations. Visit William Way for information about social events and support resources. *The Gay Philadelphia News* (www.epgn.com) Market Place is a current list of many area groups and organizations.

Medical care: Philadelphia is the birthplace of American medicine, and more than 30 hospitals offer medical services throughout the area. Philadelphia FIGHT (215–985–4448; *www.fight.org*) is a comprehensive AIDS service organization providing primary care, consumer education, advocacy, and research on potential treatments and potential vaccines. FIGHT was formed as a partnership of individuals living with HIV/AIDS and clinicians who joined together to improve the lives of people living with the disease. FIGHT provides primary care to people with HIV/AIDS at the Jonathan Lax Immune Disorders Treatments Center, which provides state-of-the-art clinical care to address the comprehensive needs of people with HIV/AIDS. Clinicians at FIGHT also conduct research to test potential therapies for HIV/AIDS. The first North American trial of a potential vaccine is also underway at FIGHT.

Nuptials: The State of Pennsylvania has a law similar to DOMA defining marriage as between a man and a woman and purports to not honor marriages between same-sex couples from other states. In 1982, Philadelphia passed an ordinance prohibiting discrimination based on sexual orientation, and Philadelphia's 1997 domestic partners law was the first in the country to provide a tax break for gay and lesbian couples. Some area employers do offer domestic partner benefits.

Getting Around Town

Public transportation: The Southeastern Pennsylvania Transit Authority (SEPTA) (215–580–7800; *www.septa.org*) provides bus, trolley, and subway services in the greater Philadelphia area. Cash fare: $2; tokens $1.35; transfer 60 cents.

Unlimited-ride transpasses: daily $5.50, weekly $18.50. SEPTA also offers rail service with fares varying by distance. Two-zone fare: $2.50; regional fare: $3–7.

Roads: I-95, I-76, I-476, Atlantic City Expressway, US1, US30

Airport: Philadelphia International Airport (airport code: PHI) (215–937–6937; *www.phl.org*), only 8 miles from the city center, is served by all major domestic carriers.

It's a Gay Life

Annual events: Philly Pride (*www.phillypride.org*) hosts Pride Day in June, Outfest in October, and Winter Pride. Philadelphia's GLBT community hosts a series of annual and special events, including the Blue Ball Weekend (*www.blueballphilly.com*) in January, Gay Black Pride (*www.phillyblackpride.org*) in April, the Philadelphia International Gay & Lesbian Film Festival (*www.phillyfests.com*) in July, and Sportsweek (*www.phillysportsweek.org*) in June. The city plays host to dozens of other annual events including Jam on the River (*www.jamontheriver.com*) in May; the Manayunk Arts Festival (*www.manayunk.com*), featuring more than 250 national artists; and the Philadelphia Fringe Festival (*www.livearts-fringe.org*), presenting works of more than 1,300 artists in theater, dance, performance art, music, poetry, puppetry, and visual arts.

Nightlife: Live music is everywhere. Classical, jazz, Blues, rock, reggae, and hip-hop can be heard in bars around town or more formally in Philly's amphitheatres and concert halls. Summer months are graced by outdoor concerts in Rittenhouse Square and along Penn's Landing. Just two blocks from the Pennsylvania Convention Center and one block from the Avenue of the Arts is the Gayborhood. This center of gay activity, commerce, and nightlife is located between 11th and Broad streets, from Chestnut to Pine streets. Here you'll discover a vast selection of shops, restaurants, galleries, and bars catering to the GLBT community. Just a few of the Gayborhood favorites include 12th Air Command (254 South Street; 215–545–8088; *www.12thair.com*), with nightly drink specials and hot weekly events; Woody's (202 S. 13th Street; 215–545–1893; *www.woodysbar.com*), offering an eclectic mix of music; and the nightclub Sisters (1320 Chancellor Street; 215–735–0735), with special events, a restaurant, and a fabulous dance environment. Visit Giovanni's Room (345 12th Street; 215–923–2960; *www.giovannisroom.com*), one of the oldest GLBT bookstores in the nation, to pick up the *Philadelphia Gay News* (*www.epgn.com*) for current listings.

Culture: Philadelphia's main stage theaters produce contemporary and classical works, and its art museums comprise one of the largest collections of art in the country. Philadelphia's vast collection of art museums starts at the peak of the Benjamin Franklin Parkway with the Philadelphia Museum of Art (26th Street and the Benjamin Franklin Parkway; 215–763–8100; *www.philamuseum.org*), the third-largest art museum in the United States. The striking, neoclassical building is an oasis of beauty, featuring more than 2,000 years of human creativity in paintings, sculpture, decorative arts, and architectural settings from Europe, Asia, and the Americas. America's first museum and school of fine arts, the Pennsylvania Academy of the Fine Arts (118 N. Broad Street; 215–972–7600; *www.pafa.org*), has a collection of American paintings and sculpture spanning three centuries and includes works by America's greatest artists. The gas light–lined Avenue of the Arts is home to more than 20 major educational and performing arts facilities, including venues for opera, ballet, jazz and orchestral music, classic drama, and musical theater. The 3-mile-long avenue, which passes through the heart of the city, is the site of the Academy of Music (Broad and Locust streets; 215–893–1999; *www.academyofmusic.com*) and the new, world-class Kimmel Center for the Performing Arts (260 South Broad Street; 215–790–7600; *www.kimmelcenter.org*). Philadelphia also has one of the largest collections of outdoor and mural art in the world, as well as a variety of galleries in which to browse and shop. Stroll through the gallery district in Old City during First Fridays (215–625–9200; *www.oldcityarts.org*) when new exhibits premiere and the streets come alive with music and entertainment.

Recreation: Philadelphia has earned its reputation as one of the country's greatest cities for sporting events and activities. Whether you're looking for the hottest pro action, top competition between rising stars, or the chance to get in the game yourself, Philadelphia has plenty of ways to get you close to the action. For those who want to participate in sports, Philadelphia offers opportunities for golf, cycling, jogging, rock climbing, boating, hiking, tennis, in-line skating, ice skating, and much more. Fairmount Park's 8,900 acres offer a collection of athletic fields and trails. Its River Drive Recreation Loop is popular for walking, biking, and running. Rowing's rich tradition comes alive on the Schuylkill River, and canoeing is popular along the Delaware River (Philadelphia Parks Alliance; 215–879–8159; *www.philaparks.org*). There's no shortage of options for spectators in Philadelphia's home teams: MLB's Phillies (215–463–1000; *www.phillies.com*), the NFL's Eagles (215–463–2500; *www.philadelphiaeagles.com*), the NBA's 76ers (215–339–7676; *www.nba.com/sixers*), the NHL's Flyers (215–218–7825; *www.philadelphiaflyers.com*), National Professional Soccer's KiXX (888–888–5499; *www.kixxonline.com*), the National Lacrosse League's Wings (215–389–WING; *www.wingslax.com*), and the Women's United Soccer Association Charge (215–467–GOAL; *www.philadelphiacharge.com*).

For the Visitor

Accommodations: One of the most wonderful things about Philadelphia is its historic architecture. In Philadelphia, hoteliers have adapted to existing structures in very interesting ways. Renovation of existing landmark properties accounts for about 80 percent of the new rooms that have opened in Center City Philadelphia since 1998. A few of Philly's gay-friendly properties include Alexander Inn (12th and Spruce streets; 215–923–3535; *www.alexanderinn.com*), a boutique hotel located in Center City; DoubleTree Hotel (237 S. Broad Street; 215–893–1600; *www.doubletree.com*), located in the heart of Philadelphia on the Avenue of the Arts, across the street from the Kimmel Center, the Academy of Music, and the Merriam Theater; Hotel Windsor (1700 Benjamin Franklin Parkway; 215–981–5678; *www.windsorhotel.com*), an all-suite hotel located in the heart of Philadelphia's business and cultural district; and Sheraton Rittenhouse Square Hotel (18th and Locust streets; 215–546–9400; *www.sheraton.com*) is the first "ecosmart" hotel in the United States, which showcases an environmentally responsible combination of high-tech features.

For More Information

Gay & Lesbian Center

The William Way Community Center
1315 Spruce Street
Philadelphia, PA 19107
215–732–2220
www.waygay.org

Publications

Philadelphia Enquirer
P.O. Box 8263
Philadelphia, PA 19101
215–854–2000
www.philly.com/mld/inquirer

Daily News
Philadelphia Newspapers Inc.
400 N. Broad Street
Philadelphia, PA 19130
215–854–2000
www.philly.com

Philadelphia Gay News
505 South 4th Street
Philadelphia, PA 19147
215–625–8501
www.epgn.com

Convention and Visitors Bureau

Philadelphia Convention and Visitors
Bureau
1700 Market Street, Suite 3000
Philadelphia, PA 19103
215–636–3300
www.pcvb.org

Chamber of Commerce

Greater Philadelphia Chamber of
Commerce
200 South Broad Street, Suite 700
Philadelphia, PA 19102
215–545–1234
www.gpcc.com

Realtor

Mark Van Cour
Realtor
Prudential Fox and Roach Realty
210 W. Washington Square, Suite 200
Philadelphia, PA 19106
215–521–1628
www.markvancour.com

## 41

Providence, Rhode Island

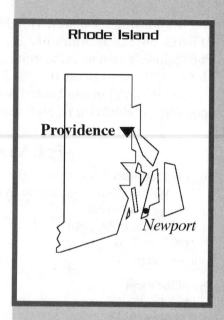

Rhode Island

Providence ▼

Newport

A Look at Providence

Providence is famous for its beautifully preserved historic architecture, having more buildings on the National Historic Register than any other American city. Historic sites, wonderful museums, and theaters compliment the current Renaissance Providence is experiencing, which has brought a new mall, Riverwalk, outdoor skating center, convention center, hotels, and more. The Moshassuck and Woonasquatucket rivers, two narrow but significant waterways that snake through Providence, are edged by cobblestone walkways and flanked by park benches, trees, flowering plants, and a series of graceful Venetian bridges connecting downtown Providence to the city's East Side. At the hub is Waterplace Park, a gathering place in the foreground of Rhode Island's State House with a stone-stepped amphitheater for summer concerts and several overlooking restaurants, as well as the world-renowned WaterFire, an installation of 100 dancing bonfires along the river. The city is home to renowned universities, including Ivy League Brown University, the Rhode Island School of Design, Providence College, and Johnson & Wales University, whose academic programs, theaters, museums, and people contribute significantly to the quality of life in the city.

Possible drawbacks: There's no gay community center, and the large college student and artist population, which brings excitement and life to the city, is transient.

▶ Nickname:
America's Renaissance City

▶ County:
Providence

▶ Area code:
401

▶ Time zone:
Eastern

▶ Population:
173,618

▶ County population:
621,602

▶ Region:
Western Rhode Island

▶ Average home price:
$232,918.00

▶ Fabulous reasons to live here:
Scenic beauty, history, culture, arts and artists, museums, recreation, large GLBT community, excellent education, strong economy

Climate

Elevation 115'	Avg. high/low(F°)	Avg. inches		Avg. # days precip.	Avg. % humidity
		rain	snow		
Jan.	37/19	4.4	9.6	11	64%
April	48/29	4.3	0.7	11	59%
July	83/63	3.4	–	9	68%
Oct.	63/42	3.9	0.1	9	67%
YEAR	60/41	47.6	35.5	124	56%
# days 32° or below: 55			# days 90° or warmer: 11		

Local Connections

Gas company: New England Gas (401–272–3330; *www.negasco.com*)

Electric company: Narragansett Electric (800–322–3223; *www.nationalgridus.com/Narragansett*)

Phone companies: Cox Communications (401–383–2000; www.cox.com); Verizon (800–870–9999; *www.verizon.com*)

Water and sewer: Providence Water (401–521–6300; *www.provwater.com*)

Cable company: Cox Communications (401–383–2000; *www.cox.com*)

Car registration/License: Rhode Island Department of Motor Vehicles (401–588–3020; *www.dmv.state.ri.us*)

You need to obtain a valid Rhode Island license upon becoming a resident. Application fee: $5. License fee: $12. Initial license is good up to two years; renewals are good for five years. New residents have 30 days to register vehicles. No sales tax charged to transfer out-of-state vehicles. Annual registration fee: $30; title fee: $25.

The Tax Ax

Sales tax: 7 percent; exemptions: prescriptions, food, some clothing, precious metal bullion, and some burial-related items

State income tax: 25 percent of federal income tax

Property tax: Local and fire district taxes are the only tax on property. Providence tax rate is $29.65 per $1,000, based on 50 percent of the full value. There is a homestead exemption for owner occupancy in the city.

Local Real Estate

Overview: Providence real estate is made up of a mix of single- and multi-family dwellings, many dating back to the turn of the 20th century. Most of the properties are in the neighborhoods that surround the downtown area, such as the East Side, Armory, Federal Hill, Mt. Pleasant, and Elmhurst neighborhoods. Areas such as the Armory and Federal Hill target the urban pioneer, with a strong tenant base. Elmhurst and the East Side are established, tree-lined street neighborhoods with a stronger owner-occupancy ratio. These properties run from a small cottage in a "transitional" urban neighborhood to multi-million-dollar listings on desirable Blackstone Boulevard in the East Side. (The East Side prices are two to three times those listed here.)

Median price for a single-family home: $265,000

Average price for a single-family home: $232,918

Average price for a 2BR condo: $307,725

Rental housing market: Providence has a strong rental market, as Rhode Island is home to several universities, hospitals, and corporations. Mt. Pleasant, the East Side, and Federal Hill all have strong rental, tenant occupancy with the average rent for a two-bedroom unit with off-street parking ranging anywhere from the mid-$800/month range to the mid-$1,200/month range in areas of the East Side.

Gay-friendly neighborhoods: The East Side of Providence, Federal Hill, and the Armory district offer strong diversity with cafes and coffee shops, as well as great shopping. Downtown, with its recent conversions of former "high-rise" office buildings to condominiums, has also targeted the gay buyer with loft-style, city living.

Nearby areas to consider: Just to the south of Providence is the suburb Cranston, the third-largest city in Rhode Island. Cranston enjoys more than 3 miles of riverfront shoreline along the Providence River. Because of affordable housing and an easy commute, the neighborhood of Edgewood in Cranston has attracted a large GLBT community. The historic Village of Pawtuxet in nearby Warwick is New England's oldest village. This nationally recognized historic district, with colonial structures and historic homes along tree-lined streets, has attracted a large GLBT community.

Earning a Living

Per capita income: $15,525

Median household income: $26,867

Business climate: Providence is ranked by *Popular Science* in the top 20 for high-tech cities. With such an eye for excellence embedded in its history, it's no wonder this city is home to the Rhode Island School of Design, one of the nation's finest art schools. Brown University and the state government comprise the other leading sources of employment, culture, and social life.

Help in starting a business: The Greater Providence Chamber of Commerce has more than 3,300 member businesses, representing all 39 cities and towns in Rhode Island. The Chamber develops a positive and productive business climate for the community through economic development, political action, and civic endeavors. The Chamber promotes programs of a civic, social, and cultural nature, and through its growing membership, provides the leadership, ideas, energy, and finances to help address major community challenges.

Job market: High-technology is on an upswing. Education provides a large number of jobs. Additionally, health and social services and manufacturing comprise almost half the market sector jobs in Providence.

The Community

Overview: Providence has a strong gay community. The influence of several area colleges and universities and a revival of downtown have brought young, art-oriented urban pioneers into the area. The GLBT community has bowling and softball leagues and many spiritual, support, and social groups.

Community organizations: The Center (The Gay, Lesbian, Bisexual and Transgender Center of Rhode Island) is, as of this writing, without a home. The Rhode Island Pride (401–467–2130; *www.PrideRI.com*) is the current area connection for information and volunteer opportunities. Check out its quarterly publication, *Kaleidoscope*, for all the current activities. Youth Pride, Inc. is a nonprofit organization providing support, advocacy, and education for youth and young adults impacted by sexual orientation and gender identity/expression through a safe space drop-in center (401–421–5626; *www.youthpride-ri.org*).

Medical care: Affiliated with and serving as a major teaching affiliate of Brown Medical School, the Miriam Hospital (TMH) (401–793–2500; *www.lifespan.org*) is a private, 247-bed, not-for-profit, acute-care general hospital providing primary, secondary, and tertiary medical and surgical services to adolescents and adults in 33 medical and surgical specialties and sub-specialties, plus a full range of cardiac, pathological, and radiology services as well as psychiatric consultation/liaison services. Rhode Island Hospital (RIH) (401–444–4000; *www.lifespan.org*) is a private, 719-bed, not-for-profit, acute-care hospital and academic medical center providing comprehensive diagnostic and therapeutic services to inpatients and outpatients, with particular expertise in cardiology, oncology, neurosciences, and orthopedics, as well as pediatrics at its Hasbro Children's Hospital.

Nuptials: The State of Rhode Island has no laws prohibiting marriages between same-sex couples.

Getting Around Town

Public transportation: Rhode Island Public Transportation Authority (RIPTA) (401–781–9400; *www.ripta.com*) provides bus and trolley services, including the free ARTrolley on the third Thursday of each month. Base fare: $1.50; transfers 10 cents; unlimited day ride pass (good for the entire state) $6; daily group pass (for up to four riders) $18.

Roads: I-95, I-195, I-295, US6, US44

Airports: T.F. Green Airport (airport code: PVD) (401–737–8222; *www.pvdairport.com*) is just minutes from downtown and serviced by more than a dozen carriers. Recent renovations have created a modern, refined, and convenient airport.

It's a Gay Life

Annual events: Pride Rhode Island (*www.PrideRI.com*) sponsors the Pride Art Show and PrideFest & Night Parade in June; Rhode Island International Film Festival (*www.film-festival.org*) in August includes a gay Filmfest series. Just a few highlights of Providence's many annual events and festivals include Providence IceFire Winter Carnival (*www.waterfire.com*), Capital City Arts Festival (*www.pwcvb.com*), Festival of Historic Houses and Candlelight Tour (*www.ChristmasinNewport.org*), Providence Jazz & Blues Festival (*www.caparts.org*), and Statewide Convergence International Arts Festival (*www.pwcvb.com*). The Providence Warwick Convention & Visitors Bureau (*www.goprovidence.com*) offers the complete list and details.

Nightlife: A city infused with the silvery light from the sea, Providence hosts many off-duty sailors from nearby Navy installations. The mix of students, sailors, artists, and professionals make for a heady bar blend. In the "Downcity" area, the Arts and Entertainment District is anchored by theaters and entertainment venues offering living and working space and fostered by tax incentives to encourage the arts. Throughout the district, nightclubs attract music-lovers of every beat. Providence has more than 20 bars, nightclubs, cafes, and restaurants catering to the GLBT community. Grouped together in Downcity are Union Street Station (69 Union Street; 401–331–2291; *www.69unionstreetstation.com*), with its piano nights and karaoke; NV@The Strand (79 Washington Street; 401–751–2700), a huge Sunday-only dance club; Wheels (125 Washington Street; 401–272–6950), with weekend DJs; and University Pub (17 Snow Street; 401–273–0951). A block away, the Yukon Trading Co. (124 Snow Street; 401–274–6620), Mirabar (35 Richmond Street; 401–331–6761; *www.mirabar.com*), and the Providence Eagle (200 Union Street; 401–421–1447) satisfy the bear, Levi, and leather crowds. For complete listings, visit Books on the Square (471 Angell Street; 401–331–9097; *www.booksq.com*) and pick up *Options* (*www.optionsri.org*), *Metroline* (*www.metroline-online.com*), and *In Newsweekly* (*www.innewsweekly.com*).

Culture: Providence has become the center of an emerging arts, cultural and entertainment community in New England. Providence is a haven for young artists and home to the largest number of working artists in the country, Providence boasts an eclectic mix of galleries, art shops, theaters, and museums. The award-winning Trinity Repertory Company (201 Washington Street; 401–351–4242; *www.trinityrep.com*), Veterans Memorial Auditorium (69 Avenue of the Arts; 401–272–4862), and Providence Performing Arts Center (220 Weybosset Street; 401–421–2997; *www.ppacri.org*) are not only historic landmarks, but also feature

Broadway musicals, children's performances, popular seasonal ballets, opera, plays, and musical concerts, including the Rhode Island Philharmonic (401–831–3123; *www.ri-philharmonic.org*). AS220 (115 Empire Street; 401–831–9327; *www.as220.org*) is an alternative arts performance, studio and living space with regular performances, readings, and gallery exhibits. Much of the visual arts influence in Providence can be attributed to the Rhode Island School of Design. The Museum of Art (224 Benefit Street; 401–454–6500; *www.risd.edu*) houses more than 65,000 works, ranging from Greek sculpture to French Impressionist paintings, Chinese terra-cotta to contemporary multimedia art. The Museum's Pendleton House is the earliest example of an "American wing" in any museum; it features an extraordinary collection of 18th-century American decorative art. Public sculpture is quite popular in Providence, with large works of art arranged in public places around the city, ranging from graceful to hulking. The third Thursday of each month is Gallery Night (401–751–2628). The free ARTrolley loops through the city and stops at 24 local galleries and museums where visitors experience Providence's emerging arts scene.

Recreation: A popular retreat is downtown's Fleet Skating Center (Two Kennedy Plaza; 401–331–5544; *www.fleetskating.com*). Three times larger than New York's Rockefeller Center, the outdoor skating center offers ice skating in the cooler months and a skateboard park during warmer months. Roger Williams Park Zoo (1000 Elmwood Avenue; 401–785–3510; *www.rogerwilliamsparkzoo.org*), situated in a 430-acre Victorian park, offers more than 156 different species of animals and is open 364 days a year. Polar bears, elephants, and a giant sea lion are among the favorites at the zoo. The parklands surrounding the zoo are great for a picnic, offering carousel rides, botanical gardens, and boat tours on the lake. Between May and October nearly 100 bonfires are set to music along the downtown rivers as part of the world-renowned WaterFire installation (401–274–3111; *www.waterfire.com*). Hop on a riverboat for a tour or sail on the Continental Sloop *Providence* (India Point Park; 401–274–7447; *www.sloopprovidenceri.org*), a replica of a Revolutionary War ship. For cycling fun, the East Bay Bike Path provides 15 gorgeous miles of nature riding on paved trails along the bay. Narrated city tours are available by foot through the Rhode Island Historical Society's Summerwalks (1110 Benevolent Street; 401–331–8575; *www.rihs.org*), or on the Conway/Grayline Trolley (800–934–8687; *www.grayline.com*) or the amphibious Splash Duck Boat Tours (corner of Fountain and Eddy streets; 401–421–3825; *www.splashducktours.com*). The Providence Civic Center (1 LaSalle Square; 401–331–0700) is home to the Providence Bruins (401–273–5000; *www.providencebruins.com*) minor league ice hockey team, affiliated with the NHL Boston Bruins. If baseball's your game, the Pawtucket Red Sox (401–724–7300; *www.pawsox.com*), Boston's minor league affiliate, play just up the road at McCoy Stadium (Ben Mondor Way, Pawtucket; 401–724–7300; *www.pawsox.com*).

For the Visitor

Accommodations: There are accommodations of every style and for every budget in the Greater Providence area, including six major downtown properties, inns and B&Bs in historic neighborhoods, airport hotels, and a variety of suburban properties located just off major highways within minutes of the city. There aren't the usual gay B&B or inn options, but the Courtyard Marriott (32 Exchange Terrace at Memorial Boulevard; 401–272–1191/888–887–7955; *www.marriot.com*), a frequent sponsor of special packages during gay community events, is situated in the historic Union Station Plaza in DownCity.

For More Information

Publications

Providence Journal
75 Fountain Street
Providence, RI 02920-9985
401–277–7000
www.projo.com

Options
P.O. Box 6406
Providence, RI 02940-6406
401–831–4519
www.optionsri.org

Convention and Visitors Bureau

Providence Warwick Convention and Visitors Bureau
One West Exchange Street
Providence, RI 02903
401–274–1636/800–233–1636
www.providencecvb.com

Chamber of Commerce

Greater Providence Chamber of Commerce
30 Exchange Terrace
Providence, RI 02903
401–521–5000
www.provchamber.com

Realtor

Thom Hammond
Realtor
RE/MAX Premier
736 Hope Street
Providence, RI 02906
401–272–2100
www.remax.com

42 ▶ Nashville, Tennessee

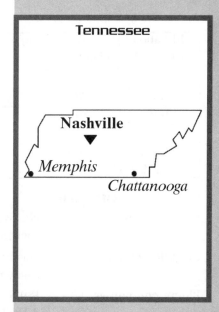

A Look at Nashville

Nashville was coined "Music City" in 1950 by David Cobb, a radio producer for WSM radio, during Red Foley's NBC radio show and it continues to live up to the reputation. The city is continually host to music events, concerts, and festivals for every type of music-lover and is consistently raising the bar for the country's music scene. Nashville's music industry generates more than $2 billion annually, but there's much more to the city. Over the last decade, Nashville has experienced an arts renaissance, with new venues opening to critical success and acclaim. Galleries, museums, a world-class zoo, opera, ballet, theaters, and two orchestras provide a growing number of nightly and annual arts events. Nashville is also home to professional, college, and amateur sports leagues, several theme parks, and championship golf courses. The Music City's arts scene is complimented by 16 colleges and universities. Many of America's major corporations are taking advantage of this well-educated workforce and below-average cost of living by relocating their headquarters and operations to Nashville.

Possible drawbacks: As population continues to increase, so increases the traffic congestion problems. High humidity and more rainfall than the Pacific Northwest create a damp, dreary environment. The area is also prone to tornados.

▶ Nickname:
Music City

▶ County: Davidson

▶ Area code: 615

▶ Time zone: Central

▶ Population:
545,524

▶ County population:
545,524

▶ Region:
Central Tennessee

▶ Average home price:
$225,000

▶ Fabulous reasons to live here:
Music and musicians; arts; fabulous nightlife; entertainment; recreation; large, active GLBT community; strong and growing economy

Climate

Elevation 400'–1100'	Avg. high/low(F°)	Avg. inches rain	snow	Avg. # days precip.	Avg. % humidity
Jan.	45/27	4.0	3.7	11	72%
April	70/46	3.9	–	11	67%
July	89/69	3.8	–	10	74%
Oct.	71/48	3.0	–	7	72%
YEAR	69/48	48.9	10.0	119	72%
# days 32° or below: 49			# days 90° or warmer: 44		

Local Connections

Gas company: Nashville Gas Company (615–734–1793; *www.nashvillegas.com*)

Electric company: Nashville Electric Services (615–736–6900; *www.nespower.com*)

Phone companies: BellSouth (615–557–6500; *www.bellsouth.com*); AT&T (800–222–0400; *www.local.att.com*); Verizon (800–483–5000; *www.verizon.com*); Adelphia Communications (615–263–1140; *www.adelphia.net*); ICG Telecom Group, Inc. (615–251–4440; *www.icgcomm.com*); Qwest Communications (800–860–1020; *www.qwest.com*); MCI Telecommunications (800–539–2000; *www.mci.com*); Sprint Communications (800–877–2000; *www.sprint.com*)

Water and sewer: Metro Water Services (615–862–4600; *www.nashville.gov/water*)

Cable company: Comcast Cable TV (615–244–5900; *www.comcast.com*)

Car registration, license: County Clerk (615–862–6251; *www.tennessee.gov/safety*)

When relocating to Tennessee you must immediately register and title your vehicle, but you have 30 days to obtain your driver's license. If you surrender a valid, out-of-state license the written and driving exams are waived. A driver's license will be issued for three to seven years, based on your age at the time of application. The fees are pro-rated with a standard, five-year license being $19.50. Title fee: $8. Passenger vehicle registration fee: $24; mailing fee $1; metro sticker: $35.

The Tax Ax

Sales tax: 9.25 percent; some foods taxed at 8.25 percent

State income tax: 6 percent, collected on dividend and interest income only

Property tax: Davidson County Property Assessor (615–862–6080; *www.padctn.com*)

Residential property is assessed at 25 percent of fair market value of the property as of each January 1st and expressed as an amount per $100. Tennessee does not have a homestead exemption.

Local Real Estate

Overview: Nashville has all home styles from Victorian and Tudor to rustic and contemporary. The current availability in Nashville is tremendous, with new housing going up all the time. Whether you want the suburbs or downtown urban living, Nashville is the place.

Median price for a single-family home: $350,000

Average price for a single-family home: $225,000

Average price for a 2BR condo: $190,000

Rental housing market: Nashville has a large number of apartments; luxury apartments are on the rise. The average rent for a two-bedroom apartment is $700.

Gay-friendly neighborhood: The local GLBT community calls most areas of Nashville home, but east Nashville attracts the largest numbers because of its many GLBT-oriented businesses and bars.

Nearby areas to consider: Just south of Nashville, the affluent suburb of Brentwood, with its rich Civil War history and many restored plantation-style homes, boasts low crime rates, median incomes almost three times the national average and excellent schools. Franklin, 20 miles southwest of Nashville, offers small-town charm and a mix of antebellum and Victorian homes. This small city with its rich history and progressive nature is attracting the GLBT community. Murfreesboro, 35 miles southeast of Nashville, has seen a 50 percent population boom in the past decade. This historic educational center offers a high quality of life, plentiful and affordable housing, and excellent schools and employment opportunities.

Earning a Living

Per capita income: $22,018

Median household income: $39,232

Business climate: *Forbes Magazine* named Nashville as one of the 25 cities likely to have the country's highest job growth over the coming five years. According to the Nashville Area Chamber of Commerce, in the past few years, companies such as Dell, Nissan, and Sprint PCS have chosen to open operations in the Nashville area because of its business climate. Nashville's business-friendly factors such as technology, logistics-friendliness, workforce, and standard of living have also earned the city high rankings in a variety of national business publications.

Help in starting a business: Nearly 93 percent of the Nashville Area Chamber of Commerce members are small businesses. The Chamber provides training, management assistance, and networking opportunities for small-business owners and their employees.

Job market: Major industries providing employment in Nashville include tourism, printing and publishing, technology manufacturing, music production, higher education, finance, insurance, automobile production, and healthcare management.

The Community

Overview: Nashville's GLBT community enjoys a combination of strength, pride, and organization. There are several major publications, a strong community center, professional and recreational organizations, and good healthcare options. The Nashville community also knows how to have fun.

Community organizations: Rainbow Community Center (615–297–0008; *www.rainbowcommunitycenter.org*) fosters personal and community growth for gay, lesbian, bisexual, transgender, queer, and questioning people in Middle Tennessee by promoting a safe environment to gather. The Center serves as an advocate and information source and provides social, educational, and service opportunities through networking and collaboration, discussion groups, support groups, and providing community services. In addition to the Rainbow Community Center, *Church Street Freedom Press* (*www.churchstreetfreedompress.com*), the local GLBT community newspaper, has a current list of the dozens of additional support, spiritual, service, and social organizations within Nashville's large and active GLBT community.

Medical care: As one of the 11 hospitals in the TriStar Health System, Centennial Medical Center (615–342–1000; *www.centennialmedctr.com*) has access to the most comprehensive healthcare network in middle Tennessee and southern Kentucky. Centennial Medical Center has been recognized both nationally and locally, including being named by HCIA-Sachs as one of the nation's Top 100 Hospitals in the areas of cardiology, stroke, orthopedics, and breast cancer management (in 2000 and 2003). Baptist Hospital (615–284–5555; *www.baptisthospital.com*) is the region's largest not-for-profit community hospital, licensed for 685 acute- and rehab-care beds. Of the 685 beds, 24 are rehab beds and 46 are adult ICU beds. Baptist Hospital has 84 basinets and 27 NICU beds. The main campus covers nearly two million square feet and spans more than six city blocks (or 38 acres).

Nuptials: Tennessee has a state law similar to DOMA defining marriage as between a man and a woman and does not honor same-sex marriages from other states.

Getting Around Town

Public transportation: Nashville Metropolitan Transit Authority (615–862–5950; *www.nashvillemta.org*) provides regional bus and trolley service. Fares: local $1.10; express $1.50; all-day pass $3.25.

Roads: I-24, I-40, I-65, I-440, US31, US41

Airport: Nashville International Airport (airport code: BNA) (615–275–1675; *www.flynashville.com*) is home to 17 airlines serving 86 markets.

It's a Gay Life

Annual events: Nashville Pride (*www.nashvillepride.org*) sponsors Pride Fest in early June, Martinis & Jazz in April, and other events throughout the year. Among the many Music City USA annual events are TACA Spring Crafts Fair (*www.tennesseecrafts.org*), Main Street Festival (*www.historicfranklin.com*), Music City Brewer's Festival (*www.musiccitybrewersfest.com*), Juneteenth Freedom Festival (*www.bellemeadeplantation.com*), American Artisan Festival (*www.americanartisan.citysearch.com*), Jack Daniel's World Championship Cook-off (*www.lynchburgtn.com*), and Uncle Dave Macon Days (*www.uncledavemacondays.com*) .

Nightlife: Every night the music scene in Nashville is vibrant and contagious. Fans rush to get a seat in the clubs, and the latecomers crowd the walls and dance floors. By late evening, the clubs are alive and rocking. Nashville doesn't have a gay quarter, and the dozen bars and nightclubs and handful of cafes and restaurants that cater to Nashville's gay community are spread around the city. Visit Davis-Kidd Booksellers (4007 Hillsboro Road; 615–385–2645; *www.daviskidd.com*) or Outloud Books & Gifts (1709 Church Street; 615–340–0034; *www.outloudonline.com*) to pick up copies of *Church Street Freedom Press* (*www.churchstreetfreedompress.com*), *Out & About in Nashville* (*outandaboutnashville.com*), or *Xenogeny/Southern X-posure* (*www.xenogeny.com*) for current community listings and events.

Culture: Every weekend, the Grand Ole Opry (2802 Opryland Drive; 615–871–OPRY; *www.opry.com*) brings the heritage of the world's longest-running radio show and an incredible mix of talent to the world. Summer is highlighted by free Opry Plaza Parties. The Nashville Ballet (615–297–2966; *www.nashvilleballet.com*) is noted for its versatility; performances include classical, contemporary, and modern works. The Nashville Chamber Orchestra (615–256–6546; *www.nco.org*) has come to be recognized as one of America's most creative and innovative orchestras, and the Nashville Symphony Orchestra (615–783–1200; *www.nashvillesymphony.org*) features a full schedule of classical, pops, children's, and special events concerts throughout the year. The Tennessee Performing Arts Center (TPAC) (505 Deaderick Street; 615–82–4000; *www.tpac.org*) is home to many of Nashville's performing arts associations and its own Broadway series, and the Tennessee Repertory Theater (615–244–4878; *www.tnrep.org*) is the state's largest professional theater company, featuring five main-stage and three off-Broadway productions annually. Over the past decade, Music City has enjoyed an art renaissance. Fisk University is home to the Aaron Douglas Gallery (1000 17th Avenue N.; 615–329–8500; *www.fisk.edu*), with its large African art collection, and the Carl Van Vechten Gallery (Jackson Steet and 18th Avenue N.; 615–329–8500; *www.fisk.edu*), housing the Stieglitz collection donated by Georgia O'Keeffe. Cheekwood Botanical Garden & Museum of Art (1200 Forrest Park Drive; 615–356–8000; *www.cheekwood.org*) is a 55-acre botanical garden and center for the arts that houses American works of the 19th and 20th centuries. The Frist Center for the Visual Arts (919 Broadway; 615–244–3340; *www.fristcenter.org*) is Nashville's newest and most expansive art exhibition. The Parthenon in Centennial Park (615–862–8431; *www.nashville.gov/Parthenon*) houses the Cowan Collection, the city's permanent art collection featuring the works of American artists and traveling exhibits. Vanderbilt University is home to the Sarratt Gallery (207 Sarratt Student Center; 615–322–2471; *www.vanderbilt.edu/sarratt*), with 10 exhibits a year of contemporary art by regional and national artists, and the Vanderbilt University Fine Arts Gallery (23rd and West End avenues; 615–332–0605; *www.vanderbilt.edu/gallery*), which houses a permanent collection spanning 40 countries and hosts five annual, themed exhibits.

Recreation: There's more than music and culture to pursue in Nashville. Blue lakes and rolling green hills surround Music City. An extensive network of public parks within the metro city limits is perfect for hiking, running, horseback riding, and exploring. Fishing, hunting, boating, hiking, water sports, and camping also lie nearby, with boat and water recreation rentals available on Percey Priest and Old Hickory lakes. Nashville's four resort golf courses feature 108 holes of championship play. The city also offers golfers more than 14 public courses. Five new exhibits have recently opened at Nashville Zoo (3777 Nolensville Road; 615–833–1534; *www.nashvillezoo.org*), including the 150,000-gallon wading pool at the African elephant habitat. For roller coasters and waterslides, visit Valley Amusement Park (2440 Music Valley Drive; 615–885–2330; *www.valleyamusementpark.com*) and Nashville Shores Water Park (4001 Bell Road, Hermitage; 615–889–7050; *www.nashvilleshores.com*). For spectators, Nashville is home to the NFL's Titans (615–565–4200; *www.titansonline.com*), the NHL's Nashville Predators (615–770–7825; *www.nashvillepredators.com*), the National Women's Football Association's Nashville Dreams (615–860–4084; *www.womensfootballcentral.com*), Pacific Coast League Baseball's Nashville Sounds (6145–242–4371; *www.nashvillesounds.com*), Arena Football League's Nashville Kats (615–254–5287; *www.arenafan.com*), the American Basketball Association's Nashville Rhythm (615–279–6666; *www.nashvillerhythm.com*), and the Nashville Kangaroos, Inc. (615–460–1401; *www.nashvillekangaroos.org*), an Australian Rules Football team. Before the pros came to play, Nashville was a college sports town, with cross-town traditions and interconference rivalries running deep through the area's 16 colleges and universities. Nashville still loves its college sports. Vanderbilt University (615–322–7311; *www.vanderbilt.edu*) takes pride in its Southeastern Conference (SEC) teams. Tennessee State University

(615–963–5841; *www.tnstate.edu*) and Belmont University (615–460–8500; *www.belmont.edu*) play Division 1-A basketball, and Lipscomb University (800–333–4358; *www.lipscom.edu*) joins the Atlantic Sun Division.

For the Visitor

Accommodations: With more than 32,000 hotel rooms, Nashville has something for everyone. There are many gay-friendly accommodations to choose from. Located in the heart of downtown, the Savage House Inn (167½ Eighth Avenue N.; 615–254–1278; *www.gaslitelounge.com*) is the only pre–Civil War residence still occupied in downtown Nashville. It's also the home of the Gaslight Lounge. Cat's Pajamas B&B (*www.bbonline.com/tn/catspajamas*) is an urban bed and breakfast in the Historic Edgefield neighborhood of downtown. This beautiful 1918 Craftsman bungalow features a fireplace, wood floors, and large bedrooms with comfortable queen-size beds, flannel sheets, down comforters, a separate side entrance, and off-street parking. A creative and delicious breakfast features organic and all-natural foods.

For More Information

Gay & Lesbian Center
Rainbow Community Center
P.O. Box 22179
Nashville TN 37202
615–297–0008
www.rainbowcommunitycenter.org

Publications
The Tennessean
1100 Broadway
Nashville, TN 37203
615–254–5661
www.tennessean.com

Church Street Freedom Press
P.O. Box 90862
Nashville, TN 37209-0862
615–582–5963
www.churchstreetfreedompress.com

Out and About Newspaper
P.O. Box 330818
Nashville, TN 37203-7505
615–596–6210
www.outandaboutnashville.com

Convention and Visitors Bureau
Nashville Convention and Visitors Bureau
211 Commerce Street, Suite 100
Nashville, TN, 37201
615–259–4700/800–657–6910
www.nashvillecvb.com

Chamber of Commerce
Nashville Area Chamber of Commerce
211 Commerce Street, Suite 100
Nashville, TN 37201
615–743–3000
www.nashvillechamber.com

Realtor
Stephanie Albright
Realtor
Crye-Leike Realtors
504 22nd Avenue E.
Springfield, TN 37172
615–335–1373
stephaniealbright.crye-leike.com

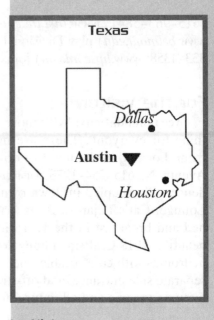

A Look at Austin

Known for being down-home and sophisticated, laid-back yet bustling with high energy, traditional and avant-garde at the same time, Austin defines coolness. Yet, Austinites remain individualistic and embrace traditions that brand the city's unique, often quirky, identity. For instance, thousands flock downtown to Congress Avenue Bridge nightly, April through October, to watch more than 1.5 million Mexican free-tail bats take flight at dusk. As home to the University of Texas and 52,000 college students, the city is awash in burnt orange and white in the fall when the University of Texas Longhorns take to the football field. Aside from politics, nothing strikes up a heated discussion more quickly than trying to name the best barbecue around. From festivals spotlighting today's arts and music to museums showcasing a rich and varied history, Austin possesses a wealth of cultural offerings. Over the past two decades, the small university town where Willie Nelson sought respite in the 1970s to brand his own unique musical style, grew into a big city with a glittery skyline and more than 1.2 million people in the metropolitan area. An incubator for creativity, the Capital City of Texas is alternately dubbed "Live Music Capital of the World," "City of Ideas," and "Silicon Hills" in tribute to a high-tech industry that includes the headquarters of Dell Computer and IBM Corp.

Possible drawbacks: Austin's economy is tightly connected to the high-tech industries. When the bubbles burst the area is severely and negatively affected.

▶ Nickname:
The Big Heart of Texas

▶ County: Travis

▶ Area code:
512

▶ Time zone:
Central (no DST)

▶ Population:
656,562

▶ County population:
812,280

▶ Region:
Central Texas

▶ Average home price:
$179,000

▶ Fabulous reasons to live here:
Affordable housing, high-tech economy, music, arts, culture, museums, nightlife, entertainment, recreation, excellent education, no income tax, active GLBT community

Climate

Elevation 501'	Avg. high/low(F°)	Avg. inches rain	Avg. inches snow	Avg. # days precip.	Avg. % humidity
Jan.	60/40	1.9	0.5	8	70%
April	79/58	2.5	–	7	71%
July	95/73	2.0	–	5	71%
Oct.	81/60	4.0	–	7	71%
YEAR	78/58	33.6	0.9	86	71%
# days 32° or below: 13			# days 90° or warmer: 109		

Local Connections

Gas company: Texas Gas Service (512-477-5852; *www.oneok.com*)

Electric companies: Texas offers consumers electric choice (Texas Electric Choice 866-797-4839; *www.powertochoose.org*) and more than twenty providers service the state. Austin Energy (512-322-6300; *www.austinenergy.com*)

Phone companies: Grande Communications (512-220-4600; *www.grandecom.com*); SBC (888-294-8433; *www.sbc.com*); Time Warner (512-485-5555; *www.timewarnercable.com/Austin*)

Water and sewer: Austin Water Utility (512-494-9400; *www.ci.austin.tx.us/water*)

Cable company: Time Warner (512-485-5555; *www.timewarnercable.com/Austin*)

Car registration/License: Texas Department of Transportation (512–424–2600 ([license]/512–416–4800 [registration]); *www.dot.state.tx.us*

If you surrender a valid out-of-state driver's license, the only exam required is the vision test to get a Texas driver's license. Fee: $24 (good for six years). (License: 512–424–2600 *www.txdps.state.tx.us*). Registration fees include a county fee ($11.50) and a weight and model year fee (starting at $41).

The Tax Ax

Sales tax: 8.25 percent

State income tax: No personal income tax in Texas

Property tax: Travis County Tax Assessor (512–854–9473; *www.co.travis.tx.us*)

Property tax rates in Texas are considered high compared to other areas of the country, based on a few factors: Texas has no state income tax, and property taxes are the base in the state for school funding. Total tax rates vary from location to location and may change from year to year.

Local Real Estate

Overview: Generally speaking, the Austin housing market is a stable market, not a buyer's or a seller's market. Housing prices stabilized over the past few years, and economic indicators are that the economy and the Austin housing market are on the upswing. All types and styles of housing are available, and there is an adequate supply of housing available to meet consumers' needs.

Median price for a single-family home: $204,000

Average price for a single-family home: $179,000

Average price for a 2BR condo: $149,000

Rental housing market: Currently the rental market in Austin is soft, and it is definitely an opportunity for tenants to make a deal in the lease market. When the economy softened, many Austinites were "right-sized" and went elsewhere to find work. Add to that the facts that "Class A" apartment construction did not stop and mortgage rates continued at historically low levels. All of these factors contributed to more supply than demand in rental housing.

Gay-friendly neighborhoods: Austin maintains its live-and-let-live attitude, so there is no gay ghetto, and most parts of the city are accepting of the GLBT community.

Nearby areas to consider: Eighty miles north of Austin is America's ninth-largest city: gay-friendly San Antonio. This large, metropolitan city in central Texas truly deserves a profile of its own, but there just wasn't room. San Antonio's large, active, well-supported GLBT community enjoys the culture, recreation, and employment opportunities afforded by San Antonio. In addition, there are dozens of fun GLBT community bars, restaurants, and shops. The Diversity Center of San Antonio (210–223–6106; *www.diversitycentersa.org*) not only provides GLBT community support, but it also maintains one of the most comprehensive lists of community social and recreational groups, as well as local health, support, and spiritual organizations.

Earning a Living

Per capita income: $19,617

Median household income: $39,927

Business climate: Austin has a highly trained workforce, renowned quality of life, moderate cost environment, and vast experience in technology, manufacturing, and research and development. *Popular Science* ranks Austin in the top 100 American high-tech cities. High-tech currently represents almost 20 percent of total non-agricultural employment. The Greater Austin Chamber of Commerce is focusing efforts on strengthening the technology sector and recruiting new industries such as automotive suppliers, medical products and pharmaceuticals, and wireless technologies.

Help in starting a business: Austin Gay and Lesbian Chamber of Commerce (*www.aglcc.org*) promotes networking, education, and support for gay and gay-friendly businesses and professionals. The Greater Austin Chamber of Commerce offers marking, networking, and educational opportunities. The city of Austin's Small Business Development Program (*www.ci.austin.tx.us/sbdp*) provides counseling and assistance to small and minority-owned businesses of all cultural backgrounds with a focus of developing and empowering small businesses in order to strengthen their business capability and survivability.

Job market: Austin's major employers include the Austin Independent School District, City of Austin, Dell, IBM Corp., Texas State University–San Marcos, and the University of Texas at Austin. Major market sectors include educational, health, and social services; professional, scientific, management, administrative, and waste management services; manufacturing; and retail trade.

The Community

Overview: Austin is truly one of America's creative class cities, with dozens of high-tech firms calling the city home and nearly two dozen colleges and universities in or near the city. This creativity draws a liberal crowd to the area, and Austin's GLBT community is large, young, and active. There's a fabulous GLBT nightlife and entertainment scene in Austin.

Community organizations: Austin has no formal GLBT center. Austin Latino Lesbian and Gay Organization (*www.allgo.org*), a Queer People of Color organization, provides cultural arts, health, and community organizing initiatives in the city. The influence of several large campus communities provides youth outreach programming and dozens of area groups offer support, spiritual, social, and recreational opportunities in Austin. The Austin Gay and Lesbian Chamber of Commerce (*www.aglcc.org*) sponsors community events throughout the year.

Medical care: Eleven major hospitals, one children's hospital, and numerous outpatient clinics, emergency medical facilities, and awareness programs are available in the greater Austin area. The total number of hospital beds is more than 2,500, with more than 2,000 licensed physicians and more than 8,000 registered nurses. The region has the most recent technology available, including specialties in neonatal care, organ transplants, in-vitro fertilization, and oncology. Seven hospitals specialize in psychiatric care and chemical dependency.

Nuptials: The State of Texas has a law similar to DOMA defining marriage as between a man and a woman. The State doesn't acknowledge same-sex marriages from other jurisdictions. Local government and many area employers extend benefits to domestic partners.

Getting Around Town

Public transportation: Area bus service is provided by Capital Metro (512–474–1200; *www.capmetro.austin.tx.us*). Fare: local service 50 cents; express service $1; transfers free. There's no daily ride pass, but the half-price card is $5 for $10 worth of rides. The downtown "Dillo" is always free.

Roads: US183, US290, SR71, SR165

Airport: Austin-Bergstrom International Airport (airport code: AUS) (512–530–2242; *www.ci.austin.tx.us/austinairport*) has a 1-acre outdoor Family Viewing Area, located near the east runway.

It's a Gay Life

Annual events: The Austin Gay & Lesbian Chamber of Commerce sponsors the Austin Pride Parade in June (*www.austinprideparade.org*). The Austin Gay and Lesbian International Film Festival (*www.agliff.or*) is the largest event of its kind in the Southwest, recently screening more than 160 films. Dozens of music and art festivals are held during the year, including Blues on the Green (*www.cityofaustin.org*), the Austin Jazz & Arts Festival (*www.diversearts.org*), the *Austin City Limits* Music Festival (*www.austincitylimits.com*), the Austin Fine Arts Festival (*www.austinfineartsfestival.com*), and the particularly Austin-flavored Eeyore's Birthday Party (*www.eeyores.sexton.com*).

Nightlife: The sound of Blues, country, rock and roll, jazz, and folk fuses into a unique genre known as the Austin sound and echoes from more than 100 venues on any given evening. The largest concentration of music venues is found downtown in the Warehouse District and along Sixth Street, a six-block stretch of bars and restaurants. Austin is also home to more than a dozen restaurants and cafes and a dozen bars catering to the gay community. Book Woman (918 W. 12th Street; 512–472–2785; *www.ebookwoman.com*) and Lobo (3204-A Guadalupe; 512–454–5406) are bookstores where you'll find *Texas Triangle* (*www.txtriangle.com*) or *Shout Magazine* (*shouttexas.com*) with current area listings and events.

Culture: The Austin Symphony (512–476–6064; *www.austinsymphony.org*), Ballet Austin (512–476–2163; *www.balletaustin.org*), and the Austin Lyric Opera (512–472–5992; *www.austinlyricopera.org*) offer a variety of programs and concerts throughout the year. Dozens of theaters present old favorites and groundbreaking new drama; dance companies, vocal ensembles, and orchestras produce events year-round. Art museums, galleries galore, and beautiful gardens replete with sculptures ease and please the eye with so many enticing shapes and colors. Umlauf Sculpture Gardens (605 Robert E. Lee Road; 512–445–5582; *www.umlaufsculpture.org*) remains one of the city's best-kept secrets. This peaceful sanctuary displays the works of the late Charles Umlauf, a world-renowned sculptor who taught at the University of Texas. Bronzes of children, animals, and religious figures and Madonna images are scattered amid the wooded setting. Each spring, Austin plays host to South by Southwest (512–467–7979; *www.sxsw.com*), an internationally acclaimed, 10-day, music, film, and multimedia event. The event features hundreds of concerts and film showings, multimedia and music industry exhibitions, educational panel discussions, and workshops examining all three industries. The University of Texas' Performing Arts Center (510 E. 23rd Street; 512–471–1444; *www.utpac.org*) and other world-class facilities attract Broadway shows and nationally and internationally renowned artists and performers through-out the year. Concerts and public events at UT's newly renovated Frank Erwin Center feature everything from the latest pop and rock artists and country music legends to the Ice Capades and the Ringling Bros. and Barnum and Bailey Circus.

Recreation: Austin stands as the gateway to the scenic Texas Hill Country—a vast region of rolling hills, sparkling lakes, and fields of wildflowers. A diverse mix of nature trails, parks, and greenbelts creates a verdant oasis in the heart of the Lone Star State. Here, you can enjoy hiking, mountain biking, and other land-based activities. Austin lies 300 miles from the ocean, but it's surrounded by water. The Highland Lakes, a series of seven manmade reservoirs along the Lower Colorado River, provide boating, waterskiing, sailing, windsurfing, row-ing, canoeing, fishing, and swimming. Town Lake bisects downtown to provide a verdant oasis with 10.1 miles of hike-and-bike trails. Zilker Park, along with being a favorite venue for outdoor music events, is also home to Barton Springs Pool. Artesian springs feed the natural pool, which remains a constant 68 de-grees year-round. Austin's naturally temperate climate and rolling hills make the area perfect for golfing, with some of the most scenic and challenging golf courses in the nation. For spectators, the University of Texas (512–471–3333; *www.texassports.com*) and the Big 12 Conference offer collegiate sports with nationally ranked programs in football, basketball, baseball, swimming, track and field, volleyball, and more. The Round Rock Express (512–255–BALL; *www.roundrockexpress.com*) is the Houston Astros' Double A affiliate; Austin Ice Bats (512–927–PUCK; *www.icebats.com*) are a WPHL professional hockey team; and the Austin Wranglers (512–491–6600; *www.austinwranglers.com*) are the Arena Football League's 19th franchise.

For the Visitor

Accommodations: With more than 22,000 hotel rooms in Austin, 5,000 rooms centered in the downtown area, there's something for every taste and budget. A few of the gay-friendly properties include the Governor's Inn (611 W. 22nd Street; 512–477–0711/800–871–8908; *www.governorsinnaustin.com*), a Neo-Classical Vic-torian Inn and a member of Historic and Hospitality Accomodations of Texas; Carriage House Inn (1110 West 22½ Street; 512–472–2333/866–472–2333; *www.carriagehouseinn.org*), a restored, two-story wooden Colonial home close to downtown; and Barton Creek Resort and Country Club (8212 Barton Club Drive; 512–329–4000/800–336–6158; *www.bartoncreek.com*), nestled within 4,000 secluded acres of rolling hills providing sweeping views of the Austin country-side, which offers a luxury spa and championship golf course.

For More Information

Gay & Lesbian Centers

Austin Gay and Lesbian Chamber of
Commerce
P.O. Box 49976
Austin, TX 78713
512–474–4422
www.aglcc.org

Austin Latino Lesbian and Gay
Organization (ALLGO)
701 Tillery Street
Austin, TX 78702
512–472–2001
www.allgo.org

Publications

Austin American-Statesman
P.O. Box 670
Austin, TX 78767
512–445–3500
www.statesman.com

The Daily Texan
P.O. Box D
Austin, TX 78713
512–471–4591
www.dailytexanonline.com

Texas Triangle
611 W. 6th Street
Austin, TX 78702
512–476–0576
www.txtriangle.com

SHOUT Magazine
500 South Congress, Suite 340
Austin, TX 78704
512–320–8678
www.shouttexas.com

Convention and Visitors Bureau

Austin Convention and Visitors
Bureau
301 Congress Avenue, Suite 200
Austin, TX 78701
512–472–5171/800–926–2282
www.austintexas.org

Chambers of Commerce

Austin Gay & Lesbian Chamber of
Commerce
P.O. Box 49976
Austin, TX 78765
512–474–4422
www.aglcc.org

Greater Austin Chamber of
Commerce
210 Barton Springs Road, Suite 400
Austin, TX 78704
512–478–9383
www.austin-chamber.org

Realtor

Bill Evans
Realtor-Broker
Austin REAL Pros, REALTORS
1310 South First Street, Suite 100
Austin, TX 78704-3060
512–458–3730
www.billevans.com

44 ▶ Bellaire, Texas

A Look at Bellaire

Bellaire was founded in 1908 as the Home Rule City. Four miles southwest of Houston, this small community offers the perfect combination of quiet, small-town America and the convenience of big city attractions. Local community members take pride in their city, enjoying annual celebrations such as Christmas with "snow" in the park and a 4th of July parade that's classic small-town America. The community also takes great pride in Bellaire High School. This flagship school of the Houston Independent School District consistently graduates high numbers of National Merit Finalists. It's a magnet school for foreign languages and is known for both its International Baccalaureate Program and for producing state-champion baseball teams. Houston's Southwest region has 13 unique neighborhoods, but many share similar qualities making for wonderful places to live. Major shopping and entertainment venues, including the Galleria, Reliant Center, Six Flags over Texas, and other amenities, mix with history, charm, and neighborly ties of the Southwest Houston communities to create a top-tier quality of life. The charms of Bellaire are enhanced by easy access to Houston, with world-class arts and entertainment, professional sports teams, exceptional medical care, more than a dozen colleges and universities, and expanding job and business opportunities.

Possible drawbacks: Property in Bellaire is expensive. Temperatures exceed 90 degrees almost a third of the year, the humidity can be quite high, and the area receives more rain than the Pacific Northwest.

▶ Nickname:
Home Rule City

▶ County: Harris

▶ Area code:
713

▶ Time zone:
Central (no DST)

▶ Population:
15,642

▶ County population:
3,400,578

▶ Region:
Southeast Texas

▶ Closest metro area:
Houston

▶ Average home price:
$518,000

▶ Fabulous reasons to live here:
High-tech economy, arts, culture, museums, nightlife, entertainment, recreation, excellent education, no income tax, large GLBT community

Climate

Elevation 40'	Avg. high/low(F°)	Avg. inches		Avg. # days precip.	Avg. % humidity
		rain	snow		
Jan.	62/43	4.3	0.2	10	76%
April	79/59	3.6	–	7	76%
July	93/74	3.6	–	9	77%
Oct.	81/60	4.0	–	8	76%
YEAR	79/59	52.9	0.4	104	77%
# days 32° or below: 12			# days 90° or warmer: 99		

Local Connections

Gas company: Centerpoint Energy (713–659–2111/800–752–8036; *www.centerpointenergy.com*)

Electric company: Texas offers consumers electric choice (Texas Electric Choice; 866–797–4839; *www.powertochoose.org*) and more than 20 service providers for the state.

Phone company: SBC Communications (888–294–8433; *www.sbc.com*)

Water and sewer: City of Bellaire Public Works (713–662–8170; *www.ci.bellaire.tx.us*)

Cable company: Time Warner Cable (713–341–1000/888–750–7890; *www.timewarnercable.com/Houston*)

Car registration/License: Texas Department of Transportation (512–424–2600 (license]/512–416–4800 [registration]); *www.dot.state.tx.us*

If you surrender a valid out-of-state driver's license, the only exam required is the vision test to get a Texas driver's license. Fee: $24 (good for six years). (License: 512–424–2600 *www.txdps.state.tx.us*). Registration fees include a county fee ($11.50) and a weight and model year fee (starting at $41).

The Tax Ax

Sales tax: 6.25 percent

State income tax: No personal income tax in Texas

Property tax: Harris County Tax Office (713–368–2000; *www.tax.co.harris.tx.us*)

Property taxes on all real and income-producing tangible personal property. Rates can change yearly. The current mil levy is 2.82125 per $100 of valuation.

Local Real Estate

Overview: The 6,000 homes in Bellaire are a mixture of 1950s and 1960s two- and three-bedroom ranch styles and brand new Georgian brick and Mediterranean stucco mansions. The practice of teardowns—replacing old frame and brick bungalows with new, larger construction—is common in Bellaire.

Median price for a single-family home: $457,000

Average price for a single-family home: $518,000

Average price for a 2BR condo: $207,000

Rental housing market: The average rent for a two-bedroom apartment is $1,150.

Gay-friendly neighborhoods: All of Bellaire is gay-friendly.

Nearby areas to consider: The Montrose district is the GLBT epicenter of Houston and a popular neighborhood for the GLBT community. Housing demand is high in Meyerland, a Houston neighborhood straddling Brays Bayou. The northeast corner of the community includes the redeveloped Meyerland Center retail development, and many institutions of Houston's Jewish community are found here, including several temples and the Jewish Community Center. The Houston neighborhood of Westbury, centered around Westbury Square with its winding pedestrian streets built in 19th-century style and lined with interesting shops, is popular with the GLBT community because of affordable housing and the neighborhood's eclectic style.

Earning a Living

Per capita income: $46,674

Median household income: $104,200

Business climate: Bellaire has recently experienced a large residential growth and commercial property revitalization. The city's proximity to Houston, home to 17 Fortune 500 Companies and ranked by *Popular Science* as one of the top 10 tech cities in the nation, offers a wealth of business opportunities. Houston offers a variety of incentives to new and expanding businesses, including property tax abatements, franchise tax refunds, and job training funds.

Help in starting a business: The Southwest Houston Chamber of Commerce serves the dozen smaller communities and cities of Southwest Houston by connecting business and community through networking, leadership training, and special events; the Greater Houston Gay & Lesbian Chamber of Commerce is an organization of broad-based members advocating the economic and cultural development of the GLBT community and supporting businesses. The Greater Houston Partnership (*www.houston.org*) provides resources, networking, and advocacy for the entire Houston market.

Job market: Industries providing employment in Bellaire include educational, health, and social services; and professional, scientific, management, administrative, and waste management services.

The Community

Overview: Bellaire is a popular city for GLBT nesters in the Houston area. Because of this popularity, a majority of local businesses fly the rainbow flag, and the local elected officials are supportive and often members of the GLBT community. Additionally, the city of Houston and the surrounding communities are among the nation's most gay-friendly areas. The Greater Houston area is an easy place to be out, as witnessed by many gay elected and appointed officials and hundreds of GLBT groups, organizations, and businesses that serve metro Houston's large and active GLBT community. Additionally, there's a growing trend in the city for "straight" businesses to fly rainbow flags and support the community through special events. *The Gay & Lesbian Rainbow Pages* (*www.rainbowpages.net*) provides a high-quality, full-color glossy, timely, and comprehensive directory of the area's gay and gay-friendly businesses and services.

Community organizations: The offices of Greater Houston's Gay & Lesbian Chamber of Commerce (*www.ghglcc.org*) are located in Bellaire, and the Bellaire Democrats (*www.bellairecemocrats.org*) continually strive for GLBT equal rights. In addition, there are several hundred GLBT recreation, support, service, political, and spiritual groups and organizations in the greater Houston area. The Houston GLBT Community Center hosts more than 30 meetings and events each month for the GLBT community and provides referrals between Houston's GLBT community and area businesses, groups, and services. The Gay & Lesbian Switchboard (713–526–4367; *www.gayswitchboardhouston.org*) also provides information and referrals for the Houston area. After Hours (*www.afterhours.org*), a late-night radio variety show, provides a permanent voice for the various GLBT communities with its varied co-hosts. Features include a News and Views segment and music by GLBT artists throughout the show; airs Saturdays from 1 to 3 a.m. on KPFT 90.1 FM.

Medical care: More than 100 hospitals and medical centers serve the region. Houston is home to the world-famous Texas Medical Center (713–791–6161; *www.tmc.edu*) as well as a sophisticated network of large and small community hospital systems that provide excellent family healthcare, cardiac care, cancer research and therapy, trauma care, and innovative treatments in hundreds of specialties. Bayou City Medical Center (713–774–7611; *www.bayoucitymedicalcenter.com*) provides community-based inpatient and outpatient care with 526 beds and more than 700 physicians on staff. Many medical and surgical services are here: cardiology, obstetrics, neonatology, pediatrics, orthopedics, physical therapy and rehabilitation, psychiatry, and infectious diseases. Memorial Hermann (713–222–2273; *www.memorialhermann.org*) operates acute-care hospitals for adults and children; a heart and vascular institute; three long-term, acute-care hospitals; a retirement community, an assisted living center, and two nursing homes; a medically based Wellness Center; rehabilitation and home health programs; and several convenient and freestanding outpatient imaging centers.

Nuptials: The State of Texas has a law similar to DOMA defining marriage as between a man and a woman. The State doesn't acknowledge same-sex marriages from other jurisdictions. Most area employers, including the City of Houston, extend benefits to domestic partners.

Getting Around Town

Public transportation: METRO (713–635–4000; *www.ridemetro.org*), Houston's city transit system, offers area wide bus and Express Shuttle Service. Fares: local $1; commuter (zone-based) $1.50–3.50; one-day pass $2. METRORail line connects Houston's major cultural and entertainment centers. Fares: single ride $1; all-day pass $2. The Trolley services in downtown Houston are free.

Roads: I-10, I-45, I-610, US59, US90, SR288

Airports: George Bush Intercontinental Airport (airport code: IAH) (281–230–3000) is presently served by 23 passenger airlines, and William P. Hobby Airport (airport code: HOU) (713–640–3000) is the largest hub airport for Southwest Airlines.

It's a Gay Life

Annual events: Pride Houston (*www.pridehouston.org*) sponsors the AIDS Walk in March and the Houston Gay Pride Festival and Parade in late June. The City of Bellaire sponsors the Fall Arts and Crafts Festival (*www.gswhcc.org*), Faire in Bellaire (*www.gswhcc.org*), Bayou City Art Festivals (*www.bayoucityartfestival.com*), and Holiday in the Park-Bellaire (*www.gswhcc.org*). The greater Houston area provides many more annual events and festivals, including the Houston International Festival (*www.ifest.org*), Houston Livestock Show and Rodeo (*www.rodeohouston.com*), and Juneteenth (*www.juneteenth.com*), a holiday unique to Texas celebrating June 19th, the day in 1863 when word finally reached Texas that President Lincoln had signed the Emancipation Proclamation.

Nightlife: Main Street is Houston's entertainment district, with street cafes and live music. Each weekend, four blocks between Congress and Capitol are closed to traffic to accommodate Houston's biggest street party: The Main Event! The bars and restaurants that line Main Street make way for live entertainment, street performers, and laser light shows. Also downtown, the Bayou Place entertainment complex (500 Texas Avenue; 713–221–8883) offers restaurants, bars, and entertainment venues including the Verizon Wireless Theater (520 Texas Avenue; 713–230–1600; *www.verizonwirelesstheater.com*) and the eight-screen Angelika Theater (500 Texas Avenue; 713–225–5232; *www.angelikafilmcenter.com/houston*). Other nightlife hot spots include Rice Village and Richmond Avenue. In larger-than-life Texas style, Houston caters to the GLBT community with 30 bars and 15 restaurants. Visit the community bookshop Lobo-Houston (3939 Montrose Boulevard; 713–522–5156; *www.lobobookshop.com*) and pick up *Houston Voice* (*www.houstonvoice.com*), *OutSmart* (*www.outsmartmagazine.com*), and *Texas Triangle* (*www.txtriangle.com*) for the latest GLBT listings and events.

Culture: Houston is one of five cities in the United States with permanent professional resident companies in the four disciplines of the performing arts: Houston Ballet (713–523–6300; *www.houstonballet.org*), Houston Grand Opera (713–228–6737; *www.houstongrandopera.org*), Houston Symphony (713–224–7575; *www.houstonsymphony.org*), and Alley Theatre (615 Texas Avenue; 713–228–8421; *www.alleytheatre.org*). All troupes have enjoyed international acclaim and prestige, including Grammy, Emmy, and Tony awards. Houston's Theater District (*www.houstontheaterdistrict.org*), a 17-block area in the heart of downtown Houston, is home to eight world-class performing arts organizations, the 130,000-square-foot Bayou Place entertainment complex, restaurants, movies, plazas, and parks. Houston boasts the fourth-largest museum district in the country, with landmark museums such as the Museum of Fine Arts, Houston (1001 Bissonnet Street; 713–639–7300; *www.mfah.org*) and the Houston Museum of Natural Science (1 Hermann Circle Drive; 713–639–4629; *www.hmns.org*) as part of the 15-institution district. Visitors to the Museum District can view one of only two Rembrandt paintings in Texas, one of the most highly renowned Surrealist collections in the country, the top collection of gems and minerals in the world, and a 7,400-square-foot model of the human body.

Recreation: The Bellaire Parks and Recreation Department (713–662–8280; *www.ci.bellaire.tx.us*) maintains 41+ acres of passive and active park areas, three community pools and the area's first dog park. The department also sponsors events and sports leagues in the city. Houston's Six Flags AstroWorld (9001 Kirby Drive; 713–799–1234; *www.sixflags.com*) and Space Center Houston (1601 NASA Road 1; 281–244–2100; *www.spacecenter.org*) are full of adventure. Explore the world's oceans from inside Moody Gardens' 12-story Aquarium Pyramid (1 Hope Boulevard, Galveston; 800–582–4673; *www.moodygardens.com*) then appreciate science and nature in the Rainforest and Discovery Pyramids. Visit Traders Village (7979 N. Eldridge Road; 281–890–5500; *www.tradersvillage.com*) on the weekends for food, fun, and great finds from more than 800 vendors. Golfers have 963 holes to discover in the greater Houston area. For history buffs, visit the San Jacinto Battleground Complex (1 Monument Circle; 281–479–2421; *www.sanjacinto-museum.org*), which marks the spot where Texas won its independence from Mexico, or the Lone Star Flight Museum (2002 Terminal Drive, Galveston; 409–740–7722; *www.lsfm.org*), a large collection of restored aircraft and photo archives housed in an aircraft hanger. There's plenty for spectators, including MLB's Houston Astros (713–259–8000; *www.astros.com*), the NBA's Houston Rockets (713–627–DUNK; *www.nba.com/rockets*), the horses at Sam Houston Race Park (7575 N. Sam Houston Parkway W.; 281–807–8700; *www.shrp.com*), or greyhounds at the Gulf Greyhound Park (1000 Fm 2004 Road; 409–986–9500; *www.gulfgreyhound.com*).

For the Visitor

Accommodations: With 55,000 rooms in the Greater Houston area, the city welcomes visitors with comfortable accommodations in every category, from elegant Houston hotels to affordable family inns and charming bed and breakfasts. A few of the popular, gay-friendly options include: Patrician Bed & Breakfast Inn (1200 Southmore Boulevard; 713–523–1114; *www.texasbnb.com*), located near downtown Houston and in the museum district, a 1919 Colonial Revival style mansion; the Lovett Inn (501 Lovett Boulevard; 713–522–5224/800–779–5224; *www.lovettinn.com*), located on a tree-lined boulevard in the Montrose-Museum District, a gracious 1923 Colonial-style home built by former Houston Mayor and Federal Judge Joseph C. Hutcheson; gay-owned and -operated Gar-Den Suites (2702 Crocker Street; 713–528–2302; *www.gar-densuites.com*), located in the heart of Montrose, which offers a heated swimming pool, a hot tub/spa, and a sun deck and private patios, all in a clothing-optional atmosphere.

For More Information

Gay & Lesbian Center
Houston GLBT Community Center
3400 Montrose Boulevard, Suite 207
Houston, TX 77006
713–524–3818
www.houstonglbtcommunitycenter.org

Publications
Houston Chronicle
801 Texas Street
Houston, TX 77002
713–220–7171
www.chron.com

Out Smart
3406 Audubon Place
Houston, TX 77006
713–520–7237
www.outsmartmagazine.com

Convention and Visitors Bureau
Greater Houston Convention and
Visitors Bureau
801 Congress Avenue
Houston, TX 77002
713–227–3100
www.houston-guide.com

Chambers of Commerce
Greater Southwest Houston Chamber
of Commerce
P.O. Box 788
Bellaire, TX 77402-0788
713–666–1521
www.gswhcc.org

Greater Houston Gay & Lesbian
Chamber of Commerce
P.O. Box 66129
Houston, TX 77266
713–523–7576
www.ghglcc.org

Realtor
Mike Copenhaver
Broker Associate
RE/MAX Metro
2626 Richmond Avenue
Houston, TX 77098
888–920–MIKE
www.mikecopenhaver.com

45 ▶ Dallas, Texas

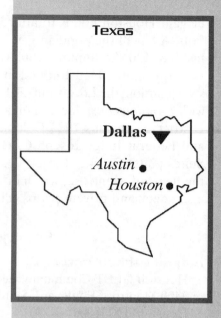

Texas

Dallas ▼

Austin ●

Houston ●

A Look at Dallas

Alive with energy and rich in diversity, Dallas is a dynamic mix of imagination, talent, and first-class attractions that make it a world-class city. Home to a vibrant economy, beautiful surroundings, and a population full of optimism and spirit, it's no wonder that Dallas is a popular international destination. Over the next decade, Downtown Dallas's Trinity River and its surrounding parks and forests will be transformed into an environmentally sensitive recreation and entertainment area. One highlight is a series of three planned sculptural bridges designed by Santiago Calatrava to span the river. The Dallas Arts District is the largest urban arts district in America, with the Nasher Sculpture Center, Crow Collection of Asian Art, the Dallas Museum of Art, and the Morton H. Meyerson Symphony, designed by I. M. Pei, as its cornerstones. Fair Park Dallas is a 277-acre national historic landmark with the largest collection of art deco building, nine museums, and home to the State Fair of Texas.

Possible drawbacks: The real estate boom of the 1990s brought the devastation of urban sprawl to greater Dallas. Endless, contemporary neighborhoods ring the city, and traffic congestion can give the area the feel of Los Angeles during rush hours.

▶ Nickname:
The Time of Your Life City

▶ County:
Dallas

▶ Area code: 214

▶ Time zone:
Central (no DST)

▶ Population:
1,188,580

▶ County population:
2,218,899

▶ Region:
Northeast Texas

▶ Average home price:
$167,000

▶ Fabulous reasons to live here:
High-tech economy; affordable housing; arts; culture; museums; nightlife; entertainment; recreation; no income tax; large, active GLBT community

Climate

Elevation 435'	Avg. high/low(F°)	Avg. inches rain	snow	Avg. # days precip.	Avg. % humidity
Jan.	52/36	2.0	1.1	7	71%
April	76/55	3.5	–	8	70%
July	96/76	2.4	–	5	66%
Oct.	78/57	4.6	–	6	70%
YEAR	70/56	37.5	2.6	81	70%
# days 32° or below: 25			# days 90° or warmer: 98		

Local Connections

Gas company: Atmos Energy (800–460–3030; *www.atmosenergy.com*)

Electric company: Texas offers consumers electric choice (Texas Electric Choice; 866–797–4839; *www.powertochoose.org*) and more than 20 service providers for the state.

Phone company: SBC Communications (888–294–8433; *www.sbc.com*)

Water and sewer: Dallas Water Utilities (214–651–1441; *www.dallascityhall.com*)

Cable company: Comcast (800–COMCAST; *www.comcast.com*)

Car registration/License: Texas Department of Transportation (512–424–2600 ([icense]/512–416–4800 [registration]); *www.dot.state.tx.us*

If you surrender a valid out-of-state driver's license the only exam required is the vision test to get a Texas driver's license. Fee: $24 (good for six years). (License: 512–424–2600 *www.txdps.state.tx.us*). Registration fees include a county fee ($11.50) and a weight and model year fee (starting at $41).

The Tax Ax

Sales tax: 6.25 percent

State income tax: No personal income tax in Texas

Property tax: Dallas Central Appraisal District (214–631–0910; *www.dallascad.org*)

Local taxing units (counties, cities, and school districts) assess and collect property taxes on all real and income-producing tangible personal property not exempt by state or federal law. Total tax rates vary from location to location and may change from year to year.

Local Real Estate

Overview: Energy and investment have returned to the historic Main Street core of downtown Dallas with new loft apartments and condominiums, retail, and entertainment. Home prices in Dallas are currently affordable and range in style from contemporary to Tudor. Most homes in the Dallas area are built on a standard 70 × 120 foot lot, but larger, luxury-estate homes are also plentiful.

Median price for a single-family home: $200,000

Average price for a single-family home: $167,000

Average price for a 2BR condo: $150,000

Rental housing market: The rental market is strong, solid, and affordable, with rentals currently averaging $800 per month.

Gay-friendly neighborhoods: Loryland, Oak Lawn, Uptown, North Dallas, East Dallas, and Oak Cliff

Nearby areas to consider: About 16 miles north of Dallas is the city of Carrollton. With a progressive city government, easy commute to the amenities of Dallas, affordable housing, extensive city services and family orientation, Carrollton attracts much of the area's GLBT community. But, this isn't a small, Dallas bedroom community: Carrollton, at more than 110,000 residents, offers its own fine collection of parks and recreation opportunities and attracts a large artist's community because of many cultural groups and institutions, such as the Repertory Dance Theatre of Texas, Carrollton Wind Symphony, and the Plaza Art Center with its fine art gallery.

Earning a Living

Per capita income: $22,183

Median household income: $37,628

Business climate: Dallas–Ft. Worth Metroplex has a highly educated, young talent pool. The area is home to 17 Fortune 500 Companies, and the Millken Institute ranks the Metroplex as the nation's second-most-influential technology sector. The Greater Dallas Chamber of Commerce reports that numerous financial incentives are available for businesses including tax abatements, fee rebates, enterprise zones, freeport tax exemptions, foreign trade zones, and expedited permitting.

Help in starting a business: The Greater Dallas Chamber of Commerce promotes the prosperity of the region through marketing, business expansion, and relocation; develops and advocates public policy positions on key issues that affect the business community; and enhances business growth and development by providing targeted quality services and programs. Stonewall Business & Professional Association (SBPA) provides networking opportunities among the gay and lesbian community while working to promote a positive image of the gay and lesbian business and professional community. Additionally, SBPA addresses workplace and human rights issues though education programs.

Job market: The Dallas Business Journal (*www.amcity.com/dallas*) has the latest news on the Dallas market. Current major market sector employment in the Metroplex region comes from professional, scientific, management, administrative, and waste management services; educational, health, and social services; retail trade; and manufacturing.

The Community

Overview: The Dallas GLBT community is large and active. Hundreds of groups and organizations provide social, health, support, and recreational opportunities. Plentiful high-tech and creative jobs, affordable housing, a lively nightlife, an art-filled community, and supportive government all create the foundation for this progressive and fun GLBT community.

Community organizations: The Resource Center of Dallas creates awareness, fosters understanding, and fulfills the needs of the gay and lesbian community through education, health, and social programs that are available to all people. The Resource Center operates the John Thomas Gay & Lesbian Community Center, the AIDS Resource Center, and the Nelson-Tebedo Health Resource Center. Two helpful Dallas resources include the Gay & Lesbian Switchboard (214–528–0022) and the Community Referral Network (214–528–9254) connecting community members with referrals for professional services, AIDS service organization, community groups, and gay-owned or gay friendly-businesses. The Referral Network also provides information on points of interest to the gay or lesbian traveler visiting Dallas/Fort Worth and contact information for the hundreds of groups and organizations within the community.

Medical care: Just two of the 26 Metroplex area hospitals are Parkland Health & Hospital System and Presbyterian Hospital of Dallas. Parkland Health & Hospital System (214–590–8000; *www.parklandhospital.com*) is often rated among the best hospitals in the United States. Home to world-renowned specialties and groundbreaking technology, many of Parkland's specialty areas have garnered national praise for excellence in care, research, and technological innovation. As the area's only Level 1 Trauma Center, Parkland is equipped to treat any injury related to trauma. Presbyterian Hospital of Dallas (214–345–6789; *www.texashealth.org*) is an 897-bed hospital located just north of downtown Dallas and a community-based hospital serving as a referral center for North and East Texas. There are more than 1,200 physicians on Presbyterian's medical staff offering a full range of care including services for cancer, cardiovascular problems, neuroscience needs, orthopedics, senior care, and women's services.

Nuptials: The State of Texas has a law similar to DOMA defining marriage as between a man and a woman. The State doesn't acknowledge same-sex marriages from other jurisdictions. Most area employers, including the City of Dallas, extend benefits to domestic partners.

Getting Around Town

Public transportation: Dallas Area Rapid Transit (DART) (214–979–1111; *www.dart.org*) provides light-rail, bus, and commuter van services. The historic McKinney Avenue Trolley and DART's trolley buses provide free rides from downtown's West End up to the West Village in uptown. Local fares: bus $1.25; bus and rail day pass $2.50. Premium fares: bus and rail $2.25; day pass $4.50. Day passes are good until 3 a.m.

Roads: I-20, I-30, I-35, I-45, SR67, SR75, SR80

Airports: The City of Dallas operates two municipal airports and a downtown heliport. Dallas Love Field Airport (airport code: DAL) (214–670–6073; *www.dallas-lovefield.com*) is a Southwest Airlines hub with daily flights to Texas, Oklahoma, New Mexico, and Louisiana cities; Dallas Fort Worth International Airport (airport code: DFW) (972–574–8888; *www.dfwairport.com*) offers 28 international non-stop locations served daily by 60 flights.

It's a Gay Life

Annual events: The Dallas Tavern Guild sponsors community events throughout the year and a GLBT parade the last weekend in September, to commemorate a local gay rights movement victory. It corresponds with an unofficial "Gay Day" at Six Flags (*www.sixflags.com*). Dallas Razzle Dazzle (*www.razzledazzledallas.org*) plans community AIDS fundraisers throughout the year. CityArts Celebration (*www.dallascityarts.com*), the Dallas Guitar Show and MusicFest (*www.guitarshow.com*), and Savor Dallas (*www.savordallas.com*) are just a few of the more than 2,000 events scheduled in and around Dallas annually including sporting events, art shows, and special events. For a complete events calendar updated daily, go to *www.dallascvb.com/media/events.php*.

Nightlife: A turn-of-the-century warehouse district in Downtown, West End is the popular site of more than 80 restaurants, shops, and nightclubs. The Oak Lawn area is the center of GLBT life in Dallas. In the middle of the many gay bars, restaurants, galleries, and shops catering to the Dallas GLBT community along Cedar Springs Avenue is Crossroads Market Bookstore & Café (2920 Cedar Springs Road; 214–521–8919). Stop in and pick up *Dallas Voice* (*www.dallasvoice.com*) and *Texas Triangle* (*www.txtriangle.com*). These publications have extensive listings of area clubs and events and cover local GLBT community news.

Culture: Dallas's Arts District (214–953–1977; *www.artsdistrict.org*) is the largest urban arts district in the nation, with the Dallas Museum of Art (1717 N. Harwood; 214–922–1803; *www.dallasmuseumofart.org*), the Crow Collection of Asian Art (2010 Flora Street; 214–979–6430; *www.crowcollection.org*), the Morton H. Meyerson Symphony Center (2301 Flora Street; 214–670–3600; *www.meyersonsymphonycenter.com*), and Nasher Sculpture Center (2001 Flora Street; 214–242–5100; *www.nashersculpturecenter.org*). Uptown offers three shopping districts; 30 boutique shops, galleries, and antique stores located within walking distance; 70 restaurants; and a wealth of Dallas history. West Village (469–547–9650; *www.westvil.com*) is a new mixture of lofts, flats, stylish merchants, dining, and a five-screen art film house on narrow European streets at McKinney and Lemmon avenues. Mockingbird Station is a new and lively multi-use development featuring residential lofts above shops, restaurants, and the Angelika Theater (5321 Mockingbird Lane; 214–841–4700; *www.angelikafilmcenter.com*). A few blocks west on Mockingbird Lane is Southern Methodist University, home of Meadows Museum of Art (5900 Bishop Boulevard; 214–768–2516; *www.meadowsmuseumdallas.org*), one of the largest collections of Spanish art outside Spain. The Sixth Floor Museum at Dealey Plaza (411 Elm Street; 214–747–6660; *www.jfk.org*), honoring the life, legacy, and untimely death of President John F. Kennedy, is one of the most-visited sites in Dallas and frequently hosts special exhibits on its newly finished seventh floor. Three blocks east of Downtown is Deep Ellum (*www.deepellumtx.com*), a Blues and jazz center in the early 1900s that has blossomed into an avant-garde district of shops, cafes, galleries, theaters, restaurants, and bars nestled in an old warehouse district. Popular by day for business lunches and bustling until the early morning hours with diners and club "hoppers," Deep Ellum provides one-of-a-kind dining, theater, and entertainment, with a wide variety of live music on the weekends.

Recreation: The Dallas Park and Recreation Department (214–670–4100; *www.dallascityhall.com*) maintains more than 21,000 park acres, including 17 lakes, 17,196 acres of greenbelt and park land, and 61 miles of jogging and bike trails at 24 locations. Dallas has more than 100 public and private golf courses and hosts the EDS Bryon Nelson Championship (*www.pgatour.com*) every May. At Dallas World Aquarium (1801 N. Griffin Street; 214–720–2224; *www.dwazoo.com*) in downtown Dallas, you can walk through a 22,000-gallon tunnel experiencing a panoramic view of reef life. The aquarium features more than 85,000 gallons of saltwater with marine life from around the world. Minutes from Downtown to the east, White Rock Lake (*www.whitrocklake.org*) features a scenic park with 9 miles of running, biking, and walking trails as well as sailing and various picnic and leisure activities. On the shores of White Rock Lake, Dallas Arboretum (8525 Garland Drive; 214–515–6500; *www.dallasarboretum.org*) features 66 acres with 11 lush display gardens that offer seasonal color all year long. Six professional sports teams provide year-round variety in football, arena football, basketball, hockey, soccer, and baseball. The American Airlines Center (2500 Victory Avenue; 214–665–4216; *www.americanairlinescenter.com*), home of the NHL's Dallas Stars (214–387–5500; *www.dallasstars.com*) ice hockey and the NBA's Dallas Mavericks (214–747–MAVS; *www.nba.com/mavericks*) basketball teams, is a popular venue bridging Uptown and the West End entertainment districts and offers a full calendar of sports, rodeos, and concerts.

For the Visitor

Accommodations: The area's current inventory of more than 70,000 hotel rooms offers luxury to budget accommodations. In the gay-friendly epicenter of

Oakland, the Melrose (2015 Oak Lawn Avenue; 214–521–5151/800–635–7673; *www.melrosehoteldallas.com*) is a historic Dallas landmark offering 184 luxury guest rooms including 21 suites and a presidential suite, each with a dramatic view of the city. At White Rock Lake, the Courtyard on the Trail (8045 Forest Trail; 214–553–6700; *www.courtyardonthetrail.com*) has antique furnishings in a beautiful, private setting. Holiday Inn Select Dallas Central (10650 N. Central Expressway; 214–373–6000/888–477–7829; *www.sixcontinentshotels.com*) is a first-class, full-service hotel known for Texas-friendly service and a host of special amenities.

For More Information

Gay & Lesbian Center

John Thomas Gay & Lesbian Community Center Resource Center of Dallas P.O. Box 190869 Dallas, TX 75219 214–528–0144 *www.resourcecenterdallas.org*

Publications

Dallas Morning News P.O. Box 655237 Dallas, TX 75265 214–977–8222 *www.dallasnews.com*

Dallas Business Journal 10670 N. Central Expressway, Suite 710 Dallas, TX 75231 214–696–5959 *www.amcity.com/dallas*

Convention and Visitors Bureau

Dallas Convention and Visitors Bureau 325 North St. Paul Street, Suite 700 Dallas, TX 75201 214–571–1000 *www.dallascvb.com*

Chambers of Commerce

Greater Dallas Chamber of Commerce 700 North Pearl Street, Suite 1200 Dallas, TX 75201 214–746–6600 *www.dallaschamber.org*

Stonewall Business & Professional Association P.O. Box 191343 Dallas, TX 75219 214–521–5342 *www.stonewall-dallas.org*

Realtor

Lory Masters CRB, CRS, e-PRO, GRI Master Realtors, Inc. 4235 Cedar Springs Road Dallas, TX 75219 214–902–9999/877–GAY–RELO *www.lorymasters.com*

46 ▶ Burlington, Vermont

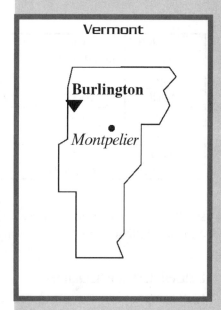

Vermont

Burlington
▼
Montpelier

A Look at Burlington

The city of Burlington, built on a hillside overlooking the lake, has a cosmopolitan flair that is complemented by one of the lowest crime rates and best air-quality measures in the nation. The region boasts excellent dining, diverse cultural events, bountiful shopping, and plentiful outdoor adventure and recreational activities in an unparalleled landscape. Lake Champlain, often called the sixth Great Lake, stretches for more than 120 miles between Vermont, New York, and Quebec. In concert with the rugged Adirondack Mountains and beautiful Green Mountains that surround it, the lake sets the stage for outdoor festivals, historic exploration, and everything from swimming, sailing, and fishing, to hiking, mountain biking, and skiing. Its mountain backdrop is one of the reasons that author and world-traveler Rudyard Kipling said Lake Champlain was one of the most spectacular places in the world to view a sunset. Burlington, Vermont, offers an outstanding quality of life that boasts a vibrant downtown with world-class shopping, restaurants, and cultural amenities, and a natural playground for outdoor activities such as golf, tennis, sailing, hiking, biking, and, of course, skiing. With its abundant festivals, events, attractions, and tremendous quality of life, Burlington and the Lake Champlain region are repeatedly recognized as one of America's most desirable places for living, working, and visiting.

Possible drawbacks: It's easy to feel a sense of isolation in Burlington because of the city's

▶ County:
Chittenden
▶ Area code:
802
▶ Time zone:
Eastern
▶ Population:
38,889
▶ County population:
146,571
▶ Region:
Northeast Vermont
▶ Closest metro area:
Schenectady, NY
▶ Average home price:
$280,000
▶ Fabulous reasons to live here:
Scenic beauty, small-town charm, fabulous recreation, affordable housing, excellent education, culture, arts, active GLBT community, strong economy

Climate

Elevation 113'	Avg. high/low(F°)	Avg. inches		Avg. # days precip.	Avg. % humidity
		rain	snow		
Jan.	27/8	2.2	19.3	15	68%
April	53/33	2.9	4.2	12	62%
July	81/60	3.9	–	12	65%
Oct.	57/39	3.2	0.2	12	70%
YEAR	55/35	36.6	78.8	155	67%
# days 32° or below: 108			# days 90° or warmer: 5		

small size and location. These feelings can increase in the winter months with almost 80 inches of snow. The city is overrun in the fall by leaf peepers.

Local Connections

Gas company: Vermont Gas Systems (802–863–4511; *www.vermontgas.com*)

Electric company: Burlington Electric Department (802–865–7300; *www.burlingtonelectric.com*)

Phone company: AT&T (802–658–9277; *www.att.com*)

Water and sewer: City of Burlington Department of Public Works (802–863–9094; *www.dpw.ci.burlington.vt.us*)

Cable company: Adelphia Cable (888–683–1000; *www.adelphia.com*)

Car registration/License: State of Vermont Department of Motor Vehicles (802–828–2000; *www.aot.state.vt.us/dmv*)

To obtain a license, Vermont law requires that out-of-state applicants must pass a vision test. The road and written tests may be waived by the examiner if the applicant holds a valid out-of-state license; however, the exam fee ($5) is still collected. Fee: four-year license $35; two-year license $23. Fee for any certificate of title, including a salvage certificate of title: $15. Registration fees are based on fuel type: gas $50; diesel $27; other fuels $86.75.

The Tax Ax

Sales tax: 6 percent; more than 40 exemptions include food, medicine, home fuels, clothes, and shoes

State income tax: 3.6–9.5 percent graduated, based on income

Property tax: Assessor (802–865–7114; *www.assessor.ci.burlington.vt.us*); Vermont Department of Taxes (*www.state.vt.us/tax*)

Property taxes support education and municipal services and vary based on school district and location of primary residence. The assessed property value is usually 80 percent of the fair market value.

Local Real Estate

Overview: Homes for urban, suburban, or rural preferences can be found ranging from the suburban ranch to stately Colonials and charming Vermont farmhouses. The most varied inventory of style is in Burlington proper. An economic hub in the 19th and most of the 20th centuries, there was housing stock created regularly at all economic levels. Suburban Burlington, comprised of scattered developments and large, single-family parcels, had intermittent construction periods over the last century. Characteristics such as location, size, acreage, views, and amenities will impact the price.

Median price for a single-family home: $265,000

Average price for a single-family home: $280,000

Average price for a 2BR condo: $190,000

Rental housing market: Average rent in Greater Burlington is $800 to $1200 monthly; however, there are always ex-college-student rental units popping up come June for less. Be sure to avoid electric heat; a cold winter month will cost approximately $500 in electricity.

Gay-friendly neighborhoods: The South End and the Hill section of Burlington plus many lake-front communities can be guaranteed to be gay-friendly, but the area's gay population is ever increasing and can be found everywhere.

Nearby areas to consider: Winooski, just across the Winooski River from Burlington, is a small city of just more than 6,000 residents. There's a large, visionary, downtown redevelopment underway that's attracting many GLBT entrepreneurs to the city. The city's comprehensive plan preserves many of the area's historic buildings, while creating a walking district environment and more than 100 acres of parkland. Bristol, 30 miles to the south, and Westord, 20 miles to the north, are two small, historic towns of approximately 3,000 residents each. These small communities are classic main street America and both are attracting the GLBT community because of their affordable, historic housing and small-town charms.

Earning a Living

Per capita income: $20,625

Median household income: $40,856

Business climate: The Lake Champlain Valley, easily reached by air, rail, car, and ferry, is Vermont's economic hub and home to more than a quarter of Vermont's population. Most businesses are "clean," small, and dispersed throughout various regions of the state. Four colleges and universities not only enrich the area's cultural and community life, but provide a well-educated workforce for several of the state's largest employers that call Burlington home.

Help in starting a business: If you're starting, growing, or relocating a business, the Vermont Department of Economic Development (802–828–3080;

www.thinkvermont.com) is the place to begin. The Vermont Small Business Development Center is another excellent organization for business development information (802–728–9101; *www.vtsbdc.org*).

Job market: Major market sectors providing employment are educational, health, and social services; retail trade; arts, entertainment, recreation, accommodation, and food services; and manufacturing.

The Community

Overview: The small town of Burlington has an active GLBT community. The university brings a large number of young people to the area, as does the State of Vermont's liberal politics. There's a strong sense of community bonds between the GLBT members, a high ratio of which are couples.

Community organizations: R.U.1.2? is Burlington's Gay Community Center addressing the social, cultural, educational, and health needs of Vermont's queer and allied communities across all races, ages, and genders through community building, social support, and civic engagement. Other GLBT organizations of note include Outright Vermont (802–865–9677) and Safespace (802–863–0003).

Medical care: Fletcher Allen Health Care (802–847–0000; *www.fahc.org*), a teaching-research-tertiary-care organization with 562 total beds and a medical staff of 590 physicians and 250 residents, is comprised of the Medical Center Hospital campus and University of Vermont Health Center campus in Burlington and the Fanny Allen Hospital campus in Colchester.

Nuptials: Vermont Secretary of State (*www.sec.state.vt.us*)

Parties to a civil union are given all the same benefits, protections, and responsibilities under Vermont law, whether they derive from statute, administrative, or court rule, policy, common law, or any other source of civil law, as are granted to spouses in a marriage. Non-Vermont residents may apply for a civil union in Vermont.

Getting Around Town

Public transportation: Chittenden County Transportation Authority (802–864–CCTA; *www.cctaride.org*) offers local bus service. Fares: one-way trip $1, monthly pass $33. Ferry service to New York is provided by Lake Champlain Ferries (802–864–9804; *www.ferries.com*).

Roads: I-89, US7

Airport: Burlington International Airport (airport code: BTV) (802–863–1889; *www.vermontairports.com*) serves nine airlines. Additionally, there are more than a dozen smaller public airports in Vermont.

It's a Gay Life

Annual events: Pride Vermont (*www.pridevermont.org*) sponsors the gay pride parade in Burlington in July. Art's Alive Annual Juried Festival of Fine Art (*www.artsalivevt.org*), Ben & Jerry's One World One Heart Festival (*www.benjerry.com*), Burlington Latino Festival Burlington (*www.hermanosproductions.com*), Lake Champlain International Fishing Derby (*www.lciderby.com*), Vermont Brewers Festival (*www.vermontbrewers.com*), Vermont International Film Festival (*www.vtiff.org*), and Vermont Maple Festival (*www.vtmaplefestival.org*) are just a few of the area's annual events.

Nightlife: Burlington and the region are home to more than 200 restaurants, serving cuisine for every imaginable taste from continental and seafood to a variety of ethnic foods, including Mexican, Chinese, Indian, Lebanese, Greek, Thai, and Cajun. No matter where one dines, the cost is a fraction of what's charged in big-city restaurants. Pubs, restaurants, and coffee houses offer up live jazz, rock, Blues, reggae, and folk. There aren't gay-specific bars and nightclubs in Burlington, but the city is very gay-friendly. Look for *Out in the Mountains* (*www.mountainpride.org*) and *In Newsweekly* (*www.innewsweekly.com*) for Vermont and New England events.

Culture: Flynn Theatre for the Performing Arts (153 Main Street; 802–652–4500; *www.flynncenter.org*) brings 100 live performances each year to the community. St. Michael's Playhouse (McCarthy Arts Center; 1 Winooski Park, Colchester; 802–654–2281; *academics.smcvt.edu/playhouse*) is Greater Burlington's professional actor's equity summer theater. The Vermont Symphony Orchestra (802–864–5741; *www.vso.org*) is a non-profit, membership-based organization that performs 45 to 50 full or chamber orchestra performances annually, as well as 100 ensemble or artist-in-residence performances. The Vermont Mozart Festival's (802–862–7352; *www.vtmozart.com*) summer concerts combine exceptional classical music with Vermont's exquisite natural beauty. It's Bourbon Street, Vermont style, during the Discover Jazz Festival (802–863–7992; *www,discoverjazz.com),* where the city comes alive with a week of small and large performances across the City. Champlain Islands is the summer home of Hermann's Royal Lipizzan Stallions of Austria (The Islands Center; 802–372–8400; *www.champlainislands.com*); a program of equestrian ballet is performed four times each week. Lyric Theatre of Burlington (802–658–1484; *www.lyrictheatrevt.org*) is community theater at its best to delight the whole family. The Vermont Stage Company (802–862–1497; *www.vtstage.org*) brings world-class theater to Vermont audiences. A few of Burlington's museums of note are the Shelburne Museum (5555 Shelburne Road; 802–985–3346; *www.shelburnemuseum.org*), Ethan Allen Homestead (1 Ethan Allen Homestead; 802–865–4556; *www.ethanallenhomestead.org*), ECHO at the Leahy Center for Lake Champlain (1 College Street; 802–864–1848; *www.echovermont.org*), Lake Champlain Maritime Museum at Basin Harbor (4472 Basin Harbor Road, Vergennes; 802–475–2022; *www.lcmm.org*), Birds of Vermont Museum (900 Sherman Hollow Road, Huntington; 802–434–2167; *www.birdsofvermont.org*), UVM's Fleming Museum (61 Colchester Avenue; 802–656–0750; *www.uvm.edu/ ~fleming*), and UVM's Francis Colburn Gallery (72 University Place; 802–656–2014; *www.uvm.edu/ ~artdept*).

Recreation: Lake Champlain provides 600 miles of beautiful shoreline and waterfront access, 70 islands, a dozen of the most popular angling species, and hundreds of historic submerged shipwrecks to explore. Lake Champlain Valley is a place of spectacular beauty and virtually unlimited summertime recreational opportunities, including kayaking, canoeing, fishing, sailing, windsurfing, waterskiing, swimming, and scuba diving. And in addition to Burlington, many smaller but equally welcoming and historic Vermont towns dot the Lake Champlain Region. Ice skating and ice fishing are popular winter activities. During the cold season there are plenty of indoor activities including tennis and racket sport facilitates, indoor swimming pools, bowling, and indoor ice and roller skating rinks. Covering approximately 9 miles on the Lake Champlain waterfront, the Burlington Bike Path offers fabulous recreational opportunities including walking, biking, jogging, and inline skating. The waterfront area is also home to the popular new Burlington Skate Park, designed for skateboarders, inline skaters, and BMX biking. Mountain and lake resort areas are readily accessible within 25 miles. The Northern spine of the Green Mountains is a short drive from the Burlington area, including such mountain peaks as Mount Mansfield (4,393 feett) and Camel's Hump (4,083 feet), offering multiple day hikes and overnight camping opportunities. An especially attractive feature of exploring Burlington and the region is that visitors needn't lug tons of gear from home and back. Local businesses rent everything from boats and bikes to in-line skates. And for those bent on acquiring new skills, qualified instructors teach everything from skiing and snowboarding to kayaking and scuba diving.

For the Visitor

Accommodations: With detailed descriptions of participating area hotels, motels, inns, and B&Bs, including amenities, price ranges, photos, and contact information, the Lake Champlain Regional Chamber of Commerce (*www.vermont.org*) provides online lodging search and booking capabilities. Residing 2,000 feet above the valley floor, the gay-owned Black Bear Inn (4010 Bolton Access Road; 800–395–6335; *www.blkbearinn.com*) offers the most panoramic views and sunsets in Vermont. The inn's 6,000 pristine private acres feature tennis courts, a crystal clear swimming pool, and miles of trails that are perfect for hiking, biking, nature tours, and horseback riding.

For More Information

Gay & Lesbian Center
R.U.1.2? Community Center Inc.
P.O. Box 5883
Burlington, VT 05402
802–860–7812
www.ru12.org

Publications
Burlington Free Press
P.O. Box 10
Burlington, VT 05402
802–863–3441
www.burlingtonfreepress.com

Publications

Seven Days
P.O. Box 1164
Burlington, VT 05402-1164
802–864–5684
www.sevendaysvt.com

Convention and Visitors Bureau

The Vermont Convention Bureau
60 Main Street, Suite 100
Burlington, VT 05401
877–264–3503
www.vermont.org

Chamber of Commerce

The Lake Champlain Chamber of
Commerce
60 Main Street, Suite 100
Burlington, VT 05401
802–863–3489/877–686–5253
www.vermont.org

Realtor

Marianne Callahan
Realtor
Lang Associates
550 Hinesburg Road
South Burlington, VT 05403
802–846–7840
www.langrealestate.com

Alexandria, Virginia

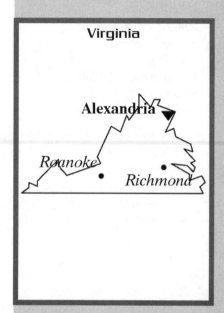

Virginia

Alexandria

Roanoke

Richmond

A Look at Alexandria

Founded in 1749 as a seaport, Alexandria, cosmopolitan yet friendly, is in the heart of the exciting Washington, DC, metro region. Alexandria was George Washington's hometown, and many early patriots spent time here, including George Mason and Thomas Jefferson, who celebrated his presidential inaugural in Alexandria. The esteemed Lees of Virginia were from here, and the most famous member—Civil War General Robert E. Lee— grew up here. From the late 18th through the mid-19th centuries, Alexandria was one of the nation's most important seaports as cargoes of tobacco, wheat, and sugar passed between the Colonies and Europe. America's Colonial seaports were known for elegance and cosmopolitan sophistication, drawing visitors from around the world. That tradition continues today throughout the Old Town historic district. The Colonial charm of 18th- and 19th-century America comes to life in the restored homes and shops throughout the city, and the preserved cobblestone streets and historic waterfront are only minutes away from Washington's majestic monuments. *Ladies Home Journal* named Alexandria the number-one city in its "Top 10 List of America's Best Cities for Women." The magazine's readers declared the yardsticks most important to them were the low-crime rate, followed by pleasant lifestyle, great public schools, plentiful job opportunities, and quality health- and childcare resources.

▶ Nickname:
The Fun Side of the Potomac

▶ County:
Alexandria City

▶ Area code: 703

▶ Time zone: Eastern

▶ Population:
128,283

▶ County population:
128,283

▶ Region:
Northeast Virginia

▶ Closest metro area:
Washington, DC

▶ Average home price:
$775,000

▶ Fabulous reasons to live here: History; architecture; beautiful setting; excellent location; music; culture; recreation; large, social GLBT community; strong, high-tech economy

Climate

Elevation 30'	Avg. high/low(F°)	Avg. inches rain	Avg. inches snow	Avg. # days precip.	Avg. % humidity
Jan.	42/26	3.3	5.5	10	63%
April	66/45	2.9	–	10	59%
July	88/69	3.8	–	10	64%
Oct.	68/48	3.3	–	7	67%
YEAR	60/47	40.7	16.6	112	64%
# days 32° or below: 75			# days 90° or warmer: 28		

Possible drawbacks: Location and excellent amenities have created a strong housing market for Alexandria, making it a very expensive Washington, DC, suburb. The city lacks the formal hub of a GLBT community center.

Local Connections

Gas company: Washington Gas (703–750–1000; *www.eservice.washgas.com*)

Electric company: Dominion Virginia Power (703–359–3300; *www.dom.com*)

Phone companies: AT&T (800–222–0300; *www.att.com*); Sprint (www.sprint.com); SBC (800–310–2355; *www.sbc.com*); Verizon (703–813–9600; *www.verizon.com*); among others

Water and sewer: Virginia-American Water Company (703–549–7080; *www.vawc.com*)

Cable company: Comcast (703–823–3000; *www.comcast.com*)

Car registration/License: Virginia Department of Motor Vehicles (866–368–5463; *www.dmv.state.va.us*)

You must obtain a Virginia driver's license within 60 days of relocating to the state. A valid out-of-state driver's license may waive the two-part knowledge exam and road skills test. Vision screening required. Licenses are valid five years. License fee: $4/year. Title fee: $10. The 3-percent motor vehicle sales and use tax based on the vehicle's sale price or $35. Your registration fee is determined by the empty weight or gross weight of your vehicle, the type of license plate you purchase, and if you register for one or two years. Passenger vehicle registration: 4,000 lbs. or less, $29.50; 4,001 lbs or more, $34.50.

The Tax Ax

Sales tax: 5 percent; prescription drugs and some foods exempt

State income tax: 2–5.75 percent bracketed, based on income

Property tax: Virginia Department of Taxation (804–367–8031; *www.tax.virginia.gov*)

The city of Alexandria bases property taxes on $1.00 per thousand of total assessed value. Assessed value is comprised of land and improvements (housing). The assessed value of property is different from the appraised value, as the appraised value is normally anywhere from 17–33 percent higher than the assessed value. The appraised value is what is normally consistent with the sales price of any particular home.

Local Real Estate

Overview: The housing selection in Alexandria is diverse. New and restored townhouses, modest semi-detached brick houses and bungalows, brick and frame Colonials, split-level and ranch-style homes in newer subdivisions, and charming old Victorians provide homebuyers with a broad range of options. The single-family homes found in Alexandria are normally located in Fairfax County.

Median price for a single-family home: $675,000

Average price for a single-family home: $775,000

Average price for a 2BR condo: $375,000

Rental housing market: Rentals for a two-bedroom range from $1,200 to $1,500 a month.

Gay-friendly neighborhoods: All of Alexandria is gay-friendly, and GLBT community members feel comfortable throughout the city.

Nearby areas to consider: Less than 20 miles south of Alexandria, in Prince William County, are Woodbridge and Lake Ridge. These two cities, of approximately 30,000 residents each, offer an easy commute to Alexandria and nearby Washington, DC. Prince William County has attracted a large, affluent GLBT community. In addition to 48 miles of shoreline and more than 50 parks and rich Civil War history, Prince William County offers a family-oriented, high quality of life that includes nationally recognized schools and pro-business policies.

Earning a Living

Per capita income: $37,645

Median household income: $56,054

Business climate: Alexandria is a thriving, historic, waterfront community. Good schools and low crime rates add to the area's high quality of life. The U.S. Department of Defense is the area's largest employer, providing a strong, constant economic base. The military influence creates a large number of high-tech opportunities. All of these factors combine to create a desirable location for small and large businesses.

Help in starting a business: The Alexandria Chamber of Commerce serves as the voice of business in the City of Alexandria through its aggressive lobbying efforts at the local, state, and federal levels. In addition, the Chamber offers a variety of programs and services to assist member firms in promoting and expanding their business base. The Alexandria Chamber is also proud to support the Alexandria Education Partnership and host the Alexandria Small Business Development Center.

Job market: Major markets providing employment include construction, manufacturing, transportation, communications, utilities, trade, finance, insurance, real estate, professional services, and, with its close proximity to Washington, DC, all levels of government.

The Community

Overview: Alexandria's location and historic charm have drawn a large GLBT community. Local government is supportive of the community, and there are many gay-owned businesses, especially in the Old Town district.

Community organizations: Alexandria is without a physical GLBT community center. The Alexandria Gay and Lesbian Community Association (Alexandria-GLCA) is a nonprofit, nonpartisan organization that strives to enhance the quality of life for the local GLBT community through social activities, political awareness, and community service.

Medical care: Inova Health System (*www.inova.org*) is a not-for-profit healthcare system based in Northern Virginia that consists of hospitals and other health services including emergency and urgent care centers, home care, nursing homes, mental health and blood donor services, and wellness classes. Two of its area hospitals include Inova Alexandria Hospital (703–504–3000; *www.inova.org*), a 339-bed community hospital that offers a full range of health care services and is dedicated to continually expanding its programs and services to help ensure the communities health care needs are met today and in the future, and Inova Mount Vernon Hospital (703–664–7000; *www.inova.org*), a 232-bed community hospital whose staff includes some of the area's most-respected physicians. Inova Mount Vernon Hospital is home to both the Inova Joint Replacement Center and the Inova Rehabilitation Center and provides a wide range of services, including cancer, emergency, psychiatric, cardiac rehabilitation, breast health, hyperbaric oxygen, wound healing, and dialysis care.

Nuptials: The State of Virginia has a law similar to DOMA defining marriage as between a man and a woman and doesn't honor same-sex marriages from other jurisdictions. Many area employers provide domestic partner benefits.

Getting Around Town

Public transportation: Washington Metropolitan Area Transit Authority (202–637–7000; *www.wmata.com*) operates buses and subway lines throughout the city. Metrobus fare: $1.25, unlimited day pass $3. Metrorail one-way fare: $1.35–3.90. The DASH bus system (703–370–3274; or *www.dashbus.com*) provides free weekend shuttle service and daily area connections. Base fare: $1; free transfers.

Roads: I-95, I-295, I-395, I-495, US1, SR7, SR236

Airports: Ronald Reagan Washington National Airport (airport code: DCA) (703–417–8000; *www.mwaa.com*), located just north of the city on the Potomac River, is only five to 10 minutes away from downtown Alexandria. Other nearby airports include Dulles International Airport (airport code: IAD) (703–572–2700; *www.mwaa.com*) and Baltimore-Washington International Airport (airport code: BWI) (410–859–7992; *www.bwiairport.com*).

It's a Gay Life

Annual events: Capital Pride (*www.capitalpride.org*) in Washington, DC, hosts 10 days of pride events and celebrations in June including a film festival, awards ceremonies, a parade, and a rally. Founded by Scottish businessmen in 1749, Alexandria celebrates this heritage with the annual Virginia Scottish Games (*www.vascottishgames.org*) in July and the Scottish Christmas Walk (*www.campagnacenter.org*) in early December. Alexandria hosts many historic garden and house tours throughout the year. The Festival of the Arts (*www.artfestival.com*) and Old Fashion Day (*oha.ci.Alexandria.va.us*) in September and Seaport Day (*www.alexandriaseaport.org*) in October are popular events in Alexandria.

Nightlife: From Colonial to Cajun, Alexandria offers a fabulous selection of wonderful restaurants and pubs. With more than 200 restaurant and pubs in a 15-block radius, there's something for everyone. Gadsby's Tavern (134 N. Royal Street; 703–838–4242; *www.gadsbystavern.org*) features Colonial-inspired regional cuisine, costumed waitstaff, and Colonial entertainment. Dessert is served in the museum ballroom, where you will enjoy 18th-century dancing, complete with musicians and your private dance master. American Heirloom Experience is a patriotic and inspiring evening that includes a private, elegant candlelight tour of George Washington's Mount Vernon Estate (3200 Mount Vernon Memorial Highway, Mount Vernon; 703–780–2000; *www.mountvernon.org*) and dinner at the charming Mount Vernon Inn (3200 Mount Vernon Memorial Highway, Mount Vernon; 703–780–0011; *www.mountvernon.org*). Colonial atmosphere and menus inspired by George and Martha make this a truly memorable event. Alexandria doesn't have a long list of GLBT bars and restaurants, but Washington, DC, just across the Potomac, provides three dozen community bars and clubs. Pick up copies of *Metro Weekly* (*www.metroweekly.com*) and the *Washington Blade* (*www.washblade.com*) for current events and listings.

Culture: Alexandria is home to the Alexandria Ballet (201 Prince Street; 703–584–0035; *www.nvfaa.org*) and Alexandria Symphony Orchestra (703–548–0885; *www.alexsym.org*). Several theaters offer live productions throughout the year, and the Alexandria Citizen Band (*www.band.alexandria.va.us*) presents concerts every Friday evening June–August in Market Square. The Alexandria Seaport Foundation (703–549–7078; *www.alexandriaseaport.org*) offers insight into the historical seaport industry. During Virginia's famous Garden Week (804–644–7776; *www.vagardenweek.org*) in April, several private homes and gardens, representing the city at its most elegant, are open. But, with its temperate climate and strong tradition of English-style gardening, the city is lovely many months of the year. River Farm, now operated as headquarters of the American Horticultural Society (7931 East Boulevard Drive; 703–768–5700; *www.ahs.org*); the exuberant gardens of Mount Vernon (3200 Mount Vernon Memorial Highway, Mount Vernon; 703–780–2000; *www.mountvernon.org*); and the 400-year-old boxwoods at Gunston Hall Plantation (10709 Gunston Road; 703–550–9220; *www.gunstonhall.org*) are among the city's fabulous garden tours. Explore the archaeology and history along the Alexandria Heritage Trail (703–838–4343; *www.ci.alexandria.va.us/recreation*), a unique 22-mile urban trail with more than 40 museums and historic parks open to the public. Home to the famed Torpedo Factory Art Center (105 N. Union Street; 703–838–4565; *www.torpedofactory.org*), Alexandria has been named one of the Top 25 Arts Destinations by *American Style* magazine, and *Arts & Antiques* called the city "Virginia's miracle mile." The seaport tradition of bounty continues with offerings ranging from French pottery to antique quilts to adorable children's wear. Antiques-lovers know to visit in March and November for two very special antiques shows.

Recreation: With the river as your companion, walk, bike, or jog the 18.5-mile Mount Vernon Trail from George Washington's Mount Vernon Estate & Gardens to Theodore Roosevelt Island. Along the way enjoy a view of the Potomac at Riverside Park, take a side trip to the Dyke Marsh wildlife habitat, or visit Jones Point Park, which features a 19th-century lighthouse. Mount Vernon Forest Trail is a nature walk through George Washington's wilderness that leads past mature Oak and Hickory trees and past Holly and Laurel shrubs and features attractions such as Washington's cobble quarry and a wooden footbridge over a 100-foot wide ravine. Interpretive signs throughout the trail list fascinating facts about the woods and wildlife. The Cameron Run Regional Park offers something for everyone: waterslide, wave pool, lap pool, batting cages and miniature golf. Times of operation vary by venue and season. In addition to Alexandria's many walking and historic trails, including the Potomac Heritage Trail and Virginia Civil War Trails, the city has 11 public parks providing baseball fields, volleyball courts, hiking, biking, swimming, gardens, soccer, and outdoor amphitheaters. (All of the sites in this section are managed by the City of Alexandria Department of Recreation, Parks and Cultural Activities; contact 703–838–4343 or *www.ci.alexandria.va.us/recreation.*)

For the Visitor

Accommodations: Alexandria offers an eclectic collection of hotels with more than 4,200 guestrooms. Choose from a European-style manor house; mid-size, full-service hotels; or a state-of-the-art resort and conference hotel, all with reasonable rates. The gay-friendly Embassy Suites Hotel Alexandria-Old Town (1900 Diagonal Road; 703–684–5900; *www.embassysuitesdcmetro.com/chevychase*), the most conveniently located hotel in Old Town Alexandria, offers you quick access to Washington, DC, attractions and Old Town Alexandria charm.

For More Information

Gay & Lesbian Center
Alexandria Gay & Lesbian
Community Association
P.O. Box 19401
Alexandria, VA 22320
703–684–0444
www.aglca.org

Publications
Washington Post
1150 15th Street N.W.
Washington, DC 20071
703–469–2500
www.washingtonpost.com

Washington Times
3600 New York Avenue N.E.
Washington, DC 20002-1947
202–636–3000
www.washtimes.com

Convention and Visitors Bureau
Alexandria Convention and Visitors
Association
421 King Street, Suite 300
Alexandria, VA 22314
800–388–9119
www.funside.com

Chamber of Commerce
Alexandria Chamber of Commerce
801 N. Fairfax Street, #402
Alexandria, VA 22313-0359
703–739–3805
www.alexchamber.com

Realtor
Maura Sullivan, Top Producer
Long and Foster Realtors
13875 Hedgewood Drive
Woodbridge, VA 22192
703–932–5870
www.umatter.biz

48 ▶ Olympia, Washington

Washington

Seattle · Spokane ·

Olympia

A Look at Olympia

Located at the southern end of Puget Sound in the beautiful Pacific Northwest, Olympia, named for the Olympic Mountains, is the state capital and the county seat of Thurston County. Majestic Mount Rainier and the rugged Cascade Mountains are nearby to the east, and Washington's Pacific Ocean coast is just an hour's drive to the west, providing countless outdoor activities and a brilliant daily-life backdrop. The rich heritage, history, and culture of Olympia are reflected in the downtown galleries, unusual shops, and specialty restaurants tucked among the historic buildings. Within walking distance are many visitor attractions, such as the Capitol Campus, the Washington State Historical Museum, the Farmers Market, and Percival Landing. Overlooking Capitol Lake, Olympia's stately legislative building, completed in 1928, stands 28 stories high and was the last great domed capitol built in the United States. Stunning buildings, landscaped seasonal gardens, greenhouses, fountains, and monuments surround the Capitol. The city enjoys a strong and stable economy and some of the state's best schools. Olympia is home to a fabulous fine arts center, restaurants, and plenty of shopping and attractions. All of this is combined in a small-town atmosphere that's progressive, open, and welcoming.

Possible drawbacks: The economy is tied to and directly affected by the government's size and spending. If you want sunny and warm,

▶ County:
Thurston

▶ Area code:
360

▶ Time zone:
Pacific

▶ Population:
42,514

▶ County population:
207,355

▶ Region:
Northwest Washington

▶ Closest metro area:
Seattle

▶ Average home price:
$233,000

▶ Fabulous reasons to live here:
Beautiful setting, recreation, music, culture, affordable housing, fabulous education, active GLBT community

Climate

Elevation 130'	Avg. high/low(F°)	Avg. inches		Avg. # days precip.	Avg. % humidity
		rain	snow		
Jan.	44/32	7.5	6.8	20	68%
April	58/36	3.6	0.1	15	74%
July	76/49	0.8	–	5	70%
Oct.	60/39	4.2	–	14	80%
YEAR	60/39	50.8	16.7	163	77%
# days 32° or below: 22			# days 90° or warmer: 0		

the Pacific Northwest isn't the place. Olympia's location on the Puget Sound and surrounding mountains create cool, wet weather most of the year.

Local Connections

Gas and electric company: Puget Sound Energy (888–225–5773; *www.pse.com*)

Phone companies: AT&T (800–222–0300; *www.att.com*); Qwest (800–244–1111; *www.qwest.com*)

Water and sewer: City of Olympia (360–753–8340; *www.ci.olympia.wa.us*)

Cable company: Comcast (877–824–2288; *www.comcast.com*)

Car registration/License: Department of Licensing (360–902–3770; *www.dol.wa.gov*)

New residents to Washington state have 30 days to apply for a driver's license and register their vehicle(s). Written, signs, and vision tests required. Fees: exam $10, license (five years) $25. Vehicle registration fees: filing $7, plates $30, license service fee $.75, decal fee $0.50–3; $15 out-of-state fee if your vehicle was most previously titled or registered in another jurisdiction; emissions test fee $15. A use tax, based on the average retail value of the vehicle, is charged at the state tax rate. Credit is given for any sales tax paid to another state or country, if proof of the tax paid is submitted, and waived if you owned and operated the vehicle in your former state of residence for 90 or more days. Vehicles powered by propane, butane, or natural gas are assessed a special fuel tax, based on gross weight.

The Tax Ax

Sales tax: 7.85 percent

State income tax: No income tax in Washington State

Property tax: Property taxes are based on 100 percent of the fair market value of the home. Depending on the area you're in the tax rates range from $9.16 to $14.69 per $1,000 of assessed value.

Local Real Estate

Overview: The Olympia area has a wide range of housing styles anywhere from contemporary to log homes, including lots of one-, two-, and multi-level homes. Currently, the Olympia market is a very strong seller's market, so homes are selling quickly.

Median price for a single-family home: $200,000

Average price for a single-family home: $233,000

Average price for a 2BR condo: $200,000

Rental housing market: If you're looking to rent, it's currently a good time. Many rental homes are available as well as apartments with landlords offering discounts on the first month's rent.

Gay-friendly neighborhoods: All of the Olympia neighborhoods are gay-friendly.

Nearby areas to consider: Tumwater, a few miles north of Olympia, is a small progressive city of approximately 13,000 residents. The city is proclaimed as a "people-friendly, people-oriented" community that has attracted a substantial GLBT population. This historic city offers a City Domestic Partner Registration. The registration doesn't provide any additional benefits. Lacey, recognized as a Tree City USA by the National Arbor Day Foundation, has a population of almost 33,000 residents. This small town about 5 miles west of Olympia is home to St. Martin's College and a large GLBT community.

Earning a Living

Per capita income: $22,590

Median household income: $40,846

Business climate: Olympia and Thurston County have a diverse economy dependent on agriculture, timber, state government, education, and a variety of commercial activities. With some of the best schools in the state and enhanced quality-of-life, Thurston County attracts and maintains a solid workforce.

Help in starting a business: The Thurston County Chamber of Commerce (360–357–3362; *www.thurstonchamber.com*) is the unified voice and advocate for area businesses. One of its many programs is the Small Business Development Center (360–753–5616), which provides information and assistance to Olympian small businesses.

Job market: Major market sectors providing employment include manufacturing; education, health, and social services; public administration; and retail trade.

The Community

Overview: Olympia is an open and supportive small town. The city offers a domestic partner registry, and there are many support and social organizations. The GLBT community is well integrated into the city, enjoys a high quality of life, and is well supported by local government.

Community organizations: The Rainbow Center (*www.rainbowcenteroly.org*) is a virtual community center for the Olympia area. It doesn't have a physical location, but it hosts the annual pride events and publishes an online magazine, maintains a calendar of community events, and more. With the absence of a physical space, several other groups supply the social support needed by Olympia's GLBT community. Stonewall Youth (*www.stonewallyouth.org*) is dedicated to providing peer support, information, and advocacy for GLBT youth and youth who have questions about their orientation, age 21 and under. Safe Schools Coalition (*www.safeschoolscoalition.org*) is a public-private partnership supporting GLBT Youth by helping schools become safe places where family can belong, where every educator can teach, and where every child can learn, regardless of gender identity or sexual orientation. Thurston Marriage Equality (*www.thurstonequalmarriage.org*) is an advocacy group promoting equal marriage for same-sex couples. Triangles is a Unitarian Universalist club providing emotional and spiritual support and a safe social environment.

Medical care: Thurston County is home to two hospitals and a number of clinics. Columbia Capital Medical Center (360–754–5858; *www.capitalmedical.com*) is a 119-bed hospital, with one general family practice clinic, serving all of Thurston and surrounding counties. It's a forward-thinking, innovative organization where trust and teamwork come together to respond to the needs of the greater community it serves. Personalized care sets this hospital apart from other healthcare organizations. Providence St. Peter Hospital (360–491–9480), part of the Providence Health System (*www.providence.org*), is a 390-bed, not-for-profit regional teaching hospital founded by the Sisters of Providence in 1887, offering comprehensive medical, surgical, and behavioral health services. Group Health Cooperative of Puget Sound (888–901–4636; *www.ghc.org*) complements the hospitals with outpatient services and two clinics in Thurston County.

Nuptials: The State of Oregon has amended its constitution, declaring same-sex marriages invalid. The City of Olympia's (*www.ci.olympia.wa.us*) Domestic Partnership Registration program (Olympia Municipal Code 2.82) allows unmarried couples in committed ongoing family relationships to document their relationships. This recognizes the diversity of family configurations, including lesbian, gay, and unmarried heterosexual couples (and their children) and unmarried elderly partners. Domestic Partnership Registration is voluntary and does not create any new or different legal rights or responsibilities, or any contractual relationships or obligations between the registrants.

Getting Around Town

Public transportation: Intercity Transit (360–786–1881; *www.intercitytransit.com*) provides area-wide bus service. Fares: one way 75 cents; daily pass $1.50.

Roads: I-5, US101

Airport: Olympia Regional Airport (airport code: OLM) (360–528–8000; *www.portolympia.com*), about 6 miles from downtown, is a general and corporate aviation facility. Seattle-Tacoma International Airport (airport code: SEA) (206–431–4444; *www.portseattle.org/seatac*) is about an hour to the north and serves 29 airlines.

It's a Gay Life

Annual events: The Rainbow Community Center (*www.rainbowcenteroly.org*) hosts Capital Pride in June, followed by the Pride Day Awards. Other area annual events of note are Arts Walk (*www.ci.olympia.wa.us*), the Boatswap & Chowder Challenge (*www.portolympia.com*), Capital Lakefair (*www.lakefair.org*), Dixieland Jazz Festival (*www.olyjazz.com*), and Olympia Harbor Days (*www.harbordays.com*). Music in the Park (*www.downtownolympia.com*), Olympia's summer outdoor concert series, is held on Fridays at noon in Sylvester Park from mid-July through August. Twilight concerts known as Music in the Dark take place in the park on Wednesday evenings during those same weeks.

Nightlife: Walking through downtown Olympia's eclectic collection of shops, bars, restaurants, and galleries is reminiscent of entering a bit of a 1950s time warp. Olympia bustles when the legislature is in session, but at other times is a rather sleepy town at night. The Spar Cafe and Bar opened downtown in 1935. This classic spot is filled with history and surrounded by local legend. Olympia has a small collection of taverns and pubs. Hannah's Bar & Grille (125 5th Avenue SW; 360–357–9890) is Olympia's only GLBT bar, and the Urban Onion (116 Legion Way SE; 360–943–9242) is a popular GLBT community restaurant. The Red Wind Casino (12819 Yelm Highway SE; 360–412–3652; *www.redwindcasino.net*) adds gaming action and live entertainment to the Olympia area.

Culture: The Washington Center for the Performing Arts (512 Washington Street SE; 360–753–8585; *www.washingtoncenter.org*) hosts the Olympia Symphony Orchestra (360–753–0074; *www.olympiasymphony.com*) and dozens of other community theater, music, and dance groups as well as touring productions. The historic Capital Theater (206 5th Avenue SE; 360–754–6670; *www.olyfilm.org*) is home to the Olympia Film Society (*www.olyfilm.org*), which offers innovative films throughout the year and an acclaimed film festival each November. The Olympic Flight Museum (7637 A Old Highway 99 SE; 360–705–3925; *www.olympicflightmuseum.com*). with its collection of old war planes and World War II memorabilia, is one of Olympia's most-visited attractions. Arts Walk (*www.ci.olympia.wa.us*) is Olympia's bi-annual arts celebration, showcasing the quality and diversity of South Puget Sound's artistic and cultural resources. Yashiro Japanese Garden (1010 Plum Street SE; 360–753–8380; *www.ci.olympia.wa.us*) is a traditional Asian garden designed in the ancient hill and pond style, honoring Olympia's sister city of Yashiro, Japan. Percival Landing Waterfront Park (360–753–8380; *www.ci.olympia.wa.us*) has a growing collection of outdoor public arts and historic interpretive sites. Olympia's historic Bigelow House (918 Glass Avenue NE; *www.bigelowhouse.org*), built during the 1850s by pioneer lawyer Daniel R. Bigelow and his schoolteacher wife Ann Elizabeth, is one of the oldest homes still standing in the Pacific Northwest. The

Bigelow House has been home to a single family—a family that saved things, so it contains a remarkable collection of original furnishings. The Hands On Children's Museum (106 11th Avenue SW; 360–956–0818; *www.hocm.org*) is one of the largest youth museums in the Northwest, with more than 10,000 square feet of exhibit space. The Museum contains four exhibit galleries with more than 50 interactive exhibits. The State Capitol Museum (211 W. 21st Avenue; 360–753–2580; *www.wshs.org/wscm*), in the historic Lord Mansion, is a few blocks south of the Capitol Campus (416 14th Avenue SW; 360–586–3460; *www.ga.wa.gov*). Featuring two floors of exhibits, the museum offers interpretations of regional Native American history and a series of interesting temporary exhibits.

Recreation: Thurston County has 52 parks providing outdoor recreation opportunities including fishing, boating, water sports, biking, camping, and rock climbing. Hiking, boating, scuba diving, and fishing are just a few of the opportunities available at Tolmie State Park (360–456–6464; *www.parks.wa.gov*). Situated next to the Olympia Brewery on the Deschutes River, Tumwater Falls Park (360–754–4160; *www.ci.tumwater.wa.us*) contains picnic and play areas, beautifully landscaped walking paths leading to an exciting view of the lower falls, and a front-row seat to the salmon run. Each fall, thousands of Chinook salmon passes through the Capital Lake Fish Ladder on their way from the ocean to the Deschutes River. Watch from the catwalk on the north side of Fifth Avenue (just before the bridge) as they school up and wait to swim through. Percival Landing is 1 1/2 miles of boardwalk with a view of Puget Sound, the Olympic Mountains, and the Capitol Dome. Artwork and interpretive displays outline the history of the harbor. A lookout tower is located along the boardwalk in Percival Park (217 Thurston Avenue SW; 360–753–8380; *www.ci.olympia.wa.us*). Priest Point Park (2600 East Bay Drive NE; 360–753–8380; *www.ci.olympia.wa.us*), a piece of the rain forest only five minutes north of downtown Olympia, provides hiking trails leading to the Puget Sound, picnic tables, and modern facilities.

For the Visitor

Accommodations: More than 1,650 hotel rooms in the Thurston County area and four campgrounds provide a pleasant mix of visitor accommodations. Ramada Inn Governor House (621 S. Capital Way; 360–352–7700; *www.ramada.com*), with an excellent downtown location, serves as the gateway to the Pacific Ocean Beaches and the Olympia Peninsula. The Ameritel Inns Olympia (4520 Martin Way E.; 360–459–8866; *www.ameritelinns.com*), serenely situated near the southernmost tip of Puget Sound, has a 24-hour indoor pool, spa, and fitness center.

For More Information

Gay & Lesbian Center
Rainbow Community Center
P.O. Box 7221
Olympia, WA 98507-7221
www.rainbowcenteroly.org

Publication
The Olympian
111 Bethel Street NE
Olympia, WA 98506
360–754–5400
www.theolympian.com

Convention and Visitors Bureau

Olympia Thurston County
Convention and Visitors Bureau
P.O. Box 7338
Olympia, WA 98507
360–704–7533/877–704–7500
www.visitolympia.com

Chamber of Commerce

Thurston County Chamber of
Commerce
1600 East 4th Avenue
Olympia, WA 98507
360–357–3362
www.thurstonchamber.com

Realtor

Kimberley Bauman
Realtor
RE/MAX Four Seasons
2627 Martin Way E.
Olympia, WA 98506
360–481–3614
www.olympiahomesbykim.com

49 ▶ Seattle, Washington

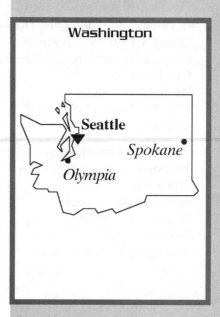

A Look at Seattle

Lush green parks and avenues have given Seattle the moniker "Emerald City." Located on the eastern shore of Puget Sound, the city is bounded by thousands of square miles of evergreen forest and hundreds of miles of salt and freshwater shoreline. With this wealth of nature at their doorstep, Seattleites concentrate much of their recreation in the outdoors. Seattle's strong maritime environment comes into sharp focus at Fisherman's Terminal, home of hundreds of purse seine and gill net boats. Residents often take time to stroll along the piers, watch fishermen mending their nets, and admire the sturdy boats. Downtown, just two blocks from the water, Pike Place Market is one of the last authentic farmers' markets in the country. A walk through the colorful old market truly becomes a sensory experience as vendors hawk their wares in a dozen different languages. The city boasts remarkable arts, cultural, educational, and community programs and international festivals. Seattle is noted for its specialty shops. Its proximity to the Orient makes an abundance of imported goods available.

Possible drawbacks: Seattle is famous for cloudy days and rainfall. Although fewer inches fall here than other American cities, there's no denying Seattle has more gray, cloudy days than just about anywhere. If prominent sunshine is important to your mood or life you'll want to look for a home somewhere else.

▶ Nickname:
The Emerald City
▶ County: King
▶ Area code: 206
▶ Time zone:
Pacific
▶ Population:
563,374
▶ County population:
1,737,034
▶ Region:
Northwest Washington
▶ Average home price:
$263,000
▶ Fabulous reasons to live here:
Beautiful setting, fabulous recreation, care of the environment, culture, arts, music, excellent education, active and politically supported GLBT community

Climate

Elevation 350'	Avg. high/low (F°)	Avg. inches		Avg. # days precip.	Avg. % humidity
		rain	snow		
Jan.	46/35	4.7	6.8	20	72%
April	58/41	2.8	0.1	15	66%
July	75/55	0.9	–	5	73%
Oct.	60/46	3.3	–	14	74%
YEAR	54/44	36.6	16.9	163	72%
# days 32° or below: 18			# days 90° or warmer: 2		

Local Connections

Gas company: Puget Sound Energy (888–225–5773; *www.pse.com*)

Electric company: Seattle City Light (206–684–3000; *www.seattle.gov/light*)

Phone companies: AT&T (800–222–0300; *www.att.com*); Qwest (800–244–1111; *www.qwest.com*)

Water and sewer: Seattle Public Utilities (206–684–3000; *www.seattle.gov/util/services*)

Cable companies: Comcast (877–824–2288; *www.comcast.com*); Millennium Digital Media (800–829–2225; *www.mdm.net*)

Car registration/License: Department of Licensing (360–902–3770; *www.dol.wa.gov*)

New residents to Washington state have 30 days to apply for a driver's license and register their vehicle(s). Written, signs, and vision tests required. Fees: exam $10, license (five years) $25. Vehicle registration fees: filing $7, plates $30, license service fee $.75, decal fee $0.50–3; $15 out-of-state fee if your vehicle was most previously titled or registered in another jurisdiction; emissions test fee $15. A use tax, based on the average retail value of the vehicle, is charged at the state tax rate. Credit is given for any sales tax paid to another state or country, if proof of the tax paid is submitted, and waived if you owned and operated the vehicle in your former state of residence for 90 or more days. Vehicles powered by propane, butane, or natural gas are assessed a special fuel tax, based on gross weight.

The Tax Ax

Sales tax: 8.6 percent

State income tax: No income tax in Washington

Property tax: Residential properties are assessed annually based on market values as determined by recent, comparable sales.

Local Real Estate

Overview: Seattle offers a great choice of neighborhoods, many with dramatic mountain or water views: funky and eclectic West Seattle and Fremont; the trendy condo high-rises of Belltown; upscale and stylish Leschi, Mt. Baker, and Greenlake; and Capital Hill, the heart of the gay social scene.

Median price for a single-family home: $355,000

Average price for a single-family home: $263,000

Average price for a 2BR condo: $300,000

Rental housing market: The rental market is currently tight in Seattle's most popular neighborhoods. Downtown studio rents start at approximately $900. Two-bedroom apartments start at $1,300.

Gay-friendly neighborhoods: Capital Hill, Central District, Kirkland, Newcastle, Bellevue, Lake Forest Park

Nearby areas to consider: Fourteen miles north of Seattle is the GLBT popular city of Mountlake Terrace. With 20,000 residents, this small city provides excellent services to its residents and businesses, and regional headquarters are also being attracted by the area's high quality of life. The easy commute to Seattle blends well with the local arts, culture, recreation, housing, education, and employment opportunities offered in the family-oriented community of Mountlake Terrace, and a substantial number of the area's GLBT community call this small town home.

Earning a Living

Per capita income: $30,306

Median household income: $45,736

Business climate: The 1962 Seattle World's Fair signaled a renaissance in the Pacific Northwest. Forestry, fisheries, and agriculture have given way to computer software manufacturers, bio-medical industries, and aerospace, which dominate the economy. With its proximity to the Pacific Rim, extensive port facilities, high-tech and communications industries, and educational institutions, Seattle is assuming the role of a primary participant in the trade and commerce with Asia that will lead the economy into the 21st century.

Help in starting a business: There are 23 area chambers of commerce in Seattle. The Greater Seattle Chamber of Commerce acts as a portal to all of those groups. Seattle's Office of Economic Development (206–684–2499; *www.ci.seattle.wa.us/economicdevelopment*) works to maximize Seattle's potential as a thriving hub for businesses, jobs, robust neighborhoods, and economic opportunity.

Job market: High-tech, computer software, shipping and imports, education, and the arts are all active employment markets. REI, Eddie Bauer, Nintendo, Starbucks, Boeing Commercial Airplanes, Amazon.com, RealNetworks, and Microsoft all call Seattle home. The world's most dynamic new companies are spinning out of the Puget Sound area, which is naturally the nation's leader in Internet business start-ups, but also a leader in business start-ups in general.

The Community

Overview: The GLBT community in Seattle is large and active both politically and socially. Capital Hill is the heart of Seattle's gay social scene, but the city's gay and lesbian population is large and progressive, and it pervades the entire city. Capital Hill Neighbors (*www.capitolhillneighbors.com*) provides extensive information on the area and community.

Community organizations: The Seattle LGBT Community Center (*www.seattlelgbt.org*) creates a meeting place for the LGBT community to grow together, increase public understanding, and celebrate diversity. There are more than a hundred GLBT groups and organizations in Seattle, ranging from support and health to social, spiritual, and recreational. The Community Center maintains the most current list of groups and organizations.

Medical care: Public Health-Seattle and King County (206–296–4600; *www.metrokc.gov/health*) is a well-designed portal with health services programs and information on area services and links to hundreds of local providers. In addition, Public Health provides a GLBT-specific referral resource on its Website (*www.metrokc.gov/health/glbt*).

Nuptials: The State of Washington has a law similar to DOMA defining marriage as between a man and woman and does not honor same-sex marriages from other jurisdictions. The City of Seattle offers a domestic partner registry (*www.ci.seattle.wa.us/leg/clerk/dpr.htm*), but it currently carries no additional rights for registered couples.

Getting Around Town

Public transportation: Metro Transit (206–553–3000; *transit.metrokc.gov*) provides bus service throughout King County on more than 180 different routes, including a free ride area in downtown Seattle. Fares: peak $1.50; off-peak $1.25; unlimited-ride, one-day pass $5. Free transfers are good for about an hour. The Seattle Monorail Service (206–905–2620; *www.seattlemonorail.com*) is a quick link from downtown to the Seattle Center (limited hours of operation). Fare: $1.50.

Roads: I-5, I-90, SR99, SR167, SR520

Airport: Seattle-Tacoma International Airport (airport code: SEA) (206–431–4444; *www.portseattle.org/seatac*) is located 13 miles south of downtown Seattle and serves 29 airlines.

It's a Gay Life

Annual events: Seattle Pride (206–322–9561; *www.seattlepride.org*) sponsors Seattle's gay pride parade and festival in June. The Seattle Center (*www.seattlecenter.com*) hosts dozens of cultural and arts festivals throughout the year. Experience 50 bands featured at the Capital Hill Block Party (*www.capitolhillblockparty.com*) in July; SEAFAIR (*www.seafair.com*) hosts a series of events in July and August, including the Blue Angel's Air Show. The Seattle LGBT Community Center (*www.seattlelgbt.org*) also sponsors special and fundraising events throughout the year. Seattle's International Film Festival (*www.seattlefilm.org*), held annually mid-May to mid-June, is the largest film festival in the country.

Nightlife: Pioneer Square, the city's preserved historic district, lies adjacent to the southern end of the downtown waterfront. Here the city has its roots centered on the original Skid Road (Yesler Way), a road used to skid timber down from the hills to Elliott Bay. Many of the fine, old brick and sandstone buildings have been painstakingly restored in recent years, and a half-dozen square blocks of the district offer excellent shopping and dining. More than 30 bars and clubs and dozens of restaurants cater to the Seattle's GLBT community. You'll discover fun places to eat, drink, and socialize in Capital Hill, the heart of the community. Visit Beyond the Closet Bookstore (518 E. Pike Street; 206–322–4609; *www.beyondthecloset.com*) to pick up *The Seattle Gay News* (*www.sgn.org*), one of the nation's oldest GLBT publications, providing information on area news, entertainment, and events.

Culture: The Crown jewel of Seattle's attractions is the Seattle Center (305 Harrison Street; 206–684–7200; *www.seattlecenter.com*), the 74-acre legacy of the 1962 World's Fair. Its distinctive 605-foot Space Needle is the city's leading landmark. From its lofty observation deck, there's a 360-degree view of the city and Puget Sound, backdropped by the snowcapped Cascade Range to the east and the Olympic Mountains to the west. Seattle Center is home to award-winning theater companies, professional sports teams, museums, an internationally acclaimed ballet and opera, a nationally recognized children's theater, and a hands-on children's museum and exciting scientific exhibitions. The Seattle Center is enjoyable in any season, but on weekends and fair weather days between April and October, it's a beehive of activity with outdoor concerts, amusement park attractions, impromptu performances, and special events. The Seattle Repertory Theater (155 Mercer Street; 206–443–2222; *www.seattlerep.org*) and the Mercer Arts Arena (363 Mercer Street; 206–684–7200) host various performances, including opera and ballet. The Seattle Art Museum (100 University Street; 206–654–3100; *www.seattleartmuseum.org*) is noteworthy for its collections of African and Native American art, Renaissance and Impressionist paintings, ancient Greek coins and pottery, and the works of Pacific Northwest regional painters and sculptors. The Seattle Asian Art Museum (1400 E. Prospect Street; 206–654–3100; *www.seattleartmuseum.org*) opened in Volunteer Park (1400 E. Galer Street; 206–684–4743; *www.cityofseattle.net/parks*) in August 1994, featuring one of the 10 top collections of Asian art outside Asia. Whether your interests run to contemporary or traditional art, aviation, Asian art, Nordic cultures, native cultures, or history, Seattle's many museums offer something for everyone. In Seattle, art *is* lifestyle. Sculpture, murals, and paintings are visible in museums and galleries as well as on manhole covers (Westlake Park), embedded in sidewalks (Broadway), and in bus tunnel stations and outdoor plazas.

Recreation: The best in urban recreation is at your toes and at your fingertips around Seattle: spectacularly scenic golf, kayaking and canoeing, fishing and clamming, hiking, and urban parks, including Discovery Park (3801 West Government Way; 206–386–4236; *www.cityofseattle.net/parks*), Seward Park (Lake Washington Boulevard and Orcas Street; *www.sewardpark.net*), and Woodland Park Zoo and Rose Gardens (5500 Phinney Avenue N. (West Gate) 750 N. 50th Street (South Gate); 206–684–4800; *www.zoo.org*). A short drive out of the city leads to skiing, snowboarding, river rafting, hiking, and some of the most scenic parks around: Mt. Rainier National Park (Tahoma Woods, Star Route, Ashford; 360–569–2211, est. 3314; *www.nps.gov/mora*), Mount St. Helens National Volcanic Monument (Milepost 43, SR504; 360–449–7800; *www.fs.fed.us/gpnf/mshnvm*), North Cascades National Park (810 SR20, Sedro-Woolley; 360–856–5700; *www.nps.gov/noca*), Olympic National Park and Rainforest (600 E. Park Avenue, Port Angeles; 360–565–3130; *www.nps.gov/olym*), and Columbia River Gorge National Scenic Area (Oregon Highway 30; 503–695–2372; *www.fs.fed.us/r6/Columbia*). Whale watching is a popular activity in the Pacific Northwest, with the three local pods of orcas (currently 84) most often observed between May and September. An unusual and uniquely northwest experience is the dinner cruise to Blake Island, a state park in the Sound that can be reached only by boat. Blake Island's Tillicum Village (2992 SW Avalon Way; 206–933–8600; *www.tillicumvillage.com*) features a Northwest Coast Indian cedar long house where Native Americans cook salmon over open-pit alder fires. Dinner concludes with a program of costumed tribal dancing. For spectators, there's Mariners baseball (206–628–0888; *seattlemariners.mlb.com*), the NFL's Seahawks (888–635–4295; *www.seahawks.com*), the Seattle Sounders soccer (800–796–5425; *www.seattlesounders.net*), the NBA's Sonics (206–281–5800; *www.nba.com/sonics*), the WNBA's Storm (206–217–WNBA; *www.wnba.com/storm*), the Western Hockey League's Thunderbirds (206–448–7825; *www.seattle-thunderbirds.com*), and the University of Washington's Husky Sports (206–543–2200; *www.gohusky.com*).

For the Visitor

Accommodations: Whether you're looking for a cozy, romantic hideaway in the islands of Puget Sound or accommodations fit for a queen in the finest luxury hotel or resort, you'll find what you're looking for among King County's 30,000 hotel rooms. The Seattle Hotel Hotline (800-535-7071), a free booking service run by the convention bureau, makes reservations at more than 40 area hotels for travelers. Just a short distance from the Capitol Hill and downtown Seattle commercial districts, Bacon Mansion (959 Broadway; 800–240–1864; *www.baconmansion.com*) is a 1909 classical Edwardian-style Tudor located in the Historical Harvard-Belmont Landmark District. With its colorful past history as the Wolf's Den boarding house and (police-raided) bordello, Capitol Hill Inn (1713 Belmont Avenue; 206–323–1955; *www.capitolhillinn.com*) is a beautifully restored, 1903 Victorian bed and breakfast, just two blocks to Capitol Hill's Broadway Avenue. The beautifully restored, 1906 four-square Gaslight Inn (1727 15th Avenue; 206–325–3654; *www.gaslight-inn.com*) combines turn-of-the-century ambiance with contemporary conveniences and features a heated pool and sundeck.

For More Information

Gay & Lesbian Center
Seattle LGBT Community Center
PMB 1010
1122 East Pike Street
Seattle, WA 98122
206–323–5428
www.seattlelgbt.org

Publications
Seattle Gay News
1605 12th Avenue, Suite 31
Seattle, WA 98122
206–324–4297
www.sgn.org

The Seattle Times
P.O. Box 70
Seattle, WA 98111
206–464–2111
seattletimes.nwsource.com

Seattle Post Intelligencer
101 Elliott Avenue W.
Seattle, WA 98119
206–448–8000
seattlepi.nwsource.com

Capital Hill Times
4000 Aurora Avenue N., Suite 100
Seattle, WA 98103
206–461–1300
www.capitolhilltimes.com

Convention and Visitors Bureau
Seattle's Convention and Visitors Bureau
One Convention Place
701 Pike Street, Suite 800
Seattle, WA 98101
206–461–5840
www.seeseattle.org

Chamber of Commerce
Greater Seattle Chamber of Commerce
1301 Fifth Avenue, Suite 2500
Seattle, WA 98101-2611
206–389–7200
www.seattlechamber.com

Realtor
Linda Hoffman
Associate Broker
Prudential Northwest Realty Associates LLC
1008 NE 108
Bellevue, WA 98005
206–979–7954
www.lindahoffman.biz

50 ▶ Madison, Wisconson

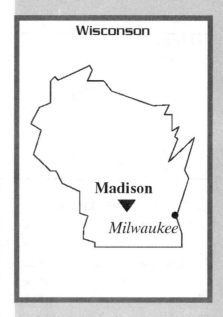

A Look at Madison

Madison combines small-town charm with a range of cultural and recreational opportunities usually found in much larger cities. Built on an isthmus between Lake Monona and Lake Mendota, Madison offers incredible natural beauty, stimulating cultural opportunities, and fabulous restaurants, shops, and attractions. Healthcare is another of Madison's strengths, with five general hospitals, more than 20 major medical clinics, and UW-Madison's medical, nursing, and pharmacy schools. Madison also maintains one of the lowest unemployment rates in the nation. Four lakes and more than 200 parks provide an abundance of year-round outdoor activities, from hiking, biking, swimming, and sailing to cross-country skiing, snow sailing, and ice fishing. The greater Madison area has so much to offer its residents, from charming historic neighborhoods and award-winning schools to a great variety of cultural and recreational activities. A host of picturesque communities, many retaining their strong ethnic heritage, surrounds the city. There's something for everyone in the Madison area: big-city action and small-town charm, a rich cultural calendar, sensational shopping, and endless recreational opportunities amid stunning natural beauty.

Possible drawbacks: As home to the University of Wisconsin, a large percentage of the residents are students and therefore transient by nature. Though home prices remain in line, rental property is at a premium and therefore expensive for the market.

▶ Nickname:
Lake City

▶ County: Dane

▶ Area code: 608

▶ Time zone:
Central

▶ Population:
208,054

▶ County population:
426,526

▶ Region:
South Central Wisconsin

▶ Average home price:
$210,372

▶ Fabulous reasons to live here:
Beautiful setting, fabulous education, recreation, culture, arts, music, active and politically supported GLBT community, strong economy

Climate

Elevation 863'	Avg. high/low(F°)	Avg. inches		Avg. # days precip.	Avg. % humidity
		rain	snow		
Jan.	26/6	1.3	10.9	10	75%
April	57/34	3.7	2.5	12	69%
July	83/59	4.2	–	10	73%
Oct.	61/37	2.5	0.3	9	73%
YEAR	56/34	35.2	44.1	122	73%
# days 32° or below:			# days 90° or warmer:		

Local Connections

Gas company: Madison Gas & Electric (608–252–7222; *www.mge.com*)

Electric companies: Wisconsin Public Power (608–834–4500; *www.wppisys.org*); Madison Gas & Electric (608–252–7222; *www.mge.com*)

Phone companies: MCI Telecommunications (888–624–5622; *www.mci.com*); TDS Metrocom (877–METROCOM; *www.tdsmetro.com*)

Water and sewer: Madison Water Utility (608–266–4641; *www.madisonwater.org*)

Cable company: Sky Cable TV of Madison (608–271–6999; *www.skycabletv.com*)

Car registration/License: Wisconsin Department of Transportation (licenses: 608–266–2353; plates: 608–266–1466; *www.dot.wisconsin.gov*)

New Wisconsin drivers have 30 days to apply for a Wisconsin driver's license. Surrender an out-of-state license and waive the written and driving exams. Fee: $18 (three years). New and transfer title fee: $35. New residents must register their cars within two days. No credit is given for unused registration on your previous state's license plate. 90-day temporary plates: $8. Annual plate fee: $55.

The Tax Ax

Sales tax: 5.5 percent

State income tax: 4.60–6.75 percent, depending upon marital status and income

Property tax: Taxes in the city of Madison are assessed at 100 percent of market value. The 2004 city of Madison tax rate was $25.35 per $1,000 in assessed value. The average tax on the average single family home would be $5,332 per year.

Local Real Estate

Overview: Styles vary from charming bungalows and older-style homes from the 1920s–40s to more modern housing of the last few decades. The city has seen substantial growth in the past 15 years. The market has been on a steady climb for more than 10 years with average appreciation greater than 7 percent per year for the past 10 years. Downtown has seen a boom in condo development, with a lot of empty nesters and young urbanites moving to the central city.

Median price for a single-family home: $178,050

Average price for a single-family home: $210,372

Average price for a 2BR condo: $174,259

Rental housing market: Fairly high-price rental housing market as the University of Wisconsin supplies the major tenants in the downtown/central city area. Prices range from $600/month for two-bedroom apartments on the east side of the city to more than $1,200/month for central and the west side.

Gay-friendly neighborhoods: Madison as a whole is very gay-friendly. As with most cities, the central city and near the east and west sides of the city have the largest concentration of gay household per capita.

Nearby areas to consider: Located on Lake Mendota, 6 miles west of Madison, is the small city of Middleton. Friendly people, low crime, small-town charm and a scenic landscape are attracting the GLBT community to this small city of 16,000 residents. Fifteen miles to the northeast of Madison is Sun Prairie, known as the Ground Hog Capital of the World. This family-oriented, town of about 23,000 residents encompasses nearly 400 recreational acres. It's one of Wisconsin's fastest-growing communities, attracting new residents because of its easy commute, quality schools, and classic downtown.

Earning a Living

Per capita income: $23,498

Median household income: $41,941

Business climate: Madison's economy remains stable because the largest employers in the area are the state government and the University of Wisconsin System. In addition, Madison is the world headquarters for General Casualty Insurance, American Family Insurance, CUNA Mutual Insurance, and WPS Insurance. All are large employers in the area and are GLBT-supportive and GLBT-friendly.

Help in starting a business: The Greater Madison Chamber of Commerce presents the annual Madison Small Business Conference. The Department of Planning and Development, sponsored through the City of Madison (*www.ci.madison.wi.us/planning*), has a multitude of resources for business owners, including the Madison Economic Department, Office of Business Resources, and a dozen other programs.

Job market: The largest employers are government and education, followed closely by health and social services and the insurance industry. Professional, scientific, management, administrative, arts, retail, and entrepreneurial trades and business also do well.

The Community

Overview: Madison's GLBT community is out and organized, and its residents are progressive and supportive of the community. Spend a short time on State Street and you'll quickly discover that this vibrant college town and state capital provide a blend of fresh, young, well-educated students with state lawmakers and longtime residents and business professionals.

Community organizations: Outreach, Inc. (*www.outreachinc.com*), Madison's GLBT center, is a vibrant and inclusive agent, dedicated to positive change for the GLBT community by providing services that nurture, strengthen, and celebrate our communities; educate and inform the public; and advocate for social justice. The LGBT Campus Center at the University of Madison (*lgbtcc.studentorg.wisc.edu*) is dedicated to offering support, resources, a safe space, and programming for all students. There are dozens of other GLBT social, spiritual, and support organizations in Madison. The Gay Madison News (*www.instepnews.com*) has an up-to-date list of groups statewide.

Medical care: University of Wisconsin Hospital and Clinics Authority (608–263–6400; *www.uwhealth.org*), UW Health, is a comprehensive system of healthcare providers serving patients at more than 60 clinical locations throughout the state, 44 of them in Dane County. Meriter Hospital Inc. (608–267–6000; *www.meriter.com*) is a 448-bed, non-profit teaching hospital that provides comprehensive health services for residents of southern Wisconsin and areas of northwest Illinois. It is a major teaching affiliate of the University of Wisconsin. St. Mary's Hospital Medical Center (608–251–6100; *www.stmarysmadison.com*) offers a full range of inpatient and outpatient treatment and diagnostic services in primary care and nearly all specialties.

Nuptials: The State of Wisconsin has a marriage law that defines marriage as between a man and a woman. Many of the area employers provide domestic partner benefits.

Getting Around Town

Public transportation: Madison Metro Bus System (608–266–4466; *www.ci.madison.wi.us/metro/metro.html*) provides extensive bus service in the metro area. Fare: $1.50; all-day pass $3. Remember to ask for a transfer; they're good for two more rides within one and a half hours of your initial trip.

Roads: I-90, I-94, US12, US14, US18, US51

Airports: Dane County Regional Airport (airport code: MSN) (608–246–3380; *www.co.dane.wi.us/airport*) is just 6 miles from downtown; General

Mitchell International Airport in Milwaukee (airport code: MKE) (414–747–5300; *www.mitchellairport.com*) is the closest international hub airport (a one-and-a-half-hour drive).

It's a Gay Life

Annual events: Pride Week (July) is organized by Madison Pride *(www.madisonpride.org)* and includes the MAGIC Picnic at Madison's beautiful Brittingham Park, a parade, a rally, and lots of fabulous entertainment; the New Year's Eve Pink Party, OutReach's New Year's Eve Celebration (*www.outreachinc.com*), is the Midwest's only major gay and lesbian New Year's event with more than 18,000 attending. Madison hosts dozens of fairs and events throughout the year. Some of the highlights are Art Fair on the Square (*www.madisonartcenter.org*), Capital City Jazz Fest (*www.madisonjazz.com*), the Dane County Fair (*www.danecountyfair.com*), and the Holiday Art Fair (*www.madisonartcenter.org*).

Nightlife: Downtown Madison is a walker's paradise. Restaurants, bars, and bookstores line State Street, University Avenue, and Main Street. This is a college town that's eclectic and energized. In addition to the vast array of offerings, there are three gay clubs in Madison: Ray's Bar (2526 E. Washington Street; 608–241–9335), Shamrock (117 W. Main Street; 608–255–5029; *www.shamrockbar.com*), and Club 5 (5 Applegate Court; 608–632–0171; *www.club-5.com*), a multi-venue space with a dance bar, large patio, restaurant, and separate bars for both men and women, Also of note is Club Majestic (115 King Street; 608–251–2582; *www.clubmajestic.net*), a converted vaudeville house that's now a fun dance bar. There are also clubs that specialize in live music, including Café Montmartre (127 E. Mifflin Street; 608–255–5900; *www.themomo.com*), a "wine and jazz" bar, and Luther's Blues (1401 University Avenue; 608–257–1184; *www.luthersblues.com*).

Culture: There's world-class entertainment to be found just about any night in Madison with performances by the Madison Repertory Theater (608–256–0029; *www.madisonrep.org),* Madison Opera (608–238–8085; *www.madisonopera.org*), and Madison Symphony Orchestra (608–258–4141; *www.madisonsymphony.org*). Overture Center for the Arts (201 State Street; 608–258–4177; *www.overturecenter.com*) and the restored Orpheum Theater (216 State Street; 608–255–6005; *www.orpheumtheatre.net*) host touring productions of all types, and there's a full schedule of performances at the University of Wisconsin-Madison's (*www.arts.wisc.edu*) many venues. Madison's "Museum Mile" is home to six museums including Circus World Museum (550 Water Street; 608–356–0800; *www.circusworldmuseum.com*) and Christopher Columbus Antique Mall Museum (239 Whitney Street; 920–623–1992; *www.columbusantiquemall.com*). You'll also discover a fine collection of galleries both downtown and around town. The Henry Vilas Zoo (702 South Randall Avenue; 608–266–4732; *www.vilaszoo.org*) is free and open year-round. Madison also offers two areas of special interest to nature lovers. Olbrich Botanical Gardens & Tropical Conservatory (3330 Atwood Avenue; 608–246–4650; *www.olbrich.org*) is dedicated to the creation, conservation, and interpretation of gardens and plant collections hardy to the American Midwest or native to the world's tropical forests for study, enjoyment and public benefit. University of Wisconsin Arboretum (1207 Seminole Highway; 608–263–7888; *wiscinfo.doit.wisc.edu/arboretum*) may at first glance look like a park, but it's a research and teaching facility that also provides a place for people to develop a positive relationship with nature.

Recreation: If outdoor recreation is important, Madison is a fabulous place to live summer or winter. There are more than 29,000 acres of recreational land and 92 miles of shoreline in Dane County. Summer water sport activities include 32 swimming areas, 40 boat-launching sites, and 48 miles of canoeing options. You'll also discover 46 miles of major hiking trails. As the bike capital of the Midwest, the Madison Area boasts more bikes than cars and more than 150 miles of bicycle trails. From world-renowned and championship courses to par-3 and miniature golf courses, the Madison area offers something for every golfer. The Madison Parks Department (608–266–4711; *www.ci.madison.wi.us*) provides more than a dozen tennis courts. Baseball fans will enjoy the minor league Madison Mallards (608–246–4277; *www.mallardsbaseball.com*) and the Summer Collegiate League, dedicated to developing young collegiate players from around the country. When the snow is falling and the temperature is cool, the greater Madison area still has a variety of outdoor activities for visitors. The many lakes, parks, and trails make for numerous opportunities including, 40 skating facilities, 240 miles of snowmobile trails, more than 100 miles of cross country skiing areas, and a downhill area with six runs.

For the Visitor

Accommodations: Madison offers many of the usual large chain hotels, but the unique bed and breakfast inns scattered throughout the picturesque settings of the city are part of the charm. The Madison Canterbury Inn (315 West Gorham at State Street; 608–258–8899/800–838–3850; *www.madisoncanterbury.com*) is a "literary" bed and breakfast housed on the second story of the historic Jacobson Building above Avol's Books at Canterbury and Dancing Grounds Cafe, a mere 60 feet off lively State Street. Save your receipts from books purchased at Avol's and redeem them for free nights at the Inn. Annie's Garden B&B (2117 Sheridan Drive; 608–244–2224; *www.bbinternet.com/annies*) hosts only one reservation at a time, allowing romantic solitude and privacy for guests in a supremely comfortable setting, with warmth and great attention to detail. Collins House Bed and Breakfast (704 Gorham Street; 608–255–4230; *www.collinshouse.com*), listed on the National Register of Historic Places as a classic example of Prairie School Architecture, is a gay-friendly inn located on Lake Mendota just eight blocks from downtown.

For More Information

Gay & Lesbian Center

Outreach, Inc.
600 Williamson Street
Madison, WI 53703-3588
608–255–8582
www.outreachinc.com

Publications

Madison Capital Times/Wisconsin State Journal
1901 Fish Hatchery Road
Madison, WI 53713
608–252–6400
www.madison.com

Madison Times
931 E. Main Street, Suite 7
Madison, WI 53703
608–256–2122
www.madtimes.com

Convention and Visitors Bureau

Greater Madison Convention and
Visitors Bureau
615 East Washington Avenue
Madison, WI 53703
608–255–2537/800–373–6376
www.visitmadison.com

Chamber of Commerce

Greater Madison Chamber of Commerce
P.O. Box 71
615 East Washington Avenue
Madison, WI 53701-0071
608–256–8348
www.greatermadisonchamber.com

Realtor

Darren Kittleson
Operating Principal/Broker
Keller Williams Realty-Madison East/
West
8001 Excelsior Drive, Suite 200
Madison, WI 53717
608–662–9501
www.darrenkittleson.com

Salt Lake City, Utah

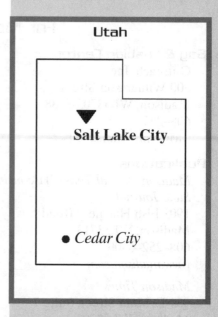

Utah

▼
Salt Lake City

● *Cedar City*

A Look at Salt Lake City

This may be a shock to many, but when big-city cosmopolitan meets rugged adventure in this clean, safe, and beautiful city, Salt Lake City has become home to a large, organized, and politically supported GLBT community. Nestled between the Great Salt Lake and a dramatic Rocky Mountain range, Salt Lake's broad streets end with dramatic views of majestic peaks. Canyons serpentine through the city's neighborhoods, creating a park-like atmosphere all year. In the midst of a major urban renaissance, creature comforts and metropolitan amenities complete the picture. Salt Lake is booming with new attractions, hotels, spas, clubs, bars, and funky shopping neighborhoods. New cooking trends are taking off in Salt Lake, introducing visitors to the flavors of the Rockies. And the city continues to shine as one of the brightest stars of the new American West. Strong economic growth during the past 20 years encouraged thousands of 21st-century pioneers to relocate to Salt Lake to build their own lives in the Rockies. Modern settlers are more likely to be young, outdoor-minded professionals attracted to close mountain recreation. Today, Salt Lake is a diverse community embracing a wide spectrum of religious, cultural, and ethnic groups.

Possible drawbacks: There's no denying that Salt Lake City rests on the religious foundation of the Mormon Church. Although the GLBT community has received encouraging support in recent years, political and social norms are determined by the city's founding fathers and the Church.

▶ Nickname:
Wasatch Front

▶ County:
Salt Lake

▶ Area code: 801

▶ Time zone:
Mountain Standard

▶ Population:
181,743

▶ County population:
898,387

▶ Region:
Northern Utah

▶ Average home price:
$170,000

▶ Fabulous reasons to live here:
Scenic beauty; recreation; temperate, dry climate; affordable housing; excellent education; culture; arts; large GLBT community

Climate

Elevation 4266'	Avg. high/low	Avg. inches		Avg. # days precip.	Avg. % humidity
		rain	snow		
Jan.	39/25	1.6	13.6	10	74%
April	61/43	2.2	5.0	10	52%
July	89/67	0.7	–	4	37%
Oct.	65/46	1.7	1.3	6	54%
YEAR	63/45	17.8	58.5	90	55%
# days 32° or below: 75			# days 90° or warmer: 57		

Local Connections

Gas company: Questar Corporation (801–324–5111; *www.questar.com*)

Electric company: Utah Power & Light (888–221–7070; *www.utahpower.net*)

Phone companies: Electric Lightwave (801–924–3000; *www.eli.net*); Qwest (801–237–5511; *www.qwest.com*); XO Communications (801–983–1600; *www.xo.com*)

Water and sewer: Salt Lake City (sewer: 801–262–2904; water 801–483–6900; *www.ci.slc.ut.us*)

Cable company: Comcast (801–485v0500; *www.comcast.com*)

Car registration/License: Utah Division of Motor Vehcicles (registration: 801–297–7780; *www.dmv.utah.gov*; license: 801–965–4437; *www.driverlicense.utah.gov*)

No written or driving exams with surrendered license. License fee: $20. To register and title in Utah for the first time costs $22 for passenger cars and light trucks plus a $2.50 driver's education fee and $1 for an insurance database fee, making the total $25.50; Emissions fee (I/M or APC Fee) between $1 and $10, depending on the fuel type. License plate fee: $9. Motor vehicles have a uniform fee in lieu of property tax based on the model year of the vehicle. The fee ranges from $10 to $150, depending on the age of the vehicle.

The Tax Ax

Sales tax: 6.6 percent

State income tax: 2.3–7 percent graduated, based on income

Property tax: Salt Lake County Treasurer (801–468–3400; *www.treasurer.slco.org*)

The taxable value of a property is 100 percent of its fair market value, less any exemptions that may be permitted. For example, the Utah Constitution permits the Legislature to exempt up to 45 percent of the fair market value of primary residential property from property taxation.

Local Real Estate

Overview: In the downtown part of Salt Lake you'll find older bungalow and Tudor-style homes. There is a lot of new construction going on in the outlying areas of the city. Average travel time to downtown ranges from 15 to 45 minutes.

Median price for a single-family home: $165,000

Average price for a single-family home: $170,000

Average price for a 2BR condo: $127,000

Rental housing market: Depending on area and size, you can find two-bedroom units from about $600–750.

Gay-friendly neighborhoods: Ninth & Ninth, Sugarhouse Avenues, and Westshire

Nearby areas to consider: About 10 miles southwest of Salt Lake City is Utah's second largest city: West Valley City. This is another popular area with Utah's GLBT community. Nestled in the Salt Lake Valley between the Wasatch and Oquirrh mountain ranges, the city's scenic beauty is enhanced by its sense of community and its commitment to provide high-quality public services for residents, businesses, and visitors. West Valley City boasts excellent public schools and short commutes to a variety of research institutions and other higher education opportunities.

Earning a Living

Per capita income: $18,185

Median household income: $45,726

Business climate: The Salt Lake area is known as the "Crossroads of the West." An east-west, north-south interstate highway system, three railroads, and an international airport provide the state with an efficient transportation system and ideal conditions for manufacturing, warehousing, and distribution facilities. Salt Lake is also an important regional trade and shipping center to the Rocky Mountain region and the West Coast. Utah's workforce has been described as smart, productive, motivated, and multilingual.

Help in starting a business: The Salt Lake Chamber is the largest business association in Utah and presents a unified voice for the business community with a full-time staff lobbyist. The Chamber is an aggressive, pro-business advocate that tackles critical issues in the areas of government, international trade, transportation, economic development, healthcare, environmental affairs, workforce issues, and education. The Chamber provides networking, advertising, referral services, and educational opportunities to its members.

Job market: Major market sectors include manufacturing; construction; government; transportation; publishing; motion picture and sound recording; telecommunications and Internet service providers; financial activities; professional and business services; education and health services; and leisure and hospitality.

The Community

Overview: A young, vibrant, highly educated GLBT community makes its home in Salt Lake City. Many community organizations provide recreation and support, well-attended annual events, and a fine collection of nightlife options—and that's just the tip of the iceberg in this mountain surrounded city. Recent local and state political actions underline the support the community receives from all levels.

Community organizations: The Gay & Lesbian Center of Utah (*www.glccu.com*) provides resources and referrals, programming, and a safe gathering place for lesbians, gay men, bisexuals, and transgender people of all ages. The Little Lavender Book (*www.lavenderbook.com*) is the local directory of groups, organizations, and gay-owned and gay-friendly businesses in Salt Lake. Many of the area groups providing support, social, recreational, and spiritual opportunities in Salt Lake use the Center as a meeting place.

Medical care: Utah has 51 hospitals that offer quality care. Major medical facilities provide short-term acute and intensive care, alcohol and chemical dependent and psychiatric care, long-term care, and rehabilitation and specialty centers (such as burn and hospice facilities). Intermountain Health Care (IHC) (801–442–2000; *www.ihc.com*) is a charitable, community-owned, nonprofit healthcare organization based in Salt Lake City serving the health needs of Utah and Idaho residents. The IHC system includes health insurance plans, 21 hospitals, clinics, and affiliated physicians. In 2003, in more than 149,000 visits, IHC hospitals, and clinics directly provided nearly $51 million in charitable assistance. A central part of IHC's mission is to provide quality medical care to persons with a medical need, regardless of ability to pay.

Nuptials: The Utah constitution declares same-sex marriages void or invalid. Recent political activities in the state and Salt Lake City have created anti-discrimination legislation protecting GLBT rights. Some area employers offer domestic partner benefits.

Getting Around Town

Public transportation: Light-rail, commuter rail, and bus services are all provided by the Utah Transit Authority (UTA) (888–743–3882; *www.rideuta.com*). With a 1,400-square-mile service area spanning six counties, UTA provides public transit to 75 percent of Utah's population. In addition to TRAX light rail in Salt Lake County, an inter-county fixed-route bus system, the agency's paratransit operation Flextrans (801–287–7433), provides curb-to-curb transportation for riders with disabilities. UTA also offers service to local ski areas during the winter months and has a comprehensive Rideshare program featuring more than 200 vanpools.

Roads: I-15, I-80, I-70, I-215

Airport: Salt Lake City International Airport (airport code: SLC) (801–575–2400/800–595–2442; *www.slcairport.com*), located 10 minutes from downtown, won the 2002 Aviation Security International Award of Excellence based on the airport's advance preparations for hosting the 2002 Olympic Winter Games.

It's a Gay Life

Annual events: Utah Pride (*www.utahpride.org*) hosts Gay Pride in June with the Utah Pride Film Festival, Dyke March, Pride Day Parade, and Pride Day Festival. The Gay & Lesbian Ski Week (877-429-6368) in January draws a large crowd. Utah Arts Festival (*www.uaf.org*), Living Traditions: A Celebration of Salt Lake's Folk & Ethnic Arts (*www.arts.utah.gov*), Greek Festival (801–328–9681), the Japanese Obon Festival (*www.slbuddhist.org*) and Snowbird's Oktoberfest (*www.snowbird.com*) are just a few of the area's additional annual events.

Nightlife: Salt Lake boasts a vibrant nightlife with more than 1,000 restaurants, brewpubs, dance clubs, and private bars. Salt Lake's thriving dining scene includes nationally recognized fine dining, cozy diners, and authentic ethnic restaurants. Salt Lake is also home to a diverse mix of nightspots including dance clubs, country/western saloons, jazz clubs, sports bars, neighborhood hangouts, martini clubs, techno-dance spots, and cigar bars. There are more than a dozen bars and clubs serving the GLBT community in Salt Lake. Most are centered downtown in the triangle formed between Temple Square, Pioneer Park, and Liberty Park. Visit Golden Braid Books (151 S. 500 E.; 801–322–1162) and pick up *The Pillar of the Gay/Lesbian Community* or the *Little Lavender Book* (*www.lavenderbook.com*) for current listings and events.

Culture: Salt Lake City offers a wide spectrum of cultural options with the nationally acclaimed Utah Symphony (Abravavel Hall; 123 West South Temple; 801–533–5626; *www.utahsymphony.org*), Utah Opera (Abravavel Hall; 123 West South Temple; 801–533–5626; *www.utahopera.org*), and Ballet West (801–323–6900; *www.balletwest.org*). The internationally acclaimed Mormon Tabernacle Choir (801–240–4150; *www.mormontabernaclechoir.org*) performs frequently throughout the year. Pioneer Theatre Company (801–581–6961; *www.ptc.utah.edu*), the Off Broadway Theatre (272 S. Main; 801–355–4628; *www.theobt.com*), the Salt Lake Acting Company (801–363–7522; *www.saltlakeactingcompany.org*), and Broadway in Utah (801–355–5502; *www.broadwayacrossamerica.com*) present a mix of classics and modern productions. Summer in Salt Lake is a music-lover's dream come true. Live concerts abound in city plazas, on mountainsides, and in public gardens. With dozens of alfresco concerts scheduled during warm weather months, the sounds of jazz, Blues, classical, or rock music fill the balmy mountain air virtually every night of the week. Built to commemorate the 2002 Games, Olympic Cauldron Park (1300 East and Guardsman Way; *www.saltlake2002.com*) is located at the University of Utah (801–581–7200; *www.utah.edu*) and was the site of opening ceremonies. The Park opened in August 2003. The Olympic cauldron towers over the park. A visitor's center houses Olympic photos and an eight-minute film ("The Fire Within"). The USANA Amphitheater (5150 S. 6055 W., West Valley City; 801–536–1234; *www.usana-amp.com*) is framed by a spectacular view of the Rocky Mountains. A great place for national tours, USANA also plays host to the "Red Hot 4th," an annual Independence Day bash featuring one of the top fireworks displays in the West.

Recreation: International exposure during the Olympic Winter Games of 2002 helped to solidify Salt Lake's close proximity to natural recreation, creating a lasting legacy for Salt Lake as an urban center and mountain retreat. Forests, lakes, streams, hiking trails, and mountain bike paths are minutes from the city center. World-class skiing and snowboarding at 10 major resorts—including Alta (8920 South Collins Road, Alta; 801–359–1078; *www.alta.com*), Brighton (12601 Big Cottonwood Canyon Road, Brighton; 800–873–5512; *www.brightonrestort.com*), Snowbird (Highway 210, Little Cottonwood Canyon, Snowbird; 801–933–2222; *www.snowbird.com*), and Solitude (12000 Big Cottonwood Canyon, Solitude; 800–748–4SKI; *www.skisolityude.com*)—are less than an hour away. In the spring, mountain hills are adorned with wildflowers and impromptu waterfalls. During summer months, hiking, rock climbing, and mountain biking are just minutes away. A blaze of brilliant foliage erupts on canyon walls in autumn. When the snow falls, visitors flock to the Ski Salt Lake resorts such as Alta, Brighton, Snowbird, and Solitude, just 35 minutes from downtown. Daily sunshine, low humidity, and mountain breezes combine for a comfortable year-round climate. Salt Lake is the gateway to western national parks including Arches (435–719–2299; *www.nps.gov.arch*), Bryce Canyon (435–834–5322; *www.nps.gov/brca*), Canyonlands (435–719–2313; *www.nps.gov.cany*), Capitol Reef (435–425–3791; *www.nps/gov/care*), the north rim of the Grand Canyon (928–638–7888; *www.nps.gov/grca*), Grand Teton (307–739–3300; *www.nps.gov/grte*), Monument Valley (928–672–2700; *www.nps.gov/nava*), Yellowstone (307–344–7381; *www.nps.gov/yell*), and Zion (435–772–3256; *www.nps.gov/zion*). Salt Lake is also home to top professional sport teams including the NBA's Utah Jazz (801–325–2500; *www.nba.com/jazz*), the WNBA's Utah Starzz (801–355–DUNK; *www.wnba.com*), AAA Baseball's Salt Lake Stingers (801–325–BASE; *www.stingersbaseball.com*), the AHL's Utah Grizzlies (801–988–8000; *www.utahgrizzlies.com*), and USL Soccer's Utah Blitzz (801–401–8000; *www.utahblitzz.com*).

For the Visitor

Accommodations: With 17,000 rooms in Salt Lake County and nearly 8,000 in the downtown area you're sure to find something to fit your taste and budget. A few of the gay-friendly options include: Hotel Monaco Salt Lake City (15 W. 200 S.; 801–595–0000/877–294–9710; *www.monaco-saltlakecity.com*) in the absolute heart of downtown is set in a meticulously refurbished landmark 14-story building and offers guests some of the most hospitable, stylish accommodations among Salt Lake City hotels; Peery Hotel (110 W. 300 S.; 801–521–4300/800–331–0073; *www.peeryhotel.com*), a historic landmark designed by prominent European hotel architect, Charles B. Onderdonk, that awaits travelers with unparalleled luxury at affordable prices; Saltair B&B/Alpine Cottages (164 S. 900 E.; 801–533–8184/800–733–8184; *www.saltlakebandb.com*) is the oldest continuously operating bed and breakfast in Utah, and the house has hosted many dignitaries.

For More Information

Gay & Lesbian Center
Gay & Lesbian Community Center of Utah
361 N. 300 W.
Salt Lake City, UT 84103
801–539–8800
www.glccu.com

Publications
Salt Lake Tribune
143 S. Main Street
Salt Lake City, UT 84111
801–237–2800
www.sltrib.com

Little Lavender Book
352 S. Denver Street, Suite 350
Salt Lake City, UT 84111
801–323–0727
www.lavenderbook.com

Convention and Visitors Bureaus
Convention & Visitors Bureau
90 South West Temple
Salt Lake City, UT 84101-1406
801–521–2822
www.visitsaltlake.com

Chamber of Commerce
Salt Lake Chamber of Commerce
Chamber of Commerce Building
175 E. 400 S., Suite 600
Salt Lake City, UT 84111
801–364–3631
www.saltlakechamber.org

Realtor
Dwight Lindsay, Realtor
Realty Brokers - Excel
150 East Vine
Salt Lake City, UT 84107
801–205–3166
www.dwightlindsay.com

Place	Local Population	Median Housing Costs	Reason to live here:
Alexandria, VA	128,283	$675,000	History; architecture; beautiful setting; excellent location; music, culture, and recreation; large, social GLBT community; strong high-tech economy
Asheville, NC	70,070	$200,000	Small-town charm, fabulous scenic beauty, culture, music, arts and artists, affordable housing, temperate climate year-round, active GLBT community
Austin, TX	656,562	$204,000	Affordable housing, high-tech economy, music, arts, culture, museums, nightlife, entertainment, recreation, excellent education, no income tax, active GLBT community
Bellaire, TX	15,642	$457,000	High-tech economy, arts, culture, museums, nightlife, entertainment, recreation, excellent education, no income tax, large GLBT community
Boston, MA	589,141	$449,000	Historic architecture, good education, strong high-tech economy, large GLBT community, history, arts, culture, recreation and style
Boulder, CO	93,051	$535,000	Scenic beauty; eco-environment; active, outdoor community; recreation, arts, and culture

Place	Local Population	Median Housing Costs	Reason to live here:
Burlington, VT	38,889	$265,000	Scenic beauty, small-town charm, fabulous recreation, affordable housing, excellent education, culture, arts, active GLBT community, strong economy
Chicago, IL	2,896,016	$739,665	Midwest at its finest; amazing architecture; proud, well-supported GLBT community; strong evolving economy; arts, culture, and recreation
Collingswood, NJ	14,326	$242,000	Family-oriented small-town charm, excellent location, growing GLBT community, fabulous schools, welcoming to small businesses and entrepreneurs
Columbus, OH	711,470	$225,000	Excellent education, nightlife, culture, music, arts, affordable housing, politically supported GLBT community, strong economy.
Dallas, TX	1,188,580	$200,000	High-tech economy, affordable housing, arts, culture, museums, nightlife, entertainment, recreation, no income tax, large and active GLBT community
DeKalb County, GA	665,865	$200,000	Charm and style; arts and culture; strong high-tech economy; entertainment; recreation; affordable housing; large, active GLBT community
Denver, CO	554,636	$210,000	Beautiful setting, affordable housing, recreation, culture entertainment, nightlife, large GLBT community, high-tech economy
Durham, NC	187,035	$223,000	Scenic beauty, culture, music, arts, history, excellent education, affordable housing, temperate climate year-round, active GLBT community, strong economy
Ferndale, MI	22,105	$120,000	Excellent location, small-town charm, affordable housing, recreation, well-organized GLBT community, supportive local government, community pride

Place	Local Population	Median Housing Costs	Reason to live here:
Guerneville, CA	2,441	$220,100	Beautiful scenery, laid-back pace, excellent recreation, integrated GLBT community
Harrisburg, PA	48,950	$150,000	Scenic beauty, history, recreation, culture, arts, affordable housing, active GLBT community, strong economy
Ithaca, NY	29,541	$170,000	Liberal, college-town atmosphere; fabulous natural beauty; recreation; affordable housing; arts; excellent education; strong economy; large, active GLBT community
Key West, FL	79,589	$950,000	Laid-back lifestyle, recreation, nightlife, artists' haven, large GLBT community, excellent weather, some of the world's most dramatic sunsets
Kihei, HI	16,749	$600,000	Perfect weather; white-sand beaches; laid-back atmosphere; casual, open GLBT community; arts and artists; recreation
Laguna Beach, CA	23,727	$3,250,000	Beautiful, sun-drenched beach setting; large arts community and arts festivals; recreation; progressive GLBT community
Lakewood, OH	56,646	$160,000	Culture, music, arts, recreation, lake views, affordable housing, large GLBT community, strong evolving economy
Las Vegas, NV	508,604	$300,000	Scenic desert beauty, entertainment, nightlife, strong growing economy, no state income tax, growing GLBT community, dry climate
Los Angeles, CA	3,694,820	$900,000	Entertainment, nightlife, arts, culture, recreation, strong economy, diverse and large GLBT community, outstanding healthcare, progressive politics
Madison, WI	208,054	$178,050	Beautiful setting, fabulous education, recreation, culture, arts, music, active and politically supported GLBT community, strong economy

Place	Local Population	Median Housing Costs	Reason to live here:
Manhattan, NY	1,537,195	$3,000,000	Arts, culture, music, theater, and entertainment; large and politically active GLBT community; strong economy fabulous public transportation excellent location
Miami Shores, FL	10,380	$350,000	Excellent weather, ocean views, recreation, culture, arts, large GLBT community, great education and continuing education opportunities, strong economy
Minneapolis, MN	382,618	$250,000	Beautiful setting, recreation, arts, culture, music, progressive local politics, large and active GLBT community, excellent education, strong economy
Nashville, TN	545,524	$350,000	Music and musicians, arts, fabulous nightlife, entertainment, recreation, large and active GLBT community, strong and growing economy
New Orleans, LA	484,674	$250,000	Nightlife, music, culture, and recreation; excellent food; large and organized GLBT community
Olympia, WA	42,514	$200,000	Beautiful setting, recreation, music, culture, affordable housing, fabulous education, active GLBT community
Palm Springs, CA	44,260	$345,000	Nightlife, arts, recreation, dry desert climate, beautiful setting, strong economy, historically accepted and integrated GLBT community
Philadelphia, PA	1,517,550	$339,000	History, culture, arts, museums, recreation, active and politically supported GLBT community, fabulous healthcare, strong economy, excellent education
Phoenix, AZ	1,421,298	$190,000	Affordable housing, growing GLBT community, nightlife, culture, recreation, outstanding medical care, solid economy

Place	Local Population	Median Housing Costs	Reason to live here:
Portland, ME	64,249	$250,000	Recreation, spectacular sea harbor views, laid-back atmosphere, excellent education opportunities, family-oriented GLBT community
Portland, OR	529,121	$183,500	Progressive environmentally and politically, scenic beauty, recreation, culture, arts, affordable housing, large and active GLBT community
Providence, RI	173,618	$265,000	Scenic beauty, history, culture, arts and artists, museums, recreation, large GLBT community, excellent education, strong economy
Provincetown, MA	3,431	$750,000	Beautiful setting, beaches, laid-back atmosphere, excellent location, nightlife, recreation, social GLBT community
Sacramento, CA	407,018	$372,000	High-tech economy, excellent healthcare, large and organized GLBT community, museums, recreation
Salt Lake City, UT	181,743	$165,000	Scenic beauty; recreation; temperate, dry climate; affordable housing; excellent education; culture and arts; large GLBT community
San Francisco, CA	789,600	$794,000	Beautiful and historic city; progressive politics; temperate climate; arts, culture, and recreation; high-tech economy; large, organized GLBT community
Santa Fe, NM	62,203	$321,000	Scenic beauty; dry climate; small-town charm; excellent education; arts and artists; recreation; large, integrated GLBT community; strong high-tech economy
Seattle, WA	563,374	$355,000	Beautiful setting, fabulous recreation, care of the environment, culture, arts, music, excellent education, active and politically supported GLBT community

Place	Local Population	Median Housing Costs	Reason to live here:
St. Louis, MO	348,189	$140,000	Strong economy, arts, museums, music, large and active GLBT community, affordable housing, historic architecture
St. Petersburg, FL	252,246	$217,800	Excellent weather, ocean views, nightlife, recreation, culture, arts, growing GLBT community, affordable housing
Takoma Park, MD	17,299	$250,000	Small-town charm, large GLBT community, city pride, good education, artist enclave, excellent location near arts, culture, recreation
Tucson, AZ	486,699	$185,000	Arts, culture, history, scenic environment, relaxed pace, affordable housing, new-knowledge-based economy
Washington, DC	572,059	$367,500	The nation's capital, museums, recreation, entertainment, nightlife, large and organized GLBT community, stable economy
West Hollywood, CA	35,716	$850,000	Progressive politics, large GLBT community, arts, entertainment, nightlife, historic setting, great weather
West Palm Beach, FL	97,708	$271,000	Tropical weather, ocean views, culture, arts, entertainment, recreation, excellent education, social GLBT community
Wilton Manors, FL	12,697	$304,000	Small-town charm, near big-city amenities, family-oriented GLBT community, significant local political support, excellent weather, recreation

50 Fabulous Gay-Friendly Resources

General

1. The **National Association of LGBT Community Centers** (*www.lgbtcenters.org*) exists to support and enhance lesbian, gay, bisexual, and transgender (LGBT) community centers, which are engines of community organizing and liberation and are crucial to the health and strength of LGBT communities.

2. The **Independent Gay Forum** (*www.indegayforum.org*) was created by a group of gay writers, academics, attorneys, and activists to advance discussion of gay-related issues.

3. **InterPride** (*www.interpride.org*) exists to promote lesbian, gay, Bisexual, and transgender pride on an international level, to increase networking and communication among pride organizations, to encourage diverse communities to hold and attend pride events, and to act as a source of education. InterPride maintains a current list of most of the nation's gay pride events.

4. **GLBTQ Encyclopedia** (*www.glbtq.com*) provides thousands of entries on more than three centuries of historic GLBT community members and culture.

Search Engines

5. **GayCrawler.com** (*www.gaycrawler.com*) is a portal providing access to more than 25,000 sites in more than 327 categories of specific interest to the gay and lesbian community.

6. **Gay Wired** (*www.gaywired.com*) is an Internet portal for the GLBT communities. Through the use of cutting-edge technology, superior design, multimedia entertainment, and dynamic content, Gay Wired is the ultimate online resource.

7. **The Original Gay Yellow Pages** (*www.glyp.com*) is the nation's pioneering lesbian, gay, bisexual, and transgender information directory. Searching online is as easy as searching the printed directory.

8. **The Pink Pages** (*www.pinkweb.com*) are the GLBT yellow pages for New England and beyond.

9. **Queery.com** (*www.queery.com*) is one of the most popular GLBT Web portals on the Internet.

News and Entertainment

10. **365Gay.com** (*www.365gay.com*) is a daily online GLBT newspaper, crammed full of news and features.

11. **The Advocate** (*www.advocate.com*) is an award-winning national gay and lesbian newsmagazine.

12. **Genre Magazine** (*www.genremagazine.com*) provides images and ideas that inspire, at the same time shedding relevant insights on the various aspects of career, culture, relationships, technology, finance, design, health, travel, transportation, and personal style.

13. **Out Magazine** (*www.out.com*) offers gay Americans advice on what to wear, where to go, and what to see.

14. **PlanetOut.com** (*www.planetout.com*) is a safe, dynamic home for lesbian, gay, bisexual, and transgender people of all ages offering the latest daily political and entertainment news, films, and relationship and dating advice.

Business

15. **The National Gay & Lesbian Chamber of Commerce (NGLCC)** (*www.nglcc.org*) is the only national not-for-profit advocacy organization specifically dedicated to expanding the economic opportunities and advancements of the LGBT business community. NGLCC membership is open to GLBT-owned businesses, professionals, students of business, and GLBT-friendly business allies.

16. **GayWork.com** (*www.gaywork.com*) is an online community for GLBT individuals looking for a job, as well as the global business community seeking GayWork.com's diverse job applicants. GayWork.com brings together the most progressive and forward-thinking employers with the most talented and creative individuals.

17. **GayBusinessWorld.com** (*www.gaybusinessworld.com*) is an online community for the GLBT professional, entrepreneur, small-business owner, or corporate executive. Features gay and lesbian business stories about your favorite topics, as well as a full, free membership system to help you in both networking and making new friends.

Family

18. **Parents, Families and Friends of Lesbians and Gays (PFLAG)** (*www.pflag.org*) promotes the health and well-being of GLBT persons and their families and friends through: support, to cope with an adverse society; education, to enlighten an ill-informed public; and, advocacy, to end discrimination and to

secure equal civil rights. PFLAG provides opportunity for dialogue about sexual orientation and gender identity and acts to create a society that is healthy and respectful of human diversity.

19. **Family to Family Inc.** (*www.fam2fam.org*) is a non-profit, nationwide international and domestic adoption agency that strives to increase and broaden the access to adoption to those couples and individuals who wish to build a family through adoption in a cost-effective, open, respectful, and ethical manner with full disclosure.

20. **ProudParenting.com** (*www.proudparenting.com*) serves as an online portal for GLBT parents and their families worldwide. Their goal is bringing family together by being the best on the Internet serving the needs and interests of the proud parenting community.

21. **2moms2dads.com** (*www.2moms2dads.com*) is a one-stop resource for GLBT parents or those interested in becoming parents through adoption, surrogacy, in vitro, egg donors, sperm donors, and so forth.

22. **Rainbow Wedding Network** (*www.rainbowweddingnetwork.com*) offers immediate access to gay-friendly wedding services, including an online registry, specifically designed for GLBT and gay-friendly couples. Their goal is to make your ceremony plans as comfortable and stress-free as possible.

Human Rights

23. **The American Civil Liberties Union (ACLU)** (*www.aclu.org*) is our nation's guardian of liberty. They work daily in courts, legislatures, and communities to defend and preserve the individual rights and liberties guaranteed to every person in this country by the Constitution and laws of the United States. Their job is to conserve America's original civic values: the Constitution and the Bill of Rights.

24. **Lambda Legal** (*www.lambdalegal.org*) is a national organization committed to achieving full recognition of the civil rights of lesbians, gay men, bisexuals, transgender people, and those with HIV through impact litigation, education, and public policy work.

25. **The Human Rights Campaign (HRC)** (*www.hrc.org*) is a bipartisan organization that works to advance equality based on sexual orientation and gender expression and identity, to ensure that gay, lesbian, bisexual, and transgender Americans can be open, honest, and safe at home, at work, and in the community.

26. **The Gay & Lesbian Alliance Against Defamation (GLAAD)** (*www.glaad.org*) is dedicated to promoting and ensuring fair, accurate, and inclusive representation of people and events in the media as a means of eliminating homophobia and discrimination based on gender identity and sexual orientation.

27. **The National Gay and Lesbian Task Force, Inc.** (*www.thetaskforce.org*) works to build the grassroots political power of the GLBT community in order to

attain complete equality through direct and grassroots lobbying to either help defeat anti-GLBT ballot initiatives and other measures or to help push pro-GLBT legislation and other measures.

28. **And Justice for All (AJA)** (*qrd.tcp.com/qrd/www/orgs/aja*) fights for equality for everyone without regard to sexual orientation. AJA seeks to achieve this goal by increasing the visibility and participation of heterosexuals in the lesbian, gay, bisexual, and transgender rights movement.

Politics and Activism

29. **National Stonewall Democrats (NSD)** (*www.stonewalldemocrats.org*) is the only national organization of gay, lesbian, bisexual, and transgender Democrats, with more than 90 local chapters across the nation. NSD is committed to working through the Democratic Party to advance the rights of all people regardless of sexual orientation or gender identity.

30. **Log Cabin Republicans** (*www.logcabin.org*) comprises thousands of members and more than 68 local chapters across the United States, all working to ensure an inclusive and fair Republican Party. This is a group of like-minded Americans who believe in limited government, a strong national defense, lower taxes, personal responsibility, and free markets.

31. **The Gay & Lesbian Victory Fund and Leadership Institute** (*www.victoryfund.org*) is recognized as the leading national political organization that identifies, trains, and supports open lesbian, gay, bisexual, and transgender candidates and officials. They are the only national organization committed to increasing the number of openly gay and lesbian public officials at federal, state, and local levels of government.

32. **The Republican Unity Coalition (RUC)** (*www.republicanunity.com*) serves as a policy forum for Republican leaders—gay and straight—to encourage greater tolerance of gays and lesbians in the party and American life and to support public policies that constructively respond to concerns of gay and lesbian Americans.

33. **The Democratic National Committee (DNC)** (*www.democrats.org*), founded by Thomas Jefferson in 1792, is the national party organization for the Democratic Party of the United States.

34. **Act Up** (New York: *www.actupny.org*; Philadelphia: *www.critpath.org/actup*; San Francisco: *www.actupsf.com*) is a diverse, non-partisan group of individuals united in anger and committed to direct action to end the AIDS crisis. Act Up advises, informs, and demonstrates.

35. **Outright Libertarians** (*www.outrightusa.org*) is primarily an organization of gay, lesbian, bisexual, transgender, and queer Libertarian Party activists welcoming anyone who believes in individual liberty, personal responsibility, a society that is tolerant of all individuals and who wishes to actively promote Libertarian ideas and ideals to all those who love differently.

36. **The Lavender Greens** (*www.lavendergreens.org*) organized as a caucus with the purpose of promoting lesbian, gay, bisexual, transgender, intersex, and queer Green issues within the Green Party.

Relationships

37. **Partners Task Force for Gay & Lesbian Couples** (*www.buddybuddy.com/toc.html*) supports the diverse community of committed gay and lesbian partners through a variety of media. The Website contains more than 250 essays, surveys, legal articles, and resources on legal marriage, ceremonies, domestic partner benefits, relationship tips, parenting, and immigration.

38. **GayMatchMaker.com** (*www.gaymatchmaker.com*) helps singles find happiness through a safe, fun, and effective online dating community. GayMatchMaker.com is a partner of the Relationship Exchange, a network of online personals sites that share a common database of millions of singles.

39. **OutPersonals.com** (*www.outpersonals.com*) is a member of the FriendFinder Network's 15 Web communities with more than 20 million registered members. People have a relaxed and safe environment to meet others all over the globe 24 hours a day.

40. **Gay.com** (*www.gay.com*) has members in more than 100 countries and services in English, French, German, Italian, and Portuguese. Gay.com offers an extensive network that connects the gay community globally. Premium personals, chat, engaging content, shopping guides, and community services have made Gay.com one of the largest gay online communities in the world.

Spirituality

41. **The Metropolitan Community Churches (MCC)** (*www.mccchurch.org*) is a worldwide fellowship of Christian churches with a special outreach to the world's gay, lesbian, bisexual, and transgender communities.

42. **Gay Spirituality & Culture** (*www.gayspirituality.typepad.com*) is a group of independent writers with interests in inner transformation, personal growth, spirituality, religion, and culture for the lesbian, gay, bisexual, and transgender community.

43. **DignityUSA** (*www.dignityusa.org*) works for respect and justice for all gay, lesbian, bisexual, and transgender persons in the Catholic Church and the world through education, advocacy, and support.

44. **The Unitarian Universalist Association (UUA)** (*www.uua.org*) represents the interests of more than one thousand Unitarian Universalist congregations, on a continental scale.

45. **Gay and Lesbian Atheists and Humanists** (*www.galah.org*) is an organization that supports equal rights for the GLBT community, educates people about atheism and humanism, supports separation of church and state, and provides freethinkers with opportunities to get to know each other.

46. **The World Congress of Gay, Lesbian, Bisexual, and Transgender Jews** (*www.glbtjews.org*), Keshet Ga'avah, consists of more than 65 member organizations around the world. They hold conferences and workshops representing the interests of lesbian, gay, bisexual, and transgender Jews with a varied focus from regional, national, continental, to global.

47. **YOESUF Foundation** (*www.yoesuf.nl/engels*) is a center for information and education about Islam and sexual diversity. The foundation is focused on the subject of Islam and homosexuality in relation to emancipation and other social questions. Target groups are public organizations and individuals, Muslims as well as non-Muslims. The foundation is not bound by nationality, ethnicity, religion, or political denomination.

Youth

48. **Gay-Straight Alliance Network (GSA)** (*www.gsanetwork.org*) is a youth-led organization that connects school-based Gay-Straight Alliances to each other and community resources. Through peer support, leadership development, and training, GSA Network supports young people in starting, strengthening, and sustaining GSAs.

49. **National Youth Advocacy Coalition (NYAC)** (*www.nyacyouth.org*) is a social justice organization that advocates for and with young people who are lesbian, gay, bisexual, transgender, or questioning in an effort to end discrimination against these youth and to ensure their physical and emotional well being.

50. **Youth Guardian Services** (*www.youth-guard.org*) is a youth-run, non-profit organization that provides support services on the Internet to gay, lesbian, bisexual, transgender, questioning, and straight supportive youth.

Gregory A. Kompes is a writer, photographer, and public speaker with a degree in English from Columbia University. Led by a natural curiosity about all things cultural and gay, he has traveled extensively throughout the United States, visiting museums, natural wonders, restaurants, bars, arenas, theaters, concert halls, and gay ghettos. His articles on gay life, entertainment, and travel have appeared online and in print publications across the country. Gregory and his domestic partner, Todd Isbell, live in Las Vegas, Nevada. For more information, visit Gregory's Website at *www.kompes.com.*

ABOUT THE AUTHOR

How to Use the Interactive CD

First, it's important to understand what's on the interactive CD. You'll find the following:

- A folder called "50 Fabulous Gay-Friendly Places," which contains a folder called "Install," which contains a file called **setup.exe**. This file is used to install the program on your computer, allowing you to search data included in *50 Fabulous Gay-Friendly Places to Live*.

- A "Chapters" folder, containing chapters for each of the 50 Fabulous Gay-Friendly places. These are in PDF format, which requires Adobe Acrobat Reader, version 6.0 or higher.

- Adobe Acrobat Reader, version 7.0, which you can install on your computer by double-clicking the icon named "AdobeReader70.exe," found in the CD's main directory, which is displayed when you view the CD on your computer. This version of Adobe Acrobat reader is for Windows XP users only. To get a version that works with other versions of Windows, go to *www.adobe.com*. If you already have Adobe Acrobat Reader version 6, you don't need to install or download anything.

- This "**How to Use**" document, which you can print or re-display as needed.

Now, let's talk about how to use the CD to set up our database search tools.

1. When you put the CD in your CD drive, the Autorun program should kick in after a few moments, and automatically run the Setup program to install the database search tools. If this doesn't happen (the use of Autorun may be disabled on your computer), choose **Run** from the Windows **Start** menu.

2. Click the **Browse** button.

3. The Browse dialog box opens. Go to the drive letter for your CD drive (this is often drive D:) and **click once on the drive letter**.

4. Click the **Open** button.

5. The **Fabulous 50 Gay-Friendly Places** folder is displayed. **Double-click** it.

6. The **Install** folder is displayed. **Double-click** it.

7. See a **Setup** file displayed in the Install folder. **Double-click** it.

8. Back in the **Run** dialog box, click **OK**. The installer program will start on its own, and you can respond to the prompts, inserting your name/company name, and then choosing "**Typical**" for the type of install you want to do.

That's all there is to it—the installation will take a few minutes, and you'll see both a Desktop and a Programs menu icon appear (in the Windows Start menu) when the process is complete.

To run the Search program, simply double-click the **50 Fabulous Gay-Friendly Places** icon on your Desktop or Start menu, and follow the instructions on the form that appears. **Note** that depending on the anti-virus or security software you may be using on your computer, you may be prompted about the safety of opening this program—choose Yes and/or Open (depending on the prompt/s that appear) and go ahead and open the program. There are no viruses or spyware included in this program, *guaranteed*.

If you ever want to uninstall this program, just go to the Control Panel (via your Windows Start menu) and double-click the Add/Remove Programs icon. Select "Search: 50 Fabulous Gay-Friendly Places to Live" from the list, and then click the Remove button. The un-install process begins and prompts you when it's completed—it's that simple.

If you have any **questions** about this program, its installation or use, please e-mail us at help@limehat.com.